Literary Citizenship in Scandinavia
in the Long Eighteenth Century

T0386123

Knowledge and Communication in the Enlightenment World

Series Editors
James Raven
Cristina Soriano
Mark Towsey

This series presents innovative studies focused on the history of knowledge transmission from c.1650 to c.1850. Books in the series address a wide range of artefacts and activities supporting texts, textual culture and textual networks and their role in the transfer of ideas across geographical, linguistic, social, ideological, and religious boundaries. In promoting explicitly global or transoceanic perspectives, the series explores how far western European periodisation of 'the Age of Enlightenment' maps onto processes of social, cultural, technological and intellectual change across the globe. The series publishes ground-breaking transnational studies of script, print, material culture, translation and communication networks that transform our understanding of the social history of knowledge in this critical period of change.

The editors welcome proposals and preliminary enquiries from prospective authors and editors for monographs and closely-curated edited collections. We are happy to consider both conventional and Open Access models of book publishing. Proposals or queries should be sent in the first instance to one of the editors, or to the publisher, at the addresses given below; all submissions will receive prompt and informed consideration.

Professor James Raven, Magdalene College, University of Cambridge, jr42@cam.ac.uk

Professor Cristina Soriano, Department of History, University of Texas at Austin, cristina.soriano@austin.utexas.edu

Professor Mark Towsey, Department of History, University of Liverpool, M.R.M.Towsey@liverpool.ac.uk

Dr Elizabeth McDonald, Commissioning Editor, Boydell & Brewer Ltd., emcdonald@boydell.co.uk

Literary Citizenship in Scandinavia in the Long Eighteenth Century

Edited by
Ruth Hemstad, Janicke S. Kaasa,
Ellen Krefting and Aina Nøding

THE BOYDELL PRESS

First published 2023
The Boydell Press, Woodbridge

ISBN 978 1 78327 779 7

Open Access:
This title is available under the Creative Commons license CC-BY-NC

The open access version of this publication was funded by
the Research Council of Norway and the National Library of Norway

The Boydell Press is an imprint of Boydell & Brewer Ltd
PO Box 9, Woodbridge, Suffolk IP12 3DF, UK
and of Boydell & Brewer Inc.
668 Mt Hope Avenue, Rochester, NY 14620-2731, USA
website: www.boydellandbrewer.com

A CIP catalogue record for this book is available
from the British Library

Contents

Illustrations

Figures

The editors, contributors and publisher are grateful to all the institutions and persons listed for permission to reproduce the materials in which they hold copyright. Every effort has been made to trace the copyright holders; apologies are offered for any omission, and the publisher will be pleased to add any necessary acknowledgement in subsequent editions.

Notes on Contributors

Jens Bjerring-Hansen is Associate Professor of Scandinavian Literature at the University of Copenhagen, specialising in eighteenth- and nineteenth-century literature. He is the author of the monograph *Ludvig Holberg på bogmarkedet* (2015). His most recent volume is *Scandinavian Exceptionalisms* (2021, co-eds T. Jelsbak and A. Mrozewicz). Currently, as the PI of the project *Measuring Modernity* (2020–4), he is engaged with the so-called 'Modern Breakthrough' in late nineteenth-century Scandinavian literature and culture.

Jon Haarberg is Emeritus Professor of Comparative Literature at the University of Oslo. His interest in the history of catechism in Denmark–Norway developed from his commentary on Petter Dass's bestselling *Catechism Songs* (1715; critical edn *Katekismesanger*, Oslo, 2013). In 2017 he published a book exploring the rise and fall of Norwegian national literature: *Nei, vi elsker ikke lenger. Litteraturen og nasjonen* (Oslo) and in 2022 a history of catechisms in Norway, *Historien om Norges viktigste bok: katekismen* (Oslo).

Ruth Hemstad is Research Librarian in History at the National Library of Norway and Associate Professor II, Department of Archaeology, Conservation and History, University of Oslo. She has published on transnational Scandinavian history, Scandinavianism and Nordic cooperation 1800–1930s. Her latest publications include *Litterære verdensborgere. Transnasjonale perspektiver på norsk bokhistorie 1519–1850* (co-eds A. M. B. Bjørkøy *et al.*, Oslo, 2019), *Frie ord i Norden? Offentlighet, ytringsfrihet og medborgerskap 1814–1914* (co-ed. D. Michalsen, Oslo, 2019), 'Scandinavian Sympathies and Nordic Unity: The Rhetoric of Scandinavianness in the Nineteenth Century', in M. Hilson *et al.* (eds), *Contesting Nordicness from Scandinavianism to the Nordic Brand* (Berlin, 2022) and 'Organizational Scandinavianism Abroad: Literature, Sociability, and Pan-Scandinavian Associational Life in German-speaking Europe 1842–1912', in M. Federhofer and S. Meyer (eds), *Mit dem Buch in der Hand* (Berlin, 2021).

Janicke S. Kaasa is Associate Professor of Scandinavian Literature at the University of Oslo. Her current research focuses on early children's magazines in Scandinavia. Recent publications include: 'Å gi sin daler med glede: Barn som forbrukere i *Ungdommens Ven* (1770)' in *Barnboken*, 42 (2019) and '"Saavel fra fjerne Lande som fra vort eget Hjem". Importert materiale i *Billed-Magazin for Børn*', in A. M. B. Bjørkøy *et al.* (eds), *Litterære verdensborgere* (Oslo, 2019).

Ellen Krefting is Professor of History of Ideas at the University of Oslo. Research interests include media, genres and forms of knowledge in eighteenth-century Europe and Denmark–Norway. She has published extensively on *Spectator*-type journals, e.g., 'Society and Sentiment. (Hi)storytelling in Copenhagen's *Den patriotiske Tilskuer* 1761–63', in K.-D. Ertler *et al.* (eds), *Storytelling in the Spectators* (Berlin, 2020), 'The Spectatorial Press in the Kingdom of Denmark–Norway' with A. Nøding in M. Doms (eds), *Spectator-type Periodicals in International Perspective* (Berlin, 2019), and *Eighteenth-Century Periodicals as Agents of Change*, with A. Nøding and M. Ringvej (eds) (Leiden, 2015).

Karin Kukkonen is Professor of Comparative Literature at the University of Oslo. She specialises in the eighteenth-century novel in a European context and is interested in how eighteenth-century reading practices compare to emerging ones of the digital age. In this context, she has published *4E Cognition and Eighteenth-Century Fiction: How the Novel Found its Feet* (Oxford, 2019), *A Prehistory of Cognitive Poetics: Neoclassicism and the Novel* (Oxford, 2017) and (with A. V. Čepič) on reading practices in *International Journal of the Book* 71.1 (2019).

Ulrik Langen is Professor of Modern History at the University of Copenhagen. He has published on a variety of subjects within the field of modern cultural history. In several prize-winning books and articles, he has focused specifically on social interaction in the urban setting of eighteenth-century Copenhagen. His latest publications include *Struensee* (Aarhus, 2018); 'The Post Office Feud. Sensing Urban Disturbance in late Eighteenth-Century Copenhagen', in *The Senses and Society*, 12:2 (2017), 'Pride and Resentment: French *Émigrés* and Republicans in the Streets of Late Eighteenth-Century Copenhagen', in E. Chalus and M. Kaartinen (eds), *Gendering Spaces in European Towns, c. 1700–1914* (London, 2019) and *Grov Konfækt, Tre vilde år med trykkefrihed 1770–73* (with H. Horstbøll and F. Stjernfelt) (Copenhagen, 2020; English edn, *The World's First Full Press Freedom: The Radical Experiment of Denmark–Norway 1770–73* (Berlin, 2022)).

Aina Nøding is Research Librarian in Book History at the National Library of Norway, PhD in comparative literature (2007, University of Oslo). Latest books include the edited volumes *Eighteenth-Century Periodicals as Agents of Change* (co-eds E. Krefting and M. Ringvej; Leiden, 2015) and *Litterære verdensborgere* (co-eds A. M. B. Bjørkøy *et al.*; Oslo, 2019) and a biography of the writer *Claus Fasting* (Oslo, 2018). Recent articles include three on Danish and Norwegian periodical fiction, published in *Oxford Research Encyclopaedia of Literature* (New York, 2017); in M. Doms (ed.), *Spectator-type Periodicals in International Perspective* (Berlin, 2019; with E. Krefting) and in K.-D. Ertler *et al.* (eds), *Storytelling in the Spectators* (Berlin, 2020).

Jonas Nordin is Professor of Book and Library History at Lund University. His latest publications include 'Northern Declarations of Freedom of the Press: The Relative Importance of Philosophical Ideas and of Local Politics', *Journal of the History of Ideas*, 81:2 (April 2020), with J. Chr. Laursen; 'Spirit of the Age: Erik Dahlbergh's Images of Sweden's Past', in B. Roling and B. Schirg (eds), *Boreas Rising: Antiquarianism and National Narratives in 17th- and 18th-century Scandinavia* (Berlin, Boston, 2019); 'From Seemly Subjects to Enlightened Citizens: Censorship and Press Freedom from the Middle Ages to the 18th Century', in *Press Freedom 250 Years: Freedom of the Press and Public Access to Official Documents in Sweden and Finland – A Living Heritage from 1766* (Stockholm, 2018).

James Raven is Emeritus Professor of Modern History at the University of Essex and a Fellow of Magdalene College, University of Cambridge. He studied the international reception of Erik Pontoppidan's *The Natural History of Norway* (1752–3) for the LitCit project. His latest books include *Bookscape: Geographies of Printing and Publishing in London before 1800* (Chicago, London, 2014) and *What is the History of the Book?* (Cambridge, 2018). He is a Fellow of the British Academy.

Thor Inge Rørvik is Lecturer in History of Ideas at the University of Oslo. He is co-author of *Universitetet i Oslo, b. 2: Vitenskapenes universitet 1870–1911* (*The University of Oslo*, vol. 2; Oslo, 2011) and author of several articles on Norwegian history of ideas in the eighteenth and nineteenth centuries, e.g. 'The Child in the Early Nineteenth-Century Norwegian School System', in R. Aasgaard, M. J. Bunge and M. Roos (eds), *Nordic Childhoods 1700–1960. From Folk Beliefs to Pippi Longstocking* (London, 2018).

Karen Skovgaard-Petersen is Dr.Philos., director of the Society for Danish Language and Literature. Her main research interests are early modern historiography and philology and the writings of the Dano-Norwegian Enlightenment author Ludvig Holberg. Recent publications in English are 'Holberg's Autobiographical Letters' and 'Journeys of Humour and Satire – On Holberg's *Peder Paars* and *Niels Klim*' in K. Haakonssen and S. Olden-Jørgensen (eds), *Ludvig Holberg (1684–1754). Learning and Literature in the Nordic Enlightenment* (London, 2017); 'A Lutheran Appropriation of the First Crusade: The Danish Historian Anders Sørensen Vedel's Apology for Editing Robert of Rheims', in J. M. Jensen *et al.* (eds), *Fighting for the Faith* (Stockholm, 2018).

Iver Tangen Stensrud is an independent historian, PhD 2018 (History, Oslo School of Architecture and Design). His main research interest is Norwegian illustrated periodicals in the mid-nineteenth century. His thesis discusses the illustrated press, architecture and urban development in nineteenth-century Oslo. Recent publications include 'The Magazine and the City: Architecture, Urban Life and the Illustrated Press in Nineteenth-Century Christiania' (PhD thesis, 2018); 'Xylography', in M. Hvattum and A. Hultzsch (eds), *The Printed and the Built* (London, 2018); 'Christiania, det gamle og det nye', *Kunst og Kultur* 102:1 (April 2019).

Frederik Stjernfelt is Professor of Semiotics, Intellectual History and Philosophy of Science at Aalborg University Copenhagen. He has published, inter alia, on cognitive semiotics and the philosophy of Charles Peirce, the intellectual history of the Enlightenment, the philosophy of science of the humanities. Recent publications include *Your Post Has been Removed. Tech Giants and Freedom of Speech* (Cham, 2019; with A. M. Lauritzen); *Grov Konfækt: Tre vilde år med trykkefrihed 1770–73* (Copenhagen, 2020; with H. Horstbøll and U. Langen; English edn, *The World's First Full Press Freedom: The Radical Experiment of Denmark–Norway 1770–73* (Berlin, 2022)); 'Conscious Self-Control as Criterion for Reasoning', *Cognitive Semiotics*, 14:1 (2021).

Jonas Thorup Thomsen obtained a PhD in History (2022) from Aarhus University with the thesis *Danish Clergymen and their Book Collections: An Investigation into Clerical Libraries, Book Distribution, and Knowledge Circulation in Denmark, c. 1685–1810*. His current project examines Danish lending libraries of the eighteenth century as arenas for the circulation of knowledge.

Acknowledgements

THE CHAPTERS INCLUDED IN this volume result from the research project *Literary Citizens of the World. Tracing Transnational Crossroads of Books in Early Modern Norway, 1519–1850* (LitCit). This international and interdisciplinary project was funded by the Research Council of Norway (RCN), hosted by the National Library of Norway (NB) between 2016 and 2021, with Aina Nøding and Ruth Hemstad as alternating managers. The chapters present concluding research results by LitCit participants as well as research from invited experts in related areas. This volume is funded in full by the RCN and NB. The editorial committee (Ruth Hemstad, Janicke S. Kaasa, Ellen Krefting and Aina Nøding) wishes to thank both institutions for their generous support. Furthermore, we should like to express our gratitude to the editors of the series *Knowledge and Communication in the Enlightenment World*, Professors James Raven and Mark Towsey, for their and the reviewers' many useful comments in the editing process. Most of all, we should like to thank the contributors for their brilliant chapters and the thought-provoking discussions that have ensued from our collaboration.

Introduction

Ruth Hemstad, Janicke S. Kaasa,
Ellen Krefting and Aina Nøding

HOW DO YOU BECOME a citizen? Ever since printing was introduced, being a member of society or a community in Scandinavia increasingly involved reading and writing. People memorised their catechism to be allowed to marry, produced and read periodicals to take part in missionary work or learn about faraway places, advocated new ideas in pamphlet wars during periods of press freedom, displayed a copy of the constitution in their living rooms, or consumed the latest fashion in continental novels to become moral and sensitive individuals. Literary practices shaped and changed identities and the organisation of society. This happened locally, as well as transnationally, as reading, writing and producing texts involved entanglements within and beyond the borders of the Northern European periphery of Norway, Denmark and Sweden.

Today, 'literary citizenship' is a term used in media, online fora, professional and academic circles to describe and encourage writers' active contributions to and promotion of literary culture and community. Furthermore, it has been applied to reading and writing in general, or more specifically to describe a work's or writer's inclusion in a literary community after crossing linguistic or national boundaries.[1] In the present volume we adapt this term to our own ends, that is, to highlight literary agency and the historicity of the local and border-crossing, social and

---

[1] See for instance L. A. May, *The Write Crowd. Literary Citizenship and the Writing Life* (New York, NY, London, 2015); R. McGill and A. Babyn, 'Teaching Critical Literary Citizenship', *The Writer's Notebook* (February 2019), <www.awpwriter.org/magazine_media/writers_notebook_view/311> (accessed 23 February 2023); M. Santana, 'Mapping National Literatures: Some Observations on Contemporary Hispanism', in B. Epps and L. F. Cifuentes (eds), *Spain Beyond Spain: Modernity, Literary History, and National Identity* (Cranbury, NJ, 2005) pp. 109–25, at p. 120.

empowering aspects of literature, used in the broadest sense of the word. We take the term 'literary citizenship' as a general frame for our historical investigations into the engagements with books and prints in Scandinavia, particularly Norway and Denmark, by readers, writers and publishers in the long eighteenth century. We seek to trace the establishment and productive interactions between the widening 'republic of letters' and 'the republic', so to speak – between the transnational communities of readers, writers and producers of publications on the one hand and society and the state in general on the other.

We start by evoking the major transitions beginning in the early sixteenth century, highlighting changes of literary language (Latin to vernacular), media technology (manuscripts and orality to printed books and periodicals), religion (Catholic to Protestant) and politics (shifting unions and degrees of autonomy). We then go on to explore the continued overlapping existence of these new and old phenomena as well as the impact the changes had on the expansion of the public sphere, reading materials and practices that resulted in an Enlightenment with Scandinavian traits. By examining multiple historical and transnational practices of writing, publishing, importing, translating, circulating, reading and interpreting texts, we aim to show how these practices have been involved in fostering individual as well as collective identities and agencies within, across and beyond national, linguistic and medial borders and communities.

Hence, rather than focus only on canonical works and genres, and their dissemination, we investigate print that has been available to different readerships and used and read for sociability and belonging, instruction, entertainment or self-improvement, profit or charity, spiritual awakening or political debate. The result is not a simple, uniform or linear history of the book in the northernmost parts of Europe. On the contrary, focusing on literary citizenship helps us discover the very different ways engagement with print, in various genres and formats, has mediated and shaped local, national and transnational networks and communities, identities and agencies of multiple sorts in an interconnected media landscape.

NORTHERN ENLIGHTENMENT

Literary Citizenship takes Early Modern and Enlightenment books and other prints in and from Scandinavia, especially Norway and Denmark, as vantage points for a wider study of the actual geographies of texts: of how they spread and shaped – and were shaped by – knowledge, ideas, emotions, politics, social practices, genres, reading and trade.[2] In doing so, we may not always escape the inherent methodological difficulties of being situated in a particular region or nation, with its nationally defined archives and collections. However, the following chapters discuss new ways of surveying these texts and their dissemination, bearing in mind Jeffrey Freedman's observation that 'books have not been as respectful of national borders as the historians who study them.'[3] Indeed, the history of what constitutes today's Scandinavian nations and languages is well suited to exploring the inherent methodological difficulties of terms such as transnational/-regional/-cultural/-lingual, conundrums that are shared by cultural historians around the world. Like so many other 'national' histories of the book – but particularly pertinent in the case of Norway – the histories of the book in Scandinavia are those of transnational and transcultural mobility, transfer and adaptation. Norway, which for four centuries was more or less politically subordinated to Denmark (1397–1814), followed by a century as an autonomous, but junior, partner in a personal union with Sweden (1814–1905), held the position as a periphery within the periphery. As an integrated part of the Danish realm since 1537 and eventually sharing the same written language, its literary field was dominated by Denmark and continued to be so during the nineteenth century. Contact and exchanges between the Swedish realm (which included Finland until 1809) and Denmark and Norway remained limited, even after 1814, with the exception of certain pan-Scandinavian literary initiatives (cf. Bjerring-Hansen in this volume).[4] These prominent features call for resisting 'methodological nationalism' and necessitate an approach that moves beyond the national, acknowledging the importance of translation and transmission across

---

[2]   Cf. M. Espagne and M. Werner (eds), *Transferts* (Paris, 1988); J. Freedman, *Books Without Borders in Enlightenment Europe* (Philadelphia, 2012); S. Frost and R. W. Rix, *Moveable Type, Mobile Nations* (Copenhagen, 2010); T. Munck, *Conflict and Enlightenment* (Cambridge, 2019); M. Ogborn and C. W. J. Withers (eds), *Geographies of the Book* (Farnham, 2013); J. Raven, *Bookscape* (Chicago, London, 2014); S. J. Shep, 'Books Without Borders: The Transnational Turn in Book History', in R. Fraser and M. Hammond (eds), *Books Without Borders*, vol. 1 (Basingstoke, 2008).

[3]   Freedman, *Books Without Borders in Enlightenment Europe*, p. 1.

[4]   R. Hemstad, '"En skandinavisk Nationalitet" som litterært prosjekt: 1840-årenes transnasjonale offentlighet i Norden', in A. Bohlin and E. Stengrundet (eds), *Nation som kvalitet: Smak, offentligheter och folk i 1800-talets Norden* (Bergen, 2021), pp. 311–32; K. H. Ekman, *'Mitt hems gränser vidgades.' En studie i den kulturella skandinavismen under 1800-talet* (Gothenburg, Stockholm, 2010); T. van Gerven, *Scandinavism. Overlapping and Competing Identities in the Nordic World 1770–1919* (Amsterdam, 2022).

political, cultural, linguistic and temporal borders, while accounting for local specificities.[5]

History is unavoidably written from specific points of view, including geographical ones. In taking our departure from Norway and its close political, linguistic and cultural ties with Denmark in the long eighteenth century, while also including the broader Scandinavian context of Sweden, we gain at least three things. Firstly, by presenting Norwegian cases and perspectives often omitted in other Scandinavian studies, this volume offers new understandings of discrepancies, interactions or parallels within the region due to differences in political power, religious practices or natural resources and conditions between the three kingdoms.[6] Secondly, we aim to escape the traditional nationally oriented history writing, particularly as found in a young modern state such as Norway, by focusing on transnational relations both within and beyond Scandinavia. Finally, an important goal is to expand opportunities for non-Scandinavian scholars to track the journeys of printed books, illustrations and news, and their social effects, further north. These transnational entanglements between centres and (semi-)peripheries offer future studies a more comprehensive material on the history of print, knowledge and communication, especially in the long eighteenth century.[7]

Books in Scandinavia were on the one hand shaped by a European market and tradition, and on the other they constitute an important and different case of regional and local adaptation. The three Scandinavian countries, constituting two different yet kindred language areas, were marked by what has been termed 'Northern Enlightenment' and later the phenomenon of Scandinavian world literature (notably featuring Ibsen and Strindberg).[8] The term 'Northern Enlightenment' points to the particular character of the Enlightenment movement in Scandinavia and the northern German states with its close ties to state administration, the Church, universities and local governments, setting its content and society apart from other

---

[5] See L. Howsam, 'The Study of Book History', in L. Howsam (ed.), *The Cambridge Companion to History of the Book* (Cambridge, 2015), pp. 1–13, at pp. 10–12.

[6] See S. A. Reinert, 'Northern Lights: Political Economy and the Terroir of the Norwegian Enlightenment', *The Journal of Modern History*, 92 (March 2020), 76–115; J. Israel, 'Northern Varieties: Contrasting the Dano-Norwegian and the Swedish-Finnish Enlightenments', in E. Krefting *et al.* (eds), *Eighteenth-Century Periodicals as Agents of Change* (Leiden, 2015), pp. 17–45.

[7] M. Werner and B. Zimmermann, 'Beyond Comparison: *Histoire Croisée* and the Challenge of Reflexivity', *History and Theory* (2006); D. Bellingradt and J. Salman (eds), *Books in Motion in Early Modern Europe* (Cham, 2017).

[8] N. Fulsås and T. Rem, *Ibsen, Scandinavia and the Making of a World Drama* (Cambridge, 2018).

regional and national Enlightenments.[9] Recurring international topics of the day, such as tolerance and defence of civil liberties (including freedom of print), were widely debated. However, in the dual monarchy of Denmark–Norway these battles took place within the framework of the absolutist state, not outside them. Furthermore, Northern Enlightenment was largely state-sponsored and loyal to the absolutist Lutheran regime. With some exceptions, critique took the form of self-critique in the 'patriotic' debates over reform, progress and human betterment. Historical writing, law and moral discourse dominated the intellectual field and the burgeoning public sphere.[10] By exploring the duality between openness to radical European and North American ideas and their local adaptation, important traits of transnational European entanglements are revealed in Scandinavian book and media history. Consequently, new light is shed on both the European and regional book markets, the development of a bourgeois and popular public sphere and the impact of new media on intellectual, social and political change.

LITERARY CITIZENSHIP, THE MEDIA LANDSCAPE AND CENSORSHIP

While 'literary citizenship' is a recent term, with a range of meanings and connotations, we apply it here as an analytical frame for exploring the historical use, development and impact of printed materials by and on individuals, communities and society as a whole. It helps us establish how religious books, from the Early Modern period, were used to forge various kinds of spiritual and cultural identities and communities, before and after the Protestant Reformation of the sixteenth century. During the 'reading revolution' of the eighteenth century – when print travelled faster and became an essential component in 'democratising' information, enlightenment and understanding even in the northern parts of Europe – it fostered new individual and collective virtues and senses of belonging. Importantly, print was key to the emergence of a modern citizen consciousness.

The term 'citizen' (*borger*) in the Dano-Norwegian context was used both in a narrow sense, designating an inhabitant of a particular town working as master merchant or artisan, as well as in a broader sense, signifying membership of a larger political community, referring for instance to 'all

[9] E. Krefting *et al.*, 'Introduction', in E. Krefting *et al.* (eds), *Eighteenth-Century Periodicals as Agents of Change* (Leiden, 2015), p. 9.

[10] K. Haakonsen and H. Horstbøll (eds), *Northern Antiquities and National Identities. Perceptions of Denmark and the North in the Eighteenth Century* (Copenhagen, 2008); H. Evju, *Ancient Constitutions and Modern Monarchy. Historical Writing and Enlightened Reform in Denmark–Norway 1730–1814* (Leiden, 2019).

the subjects in a state', in the words of the Norwegian-born playwright and historian Ludvig Holberg (1683–1745).[11] A growing number of publications, and periodicals in particular, framed the readers as 'citizens' and aimed to encourage 'citizen virtues'.[12] Ideals of good citizenship and public spiritedness (over private interest) were rooted in the dominant ideology in the Dano-Norwegian conglomerate state of the long eighteenth century, which was that of patriotism, not to be confused with nationalism.[13] The frequent references to 'patriot' and 'patriotic' in titles, dedications and forewords of publications in Scandinavia during the period attest to the link between books, citizen virtues and patriotism. Reading and writing were essential to improve the public's ability to participate as citizens in society and thereby contribute to the development and well-being of the entire state. Moreover, a growing number of publications sought to engage and educate new groups of readers to become active participants in the literary culture on different levels. Hence, the rise of religious as well as secular printed materials addressing women and child readers, for instance, impels investigations into new forms of literary citizenship. They include incorporating religious and moral models found in books and periodicals, improving sensibility through reading sentimental fiction or taking part in dramatic societies, or joining a local library to explore secret societies and sensationalist rumours from European courts. By applying transnational genres (such as the prose story, the novel, constitutions or secret histories) or shaping a local political discourse in pamphlet form, readers, booksellers and writers engaged in these new forms and networks, taking part in literary communities across borders and moulding them to better their own lives locally.

As these 'citizenships' were not limited to the book medium, the stories presented in this volume highlight the complex media relations of the period. Book history has traditionally left out many of the tangled relationships between media forms, a flaw international scholars have increasingly

---

[11] 'alle Undersaattere udi en Stad'; cf. the entry 'Borger' in the Holberg online dictionary, <www.holbergordbog.dk>.

[12] See for instance the very first issue of the Copenhagen weekly *Borger-Vennen* (Citizen's friend, 1788), declaring that it will 'write about the concept of the citizen, civic ways of thinking and acting, civic virtue and diligence in various occupations, civic well-doing and its considerable effect on the happiness of the state' ['skrive om Borger-Navnet, borgerlig Tænke- og Handle-Maade, borgerlig Duelighed og Fliid i forskiellig Virkekreds, borgerlige Fortienester og deres betydelige Indflydelse i Statens Lyksalighed']. *Borger-Vennen*, no. 3, (Copenhagen, 1788), p. 17.

[13] J. Engelhardt, 'Patriotism, Nationalism and Modernity: The Patriotic Societies in the Danish Conglomerate State, 1769–1814', *Nations and Nationalism*, 13:2 (2007), 205–23.

pointed to.[14] Media convergences are not a recent phenomenon, but rather a continuous historical process: they are present from the liturgical books of the sixteenth century (with musical sheets and illustrations) to the serialised books in periodicals, the oral repetition or singing of religious texts, the international trade in illustrations, or university lectures circulated in manuscript. This wide range of materialities and reproductions illustrates what D. F. McKenzie famously referred to as 'the sociology of texts': the shift in meaning taking place depending on the material form and historical situation of texts and reading.[15] Moreover, journals, bibliographies and pamphlets are intriguing sources that reveal how books and literature moved and shed light on the discussion of those movements, including questions of legislation and censorship. This shifting media landscape and its politics are transnational by nature, but adaptations are local and regional.

In this volume we explore interactions across media forms: books, manuscripts and periodicals, text and image, text and performance. Methodologically, the interactions of media forms here mean exploring and discussing the possibilities and limits of access to the physical objects versus the growing number of digital collections internationally, found in separate locations, languages and channels.[16] Furthermore, we study how changing legal frameworks affected the production, import and circulation of books and formed and changed literary citizenship. In Denmark–Norway the introduction of absolutism in 1660 brought strict censorship laws and procedures with profound effects on the shape and development of the media landscape and book market. Until 1770 domestic publications as well as imported theological books needed approbation by a government official, an appointed censor at the University (Denmark) or the local bishop (Norway). Violators of the laws could face torture, execution or exile. To prevent heterodoxy and opposition to royal authority, censorship mainly targeted texts on religion, politics and economics, and news. Satire and slander were also prohibited. The censorship practice was however marked by what Edoardo Tortarolo has called 'functional ambiguity', allowing for public or semi-public negotiations between authors, censors and readers.[17] Moreover, while most of the censorship practices actually targeted the

---

[14]   A. Briggs and P. Burke, *A Social History of the Media* (Cambridge, 2009); L. Brake, *Print in Transition 1850–1910* (Basingstoke, 2001); A. Thomson *et al.* (eds), *Cultural Transfer*, SVEC, no. 4 (Oxford, 2010).

[15]   D. F. McKenzie, *Bibliography and the Sociology of Texts* (Oxford, 1999 [1984]).

[16]   See for instance L. Putnam, 'The Transnational and the Text-Searchable: Digitized Sources and the Shadows They Cast', *The American Historical Review*, 121:2 (April 2016), 377–402.

[17]   E. Tortarolo, 'La censure à Berlin au XVIIIe siècle', *La Lettre Clandestine*, 6 (1997).

dissemination of undesirable print material among the broader population in particular, the learned classes could freely purchase uncensored books or import foreign literature.[18] In some cases repressive legislation seems to have had productive effects. The detailed control of the news press following the official censorship 'rescript' of 1701, explicitly prohibiting the blending of 'news' with 'opinion', opened a favourable space for the medium of journals, thriving on the exchange of opinions, especially on moral and social issues.[19]

The first freedom of the press act in the world was enacted in Sweden in 1766, lasting until 1772. Even briefer was the similar experiment in Denmark–Norway, with the first – and still unprecedented – declaration of unlimited freedom of the press made in 1770 before being abolished in 1773. Both resulted in an explosion of publications (cf. Langen, Nordin and Stjernfelt in this volume).[20] In Denmark–Norway pre-censorship was not reintroduced but replaced with post-publication censorship by the police. The conditions for writing and publishing in Denmark–Norway were further curtailed by the regulation on the boundaries of press freedom in 1799.[21] While Denmark retained its absolutist regime until 1848/49, new constitutions, in Sweden in 1809 and in the re-established Norway in 1814, constitutionally secured freedom of the press.

Foreign-language literature was subject to double standards in terms of censorship and regulations. For the most part, only the upper strata of society read languages other than Danish in Denmark and Norway, so imported or locally produced texts in foreign languages usually received lenient treatment by the authorities as they were not considered 'dangerous' for the educated to read while being out of reach for the commoner. Goethe's *Werther*, for instance, was sold and read in German but was not allowed to be printed in a Danish translation. Nevertheless, translations represented a substantial part of the Dano-Norwegian book market across media forms and genres: broadsheet ballads and romances, travelogues and scientific accounts, periodicals and pamphlets, schoolbooks and religious works, fairy tales and moral fiction etc. Furthermore, translations remained an

---

[18] J. Jakobsen, *Uanstændige, utilladelige og unyttige skrifter* (Copenhagen, 2017).

[19] E. Krefting, 'News versus Opinion: The State, the Press, and the Northern Enlightenment', in S. G. Brandtzæg, P. Goring and Chr. Watson (eds), *Travelling Chronicles: News and Newspapers from the Early Modern Period to the Eighteenth Century* (Leiden, 2018), pp. 299–318; E. Krefting *et al.*, *En pokkers skrivesyge. 1700-tallets dansk-norske tidsskrifter mellom sensur og ytringsfrihet* (Oslo, 2014).

[20] H. Horstbøll *et al.*, *Grov konfækt* (Copenhagen, 2020).

[21] L. Björne, 'Freedom of Expression in the Nordic Countries 1815–1914: Theory and Practice', *Scandinavica*, 58:2 (2019), 12–28.

entry point to the book market for women writers well versed in modern languages as translators of drama, poetry, history or hymns. From a self-censorship perspective of both sexes, it was considered safer for a writer to hide behind the political opinions of foreign authors as a translator than to advertise their own. In leading academic and literary circles, *good* translations were considered a means of strengthening the domestic literature by displaying the range of the Danish language, thus providing budding writers with good examples of texts in all genres. Nevertheless, translations (and reprints) first and foremost remained good business for printers at a time before international copyright.[22] Translations *from* Danish into major European languages were often initiated from Denmark–Norway to (self-) market an author abroad, provide printers and booksellers with tradable goods at the book fair in Leipzig, or encourage international knowledge of the kingdom's past, its society or natural resources (cf. chapters by Thomsen; Langen, Nordin and Stjernfelt; Nøding; Hemstad).[23]

LANGUAGE, EDUCATION AND RELIGION[24]

The written language in both Denmark and Norway 1500–1850 was predominantly Danish (in Norway from the sixteenth century, particularly for commerce, administration and religion). This was cemented following the Reformation, Norway's gradual loss of autonomy 1397–1537 and the introduction of print with Copenhagen as its centre. Danish prevailed even after the dual monarchy broke up in 1814, thereby retaining a major gap between spoken Norwegian and the written language encountered in school, church and other areas of public life. However, Danish in general saw a purge of foreign words during the 1700s, greatly influenced by the writings of Ludvig Holberg. Simultaneously, the importance of Latin diminished

---

[22] A. Nøding, 'Syndfloden kommer: redaktøren som internasjonal formidler' in E. Krefting *et al.*, *En pokkers skrivesyge* (Oslo, 2014), pp. 204–23; 'The Editor as Scout: The Rapid Mediation of International Texts in Provincial Journals', in E. Krefting *et al.* (eds), *Eighteenth-Century Periodicals as Agents of Change* (Leiden, 2015), pp. 62–76; 'Periodical Fiction in Denmark and Norway Before 1900', *Oxford Research Encyclopaedia of Literature* (New York, 2017), <https://doi.org/10.1093/acrefore/9780190201098.013.293>.

[23] See also A. Eriksen, 'Fedrelandskjærlighet i oversettelse. Ove Mallings *Store og gode Handlinger af Danske, Norske og Holstenere*', in A. M. Bjørkøy *et al.*, *Litterære verdensborgere* (Oslo, 2019), pp. 357–76.

[24] For a more extensive introduction, see Ch. Appel and M. Fink-Jensen, 'Introduction. Books, Literacy, and Religious Reading in the Lutheran North', in Ch. Appel and M. Fink-Jensen (eds), *Religious Reading in the Lutheran North* (Newcastle upon Tyne, 2011), pp. 1–14.

in printed works and communications, replaced by vernacular languages accessible by wider audiences, as was the tendency across Europe. While some Norwegian-born writers increasingly experimented with writing in their native language or dialect during the 1700s, the language was not systematically studied until the 1840s but then gradually implemented. The process eventually resulted in two official variants: *riksmål* (later *bokmål*) and *landsmål* (later *nynorsk*). Sami languages and other minority languages did not gain official status until the twentieth century. Written and spoken Swedish would be intelligible to most in Denmark–Norway, unlike the non-Germanic Finnish language. However, the number of original texts from the other side of the border would generally speaking amount to only a fraction of imported print, while translations were rare.

Early Modern and Enlightenment Denmark–Norway remained multilingual in terms of spoken, written or read foreign languages. A Danish gentleman (pre-Holberg) would typically use Latin for work, speak German to his dog, French with the women and Danish with his servants, according to a later, humorous poem.[25] In this 'four-language culture', German was the first foreign language (and the main language in the Duchy of Holstein and increasingly in the Duchy of Schleswig, both parts of the Danish composite state) and widely used in the military and trade. Furthermore, German and French dominated court circles in Copenhagen, and French was widely read among educated and upper-class men and women.[26] English or Dutch were known by few in Denmark–Norway, although more so in commercial circles. Non-Danish books and periodicals were imported to and published in Denmark–Norway, while local newspapers could carry texts in a number of languages simultaneously or even be entirely in German or French. Furthermore, switching between languages required proficiency in two sets of typefaces (roman and gothic/ black letter) and the two corresponding types of handwriting. Gothic was what every commoner felt most familiar with, as it was used for texts in Danish and German throughout the hand-press period, while it took more effort and practice to read the roman letters in French or English. The need for full sets of both typefaces made it a major investment for small printers, meaning some would mainly print texts in Danish.

With the Reformation, which took place 1536–7 following the conversion of Christian III, Denmark–Norway entered Lutheranism. In the shift to

---

[25] C. Wilster, 'Ludvig Holberg', *Digtninger* (Copenhagen, 1827), p. 63.
[26] This is demonstrated for instance by a publication such as *La Spectatrice danoise* (Copenhagen, 1748–50), see K.-D. Ertler *et al.* (eds), *La Spectatrice danoise de La Beaumelle. Édition commentée* (Berlin, Bern, Brussels, New York, 2020).

and dissemination of Protestantism, the book medium was central: Bibles, primers, hymnals and particularly Martin Luther's *Kleiner Katechismus* (cf. Haarberg in this volume) soon became key texts of religious instruction that would play a significant role in the spread of literacy. Studies of literacy in Denmark and Norway (*c.* 1600–1840) point to a surprisingly high percentage of the population being able to read print (to some degree), across all strata of society. All children from the age of seven were taught reading in local schools, as established by law in 1739. Writing, on the other hand, was not a government priority in children's education until the 1850s, when there was a higher emphasis on secular subjects such as writing and arithmetic. Perhaps fewer than 20 per cent could write (and read) handwriting, although there were significant local and regional differences. For most girls, handwriting was considered particularly unnecessary. These levels of literacy mirror those found in other Nordic and North-Western European countries, including Sweden.[27] While schooling was not compulsory in Sweden until the mid-nineteenth century, reading levels rose sharply in the eighteenth century to levels similar to those in Denmark and Norway.[28]

The increase in literacy rates meant larger and more varied audiences, and the eighteenth century saw an upsurge of publications in the region. In addition to texts with religious contents and purposes, a variety of texts in different genres and formats flourished, not least represented by the rise of the periodical press. Such developments were, of course, also due to the general secularisation taking place from the eighteenth century onwards. As such, the book market was now to a higher degree oriented towards new target groups in terms of age, gender and class, and with other purposes

---

[27] J. Fet, *Lesande bønder* (Oslo, 1995), chap. 2, and *Skrivande bønder* (Oslo, 2003), pp. 22–4 and 38–9; L. Byberg, 'På sporet av 1700-tallets lesere', in T. Rem (ed.), *Bokhistorie* (Oslo, 2003), pp. 82–101; Ch. Appel, *Læsning og bogmarked i 1600-tallets Danmark* (Copenhagen, 2001); H. Barker and S. Burrows, *Press, Politics and the Public Sphere in Europe and North America, 1760–1820* (Cambridge, 2002), p. 9; R. Chartier, 'Reading Matter and "Popular" Reading: From the Renaissance to the Seventeenth Century' and R. Wittman, 'Was there a Reading Revolution at the End of the Eighteenth Century?', both in G. Cavallo and R. Chartier (eds), *A History of Reading in the West* (Cambridge, 1999), pp. 269–83 and 284–312; R. Darnton, 'First Steps Towards a History of Reading', in J. L. Machor and Ph. Goldstein (eds), *Reception Study* (New York, London, 2001), pp. 160–79. See also Ch. Appel and N. de Coninck-Smith (eds), *Dansk skolehistorie*, vols 1 and 2 (Aarhus, 2013).

[28] Ch. Appel and M. Fink-Jensen, 'Introduction. Books, Literacy, and Religious Reading in the Lutheran North', pp. 6–9; M. Lyons, *A History of Reading and Writing in the Western World* (Basingstoke, New York, NY, 2010), pp. 90, 98.

than merely those of education and religious indoctrination.[29] Evidently, these expansions in the book market and media landscape did not occur in a Scandinavian vacuum but were the result of dynamic interactions with political, technological and intellectual developments in Enlightenment Europe and North America.

TRANSNATIONAL BOOK AND MEDIA HISTORY IN SCANDINAVIA

The past twenty years have seen an increased interest in Early Modern and Enlightenment studies as well as studies in book and media history in both Denmark and Norway. Tore Rem's edited volume *Bokhistorie* (2003) marked a starting point for book history in the modern sense in Norway. Along with the Danish volume *Boghistorie* (J. Bjerring-Hansen and T. Jelsbak (eds), 2010), it has served as a staple introduction to the field in Scandinavia. While the focus on literary sociology and the study of the book as a physical artefact have dominated book history studies in Sweden, the research in Denmark and Norway tends to focus more on the preconditions (censorship, education and religion) and histories of circulation (trade, reading and reception, collections and bibliography). This *histoire du livre* approach coupled with the influence of Anglo-American bibliography are evident from the chapters presented in this volume, too. Coming from literary studies, Rem and others have advocated the importance of combining literary analysis with insights into their historical and material situatedness.[30] Today book historians in Scandinavia come from a range of disciplines, in particular literature, history, history of ideas and cultural history.

However, there are few books on Dano-Norwegian and Scandinavian material available to an international readership.[31] Those taking on broader perspectives and a varied number of cases, materials and media are even fewer. Furthermore, there are few studies connecting and

---

[29] See for example J. S. Kaasa, 'Hvordan bli en tidsskriftleser? Medieoppdragelse i 1700-tallets barnemagasiner', *Arr, Idéhistorisk tidsskrift*, 31:4 (2019), 21–31.

[30] Rem, *Bokhistorie*, p. 19. Cf. J. McGann, *The Textual Condition* (Princeton, 1991); R. Chartier, *The Order of Books: Readers, Authors and Libraries in Europe between the 14th and 18th Centuries* (Stanford, CA, 1994 [1992]); L. Febvre and H.-J. Martin, *The Coming of the Book: The Impact of Printing 1450–1800* (London, 1997 [1958]).

[31] An overview in English of book history in Norway (by A. Nøding) and Denmark (by A. Toftgaard) can be found in S. van Voorst *et al.*, *Jaarboek voor Nederlandse boekgeschiedenies* (Nijmegen/Leiden, 2013), pp. 141–52 and 163–86. See also Ch. Appel and K. Skovgaard-Petersen, 'The History of the Book in the Nordic Countries', in M. F. Suarez (ed.), *The Oxford Companion to the Book* (Oxford, 2010), pp. 240–7.

comparing Dano-Norwegian and Swedish book historical developments. This volume seeks to remedy all three points by providing the latest studies in English covering the hand press period, dedicated to uncovering the interactions on the transnational book market while approaching the material with a shared interest in methods and theory specifically aimed at tracing moving texts.

Among available studies in English are Gina Dahl's presentation of *Books in Early Modern Norway* (2011), which gives an overview of the country's book market, its idiosyncrasies and transnational connections included. Her book *Libraries and Enlightenment* (2014) examines how distant regions were presented in Norwegian libraries and travelogues. A central study in the history of reading is *Religious Reading in the Lutheran North*, edited by Charlotte Appel and Morten Fink-Jensen (2011). A special issue in English and French on Scandinavian book history was published in 2022, presenting cross-sections of the field today.[32] Furthermore, a volume on German-Scandinavian book and library history, edited by Marie-Theres Federhofer and Sabine Meyer, examines some of the parallels, differences and interactions in publishing, collections, reading and writing between the two regions, from the eighteenth to the early twentieth centuries.[33]

In media history, *Eighteenth-Century Periodicals as Agents of Change* (E. Krefting *et al.* (eds), 2015) explores Northern European journals' and newspapers' contributions to changes in freedom of speech and dissemination of texts and ideas. Two articles provide overviews of serial fiction (A. Nøding, 2017) and the history of the inherently transnational publication form that was the moral weekly (Krefting and Nøding, 2020), both regarding Denmark and Norway. Censorship, freedom of the press and citizenship have attracted many interdisciplinary studies, of which the volume *Scandinavia in the Age of Revolution* (P. Ihalainen *et al.* (eds), 2011) is an excellent example. Ulrik Langen and Frederik Stjernfelt have adapted their monumental achievement, the two-volume study *Grov konfækt* (2020), into an international edition: *The World's First Full Press Freedom. The Radical Experiment of Denmark–Norway 1770–73* (2022). Moreover, Thomas Munck has made important contributions on this topic, combining it with

---

[32]   The journal *Mémoires du livre/Studies in Book Culture* featured an issue on *The Book in the Northern Countries* in the autumn of 2022, with a collection of new articles (13:1, H. Hansen and M. Simonsen (eds); French/English).

[33]   M. T. Federhofer and S. Meyer (eds), *Mit dem Buch in der Hand. Beiträge zur deutsch-skandinavischen Buch- und Bibliotheksgeschichte/A Book in Hand. German-Scandinavian Book and Library History* (Berlin, 2022).

media, print and political history in Denmark and most recently across major parts of Europe (*Conflict and Enlightenment*, 2019).

Among works in Scandinavian languages, an edited volume on Scandinavian book history is currently in-press and will be presenting a cross-section of the field today.[34] A similar collection of articles covering the period 1500–1985 was published in the yearbook *Lýchnos* (K. Lundblad and H. Horstbøll (eds), 2010). The most recent volume covering the hand press period in Norway (and to some extent Scandinavia) is *Litterære verdensborgere: Transnasjonale perspektiver på norsk bokhistorie 1519–1850* (A. M. B. Bjørkøy *et al.* (eds), 2019). The thematic scope and period, as well as a handful of the contributors, correspond with the present volume, but the chapters are on other cases and sources.

The studies mentioned above present a wide range of understudied publications and writers and unveil the important complexities of a widening, loud, theatrical, engaged, entertaining and academic public sphere, constantly negotiating the political, technological and economic framework of its reading and writing. New online bibliographies and digitised material enable further studies of these topics and allow for easy access to the material at home and abroad (see 'Recommended online resources' in the Bibliography). As editors, we are delighted to add to this scholarship by presenting twelve chapters and an afterword, written by fifteen contributors in four countries, collectively changing the image by shedding new light on and exploring the complexities of print and reading from lesser-known points of view.

HISTORIES OF READING AND WRITING

The chapters mainly follow a chronological structure, allowing the reader to track the historical trajectories of the transnational book history of Denmark and Norway in a Scandinavian context. We address these cases of moving texts and ideas from several points on Robert Darnton's 'communication circuit', including authors and readers, printers and booksellers, publishers and illustrators, legal and economic frameworks – and beyond.[35] The chapters explore how the application of printed texts had a profound influence on religion and politics, entertainment and education, exploration and diffusion of knowledge, even on life and death.

---

[34]   M. Simonsen *et al.* (eds), *Boghistorie i Skandinavien*, will be published in Aarhus in 2023.
[35]   R. Darnton, 'What Is the History of Books?', in D. Finkelstein and A. McCleery (eds), *The Book History Reader* (London, 2002), pp. 9–26.

The first three chapters deal with the shift in religious practices made possible by print in the sixteenth and seventeenth centuries. Karen Skovgaard-Petersen makes Archbishop Erik Valkendorf (c. 1465–1522) a pivotal case of early transnational exchange in Norwegian print history by examining his two liturgical books from 1519, commissioned from abroad for distribution across Norway. However, his lasting reputation was due to a manuscript (an account of Finnmark sent to the Pope), and his effort to consolidate the country's religious practices was soon obliterated following the 1537 Reformation.[36] It introduced Martin Luther's *Kleiner Katechismus* (1529), which was to be translated, commented and reprinted several hundred times. In Denmark–Norway the Lutheran catechism made up the core curriculum for children to learn by heart for the next four hundred years.[37] Jon Haarberg argues the particularly strong impact this work had on education, literacy, printing practices and language in Norway. The positive consequences in these areas, neglected in Brad S. Gregory's study of the Reformation, are remarkable.[38] By contrast, Jonas Thorup Thomsen explores the conflict of old and new religious ideas at the threshold of the Enlightenment. The Dano-Norwegian theologian Johan Brunsmand's best-selling book on demonic possessions, *Køge Huskors* (1674), engaged in a transnational and trans-confessional debate on the reality of demonic possession. It took centre stage in a court case against two Danish 'possessed', as late as in 1696. They were convicted of modelling their 'possessions' on stories from the book.

The seventeenth century saw the introduction of new media, print and reading practices in Denmark–Norway in the form of newspapers and periodicals. Following the publication of newspapers in prose and verse, in French, German and Danish, the first periodical (from 1720) was typically addressed to learned men: the literary review journal *Nye Tidender om lærde Sager* (Copenhagen). Jens Bjerring-Hansen discusses how Lübeck's *Nova literaria* from around 1700, along with later literary journals – the multi-language *Nordia* from around 1800 and the Danish-language *Det nittende Aarhundrede* (The nineteenth century) from just before 1900 – aimed to form a pan-Scandinavian literary field. While facilitating intellectual and aesthetic exchange across regional borders, they had to navigate increasingly vernacular language systems.

---

[36]   On the early attempts of the Church to consolidate worship practices through print, see E. Eisenstein, *The Printing Revolution in Early Modern Europe*, 2nd edn (Cambridge, 2005), pp. 173ff.

[37]   Cf. A. Pettegree, *Brand Luther* (New York, 2016) and Ch. Appel and M. Fink-Jensen (eds), *Religious Reading in the Lutheran North* (Newcastle upon Tyne, 2011).

[38]   B. Gregory, *The Unintended Reformation* (Cambridge, MA, 2012).

The laws and regulations of the absolutist regime in the dual monarchy of Denmark–Norway naturally dominated the politics of printing. Ulrik Langen, Jonas Nordin and Frederik Stjernfelt explore the unprecedented (but short-lived) shift from pre-censorship to freedom of print in the 1760s and 1770s in both Sweden and Denmark–Norway. In spite of the similarities of these events, taking place at roughly the same time, there was a striking lack of interconnections between the two realms at the time. The media revolution that followed in both states had a profound impact on public discourse, the public sphere and the expansion of readerships.[39] The two Scandinavian examples place other early experiences of freedom of the press in perspective, inviting new insights into their institutional and intellectual preconditions, the consequences for the public discourse and the effects on the market conditions of printers and publishers.

By the second half of the eighteenth century, reading communities and their material had broadened substantially in every way. Karin Kukkonen maps the multilingual book collections in Norway, from commercial lending libraries to school libraries and bourgeois reading societies. She discusses how they contributed to the circulation of books and ideas, for education and entertainment, and helped shape and cater to new literary citizens, what Reinhard Wittmann calls 'the institutionalised reader' of the bourgeoisie.[40] Drawing on examples ranging from Richardson's *Pamela* and Goethe's *Werther* to the German 'Geheimbundroman', she demonstrates how the practises of reading and performance that emerged around these book collections contributed to the development of the public sphere in Norway and of modern Scandinavian literature. One of the most popular works amongst bourgeois readers was Jean-François Marmontel's moral tales, *Contes moraux* (1761). Aina Nøding shows that the reception of *Contes moraux* followed two diverging paths in Denmark–Norway: one as *oeuvre* in French volumes, the other as individual stories, scattered in newspapers and periodicals in Danish and adapted to changing readerships and literary fashions. In identifying a French 'pirate' edition in Copenhagen (previously thought to be British), she argues for rethinking the binary

---

[39] H. Horstbøll *et al.*, *Grov konfækt* (Copenhagen, 2020); E. Krefting *et al.*, *En pokkers skrivesyge* (Oslo, 2014).

[40] R. Wittmann, 'Was there a Reading Revolution at the End of the Eighteenth Century?', in G. Cavallo and R. Chartier (eds), *A History of Reading in the West* (Cambridge, 1999). A catalogue of these libraries' holdings, compiled by K. Kukkonen and M. Sjelmo, is freely available for search: *Literary Fiction in Norwegian Lending Libraries in the 18th Century*, <www.nb.no/forskning/skjonnlitteratur-i-norske-bibliotek-pa-1700-tallet> (2019).

centre–periphery model of the book market in light of the transnational activities of a Dano-Swiss printer-bookseller.[41]

While moral tales became the height of fashion, so did 'immoral' ones, as cloaks for addressing topics that were not to be approached publicly. Ellen Krefting presents the genre of 'secret history' as it was imported, read and practised in Denmark–Norway. These stories and anecdotes, circulating in manuscripts and print, claimed to present 'alternative facts' of both past and present political realities by focusing on the private conduct of royals and other people of influence rather than on public affairs.[42] The anti-absolutist discourse embedded in the genre helped shape literary citizenship and political discourse, Krefting argues, as the revelations of the 'scandalous' behaviour of people in power could serve to illustrate the weaknesses of absolute monarchy as a political system. While parallel media practices (of print, manuscript and orality) were of course common in the early days of print history (cf. Haarberg and Skovgaard-Petersen in this volume), they remained – and remain – strategies for effective circulation of texts and knowledge. Thor Inge Rørvik demonstrates this with regard to university lectures in philosophy held in Scandinavia 1790–1850. The period saw preferred teaching methods alternate between textbooks, lectures and dictates, the last of the three making the students' comprehensive manuscripts their curriculum, suitable for circulation. This process of listening, writing, (re)reading and circulating played a crucial role in the students' attainment of an academic literary citizenship.

While the cases presented here often discuss the import and adaptation of ideas, genres and technologies, Scandinavia as an object of interest in its own right or as a source of texts and inspiration is apparent throughout the period. The wide appeal of Valkendorf's description of Finnmark or the international reception of Erik Pontoppidan's *The Natural History of Norway* (1752/3) and its tales of mermaids and sea monsters are testament to a continuous interest in the nature and culture of the exotic North.[43] Moreover, Norwegian politics captured the interest of the world through numerous translations of its 1814 constitution, in Britain termed 'the most

[41] S. Shep. 2015. 'Books in Global Perspectives', in L. Howsam (ed.), *The Cambridge Companion to History of the Book* (Cambridge, 2015), pp. 53–70.

[42] E. T. Bannet, '"Secret History" [...]', *Huntington Library Quarterly*, vol. 68:1 (2005), 375–96; R. Bullard, *The Politics of Disclosure, 1674–1725* (London, 2009); R. Darnton, *The Forbidden Best-Sellers of Pre-Revolutionary France* (New York, NY; London, 1996); S. Burrows, *The French Book Trade in Enlightenment Europe*, vol. 2 (New York/London, 2018).

[43] See J. Raven's chapter in the upcoming volume *Exchanging Knowledge* in the present series *Knowledge and Communication in the Enlightenment World*.

democratic constitution in Europe'.[44] Ruth Hemstad shows how it became the most famous and broadly distributed Norwegian print for the better part of the century. In addition, it served as a political argument and inspiring model in several countries and regions, not least in German-speaking areas. At home the constitution remained the pivotal national document and symbol, printed in numerous versions and formats for domestic readers, thus fostering social and national identities. By mapping the geography of the printed Norwegian constitution, this chapter demonstrates how political ideas, even in the form of a legal text, could travel far beyond borders and time, in a variety of printed formats, and adapt to different political discourses – even from periphery to centre (see also Nøding's chapter).[45]

The final two chapters centre on periodicals from the 1830s and 1840s and their significance in enabling various readerships to acquire knowledge of distant lands and peoples, presented in texts and images. While Bjerring-Hansen in his chapter depicts the learned sphere of high-end cultural periodicals, Janicke S. Kaasa explores the staging of the child reader as part of a worldwide network of religious activity in *Missionsblad for Børn* (Missionary magazine for children, 1847–8), one of Norway's first children's magazines affiliated with Christian missionary work. Missionary periodicals made up a substantial part of reading material offered to children (see Haarberg's chapter), drew both inspiration and actual material from foreign models, and forged an active and pragmatic role for the child reader as world citizen, heavenly citizen and literary citizen.[46] Similarly, Iver Tangen Stensrud's chapter is devoted to the Norwegian illustrated press of the 1830s. Stensrud examines the transnational 'social geography'[47] of the periodical *Skilling-Magazin*, which was part of a network of European 'Shilling/ Penny magazines'. While tracing the exchange and adaptations of texts and images with contemporary magazines, Stensrud furthermore highlights *Skilling-Magazin's* connections to earlier forms of publishing, placing it at a historical and geographical crossroads between Enlightenment and nineteenth-century mass publishing.

In his afterword, co-editor of the series *Knowledge and Communication in the Enlightenment World* James Raven provides perspectives on the

[44] R. G. Latham, *Norway and the Norwegians* (London, 1840).

[45] K. Gammelgaard and E. Holmøyvik (eds), *Writing Democracy: The Norwegian Constitution 1814–2014* (New York/Oxford, 2014); M. J. Prutsch, *Making Sense of Constitutional Monarchism in Post-Napoleonic France* (London, 2012), R. Hemstad (ed.), *'Like a Herd of Cattle'. Parliamentary and Public Debates Regarding the Cession of Norway, 1813–1814* (Oslo, 2014).

[46] See M. O. Grenby, *The Child Reader* (Cambridge, 2011).

[47] A. Johns, *The Nature of the Book* (Chicago, 1998).

Scandinavian cases presented here. He places the volume and its findings within the larger context of modern book history and practices of 'literary citizenship', highlighting the academic potential of the term in this field. Due to linguistic barriers and perhaps the image of Scandinavia as mysterious and peripheral, the region's texts and people have often remained inaccessible to foreign scholars with an interest in moving books and ideas. Since an international, comprehensive and openly shared platform for bibliography or online books and periodicals is still some way off, it takes the effort of scholars to connect the dots. This book is an attempt to do so, pointing to new ways of doing it, relevant beyond a Scandinavian context. We hope the windows opened here onto a few of the writers, readers and publications from Scandinavian hand presses will bring new perspectives and answers – as well as intriguing questions.

1

Early Print and Northern Exploration in the Service of the Church: On Archbishop Erik Valkendorf's Activities as Writer and Editor

Karen Skovgaard-Petersen

IN 1519 TWO LARGE liturgical books, *Missale Nidrosiense* and *Breviarium Nidrosiense*, were published in Copenhagen and in Paris respectively. The driving force behind their publication was the archbishop in Nidaros (modern-day Trondheim), Erik Valkendorf, making them the earliest printed books commissioned from Norway, if not printed there.[1] Erik Valkendorf has also left other marks on Dano-Norwegian literary history. From his hand we have a brief description also in Latin of Finnmark, the northernmost part of Norway, which he sent to Pope Leo X, probably in 1519. Here he informs the pope about the strange nature and tough living conditions at the northern edge of Christendom – and about his own efforts to convert the local inhabitants. Greenland fell within his horizon as well. From his hand we have preserved a number of notes that tell us that he was about to engage in an expedition to this distant island that was part of his diocese.

Very different as these books and writings are, they all demonstrate Valkendorf's energetic efforts to strengthen the archsee of Nidaros as part of the international Church. As we shall see, the *Breviarium* and the *Missale* form part of a common European pattern. Across the continent, high-ranking clerics like Valkendorf strove to consolidate, and control, local liturgies through the medium of print. Thus, the two Norwegian books not only bear witness to Valkendorf's awareness of the stabilising potential of the

---

[1] The *Breviarium* and the *Missale* formed the occasion for the celebration of the Norwegian printed book's 500 years' jubilee in 2019.

still relatively young printing press, they also form a remarkable instance of local adaptation of transnational, European book culture. Valkendorf's strong engagement in Greenland and his report to the pope about Finn-mark likewise illustrate his dynamic agency as promotor of local interests, commercial as well as missionary, within the international papal Church. This is the context in which his pioneering activities as writer and editor must be seen.

A SHORT BIOGRAPHY[2]

Erik Valkendorf was born in Funen (Denmark) probably in the 1460s into a noble family immigrated from Germany. After studies in Greifswald he became employed in the royal chancellery in the 1490s, and from 1499 he is entitled chancellor to Duke Christian (1481–1559), son of the Danish king Hans. In 1506 he accompanied Christian to Norway, where Christian had been invested with royal power as vicegerent. Valkendorf became a member of the Privy Council in Norway, and in 1510 he was appointed archbishop of Nidaros. He kept his position as a member of the inner circle around Christian, who in 1513 followed his father as ruler not only of Den-mark but of the Union of Kalmar between Denmark, Norway and Sweden. The Union was not, however, accepted by the Swedes, and hence they did not recognise Christian as their king.

In the late 1510s Valkendorf became involved in conflicts with the king's representatives in Bergen and Oslo over fish trade and ecclesiastical free-dom from taxes. He left Norway in 1521 to present his case to Christian II. They met in Amsterdam, but no reconciliation was obtained. Instead, Valkendorf continued to Rome in order to gain support from the pope. However, he had to wait there until the new Pope Hadrian VI would come to Rome, and in November 1522 Valkendorf died in Rome.

THE PUBLICATION OF SAXO'S *HISTORY OF DENMARK*

The first time we hear of Valkendorf's activities on the literary stage it is as trusted advisor to Christian II. It concerned the publication of a work of particular significance to the newly elected monarch, namely Saxo Grammaticus's ambitious Latin history of Denmark written *c.* 1200. It was published in Paris in 1514 by one of the renowned printers of the day, Jodo-cus Badius (1462–1535), and the editor was a Danish humanist and canon,

---

[2]   The authoritative biography of Valkendorf is L. Hamre, *Erik Valkendorf. Trekk av hans liv og virke* (Bergen, 1943).

Christiern Pedersen (*c.* 1480–1554). From the three prefaces – written by Lage Urne, bishop of Roskilde, Christiern Pedersen and Jodocus Badius respectively – it is clear that the edition was closely connected to the king himself. The edition as a whole is a manifestation of Denmark as an old and powerful monarchy, and the king himself is depicted on the title page in front of his army with the Danish coat of arms. The first letter in Saxo's own text, C, is a similar woodcut of the king with his coat of arms and the accompanying explanation: *Rex Dacie, Svecie, Norvegie, S Gothorum* [King of Denmark, Sweden, Norway, the Slavs and the Goths].

The king had demanded, Christiern Pedersen explains in his preface, that the task of printing Saxo's history should be entrusted to a knowledgeable and accomplished printer since sloppiness and errors would be unworthy of such a great author. Moreover, Pedersen goes on, 'this point was strongly supported by the reverend lord, Erik Valkendorf, Archbishop of Nidaros and legate of the Apostolic See, and the royal chancellor, the most noble magister Ove Bille, provost of the Churches of Lund and Viborg.'[3] Here, then, we meet Valkendorf as one of the driving forces behind the first edition of Saxo's history of Denmark, whose goal was to make Denmark's long and glorious history known throughout Europe. Or as Christiern Pedersen proudly puts it: 'Thereby I ensured that the text which hitherto could only be read by Danes alone – and of them only few – can now easily be brought to Italians, Spaniards, Frenchmen, Germans, in short all Christians.'[4]

Interestingly, already in 1515 we see a hint of the political use of the edition of Saxo, and here Valkendorf was involved. In the summer of 1514, the Habsburg princess Elizabeth had married Christian II by proxy in Brussels, and the following year Valkendorf headed the delegation to Brussels sent by the king to bring his bride to Denmark. A speech given to the young queen in The Hague by one of the members of the delegation, Ditlev Smither, has been preserved. Here Smither has quite ingenuously inserted a long passage from Saxo as part of his panegyric to her husband, Christian II.

---

[3]   'Norat etenim indignum fore tantum virum ineptis aut minus fidelibus characteribus impressum iri. Pręsertim id affirmantibus consultissime Reuerendissimo in Christo patre domino Erico Walkendorff Archiepiscopo Nidrosiensi et apostolicæ sedis legato dignissimo: necnon Regio Cancellario viro nobilissimo magistro Auone bille Ecclesiarum Lundensis et Vibergensis pręposito.' (Saxo Grammaticus, *Danorum regum heroumque historia*, ed. Chr. Pedersen (Paris, 1514), Chr. Pedersen's preface). Here and in the following quotations, their orthography has been retained but abbreviations spelled out. Translations from Latin into English are my own.

[4]   'Quapropter effeci vt qui ab vnis et iis paucis Danis hactenus legi potuit: ad Italos Hispanos Gallos Germanos: omnes denique christianos facile possit perferri.' (Saxo Grammaticus, *Danorum regum heroumque historia*, Chr. Pedersen's preface).

It would be reasonable to connect this use of Saxo with Valkendorf and indeed to assume that a copy of the new edition was among the presents brought by the delegation he was heading.[5]

The Saxo edition thus gives us a glimpse of Valkendorf's awareness of the potential of the printing press – a potential he would exploit further with the publication of the liturgical books of his diocese a few years later.

THE *BREVIARIUM* AND THE *MISSALE*

The *Missale Nidrosiense* and the *Breviarium Nidrosiense* came out only a few weeks apart, the *Missale* in May 1519 in Copenhagen and the *Breviarium* in July 1519 in Paris.[6] They were designed for different purposes, and so they differ considerably in their exterior appearance. The *Breviarium* is a small, thick book, 451 leaves in octavo. It was meant for the clergymen's personal use, a liturgical manual containing prayers and texts for the priests to use in the service outside mass for private praying. The *Missale*, on the other hand, contains the prayers and texts to be used in the mass itself and is meant to be placed at the altar. This is a large, stately book in folio (303 leaves).

Even though the *Missale* was published first, the preparation of the *Breviarium* appears to have been completed some years earlier. Valkendorf's preface to the *Breviarium* is only preserved in one of the surviving copies, and it is dated 1 April 1516 in Nidaros.[7] It was not originally part of the copy in question, however, but has been glued into it at a later stage. Here the *Breviarium* is referred to as finished, indeed printed. On this basis it has been suggested that the *Breviarium* was already published in an otherwise unknown first edition in 1516 and that the 1519 edition was a second edition. Though this is unlikely, the date of this preface implies that the *Breviarium* had in fact been ready for publication in 1516, albeit possibly in

---

[5]   K. Friis-Jensen, 'Humanism and Politics. The Paris Edition of Saxo Grammaticus's *Gesta Danorum* 1514', *Analecta Romana Instituti Danici*, 17–18 (Rome, 1988–9), pp. 149–62; (on the wedding, pp. 150–3).

[6]   The colophon of the *Missale* dates the final day of printing, 25 May 1519, and similarly the *Breviarium* is dated 4 July in its colophon. Both works are found in a modern digital edition: *Breviarium Nidrosiense*, ed. I. Sperber and introduction by E. Karlsen and S. Hareide (Oslo, 2019) (<bokselskap.no/boker/breviarium/titlepage>, accessed 8 March 2022) and *Missale Nidrosiense*, ed. I. Sperber and introduction by E. Karlsen and S. Hareide (Oslo, 2019) (<bokselskap.no/boker/missale/part1>, accessed 8 March 2022). The introductions by Hareide and Karlsen provide useful surveys of their contents.

[7]   The Royal Library, Copenhagen, 28a.

a less comprehensive version than the one eventually published in 1519, and apparently sent all the way to Nidaros for Valkendorf to inspect.[8]

Valkendorf's information in the two prefaces about the members of the Nidaros Chapter involved in the production of the books also confirms that the *Breviarium* was prepared before the *Missale*. One of the collaborators on the *Breviarium* was Dean Peter Stut, who died in 1515, while his successor as dean Olav Engelbrektsson (*c.* 1480–1538) oversaw the *Missale*.

The *Breviarium Nidrosiense* was printed in Paris by two accomplished printers, Jean Kerbriant and Jean Bienayse, who collaborated on several liturgical publications in this period.[9] In fact, the *Breviarium* itself gives us a glimpse into the prolonged process from the first contact between Nidaros and Paris to the finished product. In his preface Valkendorf himself tells us that he, after having commissioned his dean and arch-dean to produce a revised copy, had asked his secretary, Canon Johannes Rev (Hans Ræff), to see to the printing in Paris.

On the very last pages of the book, we find a postscript written by Johannes Rev and addressed to Valkendorf dated 1 July 1519. Rev is proud of having accomplished the task given to him by Valkendorf and looks back upon his enterprise in the Parisian book world on behalf of Valkendorf:

> And since I was not myself sufficiently experienced in the art of printing, I sought advice and help from the excellent and highly learned Jodocus Badius, who directed me to the experienced and skilled printers Jean Kerbriant, also known as Huguelin, and Jean Bienayse. By their diligent labour our work has been brought to the fortunate conclusion that has been so wished for. I ask you to receive it in a friendly spirit dedicated as it is to your most excellent and auspicious name to which it owes its entire existence, and to distribute it to your clergy whom you have thereby bound to eternal obedience and willingness to serve. [...] Goodbye, most worthy archbishop. From the printing office of the aforementioned printers in Paris, on 1 July 1519.[10]

---

[8] 'This is the unsolved problem of the Nidaros Breviary. Was a first edition finished, and bound, ready for the Archbishop's inspection, on April 1, 1516?' (L. Gjerløw, 'The Breviarium and the Missale Nidrosiense (1519)', in H. Bekker-Nielsen *et al.* (eds), *From Script to Book. A Symposium* (Odense, 1986), pp. 50–77, at p. 56).

[9] Gjerløw, 'The Breviarium and the Missale Nidrosiense (1519)', p. 57.

[10] 'In qua re, quia impressorie artis non satis eram peritus, usus sum consilio et adiutorio optimi et doctissimi viri Jodoci Badij Ascensij: qui nobis peritos et solertes impressores Joannem kerbriant alias Hugueli, et Joannem bienayse delegit. Quorum opera et accuratione opus nostrum ad felicem faustumque ac plurimum optatum sortitum est exitum: quod excellentissimo et auspicatissimo nomini tuo, cui totum debetur, dicatum benigno supercilio suspicias precamur cleroque tuo, quem

Here we learn that the contact between Valkendorf's trusted secretary Johannes Rev and the two printers of the *Breviarium* had been established by Jodocus Badius, the Parisian printer who had published Saxo's *History of Denmark* in 1514. Valkendorf, in other words, appears to have made use of his acquaintance with Badius which went back to the preparation a few years earlier of Christiern Pedersen's edition of Saxo.

Johannes Rev probably stayed in Paris in the years 1516–19 in order to supervise the publication of the *Breviarium*. He also appears to have played a central role in the publication of the *Missale Nidrosiense* in as much as the printer of the missale was his brother, Canon Poul Rev (Poul Ræff), who during these years worked as a printer in Copenhagen. A solid expression of Johannes Rev's mediating function is found in a letter dated 31 October 1520, in which he confirms to have received money from Valkendorf which the archbishop owed to his brother for the printing of the *Missale*. In the same letter he promises to see to it that the churches that have paid in advance will receive their copy.[11] As to the *Breviarium*, the costs for the printing were covered by Valkendorf himself, as the title page proclaims, and the plan was, we learn from his preface, to sell it at a fitting price to the clergy of the diocese of Nidaros.

The size of the print runs is not known. But we know that Valkendorf left behind 120 copies of the *Breviarium* when he left Trondheim in 1521 to seek out Christian II and that 25 copies were sent to the bishop in Iceland.[12] Taking into account that the books were to be used by clergymen throughout Norway with its 1,200–1,300 or so churches, it is likely that both the *Breviarium* and the *Missale* were printed in considerably larger numbers.[13]

---

eo nomine eternis obsequijs ac beneficijs deuinxisti, impertias. [...] Vale archiepiscope dignissime. Ex chalcographia prescriptorum impressorum apud parrhisiorum luteciam ad Calendas Julias: anno salutis M.d.xix.' (J. Rev's postscript, *Breviarium Nidrosiense* (Paris 1519), fol. 305v).

[11]   Letter from Johannes Rev to Erik Valkendorf, Trondheim (Nidaros), 31 October 1520 (*Diplomatarium Norvegicum* 1:1056. Gjerløw, 'The Breviarium and the Missale Nidrosiense (1519)', p. 74.

[12]   Gjerløw, 'The Breviarium and the Missale Nidrosiense (1519)', p. 74f. The 120 copies are mentioned in a survey written by Valkendorf himself of the property he left in Trondheim in 1521 (*Fortegnelse paa de Klenodier og Penge, som Erkebiskop (Erik Walkendorf) af Throndhjem dels ved sin Afreise har overleveret, dels senere hjemsendt til Officialen Mester Olaf Engelbrektssön for at anvendes til Bygning paa Domkirken*, written in Amsterdam summer 1521. Each copy is here priced at 3 Rhenish guilders (*Diplomatarium Norvegicum*, 8:500).

[13]   Å. Ommundsen, 'Books, Scribes and Sequences in Medieval Norway' (PhD thesis, Bergen, 2007), pp. 76–7.

However, it should be borne in mind that print runs of liturgical books in around 1500 only appear to have ranged from 150 to 850 copies.[14]

Nevertheless, there is another circumstance suggesting a large print run. The *Breviarium* and the *Missale* were not the only ecclesiastical printing initiatives taken by Valkendorf. He also took steps to have a book of prayers published in Amsterdam. A contract dated 30 April 1520 between Johannes Rev and the Amsterdam printer Doen Pieterszoon affirms the planned printing of a book of prayers in 1,200 copies, and this could indicate a similar number of the *Breviarium* and the *Missale*.[15]

The book of prayers was probably never printed. However, the contract is yet another indication of Valkendorf's active efforts to furnish his diocese with printed ecclesiastical books.

LITURGICAL BOOKS IN A EUROPEAN PERSPECTIVE

Valkendorf was not the first high-ranking cleric to make use of the new medium of print to publish the liturgical books of his diocese. On the contrary, he followed a widespread practice.[16] Before the invention of print, these large liturgical books had been both expensive and very time-consuming to produce, and errors of many sorts were unavoidable. With the introduction of print, bishops around Europe saw the potential offered by the new medium to secure a hitherto unachievable standardisation of the local liturgy. In the years around 1500 a large number of liturgical books

[14] N. Nowakowska, 'From Strassburg to Trent: Bishops, Printing and Liturgical Reform in the Fifteenth Century', *Past and Present*, 213 (2011), 3–31, at p. 13, where it is also underlined that information on print runs is very fragmentary.

[15] The print run may even have amounted to 1,500 copies, at least of the *Breviarium*, which is likely to have been produced in more copies than the *Missale*. See the discussion in E. Karlsen, 'Breviarium og Missale Nidrosiense – Om trykk og bokkultur i Nidaros før reformasjonen', *Det Norske Vitenskaps-Akademi Årbok* (Oslo, 2019), pp. 172–93, at pp. 185–7. Today both books are relatively rare. Eight copies of the *Breviarium* are extant, none of them complete, and fifteen or sixteen of the *Missale*, of which three are complete (Gjerløw, 'The Breviarium and the Missale Nidrosiense (1519)', pp. 51, 68). The complete copy of the *Breviarium* found in the National Library in Oslo (D Pal 7) is a modern reconstruction, composed of two incomplete copies and supplemented with reproductions of pages of copies in Stockholm, Copenhagen, and Greifswald (cf. O. Kolsrud's description of this process inserted in the book and dated 1915). This reconstructed copy forms the basis of the edition at bokselskap.no

[16] See Nowakowska, 'From Strassburg to Trent: Bishops, Printing and Liturgical Reform'. Nowakowska's study forms the basis for this section. On Swedish and Danish prints, see G. E. Klemming, *Sveriges Äldre liturgiska literatur* (Stockholm, 1879) and L. Nielsen, *Dansk bibliografi* (4 vols, Copenhagen, 1996; 1st edn, 1919–33).

were published in print on the initiative of high-ranking clericals. While it has often been emphasised how Luther and the reformators were able to exploit the printing press in the service of their cause, it should not be forgotten that the established Catholic Church was no less aware of the potential of the new medium for ensuring standardisation and control. Valkendorf, in other words, followed a pattern.

It is characteristic of these episcopal liturgical publications around Europe that the editors, the bishops, play a prominent role in the books – and so does Valkendorf. The title page of the *Breviarium* is illustrated with his coat of arms, and above it is proclaimed that this book is now printed for the first time and at his expense. Opening the book, one finds on the verso a depiction of the patron saint of Nidaros and Norway, Saint Olaf, under which is proclaimed E.W.A.N.A.S.L. that is *Ericus Walkendorf, Archiepiscopus Nidrosiensis, Apostolicæ sedis Legatus*, with Valkendorf's coat of arms (rose, swan wings). This visual connection between the local saint and the bishop is another recurrent feature of the liturgical printed books.

Throughout the *Breviarium* Valkendorf's person is present in illustrations, e.g. wood cut initials with his coat of arms, the archbishopric's arms and Norway's coat of arms. The same is true for the *Missale Nidrosiense* but on a much lesser scale. Here we find Valkendorf's coat of arms already on the title page and again in a large woodcut letter A, in which his initials and his insignia are also found (fol. A1r).

The prefaces of the liturgical books published on episcopal initiative around 1500 strike a number of common themes: the bishops express their concern that the church will be damaged because of a lack of reliable liturgical books. The existing books are few, and those that do exist are full of errors. For that reason, the bishop has appointed qualified men of learning to cleanse the texts and see to the publication of new and reliable versions. These and other *topoi* are found in the introductory texts of both the *Breviarium* and the *Missale*.

In short, Valkendorf's efforts to consolidate, control and standardise the local liturgy by means of these two books form part of a common European endeavour to ensure uniformity and control of the liturgy through the new medium of print. The same pattern can be seen in Denmark and Sweden. Here the first printed books were produced at the initiative of the Church in 1482–3, and several liturgical books came out in the following decades. However, their use in liturgical practice did not last long. Around 20 years later, in the 1520s and 1530s, the Lutheran Reformation was carried through in both Scandinavian monarchies (Sweden and Denmark–Norway), and the liturgical books of the Catholic Church fell out of use.

But their short-lived fate does not, of course, diminish the achievement of the clergymen behind their production. Indeed, seen from the perspective of a later age it is due to their efforts that medieval liturgical traditions, which would otherwise have only been fragmentarily known, have been preserved. This is very much the case with Erik Valkendorf and the Nidaros tradition, which centred around the cult of Saint Olaf – or in the words of Lilli Gjerløw: 'Erik Valkendorf's title to perennial glory will always be his rescuing of the Nidaros liturgy, in the nick of time'.[17]

GREENLAND

Valkendorf's dynamic concern for his archbishopric also encompassed its distant northern regions, Finnmark and Greenland. The Greenland bishopric of Garðar had been established in the twelfth century and subordinated to Nidaros, but contact had been lost in the later Middle Ages. Through the fifteenth century the pope kept appointing bishops of Garðar, but no bishops actually went there. It seems that some English and Portuguese expeditions were organised. In 1492 Pope Alexander VI declared that he had been informed that the populace in Greenland had given up their Christian faith.[18]

In 1514, or 1513, the Danish King Christian II announced to the pope that he would organise an expedition to 'islands at the other side of the ice sea'. On 17 June 1514 he obtained papal indulgences for the sailors who would take part in the voyage.[19] The islands referred to in the indulgence letter have traditionally been interpreted as Greenland,[20] but it has recently been suggested that these islands were in fact India.[21] In any case, from the king's request for indulgences and the pope's acceptance we can infer that the expedition must be seen in a crusading perspective, and a re-conquest of

---

[17] Gjerløw, 'The Breviarium and the Missale Nidrosiense (1519)', p. 77.

[18] See J. Møller Jensen's two monographs *Denmark and the Crusades 1400–1650* (Leiden, 2007) and *Korstoget til Grønland. Danmark, korstogene og de store opdagelser i renæssancen 1400–1523* (Aarhus, 2022).

[19] 'Et primo de indulgentiis navigantibus ultra mare glaciale ad insulas concedendis, idem Smus D. N. propter multas rationes quas in medium adduxi, acquievit copiosam concedere indulgentiam, quem [quam?] plenius intelligat Serenissima Maiestas Vestra' (Letter to Christian II from The Holy See, 17 June 1514, *Grønlands historiske mindesmærker*, 1845, III, pp. 192ff; *Diplomatarium Norvegicum*, 17:1260).

[20] *Grønlands historiske mindesmærker* 1845, III, pp. 192–3, 482; Hamre, *Erik Valkendorf*, p. 52; see also M. Richter, *Die Diözese am Ende der Welt: Die Geschichte des Grönlandbistums Garðar* (München, 2017), p. 127.

[21] Jensen, *Denmark and the Crusades 1400–1650*, p. 195, and Jensen, *Korstoget til Grønland*, p. 414.

Greenland from the heathens would in itself qualify as a crusade. The expedition came to nothing, however. But the pope, Leo X, was clearly interested in Greenland. In 1519 he appointed a new bishop of Garðar and even indicated that Christian II would reconquer Garðar from the heathens.[22]

It is tempting to connect these plans with Erik Valkendorf. A number of notes from his hand presumably written in the period 1514–19 reveal that he was planning to organise an expedition to Greenland.[23] These notes are preserved as additions to a description of Greenland written or dictated *c.* 1350 by the Norwegian vicar and canon Ivar Bárðarson (Ivar Bårdsson). It was presumably Valkendorf who had Bárðarson's description translated from Norwegian into Danish.[24] Valkendorf's notes describe the sailing route from Norway and instruct the sailors how to behave towards the locals once they arrive. His primary interest was no doubt to re-establish the lost archbishopric. But it appears from the notes that he was also well aware of the commercial possibilities. He draws attention to the many kinds of valuable goods to be acquired in Greenland and mentions among them, surprisingly, sable and ermine and other animals that do not live in Greenland. It has been suggested that the reason for this misunderstanding may be that since some of these animals are found in northernmost Norway and Russia, Valkendorf may have assumed that they would be found in Greenland as well, since we know that Valkendorf held the belief, common in his day, that Greenland was physically connected to Northern Europe.[25]

---

[22] Letter to Vincent Pedersen Kampe, 20 June 1519, *Diplomatarium Norvegicum*, 17:1184. See also Richter, *Die Diözese am Ende der Welt*, pp. 127–8.

[23] Valkendorf's notes on Greenland are published in 'Om de af Erkebiskop Erik Walkendorf (henved 1516) samlede eller meddeelte Efterretninger om Grönland', *Grønlands historiske mindesmærker*, ed. Det Kgl. Nordiske Oldskrift-Selskab, vol. 3 (Copenhagen, 1845), pp. 482–504. Cf. Hamre, *Erik Valkendorf*, pp. 50–1; L. T. Engedalen, 'Erik Valkendorf og grønlandsforskningen – fra middelalderen til moderne tid' (MA thesis, University of Oslo, 2010), pp. 19–30; Jensen, *Korstoget til Grønland*, pp. 414–17.

[24] Bárðarson had been vicar for the bishop in Greenland and later became canon in Bergen. Today, Bárðarson's description is not known in its original Norse version. The most recent edition of Bárðarson's description is found in F. Jónsson's *Det gamle Grønlands beskrivelse* (Copenhagen, 1930). An older edition is published with an introduction in *Grønlands historiske mindesmærker*, ed. Det Kongelige Nordiske Oldskrift-Selskab, vol. 3 (1845), pp. 248–64. See also Engedalen, *Erik Valkendorf og grønlandsforskningen*, pp. 47–52.

[25] Hamre, *Erik Valkendorf*, p. 31. It has also been suggested that Valkendorf's list of goods to be acquired in Greenland reflects older trade contacts between Greenland and America. See the discussion in Engedalen, *Erik Valkendorf og grønlandsforskningen*, pp. 25–6.

It is to the German geographer Jakob Ziegler (*c.* 1470–1549) we owe the information about Valkendorf's geographical perception of the connection between Greenland and Norway. In his description of Scandinavia, *Schondia* 1532, Ziegler claims that Greenland stretches to Lapland and adds that 'I hold this opinion the more willingly because the old Archbishop from Nidaros forcefully confirmed that the sea there curves in an angle'.[26] The old archbishop, to whom Ziegler here refers as a particular authority on the geography of the northernmost regions, is none other than Valkendorf. From Ziegler's introduction to *Schondia*, it appears that the two became acquainted in Rome in 1522.

Apparently, Valkendorf did not have a larger readership in mind when he made his notes on Greenland. However, they caught the interest of later generations and circulated in manuscripts in learned Dano-Norwegian circles in the sixteenth to seventeenth centuries.[27] Around ninety years later, in 1607, they formed the background to the instructions given by the Danish King Christian IV (1588–1648) for the third of his Greenland expeditions,[28] and the poet Claus C. Lyschander in his poem on Christian IV's Greenland expeditions, *Den Grønlandske Cronica* from 1608, celebrated Valkendorf's pioneering efforts to seek out information on Greenland and on the sailing route from Norway.[29] More than 200 years after Valkendorf's death his importance for the emergent trade on Greenland also fascinated the Dano-Norwegian Enlightenment author Ludvig Holberg (1684–1754). In his *History of Denmark* (1732–5) he describes the Greenland expeditions of Christian IV in the early seventeenth century and finds occasion to praise Valkendorf as an important pioneer forerunner.[30] Interestingly, it is

[26]   The passage is here quoted in its context: 'Quæ narratio [a reference to Peter Martyr] non nihil causæ dedit mihi ut Gronlandiam ultra Huitsarch promontorium extenderem ad continentem Laponiæ, supra Vuardhus castrum, & id feci eò libentius quod & senior Archiepiscopus Nidrosiensis constanter affirmabat, mare illic in anconem curuari' (J. Ziegler, 'Schondia' in *Quae intus continentur Syria, Palestina, Arabia, Aegyptus, Schondia, Holmiae* (Strasbourg, 1532, fol. 92v)).

[27]   See the list of manuscripts in 'Om de af Erkebiskop Erik Walkendorff (henved 1516) samlede eller meddeelte Efterretninger om Grönland'.

[28]   The letter of instructions is edited by L. Bobé in 'Aktstykker til oplysning om Grønlands Besejling 1521–1607', *Danske Magazin*, 5th ser., 6 (1909), 303–24. See also V. Etting, 'The Rediscovery of Greenland During the Reign of Christian IV', *Journal of the North Atlantic*, 2 (2010), 151–60.

[29]   The poem is published in *C. C. Lyschander's Digtning*, eds F. Lundgreen-Nielsen and E. Petersen (Copenhagen, 1988), vol. 1, pp. 127–267. The portrait of Valkendorf is found at pp. 193–6.

[30]   L. Holberg, *Danmarks Riges Historie*, (Copenhagen, 1732–5), vol. 2, p. 600; online edition: eds N. M. Evensen and E. Vinje, *Ludvig Holbergs Skrifter* (2015) <holbergs-skrifter.no>.

the trade companies of his own day that Holberg projects back in time and ascribes to the entrepreneurial Valkendorf. From his Protestant Enlightenment perspective, Holberg has no appreciation of the archbishop's ecclesiastical interest in Greenland.

Nevertheless, Valkendorf's Greenlandic engagement must be understood within the frames of the late medieval papal Church where conquests in regions outside Christendom found their justification in the pope's recognition of the higher goal, the spread of Christianity. Valkendorf's notes on Greenland seem to have formed part of the preparations for an expedition to reconquer Greenland from the heathens.

THE DESCRIPTION OF FINNMARK

The expedition to Greenland came to nothing. However, Valkendorf went on another expedition to the north, to Finnmark, with the goal of including these distant regions in the Christian world. This is clear from a small description of his travels that he sent to the pope *c.* 1519 entitled *Breuis et summaria descriptio Nidrosiensis diocesis et specialiter cuiusdam ipsius partis, que Findmarkia dicitur, extrema aquilonaris christianitatis plaga* (A brief and summary description of the diocese of Nidaros, and in particular of the region called Finnmark, at the edge of northern Christendom).

The letter was found in the Vatican archives around the year 1900.[31] Its existence had been known all along, however, since it is mentioned in the Swedish historian Olaus Magnus's (1490–1557) famous description of Scandinavia, the *Historia de gentibus septentrionalibus*, first published in Rome in 1555. Among many other strange phenomena in Northern Scandinavia, Olaus Magnus devotes a chapter to the 'terrible monsters' (*horribilia monstra*) found in the North Atlantic Ocean, and it is in this context he refers to Valkendorf's letter to the pope. One such monster can overthrow several big ships, he declares, and goes on:

> A fitting testimony to this wondrous phenomenon is found in a long and illustrious letter by Erik Valkendorf, archbishop in Nidaros

---

[31]   The letter was discovered in the Vatican archives by the Swedish historian Karl Henrik Karlsson in the years 1899–1900. He published it in collaboration with his Norwegian colleague Gustav Storm with Storm's Norwegian translation in 1901, and since then Valkendorf's brief description of Finnmark has been regarded as Norway's earliest historical-topographical text. See E. Valkendorf, *Breuis et summaria descriptio Nidrosiensis diocesis et specialiter cuiusdam ipsius partis, que Findmarkia dicitur, extrema aquilonaris christianitatis plaga*, eds K. H. Karlsson and G. Storm, *Det Norske Geografiske Selskabs Aarbog* (Christiania, 1901), pp. 1–24.

(which is the archbishopric of the entire Norwegian realm) sent to Leo
X around 1520, accompanied by the horrible head of another monster,
laid in salt.[32]

The information here ascribed to Valkendorf is found in the description of
Finnmark that was discovered in the Vatican archives. Olaus Magnus also
reuses other passages from the letter, to which he must somehow have had
access. The letter itself does not reveal its author or the time of writing, but
Olaus Magnus's testimony does not leave any doubt that the Vatican letter
is the text that according to Olaus Magnus was written by Erik Valkendorf
around 1520. Moreover, the handwriting can be identified as belonging to
one of Valkendorf's secretaries.[33] There are some indications that Olaus
Magnus stayed in Trondheim in 1518 as representative of the papal legate
Archimboldus who travelled in the Nordic countries in this period in order
to collect indulgences. In other words, Valkendorf and Magnus probably
knew each other personally.[34]

According to Olaus Magnus, Valkendorf's letter to the pope was *clarissima*. Although we cannot determine whether the semantic weight is
on quality ('very excellent') or fame ('very renowned'), there is reason to
interpret it in the latter sense. It appears to have attracted interest in its day.

As Olaus Magnus here tells us, the letter was sent together with a salted
head of a large sea animal – and that head apparently caught people's attention. In Strasbourg, probably on its way to Rome, it was even depicted by
an unknown artist and given a (somewhat fanciful) walrus body, and this
picture was exhibited in the town hall. Next to it one could read a long
poem in German – placed into the mouth of the walrus. Here it presents
itself, its name and its special weapon, the long teeth, and finally its sad fate.
The bishop of Trondheim, i.e. Valkendorf, it sighs, had me impaled and sent
my head to Pope Leo in Rome, where many people have seen me, and also
here in Strasbourg did I cause a stir, Christmas 1519 – my strong teeth did

---

[32]   'Huic admirandæ nouitati idoneum testimonium perhibet longa, ac clarissima
epistola Erici Falchendorff, Archiepiscopi Nidrosiensis Ecclesiæ (quæ totius reg-
ni Noruegiæ metropolis est) Leoni X. circa annos salutis M.D.XX. transmissa: cui
epistolæ annexum erat alterius cuiusdam monstri horrendum caput, sale conditum'
(Olaus Magnus, *Historia de gentibus septentrionalibus* (Rome, 1555), book 21, p. 734
(in the section entitled *De horribilibus Monstris littorum Noruegiæ*).

[33]   G. Storm suggests that the handwriting belongs to the canon Thorfin Olufssøn
(Valkendorf, *Breuis et summaria descriptio Nidrosiensis diocesis et specialiter cuiusdam ipsius partis, que Findmarkia dicitur*, p. 2).

[34]   Hamre, *Erik Valkendorf*, p. 39.

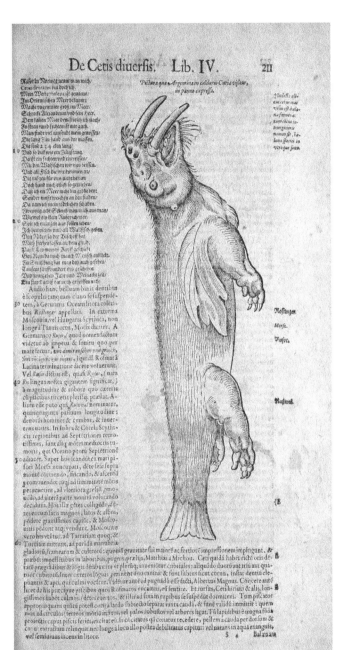

PLATE. 1.1. The archbishop of Nidaros, Erik Valkendorf, presented the pope with a salted head of a walrus. Probably while *en route* from Norway it was displayed in Strasbourg in 1519 along with a German poem, here depicted and quoted in Conrad Gessner's *Historia animalium* (vol. 4, 2nd edn, 1604).

not save me. It is the Swiss naturalist Conrad Gessner (1516–65) who quotes this poem in his zoological work *Historia animalium* (1551–8).[35]

The subject of Valkendorf's letter to the pope is the nature and inhabitants of Finnmark. The first part is about its geographical situation and the climate (midnight sun, polar rain), with an emphasis on the good fishing opportunities and the local stockfish as an important export product to other Christian nations. Next, various large creatures of the sea are in focus, among them the enormous 'troll whale', a crowd of which would once have killed me, says Valkendorf, 'had not God and S. Olaf saved me'.[36] As to the human inhabitants of Finnmark Valkendorf underlines their primitive and heathen ways of life but also informs us that those Finns who live between Russia and Finnmark have recently been christened: 'I', says Valkendorf, 'have taught them to believe in God, I have married them in Church'.[37] Throughout the small account runs the distant, strange and dangerous as a recurrent motif – as do Valkendorf's own tireless efforts to overcome the dangers and work for the expansion of the true religion among the strange peoples in the distant northern regions.

---

[35]   'Von Nidrosia der Bischoff hat
Mich stechen lassen an dem gstad.
Papst Leo meinen Kopff geschicht
Gen Rom da mich manch Mensch anblickt.
Zu Strassburg hat man den auch gesehen/
Tausent fünff hundert ists geschehen.
Und neunzehen Jahr umb Weinacht zeit/
Ein starck gebiss hat mich geholffen nicht.'

These are the final lines of the poem quoted by Gessner in his chapter on the sea animal *rosmarus* (walrus), *Historia animalium libri IV* (1st ed. 1551–8), here quoted from the second edition, vol. IV (1604), p. 211. Olaus Magnus' and Gessner's information on the walrus is discussed by E. Sandmo in 'Circulation and Monstrosity. The Sea-Pig and the Walrus as Objects of Knowledge in the Sixteenth Century', in J. Östling *et al.* (eds), *Circulation of Knowledge: Explorations in the History of Knowledge* (Lund, 2018), pp. 175–96.

[36]   'Sed Deus omnipotens et sancti Olaui regis merita me de tanto periculo eripuerunt, admirantibus non immerito cunctis rem audientibus tantum salutis discrimen me euasisse' (Valkendorf, *Breuis et summaria descriptio Nidrosiensis diocesis et specialiter cuiusdam ipsius partis, que Findmarkia dicitur*, pp. 8–11).

[37]   This is a paraphrase of a longer Latin passage: 'Finnones [...] modo christiani sunt, quorum tamen multos, qui hactenus demoniis sacrificabant, in vnum Deum credendum esse docuimus et qui coniugale fedus respuebant, matrimonialiter in facie ecclesie copulaui et copulari feci' (Valkendorf, *Breuis et summaria descriptio Nidrosiensis diocesis et specialiter cuiusdam ipsius partis, que Findmarkia dicitur*, pp. 12–14).

Leo X was known for the interest he took in exotic animals from distant places – a famous instance is the elephant Hanno, which he received from the Portuguese king in 1514.[38] It seems reasonable to regard Valkendorf's walrus head as a parallel, sent to the pope to present him face to face with the exotic and marvellous creatures found in the north. Furthermore, as the accompanying letter shows, Valkendorf's intention was to point out that the distant regions where this strange animal was found were part of Christendom, or rather were about to become part of Christendom thanks to the archbishop's assiduous efforts.

Northernmost Europe was still an unknown region in this period but subject to growing interest, not least for commercial reasons with walrus products having distinct commercial potential.[39] It is no wonder that the walrus head attracted attention in Rome and Strasbourg. Interestingly, according to Olaus Magnus, Valkendorf's accompanying letter was also widely read although it remained unprinted. It is worth noting how Valkendorf's information about the unknown territory in the far north, whether transmitted orally or in writing, reached not only Olaus Magnus, but also Jacobus Ziegler, who refers to his conversations with Valkendorf in Rome, and Conrad Gessner whose source we do not know. It is from the latter we learn about the exhibition of the walrus in Strasbourg.

Indirectly, through these three writers, who all wrote in the common European language Latin, Valkendorf's information about the nature of the northernmost parts of Europe came to influence the learned, trans-national – and eventually also transconfessional – Latin-writing republic of letters. Valkendorf's plans to launch an expedition to Greenland also had an afterlife, albeit just within Denmark–Norway, where his Danish notes about Greenland were studied in the following centuries, for instance in connection with voyages to Greenland organised by Christian IV in the first decade of the seventeenth century.

It is a paradox, then, that both Valkendorf's letter about Finnmark together with the salted walrus head and his similarly unpublished notes about Greenland seem to have had greater impact among the following generations than the ambitious and expensive printed books, the *Breviarium Nidrosiense* and *Missale Nidrosiense*. These books formed part of an international effort to establish and control liturgical standards by means of the relatively young printing medium. However, their range was only

---

[38] B. W. Ogilvie, *The Science of Describing. Natural History in Renaissance Europe* (Chicago, 2006), p. 36 with further references.

[39] Ogilvie, *The Science of Describing. Natural History in Renaissance Europe*, pp. 231ff.

Norwegian, and so they lost their practical function when the Lutheran Reformation was introduced in Denmark–Norway in 1536–7.

It is also worth noting that posterity's interest in Valkendorf's exploration of the north, both in Denmark–Norway and in the European learned republic, had to do with the commercial and exotic aspects. Even though Valkendorf himself clearly appreciated these aspects, his concern was primarily the expansion of Christianity, the strengthening of the archbishopric as part of the transnational church under its papal leadership.

2

The Case of the Norwegian Catechism

Jon Haarberg

D O BOOKS HAVE IT in their power to change the world? Or do they simply provide an account of what is already changing? Questions like these persistently resist an answer, being, most probably, versions of the causality dilemma of the chicken and the egg. Nevertheless, it seems fairly obvious that some books that influence not only individual readers but also, indirectly, the structure of society as such have a much greater impact than others. In Norwegian history one easily negligible candidate seems to eclipse the rest: Martin Luther's *Small Catechism*. It is my intention here to demonstrate why I think this must be so. Imported from Wittenberg in the 1530s, this booklet formed the religious practice of the king's subjects for centuries to come, giving rise to a specifically Norwegian literary citizenship.

Luther composed both his catechisms, the small as well as the large one, in 1529, twelve years after his first protest against Rome, at a time when he had long known that his only option was to establish a new – Protestant – church. According to the preface to the *Small Catechism*, his ambition was to create a tool to teach basic Christianity to simple folk, particularly children. Having visited some parishes in the Saxon countryside, he realised that something had to be done: 'How pitiable, so help me God, were the things I saw: the common man, especially in the villages, knows practically nothing of Christian doctrine, and many of the pastors are almost entirely incompetent and unable to teach.'[1] Luther decided that a catechism, a printed primer originating in the oral instruction of the Primitive

---

[1]   M. Luther, *Small Catechism*, anon. trans. (Saint Louis, MO, 1986), <https://catechism.cph.org>.

Church, would be the appropriate remedy. His booklet contained what he considered to be the basic Christian texts: the Ten Commandments, the Creed, the Lord's Prayer and the biblical foundations of the two sacraments (Baptism and Holy Communion), with the addition of his own succinct expositions of these texts, plus the Table of Duties: some forty pages in all.[2]

In the course of only a few years, his book spread all over the German-speaking area in innumerable editions,[3] and it was translated into a number of European languages, including Danish. Thus, when the king of Denmark–Norway decided to adopt the Evangelical-Lutheran religion in what later came to be known as the 1537 Reformation in Norway (1536 in Denmark), the *Small Catechism* soon became the key text of religious indoctrination. It maintained this position for the next four hundred years.

The history of the Lutheran catechism or *Kinderlehre* in Norway has been written several times in the past, but, until recently, only as a success story and from an ecclesiastical point of view, teleology masquerading as theology.[4] Today, what immediately strikes a student of the catechism is the rise-and-fall structure of the story: it is the story of a failed strategy leading to secularisation rather than the kingdom of God. As a historic phenomenon, the catechism now seems almost forgotten. An average Norwegian university student has only a very vague idea, if any at all, about the book and its traditional use.

A book historical version of its history must necessarily take a completely different stance. In a secular perspective Christianity has no prerogative, and so the changing dogmatics of catechetical theology, which have been the main concern of historians in the past, is of secondary interest. The essential characteristic of the book is its remarkable constancy, not change and instability.

We should, however, take into account that the political state of affairs in Scandinavia has undergone considerable changes over the centuries. In 1536 all Norwegian sovereignty was transferred to the Danish crown when the Lutheran king, Christian III, declared that the old and independent Norwegian kingdom should 'for ever' be a part of Denmark. 'For ever' turned out

---

[2] Facsimile of the Marburg edition in Herzog August Bibliothek, Wolfenbüttel: <www.zvdd.de/dms/load/met/?PPN=oai%3Adiglib.hab.de%3Appn_664786359>.

[3] A. Pettegree, *Brand Luther: 1517, Printing and the Making of the Reformation* (New York, 2016 [2015]), p. 267.

[4] The most prominent historians are (on the Danish side) bishop Jacob Peter Mynster (*Om de danske Udgaver af Luthers lille Katechismus* (Copenhagen, 1835)) and (on the Norwegian side) pastor Oscar Moe (*Katechismus og Katechismusundervisningen fra Reformationen, især i Danmark og Norge* (Kristiania, 1889)). School historians, too, tend to take the church perspective in this matter.

to be 278 years. In 1814 the kingdom of Denmark–Norway was split in two, the Norwegians having found an opportunity to establish a new national constitution while simultaneously being forced into a personal union with Sweden, lasting until 1905. Denmark had been on the losing side of the Napoleonic Wars and thus had to relinquish Norway. This means that the history of the catechism in Norway forms a part of Danish history up until 1814. After that, the Norwegian politics of church and state took their own, national course. Due to these political circumstances, we should also take into account that the written language of Norway was Danish, more or less, until 1907, in spite of considerable differences between the spoken versions of the two neighbouring languages.

In reviewing the Dano-Norwegian use of the Lutheran primer, I aim to examine (1) how it was employed as a means of religious indoctrination for more than four hundred years, (2) what part it came to play in the early phases of national print culture and (3) popular literacy, and (4) how the teaching of *Kinderlehre* was hampered by the catechetical use of the Danish language. My ambition is not to challenge the state of research on any of these points but rather to explore the adaptation of the original print phenomenon. The impact of the Lutheran catechism, I argue, can hardly be overestimated. This is the German book that made Norway into a Protestant state. Although it never succeeded in fulfilling its purpose, it not only affected the life of every Norwegian subject, it also altered the structure of society as such. Thus, the case of the Norwegian catechism may help us better understand the workings of literary citizenship, historically as well as transnationally.

SCHOOLING

In the Dano-Norwegian Reformation years 1536–7, the catechism was not yet well known. Translations into Danish did exist, although as the results of chance and haste. When Peder Palladius, bishop of Zealand, i.e. the head of clergy, had his own authoritative Danish version printed, he more or less copied the text of one of the translators who had forestalled him.[5] The Church Ordinance of 1537, the legal foundation of the reformed state, actually presupposed the existence of such a text, assigning it for daily use in church, in households and in grammar schools. The king thus relied on the *Small Catechism* in his endeavour to convert a people of habitual Catholics into zealous evangelical Christians. Pastors were supposed to explain the

---

[5]   M. S. Lausten, *Peder Palladius: Sjællands første lutherske biskop* (Copenhagen, 2006), p. 44.

five parts of the catechism in daily sermons, lasting for at least half an hour. They should also take care, the king insisted, to do so 'slowly, so that both young and old may be able to understand'.[6] In the countryside, where some 90 per cent of the population resided, the dean or, if necessary, the pastor himself, should summon both girls and boys, once a week, to teach them the catechism. In his preface Luther had already given his instructions for the method to be used. The teacher (pastor, dean or substitute) was supposed to read the text aloud to the children and then repeat it until each one of them knew it by heart, the original texts as well as the reformer's expositions of them.

The king appointed Palladius head of the clergy straight from Wittenberg. His version of Luther's *Small Catechism* appeared in 1537 and then again, in 1538 in an improved translation that held sway for almost one hundred years. A couple of years later the bishop also found time to compose the first Danish exposition of the Lutheran text, fulfilling the requirement of the Church Ordinance in that respect, too. He wrote his book in Latin and specifically addressed it to 'Norwegian pastors'. To some extent, it seems to have succeeded in reaching its readership in both main parts of the kingdom. We know that by 1550 more than half of the pastors in the bishopric of Aarhus had acquired a copy.[7]

As one might expect, the initial decades of the promotion of the Dano-Norwegian catechism lacked effectiveness. Popular as well as ecclesiastical resistance, poorly educated teachers (pastors, deans or sextons) and vast distances, especially in the Far North, contributed to what must have been a meagre result of the teaching efforts. Visitation reports suggest that the king's ambitious initiative remained rather ineffectual in some regions.[8] The miserable results seem to correspond well with those in Germany, according to the findings of the American historian Gerald Strauss. His wide-ranging study of the 'indoctrination of the young in the German Reformation' (1978) does not leave much room for doubt. Despite the prodigious proliferation of catechisms, both printed and handwritten, and the

---

[6]   *Kirkeordinansen av 1537: Reformasjonens kirkelov* (the Church Order of 1537), trans. T. Ellingsen (Oslo, 1990), p. 49, cf. p. 53.

[7]   A.V. Heffermehl, *Folkeundervisningen i Norge indtil omkring Aar 1700* (Christiania, 1913), p. 59.

[8]   Only a few episcopal visitation reports have been preserved. The most prominent one, Jens Nilssøn's diary written in the 1590s (*Biskop Jens Nilssøns Visitatsbøger og Reiseoptegnelser 1574–1597*, ed. Y. Nielsen (Kristiania, 1885)), does not give us much to go on regarding the children's level of learning.

obligatory catechism lessons that had been prescribed as early as 1531, no apparent advance had been made by the end of the century.[9]

Despite this, various Dano-Norwegian kings did not give up. On the contrary, they did what they could to intensify their efforts. In 1607 Christian IV issued a special Norwegian version of the original Church Ordinance, and in 1687 Norway received its own adapted version of the new Danish law, reiterating or tightening the provisions pertaining to the catechism.[10] In an attempt to improve the standard of the weekly catechism classes, the king decreed that all pastors should have at least two years of theological training at Copenhagen University (1621) and that the deans (*klokkere*, or 'ringers', as they were called in Norway), should preferably be students of theology (1687).[11] The most compelling decree was probably the one that made the mastering of the catechism a requirement for conducting betrothals (1645).[12] A solid knowledge of the catechism, then, marked the threshold between life as a minor and life as an adult subject. A more convincing motivation for acquiring religious instruction must have been hard to find.

The bishop of Zealand – Hans Poulsen Resen from 1615 to 1638 – was instrumental in the king's strengthened stratagem for the catechism. He issued new translations of Luther's text (1608 and 1616) and subsequently published manuals addressed to pastors and deans (1627, 1628 and 1636) on how to teach the catechism, that is the method they should use: drilling pupils by means of questions and answers. The first of these manuals, *Om Børnelærdoms Visitatz* (On the Inspection of Catechism), was often and for more than a century published as an appendix to the *Small Catechism.*

In principle, the official policy remained the same until the early eighteenth century. The king strove to teach all his subjects the catechism, also known as 'the little Bible', not only with an eschatological goal in mind, but also in order to avoid the wrath of the heavenly God on this terrestrial world. Church and school historians generally regard the onset of German pietism around 1730 as a milestone in the history of the catechism in

---

[9]   G. Strauss, *Luther's House of Learning: Indoctrination of the Young in the German Reformation* (Baltimore, MD, 1978), p. 293.
[10] *En Kircke Ordinantz* (the Church Ordinance of 1607), [1], 2v, 8v, 12, 13, 44v, 63, 65, 92v; *Kong Christian Den Femtes Norske Lov* 1687 §§ 2.4.1, 2.4.16, 2.6.1–2.
[11] University studies: *Novellae Constitutiones*, 1621, in H. Rørdam (ed.), 'Aktstykker til Universitetets historie', *Danske Magazin*, 5:I (1887–9), 37–47; deans as students of theology: *Kong Christian Den Femtes Norske Lov* 1687 § 2.15.1.
[12] Missive 22 April 1645 (V.A. Secher, (ed.), *Forordninger, Recesser og andre kongelige Breve, Danmarks Lovgivning vedkommende 1558–1660*, vol. 5 (Copenhagen, 1903), p. 445.)

Denmark–Norway. To celebrate the 200th anniversary of the Reformation, the 'state pietist' king instituted three new enterprises: (1) confirmation (1736), (2) a new exposition-type textbook (1737) and (3) board-school in the countryside (1739). However, instituting these measures did not mean that the king had broken with tradition; rather, it meant another turn of the same screw.

The German reformers of the sixteenth century had decided to skip the old church sacrament of confirmation. Its reintroduction certainly did not imply any concession to popery, the king simply wished to strengthen catechism training, which by now was well established. Confirmation was made obligatory for both sexes, involving a binding handshake with the pastor and an oath to remain a child of God until death, and taking Holy Communion also became a requirement.[13] The training should last for at least three months. Confirmation, then, meant acquiring full rights as a subject of the king: the right to marry, serve as a soldier, or receive the privileges necessary to work as a tradesman and so forth.

The new exposition-type textbook was to be the set text for both school and confirmation classes, and the king commissioned his young court pastor, Erik Pontoppidan, to write it. On closer inspection, readers have pointed out that he actually took a shortcut, abridging or partly rewriting Philipp Jacob Spener's catechism from 1677.[14] This book, *Den Christelige Lærdoms Eenfoldige Udleggelse* (Simple Exposition of the Christian Doctrine), had been translated into Danish by followers of the renowned 'father of pietism' only a few years earlier (1728). Nonetheless, the name of Pontoppidan has gone down in history as a metonymy for his book: *Sandhed til Gudfrygtighed* (Truth Leading to Piety).[15]

Before 1737 each bishop had seen to it that a suitable exposition of Luther's *Small Catechism* was available for catechetical use in his own bishopric, often taking care of the matter himself. Accordingly, Pontoppidan's book represented a marked change: a royal will for standardisation.[16] Each child in the kingdom should be answerable to the same syllabus, although the requirements varied according to the pupils' abilities. In his preface addressed to teachers, Pontoppidan explains that the 'dim-witted'

---

[13] See the Confirmation Order of 1736: *Kong Christian den Siettes II. Forordning, Angaaende den tilvoxende Ungdoms Confirmation*. Similarly, a proper knowledge of the catechism had been a requirement for participation in Holy Communion since 1629.

[14] See M. Neiiendam, *Erik Pontoppidan*, vol. 2 (Copenhagen, 1933), pp. 82–4.

[15] Pontoppidan's title contains a covert allusion to Titus 1. 1: 'the truth which is after godliness' (Authorised Version).

[16] Rescript 22 August 1738.

should be allowed to read and learn less than the competent pupil, having bracketed expendable questions, approximately one third. All in all, Pontoppidan's *Truth Leading to Piety* comprises 759 questions and answers which, ideally, should be learnt by heart, not only 'understood'. No doubt, memorising dogmatic definitions of concepts like 'justification' and 'sanctification' would be a heavy burden on anyone. This is how the book earned its dubious reputation among parroting youngsters.

The third innovation of the 1730s was board-schools (*almueskoler*). Up until then the term *school* had been reserved for grammar schools in the cities, the dean's catechism classes had not counted as such, although the purpose of the training was exactly the same: the religious indoctrination of the children of the common people. However, the decree of 1739 also introduced *reading classes* for the first time as a standard element of the syllabus. From now on pupils were supposed to learn to read, ideally also write and do simple arithmetic. Deans had given sporadic reading classes for over a hundred years, but such classes had never been a prescribed part of the training. At school children were taught to read in order to understand the catechism better. Luther's *Small Catechism* still served as a primer and Pontoppidan's exposition as a reader for advanced pupils.

This regime proved to be fairly stable for more than a hundred years, only Pontoppidan's exposition was gradually (from 1771 onwards) replaced by less ambitious abridgements and adaptations of it.[17] On the introduction of the Norwegian Education Acts of 1860 and 1889, secularisation manifested itself more strongly, transforming the old board schools into primary schools (*folkeskoler*) and subjects into citizens. Religious instruction had to yield to secular subjects such as reading, writing and arithmetic.

In spite of the liberal Norwegian Constitution of 1814, which paved the way for a steady democratisation of society throughout the nineteenth century, and in spite of the Church's loss of control over schools in 1889, the catechism continued to be an integral part of primary education until 1969. From 1911 onwards confirmation was no longer obligatory, yet almost sixty years passed before parliament formally instructed the minister of church and education that the Church should no longer count on schools to take care of its baptismal training. The last print of the current school edition of Luther's *Small Catechism* appeared in 1976.[18] The extensive educational reform of 1997 was the last even to mention the old *Kinderlehre*,

---

[17] The first abridgement was performed by Peder Saxtorph in 1771, reducing the number of questions and answers from 759 to 541.

[18] M. Luther, *Dr. Martin Luthers lille katekisme*, ed. A. Chr. Bang, 38th printing (Oslo, 1976).

proclaiming that in religious instruction 'pupils should learn the basics of the Christian faith and ethics in the light of Luther's *Small Catechism*.'[19] The book itself was hardly in use at that time. Catechism thus formed the basis of Norwegian children's schooling for more than 400 years, from 1537 to 1969. A similar, although less persistent, catechetical tradition manifested itself in the other Scandinavian countries.

BOOK PRINT

It makes sense to consider the Reformation a phenomenon of print culture. The names of Wittenberg and Luther became *brands*, according to the British historian Andrew Pettegree. Wittenberg prints spread rapidly all over Germany – and beyond. Without the printing press, the reformers' chances of success would have been scant.[20]

Having transferred all sovereignty to Denmark in 1536, when the Lutheran king Christian III ascended the throne, Norway became an integral part of the Danish dominion. Denmark, as well as neighbouring Sweden, imported their first German printer in the 1480s, which means that print culture was well established by 1537, however limited the spread of Danish prints. In the Church Ordinance of 1537 the king introduced censorship as a necessary precaution against any relapse into popery. He wanted to ensure complete control over all printing.[21] Consequently, no printer was permitted to set up shop outside the city walls of Copenhagen. It took one hundred years or so before the provinces had the opportunity to set up their own printing presses. In Norway it happened in 1643, when the first Danish printer arrived in Christiania, the capital. Bergen, the largest city by far in Norway (approx. 10,000 inhabitants in 1700), followed suit 78 years later in 1721. In both cases the catechism played a key role.

If a printer did decide to break out of the city walls of Copenhagen, he would need the king's permission. Such permission was granted in part because the king needed printers for his grammar schools (*gymnasia*) that had been set up around the kingdom to ensure the steady supply of qualified pastors to remote areas of the kingdom, far from the university in Copenhagen. Christiania's first grammar school was established in 1636. Seven years later a Copenhagen printer by the name of Tyge Nielsen arrived in Christiania. Exactly how this came to pass remains obscure. The traditional

---

[19] *Læreplanverket for den 10-årige grunnskolen* 1996, p. 98.

[20] A. Pettegree, *Brand Luther: 1517, Printing and the Making of the Reformation* (New York, 2016).

[21] Ø. Rian, *Sensuren i Danmark–Norge: Vilkårene for offentlige ytringer 1536–1814* (Oslo, 2014), p. 145.

version of the story hardly deserves credence: supposedly, a learned pastor by the name of Christen Bang, living some hundred miles north of the capital, summoned Nielsen to print his *opus magnum, Postilla catechetica*, the first significant work to be published in Norway. Bang supposedly preferred this solution to his printing problem, however expensive it must have been. However, bringing a printer to establish himself in the provinces was no matter for a mere pastor, however ambitious he may have been. Granting privileges to print was the business of the king.[22] In Christiania, like in Sorø, Aarhus and Odense in Denmark, the king needed a printer for his new grammar school.

Catechisms, hymnals and official announcements were the kinds of prints in demand by the commissioning authorities. Only a few of these articles have survived. Christen Bang's monumental *Postilla catechetica*, though, may still be read, even in a digitised version. It is arguably the world's largest catechism, an elaboration on Luther's original spanning ten volumes and some 9,000 pages. It took twenty-two years and three printers to complete it.

The lack of preserved copies of catechisms and other primers applies not only to Christiania. Having searched through all relevant libraries and collections, in 2001 Charlotte Appel was able to register only *nine* Danish-language copies of the *Small Catechism* printed in the course of the seventeenth century. Yet we know the names of 23 printers who were active in Copenhagen during these years, and that between them they produced at least sixty editions.[23] Books like these rarely became hereditary, as suggested by other print cultures, too: across the Atlantic, no copy of *The New England Primer* printed before 1727 is known today, although several hundred thousand copies were produced before that date, the first edition having been printed in the late 1680s.[24]

When Peter Nørvig, another Copenhagen printer, arrived in Bergen in the summer of 1721, it was at the invitation of the local authorities. They had summoned him to serve 'the clergy as well as the students', according to his application to the king.[25] The reason for establishing a local printing

---

[22] See E. Bjerke, '"Prentet udi Christiania". Nye perspektiver på det første boktrykker-iet i Norge', in T. Kr. Andersen *et al.* (eds), *Bokhistorie. Bibliotekhistorie: En jubile-umsantologi fra Norsk bok- og bibliotekhistorisk selskap* (Oslo, 2019), pp. 7–20.

[23] Ch. Appel, *Læsning og bogmarked i 1600-tallets Danmark*, vol. 1 (Copenhagen, 2001), pp. 165–8.

[24] See L. Price, *What We Talk About When We Talk About Books: The History and Future of Reading* (New York, 2019), pp. 41–2.

[25] A. Mohr Wiesener and H. Christensen, *Et Bergensk Boktrykkeri gjennem 200 år* (Bergen, 1921); H. Tveterås, *Den norske bokhandels historie*, vol. 1 (Oslo, 1950), p. 72.

PLATE 2.1. 'A Catechisation' as it appears in Niels Chr. Tønsberg's *Norske Folkelivsbilleder* (The Way People Live in the Norwegian Countryside) according to paintings and drawings by Adolph Tidemand (1854). The famous collector of folk tales, Peter Chr. Asbjørnsen, was commissioned by the editor to comment on this particular motif. He has no problem imagining what is going on: 'With the mien of a king and the true expression of a haughty schoolmaster the sexton is towering up among the children on the church floor. The one he is catechising, is mostly ignorant. He is one of those tall, lanky fellows who has outgrown his sense as well as his leather jacket which, slipping up from his waist, creeps over his wrists, away from his huge hands. He is hardly capable of answering "yes" and "no" in his turn. If he says more than that the result is the talk of a madman, fitting like "ax handle" as a reply to "good day, fellow". The rest of them are watching and listening with attentive, gloating or pitying expressions.'

house was the same here as it had been in Christiania: Bergen, too, needed printed catechisms, hymnals and official announcements. However, almost all of the early commissioned prints have failed to survive. What we do have from Nørvig's initial years in Norway is Petter Dass' *Catechism Songs* (probably 1722, the title page does not state a year). Nørvig must have considered it an economic necessity to go into trade publishing, having obtained privileges as a bookseller as well as a printer in 1722. Dass, the author, had passed away in 1707. Consequently, his book was not printed (in Copenhagen) until 1715. Emulating the German Johann Rist's *Katechismus-Andachten* (1656), Dass' book comprises 48 songs set to popular tunes elaborating on Luther's *Small Catechism*. It soon became a bestseller, printed more than fifty times in the course of the century. Nothing seems to suggest it was required in school or church. People wanted it for their daily devotions, as suggested by the censor, whose approbation was regularly given on page 3 or 4. Nørvig printed Dass' songs at least seven times in the 1720s, overcoming his initial financial troubles.[26]

However late its arrival, the printing press made itself useful in Norway just like in neighbouring Denmark and Sweden. What seems peculiar to the Norwegian development is the role played by the catechism, especially, as we have seen, in the early days of printing. It did not stop there. Catechetical and devotional literature continued to dominate the book market until after 1814. When Martinus Nissen, university librarian in Christiania, published his survey in 1849 of the first four decades of postcolonial Norwegian literature, 'Theology' was still by far the largest category (21 per cent), with 'Literature' as in *belles-lettres* in second place (16 per cent).[27]

LITERACY

Ever since the 1536–7 Reformation, Dr Luther's *Small Catechism* dominated the schooling of all Dano-Norwegian children. When the local authorities in Christiania imported the new medium of the printing press in 1643, catechism was the message. It comes as no surprise, then, that the catechism became instrumental in teaching the king's subjects the alphabet.

Catechism is a kind of echo, the learned Christen Bang explained, making no secret of his Greek: the teacher reads out loud Luther's text,

---

[26] J. Haarberg 'Earways to Heaven: Singing the Catechism in Denmark–Norway, 1569–1756', in Ch. Appel and M. Fink-Jensen (eds), *Religious Reading in the Lutheran North: Studies in Early Modern Scandinavian Book Culture* (Newcastle, 2011), pp. 48–69.

[27] Martinus Nissen, 'Statistisk Udsigt over den norske Litteratur fra 1814 til 1847'. *Norsk Tidsskrift for Videnskab og Litteratur* 3 (1849), 177–224, esp. pp. 180–1.

his pupils repeating it thereafter, often with one echoing voice. Learning by rote was probably the only teaching method Bang knew, Luther having prescribed it in his preface. This method certainly served as a didactic template for all teaching of the catechism after the Reformation, in Germany as well as in Scandinavia. It is a common misunderstanding that Luther championed literacy in his endeavour to enable layfolk to read the Bible on their own. The opposite is probably closer to the truth. The reformer understood early on that the risk would be much too great. Laypeople needed guidance to understand properly what they were reading, even pastors were not to be trusted.[28] Thus he insisted that the text of the catechism, including his own expositions, should always be rendered verbatim. Luther accordingly addresses his *Small Catechism* to 'ordinary pastors and preachers' as well as all heads of the family, *not* to illiterate children. Having recited the text, the preachers – or fathers – should make the children repeat it, again and again, until they knew it by heart. This plan presupposed (1) that the preacher himself had mastered the art of reading, whereas (2) his pupils had not. They would not have, nor would they need, a copy of the book until much later. Fathers should take care to examine their households once a week, Luther insists in his preface to the *Large* or *German Catechism*; if the children – or servants – had failed to learn what they were supposed to, there would be no supper.

In Denmark–Norway, learning by rote seems to have been the preferred method until the eighteenth century. Petter Dass, for instance, writing his *Catechism Songs* in the 1690s, clearly envisages his audience as listeners.[29] However, deans, pastors and parents had begun teaching the young how to read properly much earlier than that, not only to recognise a printed text they had already memorised. In this respect, Charlotte Appel has pointed to a number of enlightening paratexts. One early example is Peder Lauritzen, who in his 1594 exposition takes it for granted that his Danish-language book has layfolk among its readers.[30] Appel also demonstrates that in 1616 the bishop of Zealand, H. P. Resen, decreed that the deans should actually

---

[28] See G. Strauss, 'Lutheranism and Literacy: A Reassessment', in K. von Greyerz (ed.), *Religion and Society in Early Modern Europe 1500–1800* (London, 1984), pp. 109–23.

[29] 'Ordet indbæres [...] til Hiertet' with the editor's commentary, in Dass' dedicatory preface to his relatives (P. Dass, *Katekismesanger. D. Mort: Luthers Lille Catechismus, Forfatted I beqvemme Sange, under føyelige Melodier*, critical edn by J. Haarberg (Oslo, 2013), <www.bokselskap.no/boker/katekismesanger/tittelside>.

[30] Ch. Appel, *Læsning og bogmarked i 1600-tallets Danmark*, vol. 1 (Copenhagen, 2001), p. 183.

teach their pupils how to read 'as far as it goes',[31] his reservation clearly signalling his doubts whether the recommendation was feasible.

At least some deans did their best to follow up on the bishop's directive. From the middle of the 1600s they could find support from a new kind of primer: *The Catechism ABC*. The first we know of, still preserved, appeared in Copenhagen in 1649: one sheet (16 pp.) containing a survey of the letters of the alphabet, in lower case as well as capitals, plus the five main parts in large type.[32] The oldest preserved ABC printed in Norway dates from 1804, when secular ABCs had also entered the market.[33]

Darkness still presides over the early history of literacy in Denmark–Norway. It seems clear enough, though, that deans giving catechism lessons and parents taking their daily devotions seriously must have actively taught reading from an early date, despite the fact that they were not obliged to do so. Book-reading among the common people can hardly have been unheard of after the Reformation. In Denmark, according to Appel, the ability to read was 'more typical than atypical' by the end of the seventeenth century.[34] A significant example from Toten in Norway (approx. 70 miles northwest of the capital) tells us that the ability to read print, at least locally, must have been widespread in 1681, as the local pastor donated a free copy of his exposition-type catechism to each household in his parish.[35]

Board school (1739), confirmation (1736) and Pontoppidan's exposition-type catechism (1737) – the main instruments of Christian VI's state pietism – definitely represent a marked change in development. Teaching became more regular and systematic, and the curriculum was standardised. However, learning by rote still held sway for as long as it was unthinkable to ignore Luther's original prescription. School no longer started with pupils memorising; it ended with it, confirmation serving as a final exam. When a confirmand had passed his or her examination in church, he or she was ready for Holy Communion and life as an adult. Reading classes belonged to primary school. It was assumed that pupils would benefit from these classes in their endeavours to *understand* what they had to learn by heart: Luther's *Small Catechism* at school and Pontoppidan's 759 questions and answers as they prepared for confirmation. This massive indoctrination in the catechism continued well into the twentieth century. Admittedly, Pontoppidan's hegemony did gradually lose momentum by

[31]   *Ibid.*, p. 147.
[32]   *Ibid.*, pp. 160, 163.
[33]   D. Skjelbred, "'... de umistelige Bøger": En studie av den tidlige norske abc-tradisjonen' (PhD thesis, Oslo, 1998) and *Norske ABC-bøker 1777–1997* (Tønsberg, 2000).
[34]   Ch. Appel, *Læsning og bogmarked i 1600-tallets Danmark*, vol. 1, p. 319.
[35]   *Ibid.*, pp. 184–5.

the end of the nineteenth century. In 1911 a new Act replacing the old one of 1736 made confirmation no longer obligatory.[36] Step by step, learning by rote had to make way for the methods of modern education. Today (2020) only one private school, a relic of ancient pietism in the coastal town of Egersund in southwestern Norway, 'to some extent' still clings to Pontoppidan's old standard.[37]

Language

For centuries *Norwegian* literary culture – schooling, home devotion, printing and popular literacy – relied on *Danish* versions of 'the little Bible'. The question then arises: how did the colonial (or postcolonial) circumstances of language affect the advancement of the catechism? And, vice versa, how did the Danish catechism influence linguistic relations in the northern province of the kingdom? As is well known, Luther's Bible (1534) helped shape High German, and the King James Bible (1611) might be said to have played a similar role for English. In Denmark–Norway the Bible does not seem to have been household reading among laypeople at all before the nineteenth century. They had to make do with the catechism and the pericopes, bound as an appendix to the hymnal.

In Norway a late version of Old Norse, Middle Norwegian, was still used in writing until the sixteenth century, although modern Danish had steadily gained ground for quite some time. Historians generally place the epochal divide between Old Norse and modern Norwegian in 1523 (the disintegration of the all-Scandinavian Kalmar Union) or 1536–7 (the Danish Reformation).[38] However, the widespread idea that the decline in written Norwegian started with the transfer of national sovereignty in 1536 seems untenable. The use of written Danish in commerce and state administration was well established long before that.[39]

Spoken Norwegian differed distinctly from spoken Danish. It differed internally, too, having developed into a number of dialects, some, in the inland mountainous areas, quite unlike Danish, others, in the southern coastal districts, more easily understandable by Danes and vice versa. According to the authoritative *Norsk språkhistorie* (The History of the Norwegian Language, 2018), the period of Danish rule (1536–1814) is when the distance between writing and speech in most instances was probably

---

[36] *Odelstingsproposisjon (Ot. prp.) no. 12* (1911).
[37] According to Raimond Sleveland, headmaster of Gamleveien school in Egersund (e-mail 18.06.2018).
[38] A. Nesse (ed.), *Norsk språkhistorie*, vol. 4, *Tidslinjer* (Oslo, 2018), pp. 359–61.
[39] I. Berg, 'Reformasjonen og norsk språkhistorie', *Teologisk tidsskrift*, 7 (2018), 167–76.

the greatest in Norway. This means that Norwegian children had to cope with 'half-foreign' Danish catechisms from 1537 until the beginning of the twentieth century.[40] In theory they may have understood most of what they read (or heard recited) but in practice the output must have been sparse. The complications involved in reading, understanding and memorising religious dogmatics in a foreign language mark the history of the Norwegian catechism from beginning to end.

How do we know that comprehension was a problem? At least five factors deserve mentioning in this respect. (1) Visitation reports all testify to an alarming *unwillingness* among children and parents to commit to the catechism classes throughout the period. When examined, some might be able to recite what they had learnt by heart. The great majority, however, simply failed to show up for classes. It seems highly unlikely that more than a tiny minority acquired a proper understanding of the Lutheran dogmas.[41] (2) Establishing board schools in 1739 was primarily an attempt to bolster the *understanding* of the catechism. According to the official instruction, each schoolmaster was expected to 'teach his pupils Dr Luther's *Small Catechism* so that they first understand the meaning of every single paragraph and subsequently memorise it word for word, by rote.'[42] Moreover, (3) the exposition-type catechism, like Pontoppidan's, was generally too difficult to grasp. All pastors had to recognise that. Consequently, all revisions of Pontoppidan were abridgements. The number of questions and answers was reduced from 759 to 139 in the period between 1771 and 1891. Learning by rote, not comprehension could be sustained more easily that way. (4) Testimonies from the children themselves are hard to find, especially from the first centuries. However, there are some, especially numerous from the 1960s, when senior citizens were asked to reminisce about their childhoods some sixty to seventy years earlier, around the turn of the twentieth century. What they remembered was essentially learning by rote and punishment,

---

[40] The separation of written Norwegian from written Danish dates from 1907, when the King's Cabinet implemented the first national spelling reform (for *Bokmål*) as an Order in Council (*kongelig resolusjon*). See G.-R. Rambø, 'Det selvstendige Norge (1905–1945)', in A. Nesse (ed.), *Norsk språkhistorie*, vol. 4, *Tidslinjer* (Oslo, 2018), pp. 531–4.

[41] See e.g. A. V. Heffermehl's account of Bishop Erik Bredal's visitations to Helgeland (Northern Norway) in 1659 and 1664 (*Folkeundervisningen i Norge indtil omkring Aar 1700*), pp. 148–55.

[42] *Instruction For Degne, Klokkere Og Skoleholdere paa Landet i Norge*, 23.01.1739 (Instruction for Deans, Sextons and Schoolmasters in the Norwegian countryside), Section 10.

not mind-altering comprehension or spiritual experiences.[43] Lastly, (5) it is worth noting that the first attempts to translate the *Small Catechism* into Ivar Aasen's revolutionary norm for written 'new' Norwegian in the 1860s and 1870s were motivated by the translators' wish for the text, at long last, to be *understood* by Norwegian children.[44] Liberation from Danish rule in 1814, which also entailed liberation from absolutist theocracy, not only made the need for a national language more strongly felt, it also supposedly opened the way for Lutheran Christianity.

A comparable, only much harsher, discrepancy must have been felt by Sami children who, for a period of about a hundred years (approx. 1850– 1962), were compelled to learn and be schooled in Norwegian. At the time the use of Sami in schools was, with few exceptions, banned. Germanic Norwegian and Finno-Permian Sami are not related, which means that the essential understanding of Sami children during these years was that of the supreme authority of the Danish (or Dano-Norwegian) language to which they had to resign themselves. Written testimonies of frustrated Norwegian pastors are not hard to find. Johan Fritzner, for example, who served as a pastor in Vadsø in Northern Norway between 1838 and 1845 (and who was later to become a famous lexicographer), clearly states that the Sami children did not understand anything at all of what they had been able to memorise.[45]

In terms of language, the history of the catechism in Norway has a double conclusion. On the one hand, a severe lack of understanding among its learners can be shown, most probably due to the considerable distance between written Danish and the dialects of Norwegian children. On the other hand, Danish read by Norwegians became some sort of a hybrid, a prestigious 'recital language' too distant from everyday dialects to have any lasting effect on modern Norwegian usage.[46]

---

[43]   Two book series entitled *I manns minne* (In Living Memory) and *I nær fortid* (In the Near Past) were published on the initiative of the National Association for Public Health (*Nasjonalforeningen for folkehelsen*) in 1967–75 and 1982–7, respectively.

[44]   Cf. the prefaces to O. J. Høyem's *Barn-lærddomen eller den little katekjesen hans Morten Luther* (Nidaros, 1973) and S. Aarrestad's *Kakjesboki eller Barnalærdomen vaar* (Stavanger, 1877).

[45]   H. Dahl, *Språkpolitikk og skolestell i Finnmark 1814–1905* (Oslo, 1957), p. 23.

[46]   The hybrid was later (derogatorily) termed *klokkerdansk* ('sexton's Danish'), cf. A. Torp, 'Talemål i Noreg på 1800-talet', in A. Nesse (ed.), *Norsk språkhistorie*, vol. 4, p. 436.

AN UNINTENDED REFORMATION

I started by claiming that Luther's *Small Catechism* has a unique position in Norwegian book history. Even the Bible cannot compete with it. For 460 years, some fifteen generations, the authorities relied upon it in matters of education. Little by little, popular literacy and print culture were established thanks to this little book. In telling its story, this remarkable constancy, *la longue durée*, should not be eclipsed by our preoccupation with the historical shifts of catechetical dogmatics. Questions of dogma have certainly been of great interest and concern to theologians, but rarely of much importance to ordinary lay people. To believe first of all means to belong. Norwegians achieved this belonging in part by learning the catechism by rote. Thus, in a secular perspective the social function of the Lutheran *Kinderlehre* has been no less important than the spiritual one.

Catechism even survived the abolition of theocracy. The constitution of 1814 stated that all authority exercised by the state no longer rested in God (and His substitute, the king) but in the people themselves, implementing the Rousseauan principle of popular sovereignty. However, for as long as the monarchy remained exclusively 'Evangelical-Lutheran', fully-fledged democracy was put on hold, the clergy continuing their work as if nothing had happened.[47]

In the end, this persevering little book had to yield to secularisation. Luther got what he feared the most: 'the world' and the devil. Today (2020) 70 per cent of the Norwegian population still belong to the Evangelical-Lutheran church which, since 2017, is no longer a state church. Only a small minority claim to be true believers: 11 per cent, irrespective of religion (2008),[48] and only 50 per cent of the new-born are initiated into the church by the sacrament of baptism (2019).[49] Five hundred years after the Reformation the Norwegian or rather the Scandinavian version of Protestantism seems to be developing into some kind of 'cultural religion'. People hold on to the old rituals and traditions but refrain from mentioning God. What matters is the coming together of families and communities, the sense of belonging. Cultural religion, according to the American sociologist Phil Zuckerman, is 'the phenomenon of people identifying with historically

---

[47] The Constitution of 1814, Section 49 (the principle of popular sovereignty) and Section 2 ('Evangelical-Lutheran state religion'): <www.stortinget.no/no/Stortinget-og-demokratiet/Lover-og-instrukser/Grunnloven-fra-1814/>.

[48] L. Taule, 'Norge – et sekulært samfunn', *Samfunnsspeilet*, 1 (2014) (Statistics Norway) <www.ssb.no/kultur-og-fritid/artikler-og-publikasjoner/norge-et-sekulaert-samfunn>.

[49] Statistics Norway (SSB), table 12025.

religious traditions, and engaging in ostensibly religious practices, without truly believing in the supernatural content thereof'.[50]

After five centuries we know the outcome: Luther's grand scheme ultimately failed. His catechism did not bring about the spiritual change it was supposed to. Instead, unintendedly, it taught Norwegian children how to read. Contrary to what is often taken for granted, popular literacy was not an objective of Luther's. The reformer actually grew increasingly doubtful of the people's ability to understand his main tenets. Therefore, according to Gerald Strauss, he concentrated on 'works of popular indoctrination', the catechism, considering learning by rote a guarantee against any fanciful interpretations or outright misunderstandings of the Scripture.[51] Nevertheless, in due course the catechism became instrumental in teaching the Lutheran North its ABC. An exceptionally high literacy rate and a particularly vigorous print culture gave the Scandinavian countries a head start into the modern world.

In his acclaimed study of how 'the religious revolution' of the early sixteenth century went wrong (*The Unintended Reformation*, 2012), Brad S. Gregory fails to comment on 'good consequences' like literacy, print culture and the use of vernacular languages, exploring only the 'bad consequences' (secularised morality, privatisation of religion, relativity of doctrine, capitalism and other 'deplorable' developments). However 'unintended', literacy and print culture have proved to be a blessing to democracy and freedom, if not to Christianity as such. Thus, the case of the Norwegian catechism is an instructive historical example of how an unintended development turned out for the best after all, catechism boosting literacy as well as the new technology of printing in the Lutheran North.

---

[50] P. Zuckerman, *Society without God: What the Least Religious Nations Can Tell Us About Contentment* (New York, 2008), p. 155.
[51] G. Strauss, 'Lutheranism and Literacy: A Reassessment', p. 113.

3

Possessed by a Book:
Cultural Scripts for Demonic
Possession in Early Modern Denmark

Jonas Thorup Thomsen

Iᴺ 1696–8 ᴛʜᴇ ᴍᴀʀᴋᴇᴛ town of Thisted in north-western Jutland
became the centre of highly unusual events, in which strange symptoms
and claims of demonic possession became epidemic.[1] A total of thirteen
women and a young girl claimed they were possessed by the Devil, and the
local pastor also soon became convinced. In seventeenth-century Denmark
demonic possession was considered very real by most people, narratives
of demonic possession circulated both locally and transnationally through
translations, and even learned authorities accepted it as a possible diagnosis for strange symptoms that could not otherwise be explained. However,
it was a rare phenomenon, and there were only about twenty known cases
in seventeenth-century Denmark.[2]

---

[1] This chapter is partially based on research done in connection with my master's
dissertation, 'Besat af Djævelen: Djævlebesættelserne i Thisted 1696–98 og fænomenets kulturelle ophav' (Aarhus, 2018).

[2] Four cases involving alleged demonic possession have been published in part or in
full. In addition to the Thisted case (1696–8) examined in this chapter, surviving
court documents from the Køge case (1608–15) have been published in A. Bæksted's work, 'Indledning og noter', in *Køge Huskors* (Copenhagen, 1953). Several court
documents from the events at Rosborg (1639) have been published in Chr. Villads
Christensen and Fr. Hallager's work, 'Besættelsen På Rosborg', *Samlinger Til Jydsk
Historie Og Topografi* 3, no. 2 (1900), 225–60. The third case, which took place in
Nibe in 1686, has been published in J. C. Jacobsen's work, *Besættelse og Trolddom i
Nibe 1686* (Copenhagen, 1973). In addition to the published cases, Danish historian
Louise Nyholm Kallestrup has found evidence of fourteen cases in the protocols
of the High Court of Northern Jutland. She sets the total at twenty known cases of
demonic possession ('Knowing Satan from God: Demonic Possession, Witchcraft,

56   JONAS THORUP THOMSEN

This chapter revisits the case of the demonic possession in Thisted, which is well-known in the historiography of early modern Denmark–Norway. The most thorough investigation is still Danish runologist and curator Anders Bæksted's two-volume doctoral thesis, published 1959–60, in which he included many of the original court documents and other archival sources, some in full, others as excerpts.[3] Since Bæksted's book, the case has been treated academically several times.[4] The most detailed portrayal of the Thisted case since Bæksted's is Danish historians Charlotte Appel and Morten Fink-Jensen's micro-historical investigation of 2009, which focused on pastor Ole Bjørn's involvement in the case.[5]

Historians have long attempted to explain the peculiar phenomenon of demonic possession. In the early modern period sceptics were already trying to expose the so-called demoniacs as impostors and frauds. This also happened in the Thisted case, for instance in the anonymously-published satirical account *Kort og sandfærdig Beretning* (1699), which represented the official stance on the matter.[6] Long-standing alternative explanations have been that the demoniacs really suffered from early modern diagnoses such as melancholia, hysteria and epilepsy or that the cases were a combination of deception and mental illness.[7] More recently scholars have begun to move away from trying to diagnose the would-be demoniacs as mentally ill.[8] There are good reasons for this, namely that it is difficult to diagnose historical individuals with any certainty, that it is arguably ahistorical to

and the Lutheran Orthodox Church in Early Modern Denmark', *Magic, Ritual, and Witchcraft*, 6:2 [2011], 179–80).

[3] A. Bæksted, *Besættelsen i Tisted 1696–98*, vol. 1 (Copenhagen, 1959); A. Bæksted, *Besættelsen i Tisted 1696–98*, vol. 2 (Copenhagen, 1960).

[4] See, for instance, G. Henningsen, 'Trolddom og hemmelige kunster', in A. Steensberg (ed.), *Dagligliv i Danmark. I det syttende og attende århundrede* (Copenhagen, 1969), pp. 161–96; K. Gørlitz and O. Hoffmann, *Djævlen i kroppen. Synden i hjertet* (Copenhagen, 1987).

[5] See their chapter 'Præsten og de besatte: Ole Bjørn, præst i Thisted, 1693–1698', in Ch. Appel and M. Fink-Jensen, *Når det regner på præsten. En kulturhistorie om sognepræster og sognefolk. 1550–1750* (Højbjerg, 2009), pp. 195–232.

[6] Á. Magnússon, *Kort og sandfærdig Beretning, om den viit-udraabte Besettelse udi Tistæd* (Copenhagen, 1699). This small book was written by Árni Magnússon based on the court documents, and he was encouraged by Matthias Moth, one of the judges (Bæksted, *Besættelsen i Tisted*, 1960, vol. 2, pp. 307–12).

[7] For instance, see D. P. Walker, *Unclean Spirits: Possession and Exorcism in France and England in the Late Sixteenth and Early Seventeenth Century* (Philadelphia, 1981). Psychiatrist Fr. Hallager also explained the Thisted case as a manifestation of mental illness (*Magister Ole Bjørn og de besatte i Thisted* [Copenhagen, 1901]).

[8] See, for instance, H. C. Erik Midelfort, *A History of Madness in Sixteenth Century Germany* (Stanford, 1999); H. C. Erik Midelfort, *Witchcraft, Madness, Society, and*

do so as early modern people did not have a modern concept of mental illness, and that it does not further our understanding of the phenomenon. Instead, I contend that we must understand early modern demonic possession as a transnational, religious and cultural phenomenon that was very real to people in the past.

Scholars of early modern witchcraft and demonic possession such as Stuart Clark, Brian P. Levack and Philip C. Almond have convincingly argued that cases of demonic possession played out similarly to theatrical performances, where individuals performed as part of a group. According to these scholars, possession is best understood as following a kind of cultural script – a set of common religious and cultural beliefs.[9] Cultural scripts offered ways to interpret strange events and symptoms, and they may have determined how a case of demonic possession played out by assigning certain roles to those involved and possible ways to act and react. Although scripts did not determine how people acted, they established ways in which individuals could act when faced with possible demonic possession. Approaching demonic possession from the perspective of cultural scripts and studying their possible origins allows a dynamic examination of how beliefs about the supernatural were circulated and transformed in early modern Europe.

In the Thisted case, several agents seem to have found a useful script in the possession narratives of *Køge Huskors* (1674).[10] Indeed, I argue that this book and the cultural script it provided had a significant effect on the events in the case and that it functioned as a kind of agent of change or catalyst, shaping beliefs and even actions of individuals involved in the case. This approach highlights the role books and texts played in this process. Although *Køge Huskors* had no intention of its own, it still had an effect on events as the provider of a cultural script.[11] The connection between *Køge*

Religion in Early Modern Germany (Farnham, 2013); D. Lederer, *Madness, Religion and the State in Early Modern Europe: A Bavarian Beacon* (Cambridge, 2006).

[9] S. Clark, *Thinking with Demons: The Idea of Witchcraft in Early Modern Europe* (Oxford, 1997); B. P. Levack, *The Devil Within: Possession and Exorcism in the Christian West* (New Haven, CT, 2013); P. C. Almond, *Demonic Possession and Exorcism in Early Modern England: Contemporary Texts and Their Cultural Contexts* (New York, 2004).

[10] J. Brunsmand, *Et forfærdeligt Huus-Kaars, eller en sandferdig Beretning om en gruelig Fristelse aff Dieffvelen* (Copenhagen, 1674). Because of its long title, this book was usually referred to simply as *Køge Huskors*, which is how I will also refer to the book in this chapter. Also see the scholarly edition: J. Brunsmand, *Køge Huskors*, ed. A. Bæksted (Copenhagen, 1953).

[11] The relationship between print, physical books and demonic possession has also been examined in S. Ferber's work, *Demonic Possession and Exorcism in Early*

PLATE 3.1. The Devil at work in Køge. Note the animal motifs and the levitating boy in the background. Frontispiece from the German edition of *Køge Huskors, Das geängstigte Köge* (Leipzig, 1696).

Huskors and the Thisted case has been made before. Bæksted highlighted the references to it in the Thisted case, and Appel and Fink-Jensen briefly commented on it.[12] Most recently, Norwegian cultural historian John Øde-mark identified the Thisted events as a watershed in two articles that investigated how *Køge Huskors* underwent a genre shift, from historical account to fiction, over the course of its many editions.[13] However, the significance of this book in the concrete events of the Thisted case has not yet been fully investigated. By applying the concept of a cultural script in an analysis of the court documents of the case, I intend to change this.[14] Moreover, the case presents an opportunity to examine how 'ordinary people' read, used and interpreted books in early modern Denmark–Norway and how they became part of a literary community. It also shows how texts such as the transnational genre of possession narratives could foster new social identities and give agency, or 'literary citizenship', to individuals who otherwise did not have a voice in early modern society.

THE EARLY MODERN 'BESTSELLER' *KØGE HUSKORS*

Køge Huskors was first published in 1674 by Johan Brunsmand (1637–1707), a Norwegian-born author, pastor and theologian, and given its five editions in thirty-six years, it may be characterised as an early modern 'bestseller' in Denmark–Norway. The book was both an account of demonic possession and a defence of the reality of the phenomenon, published at a time when such views were challenged by increasing scepticism and emerging Enlightenment philosophy.[15] The central story, referenced in the title, con-

---

Modern France (London and New York, 2004); M. Gibson's *Possession, Puritanism and Print: Darrell, Harsnett, Shakespeare and the Elizabethan Exorcism Controversy* (London, 2006) and A. Cambers' 'Demonic Possession, Literacy and "Superstition" in Early Modern England', *Past and Present*, no. 202 (2009), 3–35.

[12]   A. Bæksted, 'Indledning og noter', p. 69; Ch. Appel and M. Fink-Jensen, 'Præsten og de besatte', p. 212.

[13]   J. Ødemark, 'Djevelbesettelsen i Køge og ånden fra Thisted: bokhistorie, kulturelle skript og virkelighetsforståelse', in B. Lavold and J. Ødemark (eds), *Reformasjonstidens Religiøse Bokkultur. Tekst, visualitet og materialitet* (Oslo, 2017), pp. 71–109; J. Ødemark, 'Inscribing Possession: Køge Huskors and Other Tales of Demonic Possession across Genres and Cultural Fields in Denmark–Norway (1647–1716)', *Ethnologia Scandinavica*, 47 (2017), 1–20.

[14]   Ødemark also used the concept of a cultural script, but he applied it to the texts and narratives found in *Køge Huskors* and Magnússon's 1699 account of the Thisted case ('Djevelbesettelsen i Køge', pp. 96–103), not to the events of the case.

[15]   Scepticism about supernatural phenomena such as witchcraft and demonic possession were on the rise in learned circles in Europe at the time. Brunsmand's book was a Lutheran-Orthodox defence against such ideas.

cerned the demonic possession of a house and its inhabitants in the Danish town of Køge at the beginning of the seventeenth century. The central narrative was, according to Brunsmand's preface, recounted by Anna Hans Bartskærs (d. 1642), the mother in the possessed household, and it includes vivid descriptions of demonic possession.[16] Here she describes how a young boy was tormented by the entity possessing him:

> The evil spirit ran up and down in him like a pig, and it raised his stomach. It was a horrible sight: it shot his tongue out of his neck and curled it like a piece of cloth, so blood ran from his mouth. It joined his limbs together so that four strong men could not pull them apart. He crowed like a rooster and barked like a dog, and he was borne up to the ceiling joists in the living room [...].[17]

The symptoms described above (characteristically for this text, invoking many images of animals) conform to several common signs of demonic possession: convulsions, expulsion of blood, rigid limbs, supernatural strength, inhuman voices and levitation. The book also includes examples of a demon apparently speaking through the demoniac's mouth, which included displays of supernatural knowledge and uttering blasphemies, all common signs of demonic possession throughout early modern Europe. In addition, the demon revealed that Anna's husband Hans Bartskær was the original target of the possession.[18]

In the book Anna Hans Bartskærs' tale was flanked by Brunsmand's own writings. This was preceded by an introduction in which he explained how Anna's story should serve as a warning against witchcraft and a declaration by two mayors and a council member of Køge town council that affirmed the account's truthfulness. Following Anna's story, Brunsmand supplied a historical account based on his own investigation into the documents from the subsequent witchcraft trials as well as a theological reflection on Anna's

---

[16] Brunsmand obtained the story from several circulating manuscripts, but the original from Anna's hand was not available to him. Similar manuscripts may be found in the Royal Library in Copenhagen, e.g. one from 1663, see A. Bæksted, 'Indledning og noter', pp. 28–32.

[17] J. Brunsmand, *Et forfærdeligt Huus-Kaars* (1674), pp. 44–5. My translation. The original wording is: 'Den onde aand løb op oc ned i hannem som en griis, oc reyste hans bug op, at det var grueligt at see: skiød tungen ud aff hans hals, oc trillede den tilsammen som et klæde, saa blodet fløed aff munden. Hand smaskede i hans bug som en griis, oc knytted hans lemmer saa hart tilsammen, at fire føre karle vare ikke sterke nok til at skill dennem fra hin anden. Hand goel som en hane, giødde som en hund, førde hannem op paa vore bielker i stuen [...].'

[18] For a list of common symptoms, see B. P. Levack, *The Devil Within*, pp. 6–15.

story. In addition to the Køge account, Brunsmand's book also included five narratives of possession in an appendix. Four of these were translated by Brunsmand from German texts by Lutheran theologians Andreas Hondorff, Andreas Angelus and Johann Dannhauer; they described cases of demonic possession in the German-speaking world. The final narrative, which played out in Bergen in Norway, was translated from a Latin text by Thomas Bartholin.[19] Brunsmand's translation of them into Danish made them and the transnational genre of possession narratives available to a Danish and Norwegian readership, exemplifying the importance of translation in the transnational circulation of texts.[20]

The many editions of *Køge Huskors* printed in Copenhagen in the seventeenth and eighteenth centuries indicate that it was a very popular book. The first edition of the small book, in octavo format, was published in 1674 and comprised 135 pages of text.[21] Brunsmand published a second edition in 1684 with two additional narratives of possession from northern Germany which he had received from his friend Christian Kortholt (1633–94), professor of theology in Kiel, and expanded the text to 153 numbered pages.[22] The third edition (1691) was essentially a reprint of the second edition, which probably indicates that the original print run sold out.[23] The fourth edition (1700) had further additions but was mostly a modernised and decorated print of the third.[24] The fifth edition, a reprint with an added index, was published in 1710 following Brunsmand's death in 1707.[25] Five editions in thirty-six years suggest that it was a steady seller and that Brunsmand's warning against demonic possession reached a wide audience in Denmark–Norway.[26]

[19] According to A. Bæksted, the original texts were Andreas Hondorff, *Promptuarium illustrium exemplorum* (Leipzig, 1582); A. Angelus, *Wider- Natur- und Wunder-Buch* (Frankfurt am Main, 1597) and Th. Bartholin, *Epistolarum Medicinalum: Centuria III* (Copenhagen, 1667). The text by Johann Dannhauer cited by Brunsmand has not been identified (Bæksted, 'Indledning og noter', pp. 287–8).

[20] On the transnational circulation of texts in early modern Europe, see W. Boutcher, 'Intertraffic: Transnational Literatures and Languages in Late Renaissance England and Europe', in M. McLean and S. Barker (eds), *International Exchange in the Early Modern Book World* (Leiden, Boston, 2016), pp. 343–73.

[21] J. Brunsmand, *Et forfærdeligt Huus-Kaars* (1674).

[22] J. Brunsmand, *Et forfærdeligt Huus-Kaars* (Copenhagen, 1684).

[23] J. Brunsmand, *Et forfærdeligt Huus-Kaars* (Copenhagen, 1691).

[24] J. Brunsmand, *Et forfærdeligt Huus-Kaars* (Copenhagen, 1700).

[25] J. Brunsmand, *Et forfærdeligt Huus-Kaars* (Copenhagen, 1710).

[26] The sixth edition (1757) was another reprint but was advertised as a superstitious relic of the past ('Da den for lang tid siden...', *Kiøbenhavnske Danske Post-Tidender*, 27 May 1757; J. Brunsmand, *Et forfærdeligt Huus-Kaars* [Copenhagen, 1757]). Subsequent editions (1820, 1870) drastically abridged the book and reassigned its

Brunsmand's book crossed linguistic and territorial boundaries when it was translated into Latin and published in Amsterdam (1693), Leiden (1693) and Leipzig (1695) under the title *Energumeni Coagienses* (...).[27] It was also translated from Latin into German and printed in Leipzig (1696) as *Das geängstigte Köge*.[28] All four editions were printed in the small duodecimo format. It reached a transnational audience, among them the Dutch sceptic Balthasar Bekker, who criticised it harshly in the fourth book of his Cartesian work *De betoverde Weereld* (1691–3).[29] *Køge Huskors* became part of a transnational polemic on the reality of witchcraft and demonic possession, both highly transnational phenomena.[30] By the time of the possession in Thisted, it had been published thrice in both Danish and Latin and once in German.

The translations did not have the same popular impact as the Danish version did in Denmark. Most translations were in Latin, which made them available to a transnational community of learned men, but not to the general populace. The translations also came rather late, at a time where the ideas presented in the text were challenged by new scepticism and early Enlightenment thought. Its narrative was no longer accepted as fact, at least not by its learned readership. Other possession narratives had a greater popular impact. Philip C. Almond has shown how English possession narratives influenced each other and became an established genre that was used as propaganda in a confessional battle between the Church of England, Puritan preachers and Catholics.[31] Furthermore, Brian P. Levack highlights how the possession of the Throckmorton children in 1589–93 was used as a model for other possession cases and how the narrative of

genre from edifying literature with a sincere warning against witchcraft, to fiction (J. Brunsmand, *Kiøge Huuskors en original dansk Folke-Roman i 8 Kapitler* [Copenhagen, 1820]; J. Brunsmand, *Et forfærdeligt Huus-Kaars*, ed. L. Pio [Copenhagen, 1870]). This change corresponds closely to historian Henrik Horstbøll's analysis of how certain 'stories' were gradually shortened throughout the eighteenth century to save on paper costs and reach a broader audience. The story of Faust, for example, went through changes very similar to *Køge Huskors*' (H. Horstbøll, 'De 'Små historier' og læserevolutionen i 1700-tallet', *Fund og Forskning*, 33 [1994], 77–99). Also see A. Bæksted, 'Indledning og noter', pp. 46–85.

27 J. Brunsmand, *Energumeni Coagienses* (Amsterdam, 1693); J. Brunsmand, *Energumeni Coagienses* (Leiden, 1693); J. Brunsmand, *Johannis Brunsmanni Energumeni Coagienses* (Leipzig, 1695).
28 J. Brunsmand, *Das geängstigte Köge* (Leipzig, 1696).
29 B. Bekker, *Der betoverde Weereld*, vol. IV (Amsterdam, 1693), pp. 226–34.
30 This is perhaps best illustrated by the fact that the instances of demonic possession in Thisted occurred at the same time as the notorious Salem witch trials, which were also the outcome of claims of demonic possession.
31 P. Almond, *Demonic Possession and Exorcism in Early Modern England*, pp. 1–42.

Thomas Darling's possession 1596–1600 firmly linked possession with witchcraft, which also influenced later cases of demonic possession in England.[32] *Køge Huskors* had a similar impact, but only in Denmark.

A USEFUL SCRIPT FOR DEMONIC POSSESSION: *KØGE HUSKORS* IN THISTED

Beliefs about the supernatural were rife in early modern Denmark–Norway. However, they were not static, and certain agents could influence them. Several incidents in the case of the demonic possession in Thisted suggest that *Køge Huskors* functioned as a catalyst and provided a cultural script for the events that followed. Without this book, the case may have taken a completely different turn.

The events concerning the possession in Thisted began in January 1696, when a young woman named Maren Spillemands came to the market town of Thisted to seek the council of Ole Bjørn, who had recently been made pastor of Thisted. For the preceding twelve years she had displayed ambiguous symptoms of an unknown illness, starting with pains in her thigh. Some had long held her to be possessed, and because a local woman, Maren Christensdatter, was the first to claim this, she was suspected of having caused possession by witchcraft.[33] Kirsten Langgaard, a nine-year-old child, had also displayed strange symptoms for the past year. Her schoolteacher described her condition as either a strange childishness (she was seven or eight at the time) or the result of a natural illness.[34] Others, including local pastor Palle Madsen, described symptoms more consistent with those of demonic possession. This is evidenced in a letter he wrote to Kirsten's father in 1695 in which he described the young girl's partial recovery, stating that she was less afflicted than before and could now stand on her feet, eat bread and utter the name of Jesus. This implies she was unable to do this during her 'attacks', during which she would scream, experience pains, open her mouth wide and stretch her body. Kirsten was in Pastor Madsen's house for treatment at the time, but ultimately it was unsuccessful, leading her father to seek Ole Bjørn's council in early 1696.[35]

Maren's and Kirsten's early symptoms appear vague, they were open to interpretation and they seem similar to those in other cases in Jutland, in which common people used the term 'possession' synonymously with

[32] B. Levack, *The Devil Within*, pp. 148–51.
[33] National Archives, Copenhagen, Bilag til jysk missive af 7. november 1696 ang. Kommissionen i den thistedske besættelsessag, pp. 976–7.
[34] *Ibid.*, pp. 994–5.
[35] National Archives, Copenhagen, 1697 Protokol B, p. 450.

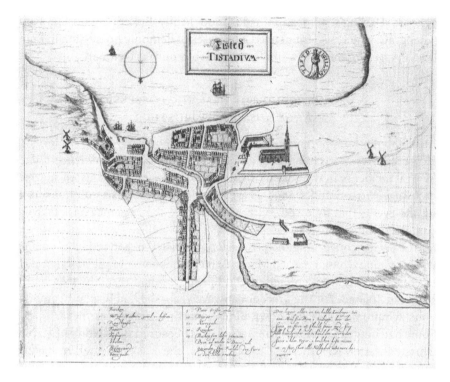

PLATE 3.2. The town of Thisted as seen from the south, including the church in which some of the events took place. The copperplate was initially produced in 1677 for Peder Hansen Resen's (1625–88) *Atlas Danicus*, never published in full.

unexplained illness perceived to be the result of witchcraft.[36] The symptoms did not necessarily match those of the theological definition of demonic possession, and there seems to have been no consensus that they were possessed. However, this was about to change. Pastor Ole Bjørn quickly took charge of events and announced that Maren and Kirsten were genuinely possessed by the Devil. Although this diagnosis was a distinct possibility, according to the official guidelines of the *Church Ritual* (1685), the swiftness and firmness of this conclusion went directly against the guidelines, which stipulated that pastors who encountered people who claimed to be possessed should be cautious and sceptical, as genuine cases of demonic possession were rare. They were also ordered to consult doctors to rule out natural causes of the symptoms, and the only action a pastor should

[36] Louise Nyholm Kallestrup has found several such cases ('Knowing Satan from God', pp. 179–80).

take to cure a demoniac was to pray for them. However, Ole Bjørn brought the possessed into the church, attempted to exorcise them, and spoke with them in a performance with the whole congregation as an audience; all of this went directly against the instructions outlined in the *Church Ritual*.[37]

Instead of adhering to the official guidelines, Ole Bjørn seems to have found an alternative script for the Thisted case in *Køge Huskors*. He actively used the book as an argument for the reality of demonic possession, and according to witnesses, he even preached about the book and warned that the possession in Thisted would become even worse than the events mentioned in this book. Seemingly, the witnesses did not feel the need to explain to their interrogators what *Køge Huskors* was, which suggests that the book and its narrative were already well known.[38] In other words, knowledge of *Køge Huskors* circulated widely, and Ole Bjørn made sure his congregation was familiar with its narrative if it was not already acquainted with it from the many copies of the book that circulated in Denmark–Norway at the time. Even those who had not read the book themselves became involved in a literary community through Ole Bjørn's sermons. After Ole Bjørn took charge of events and offered *Køge Huskors* as a script for a true possession, the demoniacs' symptoms seem to have worsened, and they began to mirror those described in the book, which more clearly corresponded to the theological description. Now convinced by Ole Bjørn and the women, several witnesses reported seeing the demoniacs levitating, displaying unnatural strength, experiencing convulsions and making animal noises,[39] all things described as signs of possession in the book.[40] Witnesses also began seeing strange animals such as bewitched hares and white rats, sometimes glowing as though they were on fire.[41] Such sightings of unnatural animals, especially rats, were the first signs of the supernatural that heralded the strange events in *Køge Huskors*.[42] The two demoniacs attracted large audiences, which seems to have only worsened their symptoms. Soon the indications of possession apparently spread to other local women – almost like an epidemic – and six months later twelve women claimed that

---

[37] The relevant paragraphs are found in chapter 6, article 3 (*Danmarks og Norgis Kirke-Ritual* [Copenhagen, 1685], pp. 226–45). ProQuest has digitised a copy of the original quarto edition from 1685, for the Royal Library, Copenhagen.

[38] National Archives, Copenhagen, Bilag til jysk missive af 7. november 1696 ang. Kommissionen i den thistedske besættelsessag, pp. 55–61.

[39] *Ibid.*, pp. 558–74, 659–63, 710–15, 852, 995–7.

[40] J. Brunsmand, *Et forfærdeligt Huus-Kaars* (1674), pp. 27–8, 44–5.

[41] National Archives, Copenhagen, Bilag til jysk missive af 7. november 1696 ang. Kommissionen i den thistedske besættelsessag, pp. 88, 387.

[42] J. Brunsmand, *Et forfærdeligt Huus-Kaars* (1674), pp. 23–5.

they were possessed by devils. Ole Bjørn and other local pastors took turns trying to help, and sometimes exorcise, them.[43]

The most important change in the affected women in Thisted was that the possessed began to speak as though devils were speaking through their mouths in deep, guttural voices, and apparently displayed supernatural knowledge. To an audience they could very exactly predict their fits, something that was also reported in *Køge Huskors*.[44] In other words, their possession became verbal after Ole Bjørn became involved. The women assumed new social identities by following the cultural script of the text, and as demoniacs they now had a voice and an audience. The demoniacs, or rather the devils inside them, claimed to have been cast into their victims by a witch, Anne Christensdatter, and stated that they would not leave until she had been burned at the stake.[45] Such executions were what finally cured the demoniacs in *Køge Huskors*. Inspired by the book, Ole Bjørn quickly had Anne Christensdatter imprisoned and tried, hoping to achieve the same results.[46] Later on, similar allegations were made against Anne Vert, another local woman, and she too was tried. However, in all known cases of demonic possession in seventeenth-century Denmark, witness statements from demoniacs were used as evidence only twice: in the witchcraft trials in Køge (1608–15) that were described by Brunsmand in *Køge Huskors* and in the trials brought by Ole Bjørn.[47] This was because such statements were regarded as having been made by the Devil – who, according to theology, was a notorious liar – making them inadmissible as evidence in a Danish trial.[48] Because of this, both women were later acquitted at the High Court of Northern Jutland.

On 18 April 1696 Ole Bjørn wrote a letter to his superior, the bishop of Aalborg Jens Bircherod, reporting that demonic possession had become epidemic and asking for the assistance of neighbouring pastors. In the letter he explicitly compared the possession in Thisted to *Køge Huskors* and used it to argue that he should be granted support:

[43]   National Archives, Copenhagen, Bilag til jysk missive af 7. november 1696 ang. Kommissionen i den thistedske besættelsessag, p. 387.
[44]   *Ibid.*, pp. 989–1; J. Brunsmand, *Et forfærdeligt Huus-Kaars* (1674), pp. 32–3.
[45]   National Archives, Copenhagen, Bilag til jysk missive af 7. november 1696 ang. Kommissionen i den thistedske besættelsessag, pp. 997–9.
[46]   *Ibid.*, p. 982.
[47]   L. Kallestrup, 'Knowing Satan from God', p. 169.
[48]   Jens Christian V. Johansen, *Da Djævelen var ude... Trolddom i det 17. århundredes Danmark* (Odense, 1991), pp. 32–3.

It seems to me that this case is very similar to the well-known story of *Køge Huskors*; indeed, in many ways it is more terrible, as the evil spirit has also spoken against me publicly, here in the church, while I was in the pulpit in a professional capacity, not just from the mouth of the possessed (as often has happened), but also from the arches of the church.[49]

The wording suggests that *Køge Huskors* was well known, at least to Ole Bjørn and his peers, and that it influenced Ole Bjørn's beliefs about what was happening in his congregation. In the letter Ole Bjørn listed all the classic symptoms of possession that the case now presented; all that was missing was the victims' ability to speak foreign languages such as Latin and Greek.[50] However, a lack of knowledge of Latin was also mentioned in *Køge Huskors*, where a pastor's Latin speech led the Devil to respond that he did not want to occupy his mind with such things.[51] Another parallel with *Køge Huskors* was that the devils, probably inspired by the book, revealed that Ole Bjørn was the original target of the possession, as Hans Bartskær had been in the book.[52] Bircherod was initially supportive and apparently convinced by Ole Bjørn, but he soon became more sceptical as the pastor and the demoniacs were unable to reproduce the supernatural symptoms before him and a rural dean at a meeting in Hillerslev. Ole Bjørn also attempted to get the devils occupying Maren and Kirsten to converse in Latin, but all they managed were three disconnected words: 'gloria', 'diabolus' and 'victoria', which was not enough to convince either

---

[49] My translation. The original reads: 'Ellers synes mig at denne Handel meget ligner den bekendte Historie og Beretning om Kiøge Huskaars, ja i mange Maader over-gaar den i Forskrekkelse, saa at den onde Aand end ogsaa offentlig her i Kirken haver ladet sig høre imod mig, da jeg stod paa Prædikestolen i mit Embedes Forretning, ikke alene af den Besættes Mund, (som tit er skeed) mens end og af Kirke-Hvelvin-gen [...]': (National Archives, Copenhagen, Bilag til jysk missive af 7. november 1696 ang. Kommissionen i den thistedske besættelsessag, p. 387).

[50] Ole Bjørn's report seems to reference a list of signs needed to prove demonic possession, as he quotes their description in Latin. His source for this list is unclear, but it corresponds closely to a list in the first draft of the *Church Ritual* and generally accepted lists of symptoms (S. Borregaard, *Danmarks og Norges kirkeritual af 1685* [Copenhagen, 1953], pp. 39–46; B. Levack, *The Devil Within*, pp. 6–15).

[51] J. Brunsmand, *Et forfærdeligt Huus-Kaars* (1674), p. 53.

[52] National Archives, Copenhagen, Bilag til jysk missive af 7. november 1696 ang. Kommissionen i den thistedske besættelsessag, pp. 527–31; J. Brunsmand, *Et forfær-deligt Huus-Kaars* (1674), p. 30.

Bishop Bircherod or his assistant, Christoffer Mumme, of the presence of demonic possession.[53]

THE SCRIPT REJECTED: ALTERNATIVE EXPLANATIONS

Following the meeting in Hillerslev, Bircherod asked the authorities for help, which was soon granted when by royal decree he was made the head of a commission tasked with determining the truth in the Thisted case. The women, and later also Ole Bjørn, were brought to Aalborg for examination and questioning. However, even though the authorities were now clearly sceptical, several women continued to display symptoms of demonic possession that mirrored those in *Køge Huskors*, as several witnesses testified. The symptoms were most vividly described by Lorends Mein, who was tasked with transporting Maren Spillemands from Thisted to Aalborg and observed one of her fits:

> [She] barked like a dog, crowed like a rooster, and her breast and stomach were distended, as though she were pregnant with twins. [...] She was attacked so badly that two men could not hold her down, and she soared two feet above the ground.[54]

This description is so similar to the description found in *Køge Huskors* discussed above that it almost seems a direct reference to the book.[55] After multiple interrogations several women, including Maren Spillemands, admitted to faking their fits and having been coached to do so by Ole Bjørn and his assistants. Maren later retracted her confession, stating that it was made under duress. On 14 May 1697, after a long investigation and trial during which many witnesses were interrogated, the commissioners ruled that Ole Bjørn and most of the women were frauds, and they received severe sentences, including death for some.[56] However, the case did not end there.

---

[53]   Det Kongelige Bibliotek, Jens Bircherod, Til en anden Biskop i Jylland angaaende Besættelsen i Thisted, 1696; National Archives, Copenhagen, Bilag til jysk missive af 7. november 1696 ang. Kommissionen i den thistedske besættelsessag, pp. 434–8.

[54]   My translation. The original reads: '[Hun] gøede som en hund, galede som en hane, og brystet tillige med maven blev opblæst, som hun kunde lavet fremmelig til barsel, så fuldkommelig som vi vel har set mange dannekvinder har gået med tvende børn [...] blev hun angreben, så at tvende karle måtte holde hende, og gik op fra jorden over alenhøj [...]': (National Archives, Copenhagen, Bilag til jysk missive af 7. november 1696 ang. Kommissionen i den thistedske besættelsessag, pp. 545–7).

[55]   Compare with J. Brunsmand, *Et forfærdeligt Huus-Kaars* (1674), pp. 44–5.

[56]   National Archives, Copenhagen, Bilag til jysk missive af 7. november 1696 ang. Kommissionen i den thistedske besættelsessag, pp. 1266–83.

Ole Bjørn appealed to the Supreme Court in Copenhagen, where the case was retried. The women were brought to the capital, where they were imprisoned under harsh conditions. The final verdict was returned on 26 February 1698, and although it was generally the same as the earlier one, Ole Bjørn, not the women, was judged to be the primary offender. He was sentenced to imprisonment for life, but this was later reduced to exile from Denmark. The women received various sentences, as some had admitted to fraud or were perceived to be ill, whereas the more stubborn of them, including Maren Spillemands, were sentenced to forced labour.[57] The fifteen judges of the Supreme Court all gave detailed written opinions on the case as they saw it. Five of the judges viewed the possession as purely fraudulent, seven saw it as a combination of fraud and mental illness (mainly hysteria), three found it to be solely the result of illness, not fraud, and two of those did not rule out the possibility that the Devil was somehow involved.[58] While the judges rejected demonic possession as an explanation, their scepticism was specific to this case and was not a complete rejection of the possibility of demonic possession.

<h2 style="text-align:center">HAUNTED BY KØGE HUSKORS:
REFERENCES TO THE TEXT IN THE THISTED CASE</h2>

Throughout the incidents surrounding the alleged possessions at Thisted, Ole Bjørn continued to refer to *Køge Huskors*; it seems he was unable to relinquish the cultural script he had found in it, and the influence of it was so powerful that at least three statements in the witness reports seem to be direct quotations from the book. The first of these references occurred when, on multiple occasions, the demons said that they were not allowed to leave the bodies of their victims, according to 'the big man', by which they meant God.[59] They apparently had to use this expression, as they could not utter holy words. One of the witnesses, Bishop Bircherod's assistant Christoffer Mumme, explained to the court that it meant 'God'.[60] This phrase was used in *Køge Huskors* in exactly the same manner, and the exact same explanation was given by its author, Johan Brunsmand, who in a note added that it referred to God.[61] As both Mumme and Brunsmand found it necessary

[57] National Archives, Copenhagen, Appendix til høyesterets Protocoll af anno 1697, fols 245–249v; Bæksted, *Besættelsen i Tisted*, 1960, 2, pp. 353–6.

[58] National Archives, Copenhagen, Appendix til høyesterets Protocoll af anno 1697, fols 2–245.

[59] National Archives, Copenhagen, Bilag til jysk missive af 7. november 1696 ang. Kommissionen i den thistedske besættelsessag, pp. 434–8, 544–52, 847–9, 999.

[60] *Ibid.*, pp. 434–8.

[61] J. Brunsmand, *Et forfærdeligt Huus-Kaars* (1674), p. 30.

to explain the expression, it is highly unlikely that it was in common usage. Instead, it was probably borrowed directly from the book.

The second textual reference to *Køge Huskors* occurred when the audience who witnessed the women acting as though they were possessed decided to sing the Danish translation of the Martin Luther psalm, 'A Mighty Fortress is Our God'.[62] In *Køge Huskors* people are mentioned as having sung the same psalm to battle the Devil and deliver the demoniacs from possession. The psalm mentions the Devil as an active figure, which may explain why they sang it, but the fact that they chose this specific psalm from the many available may indicate that they were inspired by the events in the book.

The third textual reference is found in the name by which one of the devils identified himself in Thisted. It is very similar to one noted in the appendices of *Køge Huskors* where, through his victim's mouth, the demon reveals his name as 'Lucifer'.[63] In Thisted the devil possessing Maren Spille-mands was identified as 'Luser' – a popular version of the same name.[64] The demoniacs were probably inspired by *Køge Huskors* when uttering this name and when referring to the accused witches as their mothers – another similarity between the Thisted case and the book, although this is also seen in other witchcraft trials.[65] The phrase 'the big man', the choice of the psalm, 'A Mighty Fortress is Our God' and the name 'Luser' appear to be textual references to *Køge Huskors* made by the demoniacs and their witnesses – consciously or otherwise. Given how the possession in Thisted began to mirror the possession depicted in *Køge Huskors* and how direct references

---

[62] 'Vor Gud hand er saa fast en borg'. Brunsmand, *Et forfærdeligt Huus-Kaars* (1674), pp. 46–7. National Archives, Copenhagen, Bilag til jysk missive af 7. november 1696 ang. Kommissionen i den thistedske besættelsessag, pp. 847–9.

[63] J. Brunsmand, *Et forfærdeligt Huus-Kaars* (1674), p. 83.

[64] National Archives, Copenhagen, Bilag til jysk missive af 7. november 1696 ang. Kommissionen i den thistedske besættelsessag, pp. 994–7; Ch. Appel and M. Fink-Jensen, 'Præsten og de besatte', p. 203. Alternate spellings in the court documents include 'Ludtzer', 'Lutz' and 'Luts'.

[65] The idea of witches' *lads* [*drenge*], meaning assistant devils, who did a witch's bidding and helped her to carry out her witchcraft-related activities was common in Danish witchcraft trials. However, their names were usually based on an attribute, an animal or a thing, for instance 'Raven' or 'Spot', rather than 'Lucifer'. See J. C. V. Johansen, 'Denmark: The Sociology of Accusations', in B. Ankerloo and G. Henningsen (eds), *Early Modern European Witchcraft. Centres and Peripheries* (Oxford, 1990), pp. 358–64; L. N. Kallestrup, 'Women, Witches, and the Town Courts of Ribe: Ideas of the Gendered Witch in Early Modern Denmark', in M. G. Muravyeva and R. M. Toivo (eds), *Gender in Late Medieval and Early Modern Europe* (New York, London, 2013), pp. 130–5; L. N. Kallestrup, *Agents of Witchcraft in Early Modern Italy and Denmark* (Houndmills, Basingstoke, Hampshire, 2015).

were made to the book, I contend that this book served as a recipe for demonic possession. By providing a useful cultural script and a vocabulary for the Thisted case, the book had a direct influence on how the demoniacs acted, how the local congregation became convinced of its reality, and on the initiation of witchcraft trials as a solution to the demonic possession.

CONCLUSION

Early modern beliefs that were common and widely accepted were rarely expressed, and seldom written down. However, when beliefs are challenged and discussed, they are made explicit and become available for historical investigation. *Køge Huskors* was published as a defence of the reality of demonic possession against the growing scepticism that emerged from early Enlightenment philosophy. The possession in Thisted marked an official break with such beliefs in Denmark, although witness statements were rife with beliefs more consistent with those found in *Køge Huskors* and other possession narratives. Studying incidents of demonic possession as cultural events that echo theatrical performances and follow cultural scripts allows a dynamic analysis of early modern beliefs, revealing how they circulated, were transformed and were influenced by external forces such as books, in which possession narratives could circulate transnationally through translation. Before Ole Bjørn became involved in the Thisted case, symptoms were vague and interpretations varied, as there was no clear script that the local residents could use to interpret the women's conditions. However, in *Køge Huskors* Ole Bjørn and his followers found a formula for how a demonic possession could play out and be resolved. The case began imitating the events described in *Køge Huskors*, and witness statements closely conformed to descriptions in the book.

The influence of *Køge Huskors* manifested itself in explicit references, structural similarities in observations and certain textual references to the book made by witnesses. The demoniacs mirrored the book's depictions of demonic possession, and the witchcraft trials were inspired by the book. Thus, *Køge Huskors* had real significance for a specific course of historical events. By reading *Køge Huskors* and using it to interpret their own experiences, the inhabitants of Thisted became part of a literary community with improved agency; in other words, they received 'literary citizenship'. People who did not necessarily have a voice in early modern society gained one when they assumed the identity of the demoniac. Even those who did not physically read the book became involved in a transnational literary world through the demoniacs' and Ole Bjørn's references to the book.

Ultimately, the script Ole Bjørn found in *Køge Huskors*, and wanted the Thisted case to follow, was rejected by the authorities because of growing scepticism in learned circles. The women Ole Bjørn accused of witchcraft were found innocent. Instead he became the accused, and was ultimately convicted as a fraud. During this process the authorities pointed out that his script was indeed a script – not reality. The anonymously published, but officially sanctioned, version of these events even blamed Ole Bjørn and *Køge Huskors* for spreading what it deemed to be superstitions. Following this, the book gradually underwent a genre shift, from description of historical events to popular fiction, although this change was gradual, and belief in witchcraft and demonic possession persisted for generations among parts of the population in Denmark–Norway. Ole Bjørn's interpretation and use of *Køge Huskors* backfired on him, and it even fostered political change. The possession in Thisted became the last official witchcraft trial in Denmark, and it communicated a shift in the opinion of the authorities, as the published satirical description of events became the official narrative. Indirectly, *Køge Huskors* brought about political change, even though the outcome was not intended by its author.

4

A Northern Republic of Letters?
Transnational Periodical Cultures
around 1700, 1800 and 1900

Jens Bjerring-Hansen

FRAMING SCANDINAVIAN PRINT CULTURE in the period covered by this book was a megatrend of 'vernacularisation'. An increasingly close relationship between language and nation from the middle of the eighteenth century onwards led the cultural historian Peter Burke to talk about a 'nationalisation of language'.[1] Before that, and along the same lines, in his classic study of the social construction of nation states, the historian Benedict Anderson had highlighted the consolidation of vernacular languages, Danish, Norwegian, Swedish etc., as a prerequisite for notions of the 'nation' and 'nationalism', while, importantly, stressing the importance of the book market in this development. The modern Western European nations, which took form around 1800, relied on a 'convergence of capitalism and print technology on the fatal diversity of human language', according to Anderson.[2] The Scandinavian situation generally conforms to this broad picture. In the first book printed in the Danish language, *Den danske Rimkrønike* (1495), a chronicle of the kings of Denmark written in verse, the patriotic agenda is clear.[3] In the eighteenth century, in spite of his

---

[1] P. Burke, *Languages and Communities in Early Modern Europe* (Cambridge, 2004), pp. 163–9. On Scandinavia in this development, see I. Berg, 'The Making of the Scandinavian Languages', in G. Rutten and K. Horner (eds), *Metalinguistic Perspectives on Germanic Languages. European Case Studies from Past to Present* (Oxford, 2016), pp. 35–55.

[2] B. Anderson, *Imagined Communities*, 2nd edn (London, 2006 [1983]), p. 46.

[3] P. Hermann, 'Politiske og æstetiske aspekter i Rimkrøniken', *Historisk Tidsskrift* 107:2 (2007), 389–411.

international agenda and renown, Ludvig Holberg (1684–1754), the foremost Dano-Norwegian representative of the early Enlightenment as well
as a reformer of the book market, can be considered the spiritual father of
mid-eighteenth-century patriotism through his insistence on the Danish
language for most literary purposes.[4] The radical nationalisation of language and print in the nineteenth century finally becomes evident when
comparing with the previous century. The multilingual print culture (with
publications in Danish, Latin, French, German, including Low German
etc.) was largely abandoned in favour of Danish (and after 1814, Norwegian,
which for decades hereafter would be identical to Danish).

In this chapter the focus is on three interregional, or with an anachro-
nism from the early nineteenth century, more or less 'Scandinavian', literary journals, the Latin *Nova literaria* from around 1700, the bilingual
Danish-Swedish *Nordia* from around 1800 and, finally, the Danish *Det
nittende Aarhundrede* [The nineteenth century] from just before 1900. The
aim is to address the strategies of language and distribution of these more
or, mostly, less successful border-crossing ventures against the backdrop
of the increasing nationalisation, intertwining the book market and the
cultural politics of language. Historical light will be shed on the cultural
transfer as well as the contestation and conflict between different 'modes'
of circulation (Alexander Beecroft) in which Scandinavia took part – and,
mutatis mutandis, still does – that is, the national, the regional, the global.[5]
In the examination of the journals, special attention will be given to the
'paratexts' (Gérard Genette), such as prefaces, subscription adverts etc.,
which frame and present the scope of the journals.[6] Before addressing the
particular publications, the periodical as medium or genre will be considered, especially in terms of its transnational nature and its ability to involve
new readerships.

THE SOCIOLOGY OF PERIODICALS

From a historical perspective it can be argued that the periodical (and not
the book) was the first original and qualitatively new genre to emerge in the

[4]   See O. Feldbæk, 'Kærlighed til fædrelandet. 1700-tallets nationale selvforståelse',
       Fortid og Nutid, 31 (1984), 272; J. Bjerring-Hansen, *Ludvig Holberg på bogmarkedet*
       (Copenhagen, 2015).
[5]   A. Beecroft, 'World Literature Without a Hyphen', *New Left Review* 54 (2008), 87–
       100.
[6]   G. Genette, *Paratexts, Thresholds of Interpretation*, trans. J. E. Lewin (Cambridge,
       1997).

wake of Gutenberg's revolutionary invention of the printing press.[7] Further, as James Wald has pointed to, the periodical was 'in a sense the un-book, even the anti-book'. It shared the codex form with the book, but was less weighty and, like ephemera, destined for use at a specific time. In a comparative definition Wald stresses some distinctive traits of the periodical *vis-à-vis* the book, of which the most important are: 'fragmentary, open-ended' (and not 'complete'), 'collective' (and not 'individual'), 'derivative' (and not 'creative'), and 'ephemeral' (and not 'permanent').[8]

In terms of scope and contents, periodicals are often emphasised as vehicles for innovation and experimentation, regularly and naturally, by stressing the interconnection between the rise and development of the medium and the progressive agenda of the Enlightenment as is the case in recent ground-breaking explorations of the Dano-Norwegian journals of the eighteenth century.[9] Within this framework, particular attention has been given to the *Spectator*-like journals in the tradition of Joseph Addison and Richard Steele (with *The Tatler*, 1709–11, and *The Spectator*, 1711–12), whereby 'learned' and 'literary' as well as scientific journals have gone relatively unnoticed. A way of encompassing these publications, which in a Dano-Norwegian context vastly outnumber the *Spectator* journals, is to look more broadly at the Enlightenment. As well as a pivotal era in the history of ideas, Enlightenment was also, with a formulation by Clifford Siskin and William Warner, 'an event in the history of mediation'.[10] Thus, Enlightenment thinking and practices were also directed at that which 'intervenes, enables, supplements, or is simply in between',[11] or, in other words, questions of infrastructure ('how'?) and pragmatics ('for whom?'). Print entrepreneurs took full advantage of developments in the nation's infrastructure for transportation and communication, as Paula McDowell has pointed to as an explanation for the flourishing of new kinds of serial publications.[12] This link between periodicals and infrastructural reasoning

[7] J. Wald, 'Periodicals and Periodicity', in S. Eliot and J. Rose (eds), *A Companion to the History of the Book*, 2nd edn, (Hoboken, NJ, 2020), p. 618.

[8] *Ibid.*

[9] See E. Tjønneland (ed.), *Opplysningens tidsskrifter. Norske og danske periodiske publikationer på 1700-tallet* (Bergen, 2008), E. Krefting *et al.*, *En pokkers skrivesyge. 1700-tallets dansk-norske tidsskrifter mellom sensur og ytringsfrihet* (Oslo, 2014), and E. Krefting *et al.* (eds), *Eighteenth-Century Periodicals as Agents of Change. Perspectives on Northern Enlightenment* (Leiden, 2015).

[10] C. Siskin and W. Warner, 'This Is Enlightenment. An Invitation in Form of an Argument', in C. Siskin and W. Warner (eds), *This Is Enlightenment* (Chicago, 2010), p. 7.

[11] *Ibid.*

[12] P. McDowell, 'Media and Mediation in the Eighteenth Century', *Oxford Handbooks* (2018), DOI: <10.1093/oxfordhb/9780199935338.013.46>.

is famously expressed by Richard Steele in the inaugural issue of *The Tatler* (1709), where he announced that the journal would be published 'every Tuesday, Thursday, and Saturday, in the Week, for the Convenience of the Post'.[13] As we shall see, postal routes, by wagon and ship, and questions of infrastructure and distribution were integral to the editorial concepts in transnational journal enterprises.

The pragmatic proposition of periodicals has been stressed by Aina Nøding: 'The periodicals were often targeted at a specific audience.'[14] Thus, already on title level such thematisation of the audience was evident in European periodical literature from the very beginning, as witnessed by the circular reasoning of the title of the famous *Journal des Sçavans* (from 1665), 'journal for the learned'. During the course of the eighteenth century the output of printed matter vastly multiplied,[15] and the trend was accompanied by a socio-cultural differentiation and segmentation of the reading public, as reflected and, possibly partly, triggered by the journals, whose editors quickly adapted to the demands of new readers. This can be exemplified by the periodical experiments of the entrepreneurial Danish publisher Jens Kragh Høst, who established journals particularly addressing, among others, women, doctors, Germans, Swedes and, as we shall see, Scandinavians.

Thus an additional element to the definition of periodicals can be proposed, addressing the sociology of the publications. They aim to involve new readers in the literary field by expanding or rearranging the field, socially or geographically.

The European journal system in Denmark–Norway

In the early period three types of journals stood out, forming what could be called the 'European journal system'. The promptness with which this system was imported and adapted to local settings in the conglomerate state of Denmark–Norway is striking. *The learned journals* in the tradition of the Paris-based *Journal des Sçavans* (1665) had somewhat of a counterpart in the *Nova literaria Maris Balthici* (1698–1708), *the (multi)scientific journals* such as the pioneering *Philosophical Transactions* of the British Royal Society (from 1665) inspired the *Acta Medica et Philosophica Hafniensia* (1673–80), while, finally, adaptations of *the moral weeklies* in the

---

[13]   R. Steele, *Tatler*, no. 1, 12 April 1709.
[14]   A. Nøding, 'Hva er et 1700-tallstidsskrift?' in *Opplysningens tidsskrifter. Norske og danske periodiske publikationer på 1700-tallet*, ed. E. Tjønneland (Bergen: 2008), p. 4.
[15]   Bjerring-Hansen, *Ludvig Holberg*, pp. 60–1.

style of Addison and Steele's *Tatler* and *Spectator* would appear from the 1720s onwards.

From a quantitative perspective the number of journals published in Denmark (excluding Norway) from the beginning in 1673 to 1850, when the handpress period was coming to an end and when newspapers were taking over many of the functions of the journals, totals around 900.[16] Strikingly, around 35 per cent of the titles were published for less than a year (often in only one to three issues), which speaks to the ephemeral and momentary character of the periodicals as such while also seeming to indicate an excessive idealism and/or moderate market know-how on behalf of the publishers. More positively, the short-livedness can be seen as a proxy for experimentation and innovation, unwarranted or not within the constraints of the small-sized Dano-Norwegian book market. A comparison with numbers from the major book markets (the British, German or French) could illuminate whether we are dealing with a case of Scandinavian conformism or exceptionalism in the adaption of the journal system.

Longue durée perspectives on the journals are challenged by the dynamics of experimentation but also by the principal hybridity of the medium, which meant that the boundaries between books, newspapers and journals were not firmly established before late in the eighteenth century.[17] The boundaries between the three principal types – a typology not all scholars would necessarily agree on in the first place – were blurred by historical change with subtypes developing from them and new types of journals (including magazines) appearing. This generic instability can be exemplified by the many names for the type of journals inspired by *The Spectator* ('political', 'essay' or 'Spectator' journals, 'moral weeklies' etc.), which in the Danish national bibliography, the *Bibliotheca Danica*, as an expression of understandable resignation on behalf of the cataloguers, are bundled into the category of 'Miscellanies' [*Blandede tidsskrifter*] together with other kinds of journals far away from the tradition of Steele and Addison.

Similar problems of designation are related to the type of journal in focus in this chapter. The category of 'learned journals' only makes historical sense in relation to late seventeenth and early-to-mid eighteenth-century cultural practices. Scholarly specialisation and institutionalisation lead to a diffusion of the broad-ranging agenda of the learned journals into different kinds of journals, literary journals, review journals, scientific journals.[18]

---

[16] The journal titles are primarily extracted from the National Danish Library Catalogue, *Bibliotheca Danica* [ranging from 1482 to 1830] and its *Supplement* 1831–40.

[17] See A. Nøding, 'Hva er et 1700-tallstidsskrift?'.

[18] See S. B. Barnes, 'The Editing of Early Learned Journals', *Osiris*, 1 (January, 1936), 155–72; on Scandinavian, especially Swedish learned journals, see I. Oscarsson, 'En

An overarching term for this, too rather mixed, category could be 'literary journals', whereby, however, the concept of literature was object to crucial historical change and specialisation in a related cultural trajectory. From denoting writing as such, the concept of 'literature' would increasingly become synonymous with *belles lettres*, fiction and poetry. Tellingly, journals played a role in this redefinition of literature.[19]

The question of publication language is of course crucial to gaining an understanding of the way in which the European infrastructure of journals was culturally translated to Scandinavian conditions. If we look at the learned or literary journals published in Denmark (not including Norway until 1814), a total of 61 can be identified. Out of these, 38 were in Danish, 18 in German, 3 in French and 2 in Latin. If we zoom in on 18 of the journals published from 1800 to 1850, 15 out of these were in Danish, 2 in German and 1 in French. The trend of nationalisation is clear, in other words, whereby three central shifts and corresponding *Grossperioden* can be identified: the aftermath of Humanism with Latin as the *lingua franca*, followed by the Enlightenment with the introduction of modern European languages, German, French and of course vernacular Danish, and finally the age of Romanticism and (romantic) nationalism with Danish totally dominant.

Nova literaria Maris Balthici et Septentrionis (1698–1708)

The European journal boom in the decades around 1700 was first and foremost a flourishing of learned journals. Among the most famous titles besides the *Journal des Sçavans* (1665–) are the *Acta Eruditorum* in Leipzig (1682–1782), Pierre Bayle's Amsterdam publication *Nouvelles de la République des Lettres* (1684–1718) and the Roman *Giornale de' letterati d'Italia* (1668–81). At least 300 such journals were founded before 1730.[20] They provided a growing readership with abstracts and notices of recent publications from a growing literary marketplace along with news from the

---

revolution i offentligheten: om lärda tidskrifter i Europa under tidigmodern tid och om hur svensk vetenskap representerades i dem', *Sjuttonhundratal* (2011), 93–115; on review journals, see T. Munck, 'Eighteenth-Century Review Journals and the Internationalization of the European Book Market', *The International History Review*, 32:3 (2010), 415–35.

[19]   See L. Morrissey, *The Constitution of Literature. Literacy, Democracy, and Early English Literary Criticism* (Stanford, 2008) and R. Rosenberg, 'Eine verworrene Geschichte. Vorüberlegungen zu einer Biographie des Literaturbegriffs', *Zeitschrift für Literaturwissenschaft und Linguistik*, 77 (1990), 36–65.

[20]   Barnes, 'The Editing of Early Learned Journals', p. 155.

Republic of Letters, supplementing the epistolary networks as a powerful new tool for knowledge transfer among European intellectuals.

In 1701 the editor of the *Acta editorum*, Otto Mencke, complained about the complete absence of Swedish books in Leipzig. In Holland Pierre Bayle similarly noted that it was almost impossible to obtain knowledge about what was printed in Poland, Sweden and Denmark.[21] So, from the perspective of the dominant centres of the republic of letters this international intellectual community should ideally cover the northern parts Europe as well. However, the most important initiative in that regard came from the periphery itself in form of the Lübeck-based monthly *Nova literaria Maris Balthici et Septentrionis* [Literary or learned news from the Baltic Sea and the North], 1698–1708 (edited by the Lutheran priest and antiquarian Jakob von Melle and the lawyer Achilles Daniel Leopold).

Evidently, this interregional journal had a broader geographical base than what would later be understood as 'Scandinavia' although, as Ingemar Oscarsson has pointed out, it should be considered as a predecessor to the more nationally constrained journals, which saw the light of day in Denmark (*Nova literaria*, 1720) and Sweden (*Acta literaria Sueci*, 1720).[22] The journal contained registrations and summaries of newly published literature but also original contributions within all sorts of sciences, for instance find reports related to natural history and antiquarianism. Everything was structured according to place of publication or discovery, as illustrated in the inaugural issue: Wismar, Rostock, Greifswald, Gdansk, Riga, Uppsala, Stockholm, Copenhagen, Ribe, Kiel and, finally after this counter-clockwise tour around the Baltic and Nordic regions, Lübeck.

The motivation behind the publication was determined in the inaugural issue of the journal:

> For in those journals [diariis] of learned men [...] you may very sparingly, and infrequently enough to be counted, see mentions of those things, which are going on at these more remote shores of the Baltic Sea.[23]

---

[21] Oscarsson, 'En revolution i offentligheten', p. 98.

[22] *Ibid.*, p. 111.

[23] [Preface], *Nova literaria Maris Balthici et Septentrionis* (January 1698), p. [3]. At alia nobis est, erritque omnibus, haec nostra paullo attentius confiderantibus, sententia. Latin orig.: 'In illis enim, quæ diximus, hominum eruditorum diariis, licet ea fatis diligenter afferantur, quæ vel apud exteros cultioris Europae populos, vel in superiori Germania iis vicina accidunt; parce tamen admodum, satisque infrenquenter ea recenseri videas, quæ ad remetiora hæc Balthici maris littora.'

Thus the *Nova literaria* questioned the common understanding of cultural centres and peripheries and stressed the Baltic Sea and Nordic regions with Northern Germany, the Baltic States, Denmark–Norway and Sweden as an own, hitherto forgotten part of the Republic of Letters. However, the intentions were peaceful. The editors merely pointed to a practical problem of transnational scholarly communication, which of course was even more present for the scholars of the north. However, there were no accusations of hegemony, parochialism etc. against the scholarly community in the centres of the Republic of Letters. This atmosphere of tolerability is very much in line with Ingemar Oscarsson's impression of the learned journals as open fora for different networks and interest groups, where the cultural polarisations of the time – such as North vs. South, scholarly centres vs. peripheries, humanistic vs. scientific, Protestant vs. Catholic etc. – were more or less suspended.[24]

Against this backdrop, a remarkable thing is that this Baltic community with its new organ was born and thrived well during a time of political division and crisis in the region. It was the time of the so-called 'Great Northern War' with the two most warring nations in the history of Europe, Sweden and Denmark, as belligerents.[25] The scholarly exchange between Swedes and Danes continued, as witnessed in the journal as well as in correspondence from the time.[26] In other words, relating to the concepts from Alexander Beecroft, the *Nova literaria* succeeded in a seamless integration of tensions between global and regional and in contesting national systems of literary circulation. Crucial in this regard was the common language of Latin, which at the time was the default choice, at least outside the domains of the major languages. The members of the Republic of Letters often had Latinised names, read Latin and wrote in Latin, even in correspondence with compatriots. Unfortunately, there is no bibliographical information available concerning print runs or the numbers of subscribers. However, the fact that the *Nova literaria* offered a densely printed octavo sheet each month for ten years (totalling almost 20,000 pages) and that it had a steady influx of contributors indicates that the journal was not only a demanding and possibly tiring enterprise, but also a viable one.

During the eighteenth century, Latin would lose ground as a *lingua franca* whereby the editor of a literary journal was facing a critical choice

[24] Oscarsson, 'En revolution i offentligheten', p. 99.
[25] As a term 'The Great Northern War' originates from the latter part of the eighteenth century. It covers a series of wars in which Sweden and Denmark were on opposing sides, fighting for control of the Baltic Sea area, *dominium maris baltici*, see D. H. Andersen, *Store Nordiske Krig*, vols 1–2 (Copenhagen, 2021).
[26] H. Ilsøe, 'Peder Resens nordiske bibliotek', *Fund og Forskning*, 30 (1991), 27–50.

regarding the language of publication as testified as early as in 1720 in an advertisement for a new Copenhagen-based journal under the same title as the pioneering enterprise of the region, *Nova literaria*. According to the two editors, the university professor Andreas Hojer and the publisher Joachim Wielandt, the journal would 'for the sake of Europe be in Latin' and 'for the sake of the Nordic home audience render an overview of every publication and activity in the learned world'.[27] With only thirteen issues, the new *Nova literaria* belongs to the group of short-lived journal enterprises. Part of the explanation for its failure could very well be both the choice of Latin, which discouraged a broader national readership from reading, and the high expectations for both international interest and Nordic agreement in literary matters, which at this point in time seemed anachronistic and unwarranted.

NORDIA (1794–5)

Fast forward a hundred years, we have the short-lived but ambitious journal *Nordia* established by the energetic editor and author Jens Kragh Høst. It was part of a short but remarkable blossoming of cultural Scandinavianism in the 1790s, fuelled by Danish intellectuals, not least Høst.[28] The editor presented the project as follows in the subscription plan, which was bilingual Swedish-Danish in its original form, printed in two columns:

> However, few means would be able to contribute to a mutual literary knowledge as fast and as effective as a monthly, which was common to the literature of both people. [...]

> This monthly shall in accordance with its intent deliver, first, hitherto unpublished works of poetry as well as articles of common interest in prose, second, Danish translations of remarkable Swedish poetry and scholarship, and vice versa.

---

[27] Quoted after P. M. Stolpe, *Dagspressen i Danmark, Dens Vilkaar og Personer indtil Midten af det attende Aarhundrede*, vol. 2 (Copenhagen, 1881), pp. 120–1.

[28] In 1796, after giving up on *Nordia*, Høst, along with the literary historian Rasmus Nyerup and the poet Jens Baggesen, founded *Det Skandinaviske Literaturselskab* (Scandinavian Literary Society) with its own periodical, *Skandinavisk Museum*, irregularly published in seven volumes 1798–1803. On these early efforts of 'Scandinavianism' within periodical culture, see R. Hemstad, 'I 'Tidens Fylde'. Panskandinaviske publisister og transnasjonale tidsskrifter', in A. M. B. Bjørkøy *et al.* (eds), *Litterære verdensborgere: Transnasjonale perspektiver på norsk bokhistorie 1519–1850*, (Oslo, 2019), pp. 377–404, especially pp. 382–4.

Furthermore, *Nordia* shall bring an overview of literature, theatres, and political events of both states. The original content comprises of a mixture of Swedish and Danish, and, to ensure a complete understanding of everything for all readers of both nations, a Swedish dictionary for Danes and vice versa, which is offered for free to subscribers of the journal in separate sheets.

Copenhagen, 20 Dec. 1794, Jens Kragh Høst.[29]

Clearly, the belief that a monthly journal was the most effective means of knowledge sharing lingered from the first generation of literary journals. Regarding the contents of the journal, a principal difference compared to the *Nova literaria* is the extent to which a definition of 'literature' comprised poetry and imaginative writing. However, the most interesting and experimental aspect of the make-up of the journal is the language policy and the practical and didactical measures connected to it. Whereas all the intended readers of the *Nova literaria* would understand Latin, the bilingual concept of *Nordia*, with contributions in both Swedish and Dano-Norwegian (in translation when at hand), was more tentative, risky in fact, from the outset by anticipating problems of understanding due to linguistic barriers. Hence, interim two-way dictionaries on separate sheets were offered free of charge to the subscribers of the journal.

The transnational character was of course completely different to the early literary journals. It was not a matter of promoting scholarship and connecting to Europe. The ambition was to strengthen the sense of community between Sweden and Denmark–Norway, something which was emphasised again and again in the rather vague and bleak poems of the journal, full of symbolic subtleties: the opening poem addressed Nordia as a Nordic muse, invoking an antiphony by the Nordic goddesses of singing, Svea and Dania.

With only four issues in total, *Nordia* is yet another short-term publication in Dano-Norwegian periodical literature. But what went wrong in

---

[29] J. Kragh Høst, 'Subskribtionsplan. Nordia', *Kiøbenhavnske lærde Efterretninger*, no. 3 (1795), 46–7. Danish orig.: 'Men faa Midler vilde virksomt og hastigt kunne bidrage til indbyrdes literarisk Bekjendtskab, som et Maanedsskrift, der blev fælles for begge Folkeslags Literatur. [...] Dette Maanedsskrift skal i Overensstemmelse med sin hensigt levere hidtil utrykte Arbejder saavel Poesier, som prosaiske Afhandlinger af almeeninteressant Indhold, deels Dansk Oversættelse af mærkelige svenske Poesier og Afhandlinger, og omvendt. Desuden skal *Nordia* meddele en Udsigt over begge Staters Literatur, Skueplads og politiske Begivenheder. Det Originale indrykkes i Flæng paa Svensk eller Dansk, og for at gjøre det alt forstaaeligt for samtlige Læsere af begge Nationer, udkommer en Svensk Ordbog for Danske og omvendt, som arkvis overlades Maanedsskriftets Subskribenter gratis.'

this case? In his memoirs from the 1830s, Høst the editor mentions several factors, most importantly the impact of the great fire in Copenhagen in 1795, but also more self-critically: the drop in renown of the contributors as well as in the quality of the contributions.[30] The latter was definitely a valid point, but actually one that could be raised against the inaugural issue as well, offering a lot of rhetorical talk of the idea of a pan-Scandinavian literary culture but no actual contributions to it. His opinion was shared by the polite reviewer of the *Kiøbenhavnske lærde Efterretninger* (i.e. Copenhagen learned/literary news), who praised the idea of the journal rather than its content. Of more interest are the reviewer's complaints about the poor infrastructure of the Scandinavian book market, particularly the ties between Denmark and Sweden:

> when a newly published publication makes headlines in Hamburg and arrives two days later in Copenhagen, so would a shipment of every interesting book published in Stockholm or Uppsala immediately be on its way to Denmark by waggon post [...] the reality is that the books are upheld by wind, weather, season, or the business of shipbrokers.[31]

Thus, important obstacles to a pan-Scandinavian journal were of a practical nature. There were linguistic problems. At first sight, the accompanying dictionaries seemed a luxurious service, but they were also addressing a fundamental problem of language barriers. And there were geographical hindrances. Denmark was better connected with Germany than with Sweden. However, the map sketched by the reviewer, pinning out the Northern European literary centres of Hamburg, Copenhagen, Stockholm and Uppsala was also a mental one. In the review a subtle, epochal animosity towards German cultural hegemony is expressed, as seen for instance in the complaint that Danish readers were familiar with the most insignificant notices in Hamburg journals but not with the significant works by Swedish writers.[32]

From this perspective, the efforts of regionalisation in *Nordia* can be seen as measures to counter German domination of the Danish literary

---

[30] J. Kragh Høst, *Erindringer om mig og mine Samtidige* (Copenhagen, 1835), pp. 33–4.

[31] [anon.] 'Nordia', [Review] *Kiøbenhavnske lærde Efterretninger*, no. 9 (1795), 128–9. Danish orig.: 'ligesom naar et nyt udkommen Skrift gjør Sensation i Hamborg, det om to Dage er i Kjøbenhavn, saaledes vilde ogsaa af hver en interessant Bog, som udkom i Stockholm eller Upsal [*sic*], ufortøvet afgaae et Partie Exemplarer med agende Post ned til Danmark, og ikke have nødig at oppebie den saa langsomme og af Vind og Vejr Aarstid og Mæglers dependerende Skibsleilighed.'

[32] *Ibid.* p. 129.

culture as well as the book market.³³ In terms of the journal's impact in this regard, the reviewer is realistic but hopeful: 'Rome was not built in one day.'³⁴ He expressed a hope that enterprises like Høst's journal would improve cross-national reading skills, granting Danish and Swedish publishers 'the pecuniary advantage' of doubling their area of interest.³⁵ During the course of the nineteenth century further attempts were made to unite the Scandinavian book market, with some success as Tor Ivar Hansen has argued. While the movement aiming to unite the Scandinavian countries, which later would be known as 'Scandinavianism', failed on an institutional level and as a large-scale political project, it succeeded in creating a common literary consciousness,³⁶ even though, you could add, robust infrastructural successes such as pan-Scandinavian publishers, book series or journals were absent.

Det nittende Aarhundrede (1874–7)

A final example of the challenges of establishing a transnational journal, and thereby formalising regional co-operation and understanding across cultural and linguistic domains, is the Copenhagen-based monthly *Det nittende Aarhundrede. Tidsskrift for Litteratur og Kritik* [The nineteenth century. Journal for literature and criticism], edited by the brothers Georg and Edvard Brandes throughout its relatively long life, 1874–7. This was before the remarkable European breakthrough of Scandinavian literature and what Tore Rem and Narve Fulsås have called 'the Scandinavian Moment in World Literature'.³⁷ Or, to be more concrete, before Henrik Ibsen's remarkable success with *Pillars of Society* in Germany 1877 and before the more prolific of the two Brandes brothers, Georg, moved to Berlin the same year to establish himself as a European journalist and critic. The journal is from the early days of the so-called 'Modern Breakthrough' in Scandinavia, a term later invented by Georg Brandes denoting a social and literary movement

---

³³ For more on this cultural and mental turn from Germany towards Sweden and Scandinavia, see for example Rasmus Glenthøj, e.g. *Experiences of War and Nationality in Denmark and Norway 1807–1815* (Basingstoke, 2014), pp. 1–27, and Vibeke Winge, 'Dansk og tysk 1790–1848', in O. Feldbæk (ed.), *Dansk identitetshistorie*, vol. 2 (Copenhagen, 1991), pp. 110–49.
³⁴ [anon.], 'Nordia', p. 131.
³⁵ *Ibid.* pp. 131–2.
³⁶ T. I. Hansen, 'Bøker og skandinavisk forbrødring. Et forsøk på en bokhistorisk tilnærming til skandinavismen', in R. Hemstad *et al.* (eds), *Skandinavismen. Vision og virkning* (Odense, 2018), pp. 163–86.
³⁷ N. Fulsås and T. Rem, *Ibsen, Scandinavia and the Making of a World Drama* (Cambridge, 2018), p. x.

or current which reacted against cultural and political conservatism. On these grounds rather than the earlier idealistic notions of Scandinavianism, the journal was founded as a Nordic enterprise.

The biographical backdrop to the journal project was that in 1871 Brandes had been denied a vacant professorship in aesthetics at the University of Copenhagen, for which he was the obvious candidate, as well as access to the press, which was dominated by conservative newspapers. His first idea for a strike-back was to start a liberal newspaper, but he soon gave that up and instead came up with the idea of a regional journal. A subscription plan was printed in the only Brandes-friendly national newspaper of the time, *Morgenbladet*. According to this, the aim was:

> to disseminate the knowledge of the most prominent personalities and schools of thought of our time within the realms of literature, art, and science, which by nature demands the participation of all educated members of society. Particularly the journal will be preoccupied with everything of special interest to Denmark and the North [Norden]. This aim will be pursued by the publication of comprehensible theses, critical reviews, and poetical contributions by renowned authors and scholars.[38]

Looking at the contents of the journal over the six volumes, totalling more than 2,900 pages, it is safe to say that the transnational ambitions were poorly executed: there were almost no contributions from Swedes, and the few that were indeed included were in Danish translation. A review of the first issue in a liberal Stockholm newspaper includes some interesting reflections on the Swedish dimension of the journal:

> a Danish journal, for which Sweden is not, regarding literature, a *terra incognita*, a Danish journal, which has finally discovered, that even the mainland of the North owns a literature, that blossoms in many

---

[38] 'Det nittende Aarhundrede. Subskriptions-Indbydelse', *Morgenbladet*, 21 October 1874. Danish orig.: 'at udbrede Kundskaben til de Personligheder og Aandsretninger, der i vor Tid fremtræde paa Literaturens, Kunstens og Videnskabens Omraade, og som efter deres Natur have Krav paa alle dannedes Deltagelse. Særligt vil Tidsskriftet beskjæftige sig med alt, hvad der fortrinsvis kan interessere Danmark og Norden. Sit Maal vil det søge naaet ved meddelelse af almenfattelige Afhandlinger, kritiske Artikler og poetiske Frembringelser, og Udgiverne have dertil sikret sig Hjælp af ansete Forfattere og Videnskabsmænd.'

fields [...] this will truly be both rare and welcome, something, which Scandinavianism, to its own harm, failed to accomplish. [...].[39]

In a historical perspective the reviewer denounced the value and effects of the old romanticist Scandinavianism. And at the same time, in an efficient rhetorical way, he wanted to take Brandes by the word while also keeping an eye on him to see whether he delivered on his promise: 'We will follow this with great interest', he continued. In the context of the review this should be read as a threat. Involve Sweden more, or we will lose interest in the journal. The 'Danish journal' did not deliver, hence the threat was effectuated. At least seemingly only the first issue was noticed by Swedish newspapers.

Whereas the Swedish reaction to *Det nittende Aarhundrede* took the form of a contestation between the two major languages and literatures of Scandinavia, the Norwegian feedback, as testified by Georg Brandes's correspondence with Norwegian authors regarding a possible co-operation, was addressing issues of transnationality more on matter of principle. Brandes tried to convince them to contribute, which some did, but the most prominent and promising were highly critical. Like Bjørnstjerne Bjørnson, Jonas Lie did not agree to co-operate. Unlike Bjørnson,[40] this was not due to ideological reasons but rather a difference of perspective between him and Brandes. Lie feared that the regional co-operation would not be firmly grounded in the Scandinavian cultures but would instead be preoccupied with broader European debates: 'I am to Norwegian simplicity, what Brandes is to the manifoldness of European criticism. We two cannot work together', as he explained in a letter to the publisher of the journal, F. V. Hegel at Gyldendal, quoted in Brandes's autobiography.[41] Hegel was also the publisher of both his and Brandes' books.

Similarly, Henrik Ibsen addressed the asymmetry and arrogance of Brandes's proposed journal, but more directly and with an eye for the sociology and demography of the project. He translated Brandes's Europeanism

---

[39]   C.V.B. [= Carl von Bergen], 'Det nittende Aarhundrede', [review] *Stockholms Dagblad*, 18 November 1874. Swedish orig.: 'en dansk tidsskrift, för hvilken Sverige ej i literärt hänseende är och förbliver en terra incognita – en dansk tidsskrift, som omsider upptäckt, att äfven Nordens huvudland äger en på de flesta områden blomstrande och iderik literatur [...] detta bliver i sanning någonting lika sällsynt som välkommet, något som skandinavismen, till dens egen skada, hitills ej lyckats åvägabringa.'

[40]   Letter from Bjørnson to Brandes, 16 June 1879, in M. Borup *et al.* (eds), *Brdr. Brandes Brevveksling med nordiske Forfattere*, vol. IV (Copenhagen, 1940), p. 70.

[41]   G. Brandes, *Levned*, vol. 3 (Copenhagen, 1908), p. 126.

into Copenhagen parochialism and accused him of ignoring the 4 million Swedes, the 2 million Norwegians, the 1 million Finns, and the almost equally large Scandinavian population in America. 10 million people all together. 'Abandon all Copenhagen particularism; write for them all, then I will join you.'[42] To begin with, Ibsen's dynamic mapping of the ideal readership of the journal is remarkable by including the Scandinavian diaspora in America and the Finns. Hereby he is teasingly challenging Brandes' internationalist ideology by taking him at his word. In the subscription plan the concept of the 'North' was used to designate the journal's area of interest. Now Ibsen is relating Brandes to a static and outdated conception of Scandinavia, just as the Swedish reviewer did. With Ibsen's critical proposal, Brandes was put in a 'catch-22' situation. The chosen model was not satisfying, but on the other hand the idea to include the Finns was extremely difficult to apply, at least without translation, and it was the translation of Swedish texts in the journal that had triggered Ibsen's critique. Actually, Brandes himself was very keen to establish connections to Finland, and in an interesting review article from 1877 on Scandinavian journals – published in his own journal – he would stress the similarities between Denmark and Finland: even though Finland is far away from Denmark in space, the Finnish national spirit resembles the Danish, 'more familiar to us than the Swedish'.[43] So, unsurprisingly Brandes's Scandinavianism was undermined by himself. 'Scandinavia' was not really a meaningful concept to him, which was of course problematic when proposing and editing a Scandinavian journal.

The basic rhetorical question Ibsen was posing to Brandes in an attempt to convince him to rethink things was what kind of journal he was projecting, 'Danish or a Scandinavian?', claiming that 'Danish *literati* want subscribers and readerships in all of the Nordic countries, while only living and breathing and feeling in the air of Copenhagen'.[44] The Ibsen scholars Narve Fulsås and Tore Rem have convincingly interpreted the dispute over the journal as an example of the contestation between an avant-garde of successful Norwegian authors having risen above 'the

---

[42]   Letter from Ibsen to Brandes, 20 April 1874, N. Fulsås *et al.* (eds), *Henrik Ibsens Skrifter: Brev*, <www.ibsen.uio.no/BREV_1871-1879ht%7CB18740420GB.xhtml>. Norwegian orig.: 'opgiv al københavnsk partikularisme; skriv for dem allesammen, så skal jeg være med.'

[43]   G. Brandes, 'Nye skandinaviske Tidsskrifter', *Det nittende Aarhundrede* (April 1877), p. 73.

[44]   Letter from Ibsen to Brandes, 20 April 1874. Norwegian orig.: 'De danske literater vil nok have abonnenter og læsekreds i alle de nordiske lande; men de lever og ånder og føler kun i den københavnske luft.'

provincialism of the old centres, particularly what they perceived as Copenhagen's hegemonic pretentions'.[45]

While Fulsås and Rem do not go into bibliographical details about the journal, Ibsen himself did, and in this he might have missed a point when suggesting that the projected journal was not viable and profitable. The scarce Norwegian and Swedish mentions of the journal seem to indicate a modest number of non-Danish Scandinavian subscribers, and the Danish-biased pan-Scandinavian journal would reach more than 1,500 subscribers, which was apparently enough for Gyldendal and Hegel to let it run for six volumes before it closed in 1877, when Brandes moved to Berlin.[46] In his autobiography there are no details about the journal's commercial success. Interestingly however, all specificity concerning the precarious question of the transnational ambitions and intended audience is missing as well. *Det nittende Aarhundrede* is mentioned as a monthly with the ambition of 'getting closer *to the reading public* in a more intimate way than books allowed for', nothing more, nothing less.[47]

CONCLUSIONS

To conclude: while perhaps somewhat ignoring the practical and financial difficulties involved, the critical remarks on Brandes's journal by Ibsen as well as other Norwegians and Swedes highlight two crucial and interconnected issues involved in the making of a transnational journal: language and readership. All three pan-Scandinavian journals examined here aimed, each in their own way, to rearrange the literary marketplace by involving new readers and contributors, a pragmatic aspect of the periodical arguably in part defining it as media. Around 1700 the common European sociolect of Latin made things easy for the *Nova literaria*. Around 1800 the bilingual Dano-Swedish language policy was part of the explanation for *Nordia*'s failure, while around 1900 the monolingualism of *Det nittende Aarhundrede* can explain both its relative longevity and its parenthetical status in the history of the 'Modern Breakthrough' as a pan-Scandinavian phenomenon. A final point, prompted by the three more or less Scandinavian journals, relates more broadly to the question of transnationalisation of print culture. Famously and importantly, pioneering historians of the book such as Roger

[45]   N. Fulsås and T. Rem, 'From Periphery to Center: The Origins and Worlding of Ibsen's Drama', in M. Jalava *et al.* (eds), *Decentering European Intellectual Space* (Leiden, Boston, 2018), p. 50.
[46]   M. Zerlang, 'Det moderne gennembrud 1870-1900: Presse og magasiner', The Royal Library (Copenhagen, 2010). http://www2.kb.dk/elib/mss/dmg/presse/index.htm
[47]   G. Brandes, *Levned*, vol. 2 (Copenhagen, 1907), p. 163.

Chartier and Robert Darnton have stressed the inherent international nature of the book and its constitutive impulse to defy borders. However, this perception of the book as a 'cosmopolitan agent' (Matt Cohen)[48] should be complemented with trajectories of regional efforts of transfer and transnationalism in the margins of the international or global system of literary circulation, which did not last, did not succeed, or did not happen at all.

[48] For a discussion on the internationalisation of book history, see M. Cohen, '"Between Friends and Enemies": Moving Books and Locating Native Critique in Early Colonial America', in S. Richard Lyons (ed.), *The World, the Text, and the Indian: Global Dimensions of Native American Literature* (New York, 2017), pp. 103–28.

5

Implementing Freedom of the Press in Eighteenth-Century Scandinavia: Perspectives on a Surprising Lack of Transnationalism

Ulrik Langen, Jonas Nordin and Frederik Stjernfelt

O NLY A FEW YEARS apart in the late 1700s, the kingdom of Sweden and the dual monarchy of Denmark–Norway introduced freedom of the press. These were unique experiences in many ways, even in a global comparison. The result of the liberation of the press was similar in the two cases: a tremendous increase in political pamphleteering led to an intensified and radicalised political discourse. The initial enthusiasm was followed by more ambiguous attitudes, and within a few years freedom of the press was once again restricted. In both cases, however, it proved difficult to close Pandora's box once opened, and the short periods of freedom of the press proved to have long-lasting effects in both Denmark–Norway and Sweden.

Many observers would probably expect interdependence between these two experiences but, as we aim to demonstrate, it is more a matter of historical coincidence or parallelism than mutual inspiration between the two cases. The constitutional framing of these countries was nearly dichotomous at the time, and this created very different roles for public discourse. Furthermore, for political and historical reasons, references to the neighbouring realm were often regarded with suspicion in either context. If anything, these two cases and their varying conditions may serve to prove how rapidly freedom of expression had become a core question in the European Enlightenment, whether 'moderate' or 'radical', in the course of the eighteenth century. Many of the central ideas and arguments were already framed around the beginning of the century. The traditional notion that freedom of speech was an idea born with the American and French revolutions has long been abandoned by historians, but we still need local case studies to see how this concept converged and diverged and was instantiated in very different ways and contexts, both diachronically and synchronically, before the Age of Revolutions.[1]

This chapter highlights the different paths to freedom of the press in the two states and discusses the surprising lack of connection and mutual discussion between the two parallel initiatives. We focus on the limited periods of press freedom in the strictest sense (1766–72 and 1770–3 respectively) in order to highlight the sudden stimulation of literary citizenship brought about by the introduction of freedom of the press in Sweden and Denmark–Norway.

A WELL-PREPARED IMPLEMENTATION OF PRESS FREEDOM: SWEDEN

In 1766 Sweden acquired the first government-sponsored freedom of the press anywhere in the world. This was no haphazard occurrence but the outcome of a decades-long political development. During this period, the so-called Age of Liberty, Sweden was a republic in all but name. In the 1719/20 Instrument of Government, political power was transferred from the monarch to the Council of the Realm, and from the late 1730s it was gradually conveyed to the Swedish Diet, *Riksdagen*.[2]

Riksdagen, which convened at least every three years, was composed of the four estates of the Nobility, the Clergy, the Burghers and the Peasantry. In the late 1730s two opposing parties had emerged and operated within the Diet: the Hats and the Caps.[3] Decisions were taken by a majority among the four estates, but the party divisions ran within all four of them. This called for intense negotiations and bargaining between the estates, and although consensus decision-making was still the ideal, political dissent on most matters was in reality the norm.[4] This called for a free and open

---

[1] See, e.g., E. Powers (ed.), *Freedom of Speech: The History of an Idea* (Lewisburg, 2011); on 'moderate' and 'radical' Enlightenment, see J. Israel's contribution in *ibid.*

[2] The best summary of the period in English is still M. Roberts, *The Age of Liberty: Sweden 1719–1772* (Cambridge, 1986). For recent perspectives on the political culture in the Scandinavian realms, see P. Ihalainen *et al.* (eds), *Scandinavia in the Age of Revolution: Nordic Political Cultures, 1740–1820* (Farnham, 2011).

[3] Hats favoured an aggressive foreign policy in alliance with France against Russia; Caps pulled closer to Great Britain and were less demonstrative towards Sweden's former enemies. Over time, diverging opinions on domestic politics and economy increasingly came to the fore.

[4] For the function of the parliamentary system, see M. F. Metcalf, 'Parliamentary Sovereignty and Royal Reaction, 1719–1809', in H. Schück (ed.), *The Riksdag: A History of*

debate, which had been unheard of in previous forms of government, but Swedish politicians soon found many similarities with the British parliamentary system, and it is obvious that this affected the discussion on freedom of the press.

Sweden had had an instituted system of pre-publication censorship since 1661, and an office of *censor librorum* was established as part of the Chancellery in 1688. The first proposition to abolish this control system was presented to the Diet in 1727 by a young member of the Burgher estate, Anders Bachmansson (1697–1772), better known under the name Nordencrantz, which he bore from 1743 when he received a knighthood. His motion opened with an historical exposé of the Swedish people, whose disgruntled and bitter character stretched back seven or eight hundred years. A major reason for their nasty temperament was the lack of enlightenment, for which Bachmansson Nordencrantz saw an efficient remedy: 'A free and unhindered printing of books is therefore the artificial means and the noble light that is wholly indispensable for enlightening the natural intellect.'[5] He saw the prevailing censorship as an anomaly under the new constitution, which had removed absolutism: 'in spite of us now having become a free people, [liberty of the press] is still being withheld, so we still do not seem to know the full extent of our freedom.'[6] Nordencrantz also adduced economic arguments: the restrained press forced Swedish youth to travel abroad, and the importation of books ruined the domestic printing industry. This first proposal was soon followed by another, which extended the arguments.

Nordencrantz's motion on freedom of the press was well received by the Burghers. Many members gathered to read it and owing to its national importance the group that handled the proposition suggested that it should be printed and distributed to the other estates. Ironically, this request had to pass the censor, Johan Rosenadler, who turned to his superiors for advice on how to handle the matter. The answer was as expected: as long as an author avoids blasphemous, seditious and immoral subjects, he will have no trouble with the censor, thus Swedish writers already enjoy freedom of the press. Having thus received neither a yes nor a no, Nordencrantz sent a draft copy to the censor, but Rosenadler replied that he could not assess

---

the Swedish Parliament (New York, 1987).

[5]   'Et frit och oinskränkt Boktryckerij hyser fördenskull det artificielle medlet och det ädla liuset som till det naturliga förståndets uplysande helt oumgengeligt är'. Undated draft [March 1727] with many amendments in Swedish National Archives, Stockholm, Börstorpsamlingen, E3011: Anders Nordencrantz' arkiv, koncept (tidiga).

[6]   'Men sådant är, oaktat wi blifwit et frit folk, ännu likwäl betagit, så at wi tyckes ännu icke rätteligen kienna wår frihet', ibid.

a yet unfinished manuscript. The matter was reiterated in the Chancellery some months later, but at that point Nordencrantz had refocused on other, more mundane tasks: a few weeks earlier the Chancellery had approved his application to become consul to Lisbon, which kept him away from domestic politics for more than a decade.[7]

Although this first attempt vanished into obscurity, Nordencrantz returned to the subject in several writings and became one of the most persistent and important advocates for freedom of the press.[8] Nordencrantz had lived in London for eighteen months in the early 1720s, which had made a deep impression on his political views. In his first book he declared that 'the greatest enemies of mankind are those who forbid freedom of speech' and those who 'with violence and threats suppress and persecute man's only guide: *reason*'.[9] The book came out in 1730, but he had begun the manuscript during his stay in England. Another manuscript, written at the same time but unpublished until 1767, revealed one of his sources in the long title: *Thoughts, on freedom in print, and its usefulness and harm; which in 1730 was translated from the English periodical, called Craftsman; but could not be promoted to the press, until the realm's praiseworthy estates paved the way, with the ordinance of the 2 Dec. 1766. A short preface, on the proper value and property of freedom of the press, is also attached.*[10]

Nordencrantz's inspiration *The Craftsman* was initiated in 1726, 'against a

---

[7] *Borgarståndets riksdagsprotkoll från frihetstidens början*, 3: *1726–1727* (Stockholm, 1956), ed. N. Staf, pp. 199f, 3 March 1727. Swedish National Archives: 'Hörsamt memorial', no. 325, 11 March 1727, Borgarståndets arkiv 1726–1727, vol. 5, R 1207; Johan Rosenadler to the Chancellor of the Realm, n.d., (received 12 June 1727), Kanslikollegium E IV:17; Chancellery minutes, 9, 27 June, 11 November 1727, Kanslikollegium A IIa:39, fols 281, 289, 691f. G. Nilzén, 'Anders Nordencrantz som konsul i Portugal: En studie över bitterhetens ideologiska följder', *Personhistorisk tidskrift*, 83 (1987), 38–49. See also Anders Burius, *Ömhet om friheten: Studier i frihetstidens censurpolitik* (Uppsala, 1984), pp. 231f.

[8] On Nordencrantz, see L. Magnusson, 'Anders Nordencrantz', in B. Wennberg and K. Örtenhed (eds), *Press Freedom 250 Years: Freedom of the Press and Public Access to Official Documents in Sweden and Finland – A Living Heritage from 1766* (Stockholm, 2018), pp. 77–87.

[9] '[...] menniskiosläktets största fiender, äro de, som förbiuda frihet i tal och swar, at med wåld och twång trycka och förfölja menniskians enda wägledare *förnuftet*': A. Bachmansson (Nordencrantz), *Arcana oeconomiæ et commercii, eller Handelens och hushåldnings-wärkets hemligheter: Undersökte och på det möjeligaste sätt utforskade, pröfwade och ändteligen framstälte uti åtskilliga capitel och materier* (Stockholm, 1730), preface.

[10] *Tankar, om friheten i tryck, samt desz nytta och skada; hwilke år 1730 blifwit öfwersatte ifrån den engelska periodiska skriften, kallad Craftsman; men ej kunnat til trycket befordras, förrän riksens höglofliga ständer dertil banat wägen fri, med*

backdrop of censorship and the resultant tame journalism, and became the leading opposition newspaper to Robert Walpole's long ministry 1721–42.[11] It must have been easy for Nordencrantz to relate to Swedish politics and Chancellor Arvid Horn's equally long ministry, 1720–38; drafts and excerpts in his private papers corroborate Nordencrantz's claim that the translation lay hidden in his desk drawer for nearly four decades.[12] In the meantime he had returned to the subject in several books and pamphlets and became the inspiration for many others working both within and outside the political system.[13]

The next time we hear of freedom of the press is at the Diet of 1738–9. The nobleman Henning Adolf Gyllenborg argued that 'among a free people a free press should be allowed'.[14] This would not only promote culture and general instruction but also vitalise political discourse:

> That each and every citizen without constraint or supervision may put his thoughts under the free judgement of the public, it drives away the barbarian darkness in a country, it encourages competition between cultured writers, through whom the truth more and more comes to the fore, and it helps a free people to know itself, its strengths and its weaknesses. Through freedom of the press, the fumes and blindness are averted, which are often held before the eyes of the public by powerful deceivers, and through the freedom of the press, everyone has the opportunity to defend a wounded innocence and a repressed powerlessness.[15]

---

förordningen af den 2 dec. 1766. Härwid bifogas jämwäl et kort företal, om tryck-frihetens rätta wärde och egenskap (Stockholm, 1767)

[11] S. Varey, 'The Craftsman', Prose Studies, 16 (1993), 58–77, quote p. 63.

[12] A. Burius, Ömhet om friheten, p. 378, n. 65.

[13] See e.g. A. Nordencrantz, Oförgripelige tankar, om frihet i bruk af förnuft, pennor och tryck, samt huru långt friheten derutinnan i et fritt samhälle sig sträcka bör, tillika med påfölgden deraf (Stockholm, 1756).

[14] 'hos et fritt folk ett fritt tryck bör tillåtas', Sveriges ridderskaps och adels riksdags-protokoll från och med år 1719, 11: 1738–1739, 3 (Stockholm, 1889), p. 348.

[15] 'At hvar och en medborgare utan tvång och upsyningsman får lägga sina tanckar under det almännas fria omdöme, det bortjagar det barbariska mörckret i et land, det främjar täflingen mellan vittra pennor, hvarigenom sanningen altmer och mer upbläncker, och det hielper et frijt folck till at kiänna sig sielf, sin styrcka och sin svaga. Genom tryckfrijheten hindras de dunster och förblindelser, som ofta genom konster slås det almänna för synen af mäcktige förledare, och genom tryckfriheeten har hvar och en tilfälle at försvara en sargad oskuld och en förtryckt menlösheet.' Sveriges ridderskaps och adels riksdags-protokoll, 11:3, pp. 348f.

Gyllenborg's juxtaposition of a free people and a free press is reminiscent of Nordencrantz's argument, but there is no established connection between the two proposals. If anything, there is reason to believe that Gyllenborg's was inspired by his uncle Carl, who became guardian of his nephew in 1728. Carl Gyllenborg had spent thirteen years at the Swedish legation in London and was well acquainted with British politics. In 1722, soon after his return to Sweden and only a couple of years after the establishment of the new republican form of government, Carl Gyllenborg argued in the Chancellery that 'in a free state no one should be forbidden to reason publicly about social life, especially as this is a means to uncover the truth'.[16]

However extensive the inspiration from Great Britain may have been in Sweden at this point, it seems to have been the comparable political circumstances that caught the attention, not principled tracts like David Hume's *Of the Liberty of the Press*, which was not published until 1741. At a later point, periodicals like *En fri swänsk* (A Free Swede) wrote about freedom of the press as a fundamental right in all free societies, but the empirical examples were limited to ancient Rome and Great Britain, where liberty was defended and abuse and heresy were punished. The anonymous editor, an elderly law clerk named Magnus Pihlgren, approvingly quoted Eustace Budgell of *The Spectator*, that while the liberty to discuss the nature of butterflies or the force of the magnet was guaranteed even in the most oppressive states like Turkey or Denmark, proper freedom of the press entailed the liberty to discuss political matters.[17]

En fri swänsk connected to a movement that turned press freedom into a major question in the early 1760s. Following motions from members of the Cap Party, the Diet in 1760 formed a committee with representatives from all four estates to explore how a 'reasonable freedom of the press' could be introduced. Although it worked for over two years and presented several propositions, it never reached any conclusion. It was apparent, however, that freedom of the press would be a major issue at the next gathering of the Diet.[18]

In August 1765 a new committee was formed, and it worked for eleven months to prepare the matter. *Censor librorum* Niclas von Oelreich was

[16] 'uti en fri stat bör ingen förbjudas, att uti allmänna saker, som angå alla få publique raisonera, helst som sanningen derigenom kommer fram', quoted from A. Burius, *Ömhet om friheten*, p. 214.
[17] *En fri swänsk* (1761), no. 6, see also e.g. nos 3, 17, 46. Cf. Otto Sylwan, *Svenska pressens historia till statshvälfningen 1772* (Lund, 1896), pp. 412f; A. Burius, *Ömhet om friheten*, pp. 254f.
[18] M. Skuncke, 'Press Freedom in the Riksdag 1760-62 and 1765-66', in B. Wennberg and K. Örtenhed, *Press Freedom 250 Years*, pp. 109-16.

co-opted to the committee as an expert and to describe his work in detail – he is an ambiguous figure, not unlike the French censor Chrétien-Guillaume Malesherbes, but seems to have been intent on making his own office redundant.[19] The committee assembled a large collection of domestic legislation as well as previous memorials and motions presented to the Diet, but the minutes from the committee's 21 sessions only record one reference to experiences from other countries. It was during a discussion about the right to print the minutes and proceedings of the Diet. The committee presumed that few members of the Diet would object,

> since nothing honours an upstanding member of the Diet more than when his thoughts are made public, and nothing holds the crooked within the bars of reason [like public demonstration]. *Nota Bene*: England's example.[20]

This opinion was not necessarily based on actual insights into the British political system but might as well have been a rhetorical stance that alluded to the widespread preconceptions of its supposed liberal character. For instance, China was often highlighted as a model society in Swedish discourse, and there were few who could challenge such statements with reference to first-hand experiences.[21] Furthermore, at this point the political conditions in Great Britain were far from being as exemplary as some Swedish opinion leaders claimed (see below). The committee's close scrutiny of Swedish legislation and the fact that no other references were made to the situation in other countries imply that the preparation of the freedom of the press legislation was first and foremost rooted in domestic conditions. This observation is in line with several studies that have demonstrated that Sweden's rather turbulent constitutional history between the seventeenth century and the beginning of the nineteenth century rarely drew inspiration from international examples other than on a general ideological level. Swedish politicians were familiar with all the standard works, from Aristotle to Montesquieu, but their ideas seldom survived in

---

[19]   The deliberations can be followed closely through the proceedings of the legislative committee: R 3405: Tredje utskottet 1765–1766, protokoll och bilagor, Swedish National Archives. On Malesherbes, see R. Chartier, *The Cultural Origins of the French Revolution* (Durham, London, 1991), ch. 3.

[20]   'emedan ingen ting mera hedrar en redelig Riksdagsman än då dess tankar blifwa bekantan och deremot ingenting håller en annors sinnad inom billighetens skrankor. NB: Änglands Exempel', R 3405, 12 December 1765, fol. 371r.

[21]   See L. Rydholm, 'China and the World's First Freedom of Information Act: The Swedish Freedom of the Press Act of 1766', *Javnost – The Public*, 20 (2013), 45–64.

any substantial way the confrontation with a political culture that had been chiselled out through negotiations between the four estates ever since the Middle Ages.[22]

The committee presented a proposition to the Diet in the summer of 1766. It suggested that all censorship should be abolished. However, in the deliberations of the four estates it soon became apparent that the Nobility would not consent to the law. To be adopted, a bill needed a majority of three estates, and the Clergy also showed hesitation. In order to avoid a complete rejection, the Burghers and the Peasantry had to accept that clerical authorities maintained pre-censorship in the domain of religious writings.[23]

With this major exception, the Freedom of the Press Ordinance was signed by the king on 2 December 1766. It preserved censorship in religious matters, and it made four topics liable for prosecution: blasphemy, seditious libel, defamation and obscenities.[24] In spite of these restrictions, it is important to recognise that only violations on these four clearly defined grounds were subject to indictment. The Ordinance was formulated according to the principle of *nulla poena sine lege*, no penalty without a law, which singled out the Swedish legislation rather substantially from the arbitrary legal situation in countries with otherwise wide margins for the press, such as Great Britain and the Netherlands.[25]

The most remarkable feature of the Freedom of the Press Ordinance is at any rate that it also contained a freedom of information clause. It provided that all citizens should have free access to all deliberations or minutes from the legal courts, the civil authorities, the Diet, and even from the Council of the Realm, i.e. the government. The only exception was matters of national security. All official acts and documents that were open to examination

---

[22]   Cf., e.g., F. Lagerroth, *Frihetstidens författning: En studie i den svenska konstitutionalismens historia* (Stockholm, 1915); L. Thanner, *Revolutionen i Sverige efter Karl XII:s död: Den inrepolitiska maktkampen under tidigare delen av Ulrika Eleonora d.y:s regering* (Uppsala, 1953); A. Brusewitz, *Representationsfrågan vid 1809–10 års riksdag: En inledning till representationsreformens historia* (Uppsala, 1913).

[23]   M.-C. Skuncke, 'Press Freedom in the Riksdag 1760–62 and 1765–66', pp. 116–34.

[24]   'His Majesty's Gracious Ordinance Relating to Freedom of Writing and of the Press' (1766), transl. P. Hogg, in *The World's First Freedom of Information Act: Anders Chydenius' Legacy Today*, ed. J. Mustonen (Kokkola, 2006), pp. 8–17. J. Nordin and J. C. Laursen, 'Northern Declarations of Freedom of the Press: The Relative Importance of Philosophical Ideas and of Local Politics', *Journal of the History of Ideas*, 81 (2020), 223–5.

[25]   J. Nordin, 'From Seemly Subjects to Enlightened Citizens', pp. 45–56, and R. Nygren, 'The Freedom of the Press Act of 1766 in its Historical and Legal Context', pp. 167–201, in B. Wennberg and K. Örtenhed, *Press Freedom 250 Years*.

were also free to publish. The extent of this freedom of information is notable even with today's standard in many democratic countries, and it was quite exceptional at the time. For example, it was only through the intervention of John Wilkes in 1771 that it became permissible to publish literal transcripts from the English parliament, and this right never extended to the proceedings of the Privy Council or the Cabinet.[26]

A SUDDEN IMPLEMENTATION OF PRESS FREEDOM: DENMARK–NORWAY

Prior to the introduction of freedom of the press in the absolute monarchy of Denmark–Norway in September 1770, censorship was generally carried out, since 1537, as pre-publication censorship of book manuscripts by the professors of the Academic Council at the University of Copenhagen, with theologians being the most influential. Newspapers were censored by officials appointed by the government. The only exceptions were closely monitored and circumscribed. A few recent institutions, the Royal Danish Academy of Science and Letters (1742) and the Academy at Sorø (1749), were allowed to self-censor their publications by peer review. In the 1750s the government launched a limited public debate on the common good and lent its support to the communication of economic information on a larger scale than had been the case previously. The government tried to benefit from the expanding public sphere and monitor the development of publicity. A general invitation to participate in a supervised patriotic debate on economic matters was issued in 1755, and the 'most useful' treatises would be printed in a government-sponsored journal without regard to personal standing and without cost to the author.[27]

Although certain institutions were exempted from censorship – and although many broadside ballads and minor pamphlets managed to pass censorship because the censors did not care to read them – the introduction of freedom of the press in 1770 was completely unexpected.[28] There had been no thoroughgoing debate on government level of such matters, as

[26]   P. D. G. Thomas, *John Wilkes: A Friend to Liberty* (Oxford, 1996), pp. 125–40.

[27]   On the 1755 invitation, see J. Maliks, *Vilkår for offentlighet. Sensur, økonomi og transformasjonen af det offentlige rom i Danmark-Norge 1730–1770* (Trondheim, 2011).

[28]   On Dano-Norwegian censorship, see Ø. Rian, *Sensuren i Danmark-Norge: Vilkårene for offentlige ytringer 1536–1814* (Oslo, 2014); J. Mchangama and F. Stjernfelt, *MEN: Ytringsfrihedens historie i Danmark* (Copenhagen, 2016) and J. Jakobsen, 'Uanstændige, utilladelige og unyttige skrifter: En undersøgelse af censuren i praksis 1746–1773' (Unpublished PhD thesis, the Saxo Institute, University of Copenhagen, 2017).

was the case in Sweden. The press freedom ordinance was the first action of the silent coup by Johann Friedrich Struensee, the personal physician of Christian VII. The German-born Struensee had gained power by way of his personal influence on the king and through his love affair with Queen Caroline Matilda who was a sister of the English king, George III. The Struensee reign lasted 16 months, during which a string of reforms was launched. The reign was put to an end by a group of coup plotters formally lead by Queen Dowager Juliana Maria and Hereditary Prince Frederick, who seized power during the night of 17 January 1772. In the initial phase Struensee was supported by top militaries such as P. E. Gähler and S. C. Rantzau, who had been plotting against State Council rule since the mid-1760s, and most likely, press freedom had been a theme in the secret discussions of this group. The day after the introduction of freedom of the press, the State Council was purged, and later the same winter, it was dissolved completely, while the practical effects of press freedom in the public were busily exploding.

If we take a closer look at the few sources shedding some light on the decision to introduce freedom of the press, it is striking how a very brief royal order was transformed into an elaborate ordinance, written by the Cabinet Secretary, reflecting the idea of an enlightened general public and the proper patriotic use of the press freedom. On a list of six orders from the king to his secretary, we find this in the king's own handwriting: '(To write) 3. Furthermore, an order to the chancellery that gives complete freedom of the press so that books can be printed without any kind of censorship.'[29] Within what must have been only a few hours on 4 September, this brief order was rephrased by the Cabinet Secretary and appeared as a law ten days later, on 14 September. Struensee no doubt monitored the process carefully if not actually wielding the pen of the king and his secretary:

> We are fully convinced that it is as harmful to the impartial search for truth as it is to the discovery of obsolete errors and prejudices, if upright patriots, zealous for the common good and what is genuinely best for their fellow citizens, because they are frightened by reputation, orders, and preconceived opinions, are hindered from being free to write according to their insight, conscience, and conviction, attacking abuses and uncovering prejudices. And thus in this regard, after

---

[29] '(Ecrire) 3. Encor un ordre aux chancelleries qui donne la permission sans restriction pour la presse, que les livres doivent être imprimés sans aucune censure', Danish National Archives, Copenhagen, Kabinetssekretariatet 1766–1771: Kgl. ordrer til kabinetssekretariatet, Cabinet Order of 4 September 1770.

ripe consideration, we have decided to permit in our kingdoms and lands in general an unlimited freedom of press [...].[30]

It came after the Swedish law but was more radical in the sense that it made no room for exceptions. In a sense, it was the world's first full press freedom. The law was informed by central Enlightenment ideas about the political utility of a free press: the search for truth, the criticism of abuse, the rejection of prejudice. Like informed people in Sweden and elsewhere in Europe, the king was familiar with commonplace contents of the transnational enlightened republic of letters – an interest that he had made a public display of when he in 1768 visited the Academy of Science in Paris and made conversation with prominent Enlightenment figures such as d'Alembert and Diderot.[31]

Before becoming a royal physician Struensee had lived in cosmopolitan Altona working as a doctor employed by the city. Altona had for many years enjoyed a reputation as a safe haven for dissidents and heretics of the north German lands, liberty in Altona being considerably greater than in strictly controlled Copenhagen and indeed also greater than in neighbouring Hamburg. In Altona he learned inoculation from the Jewish doctor Hartog Gerson and J. A. Reimarus, a son of the famous Hamburg theologian and secret freethinker Samuel Reimarus, whom Struensee also became acquainted with. In brief, he became part of a North German network of Enlightenment figures, including characters such as Lessing, the reform pedagogue J. B. Basedow and the Jewish philosopher A. E. Gompertz, a friend of Mendelssohn's and the former secretary of Maupertuis and the marquis d'Argens.

Like many others in the period, Struensee admired Montesquieu and Voltaire, but his favourite authors among the emerging French High Enlightenment seem to have been Helvétius and Boulanger; the former for his scientific approach to the soul and for his support of free speech, the

---

[30]   This translation was made by J. C. Laursen and published in 'David Hume and the Danish Debate about Freedom of the Press in the 1770s', *Journal of the History of Ideas*, 59 (1998), 168; translated from the original German in *Luxdorphiana, eller Bidrag til den danske Literairhistorie*, ed. R. Nyerup (Copenhagen, 1791), pp. 1–2; also in H. Hansen, *Kabinets-styrelsen i Danmark*, 1 (Copenhagen, 1916), pp. 46f.

[31]   On Christian VII's knowledge of Enlightenment writers and his visit to Paris, see U. Langen, 'Le roi et les philosophes: le séjour parisien de Christian VII de Danemark en 1768', *Revue d'Histoire, économie et Société*, 1 (2010), 5–21, and 'Raising a Crown Prince in the Age of Reason', in V. Gancheva (ed.), *The 18th Century and Europe* (Sofia, 2013), pp. 164–9.

latter for his analysis of religion as a way of politically exploiting the fears of believers.

But Struensee also acquired hands-on experience of Dano-Norwegian censorship in addition to his grandfather's case from 1742. One of his intellectual friends was the Danish deist Georg Schade, who anonymously published a large Leibnizian treatise on natural religion and reincarnation in Altona in 1761. His anonymity was broken, however, by the powerful Lutheran heretic-hunter J. M. Goeze in Hamburg's Katharina Church. Schade was turned over to Dano-Norwegian authorities in Altona, and without a court case he was banished for life to the small Danish Baltic islet of Christiansø north of Bornholm. When in power ten years later Struensee saw to the early release of his old friend. But Struensee's own publications were also indicted by Dano-Norwegian censorship. In his periodical *Zum Nutzen und Vergnügen* (For Benefit and Pleasure) Struensee argued for medical-inspired state policies as well as the virtues of satire, and he took aim at Altona's best known and revered doctor, J. A. Unzer, founder of the successful weekly *Der Arzt* (The Doctor). Because of this article, his journal was proscribed by the Dano-Norwegian State Council. Struensee, in short, did not only harbour transnational Enlightenment ideas of press freedom on the fundamental, abstract level gleaned from the reading of contemporaneous French Enlighteners and his dinner discussions in Altona. He also had direct, personal experience of the effects of Dano-Norwegian censorship at several different levels.[32]

Unlike the Swedish case, there was no pre-legislative process which would indicate any considerations on possible uncertainties or grey zones, for instance regarding author responsibility or defamation. No clearly delimited exemptions were stated, as in the Swedish law. It was also not clear how the cancelling of all censorship would affect the existing strict limits on public expressions by post-publication punishments in the Danish Law of Christian V (1683); the new legislation did not mention these at all. In short, the discussions on the nature, the function and not least the ways of applying press freedom began only *after* the ordinance was passed. Furthermore, it is important to underline that this discussion took place within the new public sphere created by the introduction of press freedom.

---

[32]   On Struensee's intellectual foundations and the transnational networks in Altona, see H. Horstbøll *et al.*, *Grov Konfækt: Tre vilde år med trykkefrihed 1770–73*, 1 (Copenhagen, 2020), pp. 479–91. Since we wrote this chapter an abridged version of this two-volume work has been published in English by the two main authors: U. Langen and F. Stjernfelt, *The World's First Full Press Freedom: The Radical Experiment of Denmark–Norway 1770–1773* (Berlin, 2022).

THE NEW PUBLIC SPHERE

Did the freedom of the press have any effect on printing in Sweden and Denmark–Norway? There are no exact figures as to the number of prints produced in Sweden, but the national bibliography is accurate enough to give us reliable trend figures. The annual average number of prints from the middle of the eighteenth century to the second decade of the nineteenth is about 555, according to this source (see Figure 5.1). The numbers for the six years following the Freedom of the Press Ordinance are well above this average, and they were not exceeded until after 1809, when press freedom was reintroduced.

The number of printers, booksellers and other agents on the print market was not great, but in an industry that had been more or less stable for several decades, a sudden increase is evident. This is most clearly visible in the political centre, Stockholm, where the seven printers in 1766 had to compete with another three in 1771, and the number of bookshops grew from two in the early 1760s to six or seven by the end of the decade. Between 1720 and 1766 an average of 1.5 new journals were launched each year; in 1766–74 this number rose to 12.5.[33]

The primary motivation behind the Freedom of the Press Ordinance was to invigorate public discourse. 'So, the life and strength of civil liberty consist in *limited Government* and *unlimited freedom of the written word*', wrote philosopher Peter Forsskål as far back as 1759.[34] The effects of the reform are also most clearly visible in the political publications. Citizenship was exercised in the literary arena, and pamphlets, which until then had mainly been circulated in manuscript copies (which were exempt from prior censorship), were now being printed in growing numbers. The connection with political activities is clearly visible in Figure 5.2, where the years 1769 and 1771, when the Diet convened, clearly stand out.

The Freedom of the Press Ordinance did not only stimulate publishing as such, it also accelerated an already ongoing radicalisation of the political climate. A few weeks before the signing of the Freedom of the Press Ordinance, another important law was adopted which stated that changes to the constitution could only be implemented after decisions by two consecutive sittings of the Diet with intermediate elections.[35] This

---

[33] J. Nordin, 'En revolution i tryck: Tryckfrihet och tryckproduktion i Sverige 1766–1772 och däromkring', *Vetenskapssocieteten i Lund årsbok* 2020, pp. 100–3.

[34] P. Forsskål, *Thoughts on Civil Liberty: Translation of the Original Manuscript with background* (Stockholm, 2009), p. 15, emphasis in original text.

[35] *Kongl. Maj:ts Nådige Förordning, Til Befrämjande af Lagarnes behörige wärkställighet bland Rikets Ämbetsmän och öfrige undersåtare: Gifwen Stockholm i*

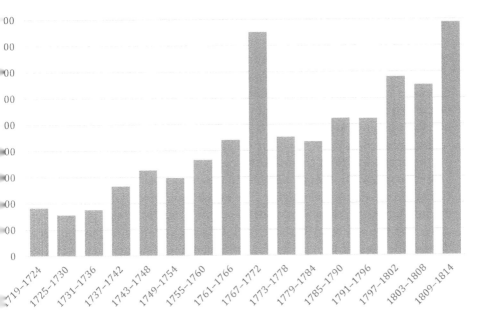

FIG. 5.1. Swedish pamphlets and books printed 1719–1814: average numbers in six-year intervals. (Source: Swedish National Bibliography, Libris: Svetryck.)

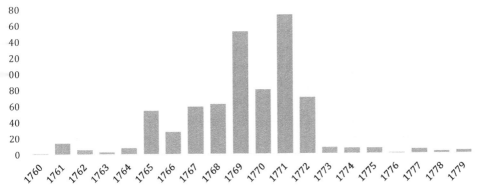

FIG. 5.2. Swedish political pamphlets 1760–79, absolute numbers. (Source: Subject headings 'General Politics' & 'Political Economy', Swedish Collection, 1700–1829, National Library of Sweden.)

was a recognition of the electorate's influence on national affairs, and such a mandate obviously required a well-informed citizenry. Furthermore, a proper citizenry could not be divided by formal inequalities. The privileges of the nobility therefore became one of the main targets of the three commoner estates, and a great number of pamphlets contained testimonies of the aristocracy's abuse of power and oppression of more humble members of society. Such opinions resonated in the government, which began to dismantle noble privileges bit by bit until they were in practice all but abolished in the early 1770s.[36]

Copenhagen, with its fifteen printing houses, was the dominant centre for the printed word in Denmark–Norway in the period of press freedom, although printing houses also existed in towns such as Bergen, Trondheim, Christiania, Aalborg and Odense. The number of printers in Copenhagen did not increase in these years, but five of the printers became particularly active and strongly contributed to the media revolution caused by the freedom of the press, which gave rise to the blending of genres, new types of periodicals, new authors, new readerships. Thus, literary citizenship was broadened considerably. Although the vast majority of pamphlets were published in Copenhagen, Norwegian printers contributed with original material and reprints. In the period after the fall of Struensee, the number of prints from Norway exceeded those printed in the Danish provinces.[37] Likewise, Norwegian authors working out of Copenhagen took part in the development of the new literary citizenship of the press freedom period. One of the most prolific writers of the period was the Norwegian J. C. Bie, who under the pseudonym of Philopatreias kickstarted public debate shortly after the introduction of press freedom by attacking grain-producing landowners, lawyers and priests in a pamphlet. The reputation of his pamphlet reached the Danish West Indies (now U.S. Virgin Islands) where it – as the sole example of so-called Press Freedom Writings – was translated into English and published in St Croix in 1771.[38]

The concept of Press Freedom Writings (*trykkefrihedsskrifter*) was a contemporary notion coined by the *Register of Press-Freedom Publications* – a new periodical that offered information on every such print published since the introduction of press freedom, including price, number of pages,

Råd-Cammaren then 12. Novemb. 1766 (Stockholm, 1766), Section 11.
[36] J. Nordin, *Ett fattigt men fritt folk: Nationell och politisk självbild i Sverige från sen stormaktstid till slutet av frihetstiden* (Eslöv, 2000), ch. 6.
[37] H. Horstbøll, 'Bolle Luxdorphs samling af trykkefrihedsskrifter 1770–1773', *Fund & Forskning*, 44 (2005), 412.
[38] [J. C. Bie], *Philopatreia's Remarks, I: On the dear Times, and Decay of Trade; II: On the Courts of Justice; III: On the Revenues of the Clergy* (St Croix, 1771).

points of sale and a short review of each separate publication. It was edited by young intellectuals and students and published by a book trader named Kanneworff; it also involved the work of the later well-known publisher Søren Gyldendal.

This literary chronology was consolidated in a collection of 914 publications gathered and bound in 45 volumes in octavo, one in quarto and one in folio, by a central civil servant, Bolle Luxdorph. The Luxdorph Collection of Press Freedom Writing is chronologically divided into two series: twenty volumes dated before the fall of Struensee in January 1772, twenty-seven after that date, plus an extra folio volume with graphic prints. This collection consists of what Luxdorph considered to be publications owing their existence to the freedom of the press. A dating of the scripts based on the first day of advertising each piece in the press constitutes a chronological reconstruction of the majority of publications in the Luxdorph Collection, and most Press Freedom Writings can now be sequentially arranged, which is important for organising the order in the many debates of the period.[39]

Immediately following the downfall of Struensee in January 1772, an avalanche of printed sermons, pamphlets and broadside ballads were published, giving a vivid picture of an alleged conspiracy conceived by Struensee. Most of these prints and sermons accentuated that the monarchy had been saved by divine intervention and by the efficiency of the Queen Dowager Juliana Maria and the Hereditary Prince Frederick, who were part of the group taking control of the government following the coup.

In contrast to Sweden, there was no explicit public debate in Denmark–Norway on freedom of the press *before* the introduction, but after its introduction the debate flourished with such a variety and detail that it is reasonable to suggest that freedom of the press in general must have been actively discussed before 1770, although covertly. Merethe Roos has pointed out that there were emergent new textual norms (and so-called 'modernising tendencies') even before press freedom, but they became much more fully expressed in the new open public sphere of the Press Freedom Period.[40] Indeed, press freedom had also been negotiated on a practical level by *Spectator* journalists pushing the limits of censorship in the 1740s.[41] Moreover, Ellen Krefting has convincingly argued that the Dano-Norwegian government adopted an implicit legal distinction

---

[39]   The Press Freedom Period 1770–3 is exhaustively investigated in H. Horstbøll *et al.*, *Grov Konfækt*, vols 1–2.

[40]   M. Roos, *Enlightened Preaching: Balthasar Münter's Authorship 1772–1793* (Leiden, 2013), p. 147.

[41]   E. Krefting, 'The Urge to Write: Spectator Journalists Negotiating Freedom of the Press in Denmark-Norway', in E. Krefting *et al.* (eds), *Eighteenth-Century Periodicals*

between news and opinion, which weakened the newspapers' editorial power so that opinions were to a great extent channelled into periodicals which, thus, became hubs of textual experiments and ultimately agents of change informed by Enlightenment discourse.[42]

Many of the Dano-Norwegian Press Freedom pamphlets and scripts mentioned press freedom as an incentive or even an excuse for publishing. There was a strong common reflexivity among the writers of the press freedom era; a permanent discussion on how to use the press freedom was followed by debates on taste, which more often than not lead to social stigmatisation of the new Grub Street writers and the new socially diverse readerships.

Two examples can illustrate how this reflexivity was present in different expressions of anticipation and disappointment, ideals and realities, normativity and practice. In January 1772 publisher Hans Holck launched the periodical *Magazin for Patriotiske Skribentere* (Patriotic Writers' Magazine), proclaiming the explicit aim of creating an arena for the application of freedom of the press. On the cover of the first issue it was stated that the king had bestowed on his subjects 'the freedom of writing which has been suppressed for so long; so, it is the intention of this magazine that anyone can have his patriotic thoughts inserted at no cost, in so far as they (without mentioning persons) are in accordance with the ordinance' (no. 1, p. 1). The entire Press Freedom Ordinance was then quoted. It is worth noticing that press freedom was perceived by Holck as a natural right that had so far been suppressed and that he offered a platform for individual exercising of this new right and the practice of literary citizenship.

Shortly after the fall of Struensee the author Niels Prahl (who was a co-editor with the above-mentioned Holck) published an account of the Struensee reign. Prahl's review of Struensee's reforms opened with the Press Freedom Ordinance, 1770, which was quoted in its entirety. Struensee was praised for the introduction of freedom of the press, but authors exercising this freedom were criticised for attacking people and entire estates. 'Instead of uncovering prejudice,' wrote Prahl, 'most people presented a whole stock of the heart's evil content. These unbound hunting writers, however, kept writing as long as someone wanted to buy their stuff'.[43] This was a pointed

---

as *Agents of Change: Perspectives on Northern Enlightenment* (Leiden, 2015), pp. 153–71.

[42] E. Krefting, 'News versus Opinion: The State, the Press, and the Northern Enlightenment', in S. G. Brandtzæg *et al.* (eds), *Travelling Chronicles: News and Newspapers from the Early Modern Period to the Eighteenth Century* (Leiden, 2018), pp. 299–318.

[43] N. Prahl, *Greve Johan Friderich Struensee, forrige Kongelige Danske Geheime-Cab-inetsMinister og Maitre des Requettes, Hans Levnets-Beskrivelse og Skiebne udi de*

critique of what Prahl considered to be a distasteful commercialisation of the public sphere stimulated by press freedom that had compromised literary citizenship.

The publication wave of the press freedom era follows a characteristic pattern: the spring of 1771 saw a first explosion and also proved the most creative in terms of new formats, new topics, new authors, new debates. After a restriction of the law on 7 October 1771 intensity began to wane, but after the coup in January 1772 it rose to new heights during the spring of 1772. From then on the new regime's increasing initiatives against freedom of the press made their mark, and in 1772–4 the number of press freedom writings quickly shrunk (Figure 5.3).

Freedom of the press changed the Copenhagen system of communication and the conditions of the public sphere for good. As Norwegian linguist Kjell Lars Berge has pointed out, the press freedom period initiated a new communication order. Radical experiments with genre and textual formats, new participants and new readerships led to new rules and new text norms. The rapid changes in the cultures of text not only opened the door to dissemination of information and knowledge (which was in line with the ordinance on freedom of the press) but became a catalyst for the expression of opinion (on every topic imaginable), also to extremes such as spin campaigns, libel and even threats.[44] In the light of the multiplicity of topics raised and genres used, the absence of reference to the Swedish press freedom legislation in the Dano-Norwegian pamphlets is striking.

Perhaps more importantly, a new market with new commercial opportunities for printers as well as writers had been established. As was the case in Sweden, the number of publications doubled as a result of the freedom of the press, and it created a permanent increase in publishing output during the following decades. The catalogue of the Royal Library registers 256 books in Danish language from the year 1769. This number grew to 438 in 1770 and reached a peak in 1771 with 730. In 1772 it decreased somewhat to 711, and the following year it was down to 337. Although these figures only have tentative and relative value, they give an idea of the increase in activity in the two main years of press freedom, 1771 and 1772.[45] The increase signalled by press freedom did not wane with the gradual introduction of new restrictions, and output levels continued to grow steadily; especially

---

sidste Aaringer i Dannemark (Copenhagen, 1772).

[44] K. L. Berge, 'Noen tekstvitenskapelige betraktninger omkring studiet av tekster, kulturer og ideologier i dansk-norsk 1700-tall', *Arr: Idéhistorisk tidsskrift*, 4 (1999), pp. 72–80; K. L. Berge, 'Developing a New Political Text Culture in Denmark–Norway 1770–1799', in *Eighteenth-Century Periodicals as Agents of Change*, pp. 172–84.

[45] See H. Horstbøll *et al.*, *Grov Konfækt*, 1, p. 53.

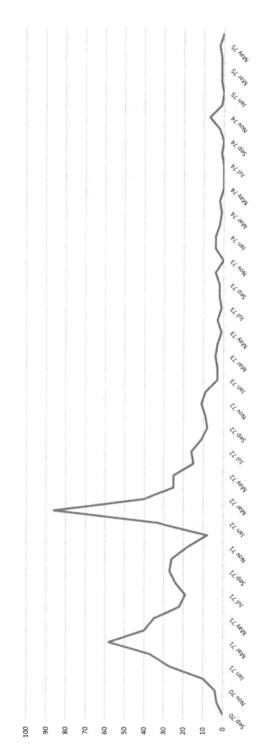

Fɪɢ. 5.3. Dano-Norwegian Press Freedom Writings per month 1770–5, absolute numbers. (Note: The graph is based on the dating of about 3/4 of the press-freedom pamphlets in the Luxdorph Collection. Dates of the first advertisements for those writings in the Copenhagen paper *Kiøbenhavns Kongelig alene priviligerede Adresse-Contoirs Efterretninger (Adresse-Avisen)* have been chosen as proxy for its publication date. See Horstbøll *et al.*, *Grov Konfækt*, vol. 1, p. 45.)

the number of periodicals in Denmark and Norway rose substantially.[46] The fact that pre-publication censorship was not reintroduced supported the growing volume of the literary market. The social expansion of Dano-Norwegian literary citizenship was consolidated and even intensified by political components during the following decades.

Even though the Swedish and Dano-Norwegian numbers in Figures 5.1–5.3 are not directly comparable, on a general level they indicate the same fact: freedom of the press fostered a considerable increase in publications, a rise that persisted even after new restrictions on the press appeared.

MUTUAL SILENCE

Much like there is no sign of interdependence between the legislation on freedom of the press in the two Scandinavian monarchies, there seems to have been little reporting in newspapers and other channels on the development of freedom of the press and the public sphere from the neighbouring country. This is a topic where more study needs to be done, and we can only offer a few preliminary observations.

Since Swedish freedom of the press preceded Dano-Norwegian press freedom, it might be expected that reporters in Sweden would have found it easier to relate the later development in Denmark. This does not seem to have been the case, however. On 25 October 1770 the Swedish semi-official newspaper *Stockholms Post-Tidningar* included a single report that censorship had been abolished in Denmark through a royal decree the preceding month. The content of the king's proclamation was rendered almost verbatim and without comment among a host of other recent decrees of seemingly lesser importance. The Swedish weekday newspaper *Dagligt Allehanda* ignored the matter altogether. There are less than a handful of pamphlets from the relevant period that discuss Dano-Norwegian politics, and we have found no mention of the freedom of the press in any of them. Again, this topic needs further investigation, but it appears as though the previous caution about expressing opinions concerning foreign powers was still prevalent, although the 1766 Ordinance expressly stated (Section 5) that it should 'be permitted to write and print material concerning the relations of the kingdom with other powers and the advantage or harmfulness of former or more recent alliances, or statements made regarding them'.

Similarly, the introduction of the Swedish Freedom of the Press Ordinance was met with silence in the Dano-Norwegian newspapers. Although

---

[46]   H. Horstbøll, *Menigmands medie: Det folkelige bogtrykk i Danmark 1500–1840* (Copenhagen, 1999), p. 347.

the Copenhagen newspaper *De til Forsendelse med Posten allene privi-*
legerede Kiøbenhavnske Tidender ('Berlingske Tidende'), which owned
the monopoly on communicating foreign news, presented lengthy reports
from the debates and decisions in the Swedish Diet, there is no sign of any
mention of the Freedom of the Press Ordinance.[47] It is not improbable that
the editors considered the news of a Swedish freedom of the press, adopted
by the Estates in a semi-republican political process, as a piece of information too controversial to be published in an absolutist Dano-Norwegian
public sphere still subject to censorship.

It seems unlikely that the two Scandinavian legislations were widely
known among the European public at large, but they did not go entirely
without notice. However, this is another question were much work remains
to be done, and at this point we can only offer a few observations. Anders
Burius has examined the reports from the Prussian, English, French, Dutch,
Danish and Imperial envoys to Stockholm. The first three did not mention
the Freedom of the Press Ordinance with a word, the Dutch representative
itemised the ordinance in an uncommented list of all decisions at the Diet,
while the Danish ambassador mentioned the decision in the passing after
the final vote in October 1766. The only one who added his own reflection
was a secretary at the Imperial legation. Nearly two months after the law
was signed by the king he made a statement on the benefits of freedom
of the press for the sciences and the arts as well as the economy. In this
general declaration he especially pointed out the Netherlands, and he told
his principals in Vienna that the initial disagreements of the Swedish Diet
had ceased now that everyone saw the benefits of a free press. This was
apparently an insinuation to his own government, so in this one instance
the Swedish ordinance might have had some, however slight, impact on a
foreign context.[48]

When it comes to foreign press reports, we can offer a closer look at
one important source: the *Gazette de Leyde*. It was a leading francophone
journal with intense coverage of European politics, including the Scandinavian kingdoms. Since it was published in the liberal climate of the Netherlands, policy matters of a potentially sensitive character probably also
stood a better chance of being reported than in environments that were
more suppressive.

To examine reports about Sweden, we have studied the *Gazette de
Leyde* from early October 1766 to the end of April 1767. The first mention of interest was on 20 January 1767 when the journal reported that

[47]   We have examined all issues printed from December 1766 to April 1767.
[48]   Burius, *Ömhet om friheten*, pp. 273f.

the Swedish king had approved freedom of the press and that a special ordinance would be published soon.[49] The *Gazette* got the date wrong by a month, but although the law was signed 2 December 1766, it took a while before it was distributed, probably due to the Christmas break. Another report on 6 February once again proclaimed that the ordinance was to be published 'before long' and that it was expected to produce a happy effect among the public.[50] On 17 March the journal published a report marked Stockholm, 27 February, which briefly announced that the ordinance was now published, but the journal's readers had to wait another fortnight before being informed of its content.

On 3 April the *Gazette* finally issued an extensive account of nearly half a page outlining the main points of the Freedom of the Press Ordinance. In line with the general news reports of the time, the content was chronicled without comments or interpretations, but the detailed account suggests that this was news of great interest. It was in fact the lengthiest report from Sweden in the seven months we have studied. Special interest seems to have been directed towards the public access to official records. In Sweden from now on, the journal conveyed:

> Everyone has the right to demand from all of the Branches of Admin-istration – from the Senate to the registrars of the smallest courts – the release of records or minutes, which contain the decisions on various matters, and to publish the content in its entirety or in extract, as well as the advice of each individual in the deliberations, and especially the verdicts of judges; and anyone who refuses to communicate the registers etc. will lose his employment. Only the Senate may refuse to disclose matters relating to foreign affairs that need to be kept secret for a certain time.[51]

49   '*le 2. Janvier, 1767*. Le Roi a approuvé la liberté de la Presse: Ainsi, il va paroître dans peu une Ordonnance à ce sujet', 'Gazette de Leyde': *Nouvelles extraordinaires de divers endroits, No. VI:* 20 January 1767, Supplement.

50   'L'Ordinnance touchant *la liberté de la Presse* va être publiée dans peu : On s'attend, qu'elle produira un effet très-salutaire au Public.' *Gazette de Leyde,* no. 11, 6 February 1767, Supplement.

51   'Chacun a droit de demander à tous les Collèges de l'Administration, depuis le Sénat jusqu'aux Greffes de la plus petite Jurisdiction, la communication des Régîtres ou Protocoles, qui contiennent la décision des différentes affaires, d'en faire imprimer le contenu en entier ou par extrait, ainsi que l'avis de chaque Particulier dans les délibérations, & sur-tout la décision des Juges; & quiconque refusera de commu-niquer les Régîstres, &c. perdra son Emploi. Le Sénat seul pourra refuser la commu-nication des délibérations rélatives aux affaires etrangères, qui doivent être tenuës sécrettes pendant quelques tems.' *Gazette de Leyde,* no. 27, 3 April 1767, Supple-ment.

In an age of cabinet politics, where governing and foreign affairs was an arcanum reserved for a chosen few, the conceding of extensive public inspection certainly stood out. The *Gazette de Leyde* was 'the European paper of record, read by Statesmen throughout the Continent'.[52] How they reacted to this news, we do not know at this point.

In the following number, 7 April, the *Gazette* returned with an addendum on how the legal responsibility was to be divided between the printer and the author according to the ordinance. The printer answered for the content if he could not produce the author's name, which he otherwise had to keep in a sealed envelope; either way, only one of them could be prosecuted. This arrangement was a clever solution to a division of responsibilities that was undefined in many jurisdictions and certainly something to ponder on for the gazette's readers.

The Danish freedom of the press a few years later did not catch the attention of the *Gazette de Leyde*, although it reported, as did many other international newspapers and periodicals, extensively on the coup against Struensee, his subsequent execution, the queen's exile and the measures of the new regime. The most notable consideration we know of remains Voltaire's famous poem celebrating the Dano-Norwegian king and press freedom in January 1771.[53]

Nevertheless, when press freedom was introduced in Denmark–Norway a few examples of Swedish inspiration and communication can be traced. One of the first new pseudonymous writers to appear after the introduction of the Dano-Norwegian freedom of the press was Gormsen Biering, who was launched as a columnist under the name of *Den danske Argus* (The Danish Argus) in the periodical *Fruentimmer-Tidenden* (Woman Times). *Den danske Argus* declared that he was inspired by *Then Swänska Argus*

---

[52]   A. Pettegree, *The Invention of News. How the World Came to Know About Itself* (New Haven, London, 2014), p. 235.

[53]   Voltaire's celebration was published in both French (18 February 1771) and Danish (8 March 1771) in Copenhagen. The French original, see *Œuvres de Voltaire*, ed. A. J. Q. Beuchot, 13 (Paris, 1833), pp. 290–9. See H. Horstbøll *et al.*, *Grov Konfækt*, 1, p. 230. On the Struensee case in the British periodicals, see M. Roos, 'Struensee in Britain: The Interpretation of the Struensee Affair in British Periodicals, 1772', in E. Krefting *et al.* (eds), *Eighteenth-Century Periodicals as Agents of Change*, pp. 77–92. Actually, the Dano-Norwegian government unsuccessfully attempted to intervene against the coverage of events in the *Gazette de Leyde*, see J. W. Koopmans, 'Dutch Censorship in Relation to Foreign Contacts (1581–1795)', in *Trade, Diplomacy and Cultural Exchange: Continuity and Change in the North Sea Area and the Baltic c. 1359–1750*, ed. H. Brand (Hilversum, 2005), pp. 220–37, at p. 231. The international reception of the Struensee case is explored in U. Langen and F. Stjernfelt, *The World's First Full Press Freedom*, ch. 12 and 13.

(The Swedish Argus), published by the litterateur Olof Dahlin in Stockholm 1732–4. Although *Den danske Argus* was a self-proclaimed press freedom writer, it was not the Swedish freedom of the press that had inspired this new venture, rather it was the snide *Spectator* style of *Then Swänska Argus*, which Biering used as a model for his literary persona. A Danish translation of *Then Swänska Argus* had been published in Copenhagen as far back as 1740, thus preceding the Danish translation of the famed *Spectator* by two years.[54]

In a private letter dating from 28 June 1771 the Danish privy archivist Jakob Langebek described the impact of press freedom in Denmark–Norway to his Swedish colleague Johan Henrik Lidén, who was a lecturer in history of science at the university in Uppsala. 'Ever since we were given the otherwise noble freedom of writing and printing,' Langebek reported, 'the entire nation has suddenly become quite political and partly so evil that hardly anything is thought of or talked or written about other than with the purpose of offending the neighbour or turning everything upside down.' 'You cannot image,' he continued, 'what a terrible and sorrowful winter we have had, and we are still not without daily fear and danger.'[55] The last part of the sentence referred to a seemingly widespread fear of becoming the target of unscrupulous writers. For his own part, Langebek had not experienced any direct attacks, but he knew of several cases among his friends and other 'brave men' who were being troubled.

In his eyes, the transformation of the public sphere since September 1770 was so overturning and the atmosphere created by the new writers was so troubling that he was convinced that the extraordinary Dano-Norwegian situation was vividly discussed in other countries. As an example of historical irony, Langebek himself anonymously wrote an aggressive pamphlet against Struensee and the king in August 1771, which was partially translated into Swedish where it was used, contrary to the author's intention, as anti-absolutist ammunition.[56] One more exception to the general rule of mutual silence is the mention of comments by Carl Linnaeus on historian Peter Frederik Suhm's cheeky public letter admonishing the Dano-Norwegian king immediately after the coup against Struensee.[57]

---

[54] On the Danish *Argus*, see U. Langen, 'Kragen ved nok hvad Soe den skal ride paa: Fruentimmer-Tidenden og trykkefrihedens første debat', *Temp: Tidsskrift for historie*, 9, 17 (2018), 67–88.

[55] 'De kan ikke forestille sig, hvad for en skreksom og sorrigfuld Vinter vi har haft, og endnu er man ikke uden daglig Frygt og Fare', H. Fr. Rørdam, *Breve fra Langebek* (Copenhagen, 1895), p. 494.

[56] H. Horstbøll *et al.*, *Grov Konfækt*, 2, ch. 27, n. 13.

[57] H. Horstbøll *et al.*, *Grov Konfækt*, 1, p. 417.

THE END OF PRESS FREEDOM

The Swedish freedom of print proved to be a short-lived experience. On 19 August 1772 Gustav III carried out a coup d'état and restored royal power. His very first proclamation was to ban the mentioning of the two opposing political parties, and he nullified all 'fundamental laws' adopted after 1680. It was unclear whether this included the Freedom of the Press Ordinance, but these moves were sufficient to hamper public debate. In the following years there were a few active attempts to explore the limits of public discourse until Gustav III issued what he labelled an 'improved' Freedom of the Press Ordinance on 26 April 1774. In essence, it was a redaction of the previous one, but with a few cunning changes he in effect reversed the content of the law. Previously, everything was permitted to be printed if it was not expressly forbidden; from now on, anything could be prosecuted if it was not expressly permitted to print. Ironically, Gustav III also referred to English press laws as exemplary because in Great Britain, in contrast to Sweden, the printer was considered as complicit as the author in violations of freedom of the press.[58]

Dano-Norwegian press freedom ended over several stages in the period 1771-3. During the summer of 1771 a surge of pamphlets appeared against Struensee and his intimate relationship with the queen. This prompted a restriction of press freedom on 7 October when a new rescript made explicit that the abolishment of censorship did not cancel the existing legislations against libel, blasphemy, lèse-majesté and the like, just as all pamphlets should indicate author or printer as legally responsible. These changes in essence provided the formerly unlimited freedom of the press in Denmark with the same kind of restrictions as the Swedish ordinance was equipped with from the start. After the coup against Struensee in January 1772 the new regime repeatedly considered the reintroduction of pre-publication censorship but finally decided on another course: the intimidation of authors and printers by a stream of small and arbitrary restrictions, threats, fines, prison sentences etc. In 1773 a handful of landmark court cases against authors and bookdealers paved the way for the final dismantling of freedom of the press by two acts of October and November, giving the police the right to prohibit published writings by decree and to punish those responsible with fines, that is, a version of post-publication censorship. This slow process of closing down took place, to a large degree, without public interest or discussion.

---

[58]   S. Boberg, *Gustav III och tryckfriheten, 1774-1787* (Stockholm, 1951), pp. 162-4.

It is a surprising fact that very little written evidence connects the two almost simultaneous press freedoms of the two neighbouring realms. Nothing in the sparse documents pertaining to the origin and subsequent developments of the Dano-Norwegian legislation mentions its Swedish predecessor, and the Swedish law was never a reference in the intense discussions on the motivation, character, reach and limits of press freedom, which ran all the way through the 1770–3 period.

Although the historical contexts were quite different – Sweden being a semi-republic, Denmark–Norway an absolutist kingdom, a fact that was revealed in the well-prepared and sudden introduction of the freedom of the press respectively – the outcome was quite similar: a vitalisation and diversification of public debate. However, the differences in the systems of government are reflected in a more profound way if we look at the idea of the public present in the two ordinances: the Swedish public ideally consisted of free citizens in open debate with each other, while the Dano-Norwegian public ideally consisted of loyal subjects debating in the pursuit of the common good. This major difference was also mirrored in the Swedish *offentlighetsprincip* (principle of public access to official documents), which was not paralleled in Denmark or Norway until much later.[59] In Sweden the citizens could claim transparency, while in Denmark–Norway government acts belonged to realm of state secrecy and were of no concern to the subjects. Another striking difference is the Swedish exemption from freedom of religious writings, which had no correspondence in Denmark–Norway. Here, press freedom was marked by a burst of pamphlets attacking clergy, church, even theology, as well as a new stream of unorthodox mysticist and prophetic writings. The termination of Dano-Norwegian press freedom put an end to this, but still it had the effect of transferring the control of the public sphere from theology professors to the police, that is, from church to state.

Epilogue

In 1809, following a coup d'état and the king's expatriation, Sweden regained freedom of the press with the new Instrument of Government (Section 86): 'With freedom of the press is understood every Swedish man's right to, without any prior restraints from official authorities, publish writings'. This paragraph was mirrored in the Norwegian constitution of 1814 (Section 100), which made Norway an independent kingdom in union with Sweden:

---

[59] See R. Hemstad and D. Michalsen (eds), *Frie ord i Norden? Offentlighet, ytringsfrihet og medborgerskap 1814–1914* (Oslo, 2019).

'Freedom of the press should prevail.' In Denmark, on the other hand, after the reaction in the 1770s the authorities had displayed a relatively relaxed attitude to the printing press in the 1780s and 1790s, whereas Swedish authorities had tightened their grip on the printers. For instance, Swedish disciples of Emanuel Swedenborg's had to take nearly two dozen of their teacher's writings that were banned in his home country to be printed in Copenhagen by Johan Rudolph Thiele. In 1792 Thiele also printed a Swedish translation of the *Déclaration des droits de l'homme et du citoyen*, which was smuggled into Sweden only a few weeks before the assassination of Gustav III.[60] However, in 1799 Danish authorities regained strict control with a Freedom of the Press Ordinance. This was the first Danish law on a par with the exhaustive Swedish ordinances and with detailed regulations on the limits of the freedom of the press and defined penalties for infringements.[61]

Curiously, this legislation, as opposed to previous laws, proved to have significant impact on the new and liberal Swedish ordinance issued in 1810. The Swedish legislators had studied the Danish ordinance closely and copied, for instance, parts of its list of crimes, its methods of determining authorship as well as its control organs. Inspiration was also drawn from the Danish lawyer Anders Sandøe Ørsted's principled treatise *Forsøg til en rigtig Fortolkning og Bedømmelse over Forordningen om Trykkefrihedens Grændser* (Attempt at a Proper Interpretation and Assessment of the Ordinance on the Limits of the Freedom of the Press, 1801).[62]

Despite the apparent inspiration, the Danish and Swedish legislations were nevertheless guided by opposing principles. The Danish ordinance was restrictive whereas the Swedish was liberal; the Danish ordinance was an administrative statute whereas the Swedish was part of the constitution. From being permanent foes, politicians and lawyers in Sweden and Denmark now formed a literary citizenry with a communal language, but their shared experiences and views nevertheless continued to be rooted in different political soils.

---

[60] The title mixes Danish and Swedish spelling: *Menneskeliga och medborgerliga Rättigheter*, p. l. [Copenhagen, 1792], National Library of Sweden, Rar. 608°. H. Ilsøe, *Bogtrykkerne i København ca. 1660–1810* (Copenhagen, 1992), pp. 172–6; T. von Vegesack, *Smak för frihet: Opinionsbildningen i Sverige 1755–1830* (Stockholm, 1995), pp. 121–3.

[61] H. Jørgensen, *Trykkefrihedsspørgsmaalet i Danmark 1799–1848: Et bidrag til en karakteristik af den danske enevælde i Frederik VI's og Christian VIII's tid* (Copenhagen, 1944).

[62] E. Nyman, *Indragningsmakt och tryckfrihet 1785–1810* (Stockholm, 1963), pp. 180f, 246, 252.

6

Multilingual Citizens of the World: Literary Fiction in Norwegian Book Collections in the Eighteenth Century

Karin Kukkonen

BOURGEOIS READERS IN EIGHTEENTH-CENTURY Norway could find literary, religious and non-fictional books in Danish (that is, the language they read as their own in the period). However, a look into the reading materials offered through libraries, reading societies and lending libraries shows that a substantial part of their reading, in particular when it comes to literary fiction, in this case novels, plays, stories and narrative poetry, was in foreign languages (mostly French, German and English). This article introduces a database of book collections in eighteenth-century Norway and outlines a range of possible analyses on its basis, connecting book history, history of reading and literary history. It thereby complements existing analyses of the publication and circulation of novels in periodicals and their evaluation in periodical criticism in the eighteenth century.[1]

If one sketches the situation in general terms, Norwegian book collections present a picture of transnational exchange similar to the one Hakon Stangerup identified for the novel in Denmark:[2] for the better part of the century, French and English, and then German, dominated the market. Even though noteworthy examples in the genre predate 1800, Danish and Norwegian novels did not emerge as a cultural force until the beginning of

---

[1]   A. Nøding, 'Vittige kameleoner: Litterære tekster i norske adresseaviser, 1763–1769' (PhD thesis, Oslo, 2007) and M. Egeland, '"De fleste Romaners Læsning er skadelig": Suhm, Sneedorff og romanen', *Edda*, 108:1 (2021), 8–21.

[2]   H. Stangerup, *Romanen i Danmark i det attende aarhundrede* (Copenhagen, 1936).

the nineteenth century. The Norwegian world of letters is closely connected to Danish publishers and book distribution networks, but its dynamics of canon-formation and transnational adaptations was not necessarily copied from Copenhagen. An analysis of book collections, which not only hold works currently published (as the materials on which Stangerup bases his analysis) but also books to be read and re-read, allows for a glimpse of the links and loops across national literatures and across time-bound publishing trends. This article attempts to trace some of the dynamics of the larger cultural horizons of Norwegian readers in the eighteenth century and beyond through case studies of *Pamela*, German popular novels and the after-effects of *Werther* in one of the first examples of the Norwegian novel in the nineteenth century.

Private and public book collections in
eighteenth-century Norway

Literacy was widespread in Norway in the period (see Haarberg in this volume). However, the population's capacity to read was not matched by the infrastructure of a modern book market steadily supplying new books in different parts of the country. A number of formats in collecting books and making them available to a wide range of readers were established across the eighteenth century in order to fill this gap. Wealthy individuals such as Claus Fasting,[3] Peter Frederik Suhm[4] or Carl Deichman would assemble impressive book collections. These private collections were often available to friends and, after the death of their owners, later made accessible to the general public. Carl Deichman's collection, for example, is today the foundational stock of Oslo City Library, still called 'Deichmanske'.[5] Schools also had their own libraries where current students and alumni could borrow books. This applies both to the 'cathedral schools' and to the military schools in the major cities. Groups of citizens started initiatives to found reading societies, where a stock of books would be bought jointly and could be borrowed for a fee. Publishers and booksellers in various towns across Norway also established commercial lending libraries as a

---

[3]   A. Nøding, *Claus Fasting: Dikter, journalist og opplysningspioner* (Oslo, 2018).
[4]   E. Krefting, 'De usminkede sannhetenes forsvar. Peter Frederik Suhms publikasjonsstrategier og offentlighetsidealer under det dansk-norske eneveldet', in A. M. B. Bjørkøy *et al.* (eds), *Litterære verdensborgere: Transnasjonale perspektiver på norsk bokhistorie 1519–1850* (Oslo, 2019), pp. 332–76.
[5]   N. J. Ringdal, *By, bok og bibliotek* (Oslo, 1985).

side business. These formats of reading societies and circulating libraries draw on well-known models, especially in Germany[6] and England.[7]

The range of book collections accessible to readers in eighteenth-century Norway is broad, and individual collections often move across the divide between the public and the private spheres. The library of the Royal Academy in Trondheim opened its doors to the public as far back as in 1766. Private collections were often made available to the public on their owner's death, like the collections of Fasting and Deichman, or donated to larger established collections, like Suhm's collection left to the Danish National Library. As momentum gathered towards the end of the century to establish a university in Norway, a solid book collection was seen as an indispensable precondition, and various citizens of Christiania (Oslo) devoted their efforts to this goal. After Norway had given itself a constitution in 1814 and the union with Denmark was dissolved, the general upsurge of new institutions and new projects also brought new reading societies, parish libraries and lending libraries across the country. The nineteenth century saw a veritable explosion of new opportunities to read in Norway.[8]

Elisabeth Eide, who has studied reading societies and book collections in nineteenth-century Norway, points to a decisive shift from foreign-language books towards books in Danish during the nineteenth century in these libraries that were now also open to artisans, manual workers and servants.[9] In the eighteenth century, however, book collections were closely tied to a 'bourgeois public sphere' and included much foreign literature in translation as well as in foreign languages.[10] The city of Bergen with its population of merchants and immigrant workers, for example, had a foreign-language lending library with a collection predominantly of German books

[6]   B. M. Milstein, *Eight Eighteenth-Century Reading Societies: A Sociological Contribution to the History of German Literature* (Bern, Frankfurt, 1972); R. Engelsing, *Der Bürger als Leser: Lesergeschichte in Deutschland* (Stuttgart, 1974).

[7]   E. Jacobs, 'Eighteenth-Century British Circulating Libraries and Cultural Book History', *Book History*, 6 (2003), 1–22; J. Raven, 'Historical Introduction: The Novel Comes of Age', in J. Raven and A. Forster, with S. Bending (eds), *The English Novel 1770–1829: A Bibliographical Survey of Prose Fiction Published in the British Isles* (Oxford, 2000), pp. 15–121.

[8]   E. Eide, 'Reading Society and Lending Libraries in Nineteenth-Century Norway', *Library and Information History* 26:2 (2010), 121–38; L. Byberg, *Brukte bøker til bymann og bonde: bokauksjonen i den norske litterære offentligheten* (2007), p. 98.

[9]   See E. Eide, 'Reading Society and Lending Libraries in Nineteenth-Century Norway', p. 132.

[10] See E. Eide, 'Reading Society and Lending Libraries in Nineteenth-Century Norway'; Byberg, *Brukte bøker til bymann og bonde*; G. Dahl, *Books in Early Modern Norway* (Leiden, 2011).

and translations into German. A bourgeois educated public, either as alumni of the cathedral schools or as members of a circle of friends around figures such as Carl Deichman, could arguably read literature in the major European languages and was interested in the latest literary trends from abroad. Eighteenth-century book collections in Norway served to keep multilingual citizens abreast of what was going on in the European world of letters.

These collections have not been as thoroughly researched as the book collections that emerged after Norway thought of itself as its own country in 1814. Some still exist, such as the collection of Christiania Cathedral School, the collection of the Trondheim Royal Academy and Carl Deichman's collection. Most eighteenth-century collections, however, can only be reconstructed from catalogues, advertisements and sales catalogues. These catalogues demonstrate that, unlike parish libraries, all these public and private collections also carried novels, plays and narrative poetry, often classified as 'literature' ('Litteratur') in the catalogues, in addition to history books, travel narratives, biographies etc.[11] In many book collections built by institutions and individuals such as Deichman, novels, plays and narrative poetry would only make up a very small proportion of the books. They account for a larger proportion of the commercial lending libraries of booksellers. In her survey of books in early modern Norway, Gina Dahl observes a similar distribution. Moreover, she highlights a related shift in the genres of entertainment literature.[12] She refers to early predominance of formats such as almanacs, ballads and broad sheets, which give way in the late eighteenth century to the novel that was supplied by the lending libraries and reading societies.[13]

Private and public book collections in eighteenth-century Norway, then, do not cover the entire reading material available to readers. They serve a bourgeois public interested in ideas and fashions from Europe and, generally, capable of reading a book in German, French and/or English.

[11] The classification of books is by no means consistent across catalogues (indeed, many of the commercial book collections are not categorised). The catalogue for Deichmanske uses the category 'Litteratur' to include novels, plays and narrative poetry. Modern literature is classified as 'skjønnlitteratur' (*belles lettres*). The Royal Academy in Trondheim uses 'Philologie og skjönne videnskaber' as a category under which it subsumes 'literature', while the catalogue of Christiania military school uses 'Aesthetik' as the larger category under which it counts 'Poesie', 'Romaner' and 'Comedier'. I have chosen 'literary fiction' as a term for the works recorded in the database, because it most clearly captures for today's users the genres featured, namely novels as well as narrative poetry and plays.
[12] G. Dahl, *Books in Early Modern Norway*, chapter 9.
[13] *Ibid.* p. 191.

These book collectors, reading societies and to some extent lending library owners can be considered 'propagators of taste' ('Geschmacksträger'), as Levin Schücking describes them: public figures and institutions who serve as brokers of literary taste in their communities.[14] For my investigation of 'multilingual readers' in eighteenth-century Norway, I will focus on the book collections used by this particular segment of society. Considering religious books and their possibly multilingual readers (in Latin, Greek and Hebrew) or considering the parish libraries with their decidedly 'practical' focus in reading materials would be a different project. However, my focus on the bourgeois multilingual reading public allows me to trace different ways in which Norway's reading infrastructure imitates models from Europe and how it imports books, reading practices and literary traditions from the European republic of letters (see also Nøding in this volume).

The basis for this investigation is a database of book collections in Norway in the eighteenth century, compiled by Marit Sjelmo and me. The database captures a representative selection of book collections of different types (private collections open to the public, school libraries, reading societies and booksellers' lending libraries) and from different areas of Norway (Christiania, Bergen, Trondheim and Drammen). It records novels, short stories, plays and narrative poetry in Danish, in foreign languages and in translation from the (published) catalogues of these book collections. The database thereby makes a selection of texts recognisable to today's readers as 'literary fiction' (see note 11). The works included are published as stand-alone books or collections of plays and stories. Works serialised in the periodicals (like Fielding's *Tom Jones* in *Det nye Magazin indeholdende Fortællinger*) could be found in the book collections, too (in this case in the Trondheim Reading Society). Identifying and recording such serialisations systematically, however, lies outside the scope of the current version of the database. The database can be accessed on the website of the National Library of Norway.[15]

Literary Fiction in Norwegian Book Collections offers a survey of novels, plays and narrative poetry in the public and private collections available to Norwegian readers before 1800. It does not cover all Norwegian book collections from the eighteenth century that have drawn up catalogues and not all texts categorised under 'literature' in the period. This would have been a much more comprehensive project. Instead, ten collections have been selected as an indicative sample, relying on previous discussions of

---

[14]   L. I. Schücking, *The Sociology of Literary Taste* (Routledge, 1966), p. 84.

[15]   <www.nb.no/forskning/skjonnlitteratur-i-norske-bibliotek-pa-1700-tallet>. A full list of the catalogues included can be found at the end of the article.

book collections in the research literature. The literary texts recorded in their catalogues are the basic entries for a database that can be searched for collections, languages and genres. We often needed to supply author names and information about the edition (where possible) ourselves, because that kind of metadata is not necessarily given (in particular in the catalogues of lending libraries). The database is openly accessible and intended to support all kinds of explorations into the popularity of certain works and authors in eighteenth-century Norway, rather than provide absolute figures.

The database records 876 titles. It gives an overview of literature available in the genres novels, plays (including libretti), narrative/epic poetry, stories (including novellas, contes and fables), as well as story collections. Miguel Cervantes' *Don Quixote*, for example, can be found in seven of the ten collections sampled, mostly in the Danish translation by Charlotte Biehl but also in French and Spanish. The library of Christiania Cathedral School even holds Lesage's French version of Avellaneda's spurious 'continuation' of the *Quixote*, which prompted Cervantes to rewrite the second part. Henry Fielding's novels are available in book form in Danish translation with the booksellers Diurendahl and Schousted, but in English at the library of Christiania Cathedral School and the military school. Sophie von La Roche's sentimental bestseller *Das Fräulein von Sternheim* is available in German in the Bergen societies and in Danish elsewhere in Norway.

The milestones of literary fiction in the eighteenth century can be found in book collections across the country, either in the original language or in Danish translation. With access to multiple collections (not only in the metropolis Christiania, but also in Bergen and Trondheim), it was possible to get a reasonably good overview of French classical drama (Racine, Molière and Corneille), but also fashionable contemporary plays from France and Germany. Readers could find a broad selection in novels and plays but also narrative poems. In the latter category Ludvig Holberg's mock-heroic *Peder Paars* dominates, but also Boileau' *Satires* and Voltaire's *Pucelle* can be found as well as Milton's *Paradise Lost* and (in multiple copies) Macpherson's *Ossian* in English or Danish translation. Norwegian readers could already navigate European literature with the works available in Danish. If they could also read German and French, it was possible to get a relatively comprehensive view of contemporary, eighteenth-century literature. Different from the recording of publication figures, as Stangerup practises it for the Danish novel, these book collections trace both current reading tastes and the broader cultural horizon. A number of unexpected findings in the database shall serve as the starting points for three explorations into book history, history of reading and literary history in what follows.

THE DISAPPEARANCE OF *PAMELA*

Samuel Richardson's *Pamela* is the novel that perhaps most comprehensively embodies mid-eighteenth-century entertainment literature.[16] It appealed to readers' sentiments, inviting them to explore their own inner life, as Diderot highlights in his 'Eloge de Richardson'. The novel makes use of letter-writing, a central cultural technology in the period, and it firmly subscribes to middle-class values to the extent that these even get acknowledged by the aristocrats Mr B— and his sister at the end of the narrative. Pretty much every aspect associated with the 'rise of the novel' can be found in *Pamela*. The complex moral ambiguities into which Richardson places his protagonist invited not only readers' reflection but also sparked a serious public debate between Pamelists (who hold that the protagonist is sincere and deserves her happy ending) and Anti-Pamelists (who hold that she is a fraud), considered as a signal of the emerging 'bourgeois public sphere'.[17] The numerous continuations and adaptations of *Pamela*, most obviously and prominently Fielding's *Shamela*, can be read as interventions in this debate.[18]

In the database we see that Samuel Richardson is available in late eighteenth-century Norway with all three of his novels. However, it is *Sir Charles Grandison* that makes Richardson's most prominent entry with five copies in Danish, French and English. *Pamela* is only available in one Danish copy at Diurendahl's lending library in Christiania, along with Eliza Haywood's *Anti-Pamela*, and in a French translation in the library of Christiania military school. *Clarissa* can be found in three copies in Danish translation. Why is Richardson's most popular novel, *Pamela*, the one that we find least often in Norwegian book collections?

The novel *Pamela*, published in 1740, appears to have coincided happily with the emergence of the circulating library. In Britain the term 'circulating library' is first recorded in 1742.[19] The circulating libraries would not only attract readers who wanted to borrow Richardson's novel but also its numerous imitations in novel and drama form.[20] If readers in the eighteenth century indeed moved from an intensive mode of reading (that is,

[16]   W. Warner, *Licensing Entertainment: The Elevation of Novel Reading in Britain* (Berkeley, 1998).
[17]   J. Habermas, *The Structural Transformation of the Public Sphere* (Cambridge, 2014).
[18]   See T. Keymer *et al.*, *The Pamela Controversy: Criticism and Adaptations of Samuel Richardson's Pamela, 1740–1750*, 2 vols (London, 2001) for an overview.
[19]   H. M. Hamlyn, 'Eighteenth-Century Circulating Libraries in England', *The Library*, 5th Series, 1 (1947), 197–222, at p. 197
[20]   A. D. McKillop, 'English Circulating Libraries, 1725–1750', *The Library*, 4th Series, 14 (1934), 477–85, at p. 484.

reading and re-reading an individual book extensively) to an extensive mode of reading (that is, going through very many books at great pace), as Rolf Engelsing proposes it, then reading societies and lending libraries were necessary to steadily supply readers with more books.[21] Indeed, Norwegian book collections from the eighteenth century also hold imitations of *Pamela*, such as Christian Fürchtegott Gellert's *Schwedische Gräfin* (1747) and Carlo Goldoni's dramatic adaptation *La Pamela fanciulla* (1750). Nevertheless, these imitations are not exactly numerous with two copies each of Gellert's novel and Goldoni's play.

Engelsing's account is not uncontested. His hypothesis echoes how eighteenth-century commentators themselves perceived the new reading practices connected to sentimental novels such as *Pamela* as extensive, superficial and fast.[22] However, it can be shown that many readers engaged repeatedly and deeply with these texts, leading to an intensive reading experience. *Sir Charles Grandison* might have better suited the practice of reading for self-cultivation, which emerged in the second half of the century, because it is thematically and narratively closer to the pattern of the *Bildungsroman*.[23] This might explain the stronger showing in the database. Generally speaking, however, multiple reading practices were at play in different contexts, including shared reading in company.[24]

For Denmark, Stangerup reports that *Pamela* was translated very swiftly into Danish (in 1743 and 1746), but observes after that a general drop in translations of what he calls 'the bourgeois novel' followed in mid-century.[25] He claims that Richardson and the bourgeois novel only came into their own with the rise of the sentimental novel in the 1780s, when we also have the first Danish translations of *Clarissa* and *Sir Charles Grandison*. Most of the editions of Richardson in the book collections sampled are indeed from the 1780s, even those in English. Perhaps *Pamela* was no longer as current as reading material in 1766, when it came to Norway.[26] The earliest catalogues in the sample included in the database are from the 1780s, so that the snapshot in the database might simply be too late. It appears, then, that *Pamela* did not have much staying power with the Norwegian reading

[21] See Engelsing, *Der Bürger als Leser*.
[22] R. Wittmann, 'Was there a Reading Revolution at the End of the Eighteenth Century?', in G. Cavallo and R. Chartier (eds), *A History of Reading in the West* (Oxford, 1999), pp. 284–312.
[23] K. Littau, *Theories of Reading: Books, Bodies and Bibliomania* (Cambridge, 2006).
[24] A. Williams, *The Social Life of Books: Reading Together in the Eighteenth-Century Home* (New Haven, 2018).
[25] See H. Stangerup, *Romanen i Danmark*, p. 227.
[26] See also A. Nøding, *Vittige kameleoner*.

public, unlike Cervantes' *Don Quixote* or Holberg's *Peder Paars*, for example. An investigation of 'long-sellers', or books with a first publication date that comes much earlier than the compilation date of the catalogue, in the database might indeed throw interesting light on canonisation processes in Norway in the second half of the eighteenth century.

Stangerup hypothesises that *Pamela* was eclipsed in Denmark by the 'adventure novels' of Le Sage, Defoe and others, which saw much higher publication figures in the period.[27] It is not certain that the same is the case for Norway, because the Norwegian book collections sampled hold only one copy of Defoe's *Robinson Crusoe* and most copies of Le Sage's novels only in translations from the 1780s. It might also be the case that Stangerup's narrow focus on the novel, instead of literary fiction more generally, limits his view on the disappearance of *Pamela*.

For Norway, Aina Nøding outlines how Pamela makes her entry into the Norwegian public sphere with a serialisation in the weekly *Norske Intelligenz-Sedler*, running from April to July 1766, so exactly the period when Stangerup records no entries for the 'bourgeois novel'.[28] The *Pamela* serialisation is not based on Richardson's novel but on Ditlevine Feddersen's Danish translation of the French version of Goldoni's *Pamela*. As Nøding shows, the serialisation probably served both as a page filler and as advertisement for a print run of the book version of Feddersen's translation.[29] However, the book also did not sell well.[30] Goldoni's *Pamela*, Nøding tells us, was performed privately in 1765–6 in Feddersen's home with the translator herself in one of the roles.[31] Norway at this time did not have a public theatre. However, private performances and convivial readings of play texts were a common occurrence.[32] Dramatic societies joined the reading societies in the late eighteenth-century cultural landscape in Norway, and some of these dramatic societies had their own libraries of play texts.[33] The popularity of dramatic societies and theatrical readings is also reflected in the holdings of many book collections. About 40 per cent of the database entries across all catalogues are play scripts or collections of plays. The most prominent collection is Holberg's *Danske skueplads* with more than

---

[27]   See H. Stangerup, *Romanen i Danmark*, p. 227.
[28]   See A. Nøding, *Vittige kameleoner.*
[29]   A. Nøding *Vittige kameleoner*, p. 164.
[30]   *Ibid*, p. 168.
[31]   *Ibid*, p. 166.
[32]   H. J. Huitfeldt-Kaas, *Christiania Theaterhistorie* (Oslo, 1876).
[33]   For the example of dramatic societies in Bergen, see the essays collected in R. M. Selvik, E. K. Gjervan and S. Gladsø (eds), *Lidenskap eller Levebrød? Utøvende Kunst i endring rundt 1800* (Bergen, 2015).

ten entries and various individual plays from that collection listed individually in addition. Norwegian readers apparently had a keen taste for reading plays. The commercial lending library Schousted in Drammen holds no fewer than four plays by Goldoni (but not *Pamela*) and four by Charlotte Biehl, his Danish translator and imitator.[34] Diurendahl's lending library in Christiania, on the other hand, only has a few play texts, probably because this demand had been met by other book collections in the city. Carl Deichman's collection had a solid holding of French contemporary plays, ranging from the sentimental to the frivolous, as well as classics such as Molière and Voltaire. The cathedral school library in Christiania held French plays as well as German and English texts in the original languages. The reading society for foreign-language literature in Bergen made available plays by Lessing, Kotzebue, Schiller, Iffland and others, but these also can be found elsewhere in Norway throughout the collections. Compared to French and German plays, English and particularly Shakespeare's plays are under-represented in the book collections sampled, with only four of the collections holding any of Shakespeare's plays.[35]

It appears to be the case that Norwegian readers interested in the theatre had access to a substantial number of play texts, which could be borrowed for an evening's entertainment (much like renting a video in more recent times) to be read together with the family and at other convivial gatherings. The serialisation of Goldoni's *Pamela* in *Norske Intelligenz-Sedler* would be ill-suited to such a practice because it only gave readers individual scenes with multiple weeks' wait between instalments. Moreover, if play texts were more or less single-use items, to be borrowed for an evening's entertainment, then only a few readers would be ready to spend significant amounts of money on a print copy of their own, and this might also account for the failure of Feddersen's project. The disappearance of *Pamela* from Norwegian book collections may then be explained by broader international moves towards reading practices suited to the *Bildungsroman* and a more particular mismatch with local shared reading practices. Narve

---

[34]   See M. Olsen, 'La Recezione di Goldini in Danimarca', in G. D'Amico and M. P. Muscarello (eds), *Terre Scandinave in Terre d'Asti* (Asti, 2009), pp. 37–49, for Biehl's artistic relationship to Goldoni.

[35]   While Danish literary criticism considered Shakespeare as lacking in command of the neoclassical rules of writing plays, Norwegian intellectuals (like Fasting; see A. Nøding, *Claus Fasting*, pp. 169–71) appeared to side with the emerging appreciation of Shakespeare's expressive qualities in German criticism. Christoph Martin Wieland for example translated twenty-two of Shakespeare's plays into German in 1762. Note, however, that the book collections sampled hold mostly English versions of Shakespeare plays and Danish translations from the 1790s.

Fulsås has argued that Norway's relative tardiness as to the emergence of the novel as a dominant literary form along with its interest in the theatre could have contributed to the literature of Norway starting as world literature, especially with Ibsen, rather than as observed elsewhere as a literature of nation-building.[36] Indeed, one could argue for a straight line from *Pamela*, and other evidence for Norwegian readers' taste for European plays recorded in the database, to Henrik Ibsen's formation as a dramatist thanks to his participation in Bergen's *Dramatiske Selskab*.[37]

German classics and German trash

In a radio play from 1932 Walter Benjamin addresses an interesting issue in the history of literature: 'Was die Deutschen lasen während sie ihre Klassiker schrieben' (What the Germans read while they were writing their classics).[38] In the second half of the eighteenth century and the first half of the nineteenth century, when Germany's literary giants Goethe, Schiller and Kleist wrote their 'classics', Benjamin suggests, most readers were engaging with completely different reading materials. Almanacs, miscellanies of ephemeral verse and short narratives as well as sentimental and shocking bestseller novels were much closer to what Germans actually read than Goethe's *Collected Works*.

The holdings of German literature we find in Norwegian book collections paint a similar picture. We have only six entries for Johann Wolfgang Goethe across all book collections, while we find eleven for Christian Fürchtegott Gellert with his sentimental novel and educational fables, as well as fourteen for Johann Gottwerth Müller with his breezy entertainment novels and nine for August Lafontaine with his edifyingly Protestant narratives. Goethe ties with contemporaries such as the novelists Sophie von La Roche and Christian Friedrich Sintenis and the dramatists Gottlieb Stephanie and August von Kotzebue. Christoph Martin Wieland fares better as a German classic still recognisable today with fifteen entries. However, thirteen of these entries come from the book collection of Christiania Cathedral School library, perhaps bespeaking the good taste of one of the librarians or of a donor more than any particular trends among readers. If

---

[36] N. Fulsås, 'Noreg som kulturell eksportnasjon', in J. E. Myhre (ed.), *Myten om det fattige Norge. En misforståelse og dens historie* (Oslo, 2021), pp. 261–308.

[37] A. S. Andersen, *Deus ex machina? Henrik Ibsen og teatret i norsk offentlighet, 1780–1864* (Oslo, 2010).

[38] W. Benjamin, 'Was die Deutschen lasen während sie ihre Klassiker schrieben', *Rundfunkarbeiten. Kritische Gesamtausgabe*, 9:1 (Frankfurt, 2017), pp. 7–19.

eighteenth-century Germans were not reading their classics, neither were the Norwegians.

Around 25 per cent of books held in Norwegian book collections were originally written in German – a substantial share compared to 30 per cent originally in French, 11 per cent originally in English and 15 per cent originally in Danish. Books in French are dominated by plays, with 151 entries ranging from classics such as Racine, Molière and Corneille to fashionable sentimental dramas from the 1780s and 1790s. The novel is represented with 86 entries, from Fénélon's *Télémaque* to Diderot's *Jacques le Fataliste*, while Marmontel (see Nøding in this volume) and La Fontaine are most prominent in the story collections. It is noteworthy that the classics of the French eighteenth-century novel are under-represented with only four copies of Prévost, none of Marivaux' *Marianne* (though several of his plays are featured), none of Rousseau's *Nouvelle Héloïse* and only one copy of Laclos' *Dangerous Liaisons* in German translation.

As seen, only few of the titles in German would actually be recognised today by non-specialists as German literature from the eighteenth century. It appears that Norwegian readers preferred educational and religious works of fiction (novels and fables) written by theologians or parish priests, such as Christian Friedrich Sintenis or Johann Martin Miller. Sintenis, for example, can be found in Diurendahl's lending library as well as in the libraries of Christiania Cathedral School and Christiania Military School. Johann Gottwerth Müller's collection of entertainment novels, called *Komische Romane aus den Papieren des Braunen Manns* (in eight volumes), can be found in Diurendahl's lending library as well as the Bergen reading society (in Danish translation). Gellert's *Fabeln* are in Christiania, Trondheim and Bergen, in the library of the Royal Academy, as well as in the lending libraries and the collections of the reading societies.

A relatively broad selection of popular German female authors such as Caroline von Wolzogen, Benedikte Naubert, Charlotte von Ahlefeld and Friederike Helene Unger could be found in the collection of the reading society for foreign literature in Bergen. Sophie von La Roche was also present in Bergen as well as in the lending libraries in Christiania and Drammen. However, female authors are massively under-represented in Norwegian book collections in German as well as in other languages. In French, only Madame d'Aulnoy and Madame de Genlis can be found in multiple libraries; in English only Clara Reeve has that distinction. Christiania Cathedral School library has the greatest diversity of female authors in English, notably dramatists. Only Charlotta Biehl, a translator and significant cultural broker in eighteenth-century Denmark, has a relatively high number of entries in Danish across collections. Benjamin's observation that German readers were attracted to popular literature rather than the 'classics' throws new light on better known accounts of gender bias in canon-formation. While Norwegian collections are indicative of the strong presence of popular literature, they are not representative of the importance of female authors in European letters.

The book collection of Bergen's reading society for foreign-language literature makes an almost ideal case for Walter Benjamin's argument. Goethe is represented with *Ältere Schriften* und *Neue Schriften* in this collection, Gotthold Ephrahim Lessing with two collections of his plays and a single copy of *Nathan der Weise* and Wieland with *Sämtliche Werke*. The only German 'classic' who goes against this trend is Friedrich Schiller. Bergen did not actually hold a copy of collected works for Schiller, but copies of his plays *Die Räuber, Die Verschwörung des Fiesco* and *Don Carlos* as well as his novella *Der Geisterseher*. The selection indicates a general interest in historical fiction in the book collection, as evidenced by entries such as Naubert's novels *Barbara Blomberg* and *Thekla von Thun*, Lafontaine's *Rudolf von Werdenberg* or Madame de Genlis' *Chevaliers du cygne* along with non-fictional works of history (not recorded in the database). However, it appears that Schiller was not just kept on the shelves of the collection as a 'classic' but was actually read in the Bergen society for another reason, namely the link between the selection of his texts and a general interest in Gothic novels and novels about secret societies documented in the reading society's catalogue.

A genre of popular literature particularly well represented in the Bergen reading society for foreign literature is the 'Geheimbundroman'.[39] The generic status of the *Geheimbundroman* is under discussion, but it appears from contemporary reviews that readers perceived the novels as a coherent trend largely modelled on Schiller's *Geisterseher*. Like Schiller's novella, these texts often included conspiracies, secret societies and supernatural challenges to Enlightenment epistemology.[40] Novels about knights and robbers, sometimes in the Gothic vein, also belong to it. Entries for the trend in Bergen include Christian August Vulpius' *Rinaldo Rinaldini*, Benzel-Sternau's *Kamillo Altiera*, Henrich Zschokke's *Kuno von Kyburg*, Johann Christoph Unzer's *Geschichte der Brüder des grünen Bundes*, Friedrich Maximilian Klinger's *Fausts Leben, Thaten und Höllenfahrt*, as well as *Der Faust der Morgenländer*, Christian Henrich Spiess' *Die Löwenritter*

---

[39] M. Voges, *Aufklärung und Geheimnis. Untersuchungen zur Vermittlung von Literatur- und Sozialgeschichte am Beispiel der Aneignung des Geheimbundmaterials im Roman des späten 18. Jahrhunderts* (Tübingen, 1987).

[40] See *ibid.*, p. 298.

and Friedrich August Grosse's *Der Genius*. We find related titles among the few works translated into German from other languages in the Bergen collection, in particular Ann Radcliffe's *The Italian* and Matthew Lewis' *The Monk*. These novels were not translated into Danish until the early nineteenth century, when they saw massive popularity in the first decade of the century.[41]

Additionally, the Bergen book collection also held non-fiction titles such as Eberhard David Hauber's *Magische Bibliothek (= Biblioteca, acta et scripta magica)*, Justus Christian Hennings' *Von Geistern und Geisterse-hern*, Ernst Keller's *Grab des Aberglaubens* and Francois Xavier Pagès' *Geheime Geschichte der Französischen Revolution*. It might appear that the Bergen reading society for foreign-language literature was assembling a starter kit for founding secret societies. However, as has been pointed out by Koselleck and others, the *Geheimbundroman* was particularly relevant for new configurations of politics and morals in the new German public sphere.[42] Norway was moving towards its own nation state at the end of the eighteenth century, and arguably many resonances with German *Sturm und Drang*, in particular through Schiller's drama, play a role in why Schiller appears to be the German classic who is actually read by Norwegians.

Moreover, Huitfeldt-Kaas reports that the Christiania dramatic society performed Schiller's *Räuber* across several seasons in 1797/8 and 1798/9 with great success.[43] The play features not only a band of robbers who undermine established authorities, but also Gothic elements like a father buried alive and a young woman in distress in a castle. The play was not officially performed in Copenhagen before 1817.[44] However, the Norwegian attraction to Schiller might be less subversive than it appears: even though Schiller paints a dramatic image of power abuse, his protagonist Karl Moor comes to realise in the end that his deeds as a robber have pushed him so far out of society that he cannot return to take his rightful place, even if he manages to triumph over his adversary Franz Moor. He gives himself up to an old, impoverished man so that the latter can claim the prize on his head. Poetic justice cannot be achieved on the terms of the rebel in Schiller's tragedy. Similarly, other texts in the Bergen collection bespeak not only the robber's rebellion against the social and political order, but also their desire to reintegrate themselves into it. Vulpius' Rinaldo Rinaldini, for

---

[41]   See H. Stangerup, *Romanen i Danmark*, p. 405.
[42]   R. Koselleck, *Kritik und Krise: Ein Beitrag zur Pathogenese der bürgerlichen Welt* (Alber, 1988).
[43]   H. Huitfeldt-Kaas, *Christiania Theaterhistorie*, p. 172.
[44]   P. Hansen, *Den danske Skueplads*, vol. 1 (Copenhagen, [1889]), p. 531.

example, wishes for 'a return to the bosom of bourgeois society.'[45] Rather than instructions to rebellion, the texts in the Bergen collection can be seen as support for a much more diversified debate.

Jürgen Habermas chooses Goethe's *Wilhelm Meister* to illustrate how the new public sphere no longer depended on theatrical representativeness of the old regime but on private persons coming together in public to negotiate their interests. 'In this sense Wilhelm Meister's theatrical mission had to fail. It was out of step, as it were, with the bourgeois public sphere whose platform the theatre had meanwhile become.'[46] Not individuals acting on stage, but dramatic societies and public debate around plays serve as the foundation of subjectivity and identity in bourgeois society. Norway's citizens at the end of the eighteenth century clearly had got that message, and they deployed plays and narratives about secret societies in order to redraw the boundaries of a public debate that until 1814 had no distinct political status in its own right. While the dramatic societies created a public within the private sphere, the imagined secret societies represented in the German popular fiction in Bergen moved what is public interest into the private, secret sphere. Indeed, Goethe's Wilhelm Meister tracks a similar path when he joins the secret 'Turmgesellschaft'. It appears, however, that such a development needs to be traced through Schiller and his lesser imitators rather than through Goethe. when it comes to Norwegian readers.

BOOK COLLECTIONS AND THE FIRST NORWEGIAN NOVEL

Circulating libraries, literature in (multiple) foreign languages and dramatic societies left their mark not only on Norwegian readers but also on Norwegian literature that came into its own in the nineteenth century. We can read about one Karoline Møllerup, who in the years 1780/1 was a young woman about town and participated in all the fashionable entertainments, such as reading sentimental novels and playing in a dramatic society. Karoline falls in love with an officer. 'He was her constant escort on every occasion. In the theatrical comedies that were so fashionable in those days, he always played the lover and she the mistress' (179).[47] When the

---

[45]   C. A. Vulpius, *Rinaldo Rinaldini, der Räuberhauptmann: Eine Romantische Geschichte* (Berlin, 2016), p. 53: 'eine Rückkehr in die Arme der bürgerlichen Gesellschaft'.

[46]   See J. Habermas, *The Structural Transformation of the Public Sphere*, p. 14.

[47]   English translation: C. Collett, *The District Governor's Daughters*, trans. Kirsten Seaver (Norwich, 1991). Citations in the main text are from this edition, followed by the page number. For a critical edition of the Norwegian original, see C. Collett, *Amtmandens Døttre (1854/1855)* (Oslo, 2013). The Norwegian original will be given

officer fails to declare himself, Karoline takes matters into her own hands and writes a love letter to him. The letter gets copied and circulated, and the young lady's reputation is ruined. She falls into madness and incessant letter-writing (p. 181). The elderly woman who tells the story in Camilla Collett's novel *The District Governor's Daughters* (*Amtmandens Døttre*) assumes that the moral is obvious: Karoline has received her deserved comeuppance for transgressing the boundaries of good behaviour. However, her listeners Georg Kold and Sofie Ramm, who belong to the younger generation, do not agree. It should be permitted to express one's feelings – even for women (pp. 182–3).

Collett enacts in this conversation the conflict between generations around which her novel revolves, namely between parents' decision-making and a young woman's choice of marriage partner. All four daughters of district governor Ramm are faced with difficulties in courtship and marriage, as Collett plays through multiple possible unhappy constellations in her novel. The main plot, however, gains a larger resonance through the links to popular reading practices and reading materials. Indeed, Collett's *District Governor's Daughters*, considered the first Norwegian novel of substance today,[48] avails itself of the reading culture we traced in the book collections in order to establish its take on love and feelings and in order to situate this perspective *vis-à-vis* the reading backgrounds of its Norwegian audience.

The novel, published in 1854/5, is set in the 1830s. Its protagonists quote (mostly) Schiller from memory throughout the dialogue, but also Heine and Goethe (with Clara's song from *Egmont*) make an appearance. Two male protagonists are associated with major authors of the turn of the century, based on two portraits they resemble: Brøcher, the suitor of Amalie Ramm, with Goethe; and Kold, the love interest of Sofie Ramm, with Byron (p. 229). Intertextual references provide characterisation, such as when Kold is given the emotional appeal of a British romantic, but they also support the motivation of the plot. When Sofie is assaulted by Lorenz Brandt, Kold comes to the rescue, and Collett's narrator comments 'No winged god of old, no hero out of the stories of Lafontaine or Clauren could, under similar circumstances, have arrived at a more perfect moment than Kold

from this edition with page numbers in the notes. Here: 'Ved alle Lystigheder var han hendes bestandige Ridder. I Komedien, som dengang var saa i Mode, var han altid Elskeren og hun Elskerinden' (p. 172).

48   T. Selboe, 'Camilla Collett (1813–1895)', in E. B. Hagen (ed.), *Den norske litterære kanon: 1700–1900* (Oslo, 2009), pp. 66–74.

did just then' (191).[49] Lafontaine, as we have seen, is well represented in Norwegian book collections as far back as the eighteenth century; in the novel even Sofie's mother reads him. (Heinrich Clauren's major commercial successes are not published until the nineteenth century and therefore do not register in the database).

Another text from the database might have served as inspiration for the entire novel: Johann Friedrich Hoche's *Des Amtmanns Tochter von Lüde* (1797).[50] The novel is registered in the Bergen reading society for foreign-language literature, so it is not possible to claim that Collett, who lived in Christiania, Copenhagen and elsewhere on the continent, came across this particular narrative in a Norwegian book collection, and I have not been able to locate evidence that Collett has read Hoche's book from her correspondence. Yet, while Collett does not copy straightforwardly from Hoche, the resonances between *Amtmandens Døttre* and *Des Amtmanns Tochter* arguably go well beyond the title.

Hoche's novel revolves around the fate of two young women, Mariane and Elise. They fall in love with their house teacher Wilhelm Wallheim, who in turn promises marriage to them both. While Elise enters a marriage of convenience after she finds out about Wallheim's duplicity and commits suicide on her wedding day, Mariane falls pregnant, is abandoned and dies in childbirth. The novel's main protagonist is Eduard, who then encounters the pregnant Mariane and hears the tragic story from her father, Amtmann Walder. After the death of Mariane, Eduard is adopted by Walder. The son of Collett's district governor is also called Edvard. The parallels are not exact, however, as Collett's main male protagonist is not Edvard, but Georg Kold, whose role is comparable to Edvard in Hoche. In Collett's novel we find not two but four daughters: Marie, who enters a marriage of convenience under pressure from her parents and dies young; Louise, who is unhappily married to the former house teacher Mr Caspers; Amalie, who reads *Ossian* (p. 209) and is engaged to the poor theologian Adolf Brøcher; and Sofie, who needs to make a choice between Georg Kold, the current house teacher, and Mr Rein, a well-established dean.

Hoche's novel is subtitled as a 'Wertheriade' (a novel written in imitation of Goethe's *Sorrows of Young Werther*). Hoche's Wallheim redoubles Werther's passion. Werther's famous yellow waistcoat is explicitly echoed, as Wallheim wears a blue waistcoat when declaring himself to Elise and a green waistcoat when declaring himself to Mariane. When his intense

---

[49] 'Ingen lafontainisk eller tromlitzsk Romanhelt kunde komme mere *á propos* end Cold i dette Øieblik' (p. 184).

[50] J. G. Hoche, *Des Amtmanns Tochter von Lüde. Eine Wertheriade* (Bremen, 1797).

feelings are rejected, he commits suicide, like Werther, with a pistol. Collett, even though she explicitly associates Georg Kold with 'Werther-like dreaming out in nature' (167),[51] is much less dramatic than Hoche. However, the two eldest daughters of her district governor are also linked to death. Marie dies young. Sofie imagines her doll Louise as dead on the wedding day of her sister Louise and Mr Caspers ('I no longer spoke to her, because she was dead. She should, she must be dead' (107).[52] She buries the doll in a ceremony not very different from what Hoche describes for Elise's funeral (p. 238). Further resonances run through the entire novel: both Elise and Sofie find refuge in a grotto, both Caspers and Wallheim are judged by their narrators for their disrespect of women's superior capacity for feeling, and both novels include in their moral argument the misguided affections of daughters as well as the failings of parents. Hoche, like Collett, chooses a different format from the epistolary novel (to which *The Sorrows of Young Werther* belongs) with a loosely plotted prose narrative where occasional letters, songs and diary entries provide moments of emotional intensity. Like Collett's Georg Kold, Hoche's Eduard also has an older female corre-spondent, who attempts to help him sort out his feelings.

Individually, each of these features is common enough in late eight-eenth-century fiction. Collectively, however, they suggest that Collett might have read Hoche's novel at some point. *Amtmandens Døttre* riffs on similar concerns and narrative figures as we find in *Des Amtmanns Toch-ter*. Collett, writing in the mid-nineteenth century, however, writes with a different ambition and historical perspective. In Hoche's novel the inter-textual references link to current literary and musical production and serve to characterise and moralise in a strictly contemporary fashion. Collett, on the other hand, chooses to combine separate literary lineages such as Byron, Lafontaine and the comedies of Karoline Møllerup to sculpt a more complex resonance chamber for the stories of her protagonists.

To all intents and purposes, Sofie chooses Mr Rein for a husband when she visits his house. She is pleased by the elegance of its eighteenth-century décor, the pastoral paintings 'in the manner of Boucher' (226),[53] the rococo mirrors and the chinoiseries as well as the dean's library that is open to anyone who wishes to use it (p. 224), much like the book collections of the eighteenth-century Norwegian bourgeoisie. Kold, on the other hand, estranges Sofie's affections when she overhears his sardonic, perhaps even

---

[51] 'nogen Trang til et werthersk Drømmerie i Naturen' (p. 160).
[52] 'Jeg talte ikke mere til hende; thi hun var jo død. Hun skulde, hun maatte være død' (p. 102).
[53] 'i Bouchers Maneer' (p. 219).

Byronic, comments on her emotional sincerity. It appears that a move into the literary past is necessary for the Norwegian 'femme emancipée' (p. 199), because in the contemporary environment her emotional life finds little respect.

Even though the portraits of Goethe and Byron are replaced by a painting of a female ancestor of the daughters in the end, literature does its service as a resonance chamber for the characters' thoughts and feelings throughout the novel, and Collett spins a complex web of national and international literary references. Lorenz Brandt, the unwelcome suitor, is 'a Norwegian of the good old sort' (190),[54] whereas Kold is linked to the project of 1814 when we learn that the copy of Byron's portrait that resembles him was printed that year (p. 229). Rein belongs to the earlier generation that cultivated cosmopolitan habits and multilingual book collections.

It is obvious that *Amtmandens Døttre* draws on the European tradition of the novel. Siv Gøril Brandtzæg has traced its links to epistolary novels featuring similar character constellations between young women, their fathers and house teachers, particularly Rousseau's *Nouvelle Héloïse* and Mackenzie's *Julia de Roubigné*,[55] while Tone Selboe foregrounds Collett's debts to Jane Austen.[56] One can also argue for *The Sorrows of Young Werther* and the *Werther* imitations as a feature in the resonance room of Collett's novel. After all, Lotte in Goethe's novel is also the daughter of a district governor (*Amtmann*). Analysing *Amtmandens Døttre* against the holdings of book collections of the eighteenth century takes us a step further in this critical project, as it underlines that the first Norwegian novel builds on the long tradition of Norwegian readers as literary citizens of the world. This tradition is also recorded by Conradine Dunker in her memoire *Gamle dage*, for example, where she chronicles bourgeois cultural life in Christiania at the end of the eighteenth century and the beginning of the nineteenth century. Dunker's *Gamle dage* was written in the 1850s, which is when Collett published her novel.[57] For Collett, the tradition of the multilingual citizen of the world includes both the fate of Karoline Møllerup and the promise of Mr Rein.

Norwegian book collections in the eighteenth century carried a broad variety of literary texts bringing the European republic of letters to the Far North. As we have seen through the three exploratory case studies of

54 'Han er en Nordmand af det gode, gamle Kuld' (p. 184).
55 S. G. Brandtzæg, '"Jeg ridsede mit Navn paa Héloïses kolde Bryst": Camilla Colletts *Amtmandens Døttre* i lys av den europeiske sentimentale roman', *Edda*, 102:2 (3 June 2015), 94–109.
56 See T. Selboe, 'Camilla Collett (1813–1895)'.
57 C. Dunker, *Gamle dage. Erindringer og tidsbilleder* (Copenhagen, 1871).

Pamela, the German *Geheimbundroman* and *Amtmandens Døttre*, these book collections contributed to cultural practices of reading and performing texts that further link Norway to developments in Europe. For reading societies in Germany, France and Britain in the late eighteenth century, Wittmann identifies two 'decisive achievements': providing an infrastructure for 'extensive reading' as well as a social organisation that reflects the 'public sphere' of private individuals.[58] We see similar 'achievements' in Norway, but our analysis of the book collections and their multilingual holdings suggest that the horizon is European, firstly because the collections mirror not simply the trends from Copenhagen, and secondly, because the Danish translations lag behind international trends recorded in the book collections. The situation will change for the book collections of the nineteenth century, as Eide has shown, when Danish comes to be the dominant language. In the eighteenth century, as well as in the representation through Collett's nineteenth-century novel, the book collections stand for a European context with and against which Norway begins to define itself as a political and literary nation.

COLLECTION CATALOGUES INCLUDED IN THE DATABASE

- *Christianiæ Læse-Sælskabs Nye Skrifter* (Christiania, 1784).
- *Fortegnelse over endeel indbundne Bøger, som ere til Leje hos Boghandler Diurendahl i Christiania* (Christiania, 1797).
- *Katalog over Cancelliraad Carl Deichmans Bibliotek; Skjenket Christiania by 1780* (Facsimile edition) (Oslo, 1979).
- *Udtog af Catalogen over det Kongl. Norske Landcadet-Corpses offentlige Bibliothek* (Christiania, 1812).*
- *Indbydelses Plan til et almindeligt Læse-Selskab for Trondhjem* (Trondheim, 1783).
- *Catalog over Det Norske Videnskabersselskabs Samlinger* (Copenhagen, 1808).*
- *Fortegnelse over Det Bergenske Læse-Selskabs samtlige Danske Bøger* (Bergen, 1791).
- *Fortegnelse over de Bøger som Læseselskabet for udenlandsk Litteratur har anskaffet i Aarene 1796–1800* (Bergen, 1800).
- Advertisements of the bookseller Schousted (Drammen) in *Norske Intelligenz-Sedler* 26 August 1789, 14 October 1789, 5 May 1790 and 6 April 1791.

---

[58] See R. Wittmann, 'Was there a Reading Revolution at the End of the Eighteenth Century?', pp. 308–9.

- Müller, Carl. *Katalog over Christiania Kathedralskoles Bibliothek* (Christiania, 1883).*

* For collection catalogues compiled after 1800 only titles published before 1800 were included in the database.

Aknowledgements

I would like thank the editors for their excellent work, Marit Sjelmo for the collaboration in compiling the database and Tone Selboe for an early conversation on Camilla Collett

7

Stolen Fruit, Moral Fiction: Marmontel's *Contes moraux* in Denmark–Norway

Aina Nøding

I T WAS A LATE Friday night in Copenhagen in May 1781. Two soldiers had been painting the town red and decided to continue the party by breaking into the storage of an off-licence. As they opened the door, the content of the storage must have been a disappointment. Instead of barrels of spirits, there were stacks of dusty and well-worn books – in French. They belonged to a public servant, Jens Nimb. Even though the soldiers' thirst mainly was of a different nature than the thirst for learning, they stole away with several volumes. Ironically, among the titles were several tomes of 'true crime' (Pitaval's *Causes célèbres* [Famous court cases]) as well as three volumes of Marmontel's *Contes moraux* [Moral tales]. Why would the soldiers bother with books they most probably could not read? According to Nimb, they were hoping to trade the books for food, which is why he advertised the theft in the local newspaper to alert shopkeepers. That is, he was only interested in retrieving a couple of them, as the rest were 'incomplete and ruined'.[1]

Nimb's advertisement points to the widespread trade in and distribution of foreign language books to readers in Denmark–Norway, albeit in an unusual fashion. That this work by Jean-François Marmontel (1723–99) would be rather dusty in the 1780s is perhaps less of a surprise. The stories first appeared between 1755 and 1759 in *Mercure de France*, a periodical edited by Marmontel from 1758. From 1761 he reprinted them as volumes

---

[1] Quote: 'ere defecte og fordærvede' (*Kiøbenhavns Adresse-Contoirs Efterretninger* (KA), 28 May 1781, p. 8). All translations by the author, unless otherwise stated.

of *Contes moraux*, continually adding stories to new editions. Critics soon questioned the label 'moral', but the stories were instantly popular across Europe. The 'tales' appealed to a wide audience with their more 'realistic' take on the genre of short prose fiction and their stylistic ease. In his preface Marmontel insisted short stories should be told efficiently, with speedy dialogues and wit, making them suitable for readings in salons and as theatre adaptations.[2]

Numerous adaptations and imitations soon followed suit across Europe and North America, including in Denmark–Norway. Of course, moral weeklies like *The Spectator* had carried short fiction aimed at instructing virtue for decades, and 'moral tales' was not a new term. However, Marmontel's *Contes* as *books* helped liberate the genre from moral philosophy (the story as an *example*), making the stories primarily literary texts within the context of a genre while carrying the label 'moral' with a gallant smile.[3] The combination of popularity among readers and the literary elite, paired with Marmontel's standing as an authority on poetics, made his work a model of the genre and raised its literary value. In Copenhagen the semi-official society for encouraging new quality literature, called *The Society of Taste* for short, launched a prize contest for the best short story in 1771. The listed models for contestants were Cicero and Marmontel.[4] Prominent writers responded, including the historian Peter Frederik Suhm (1728–98). His medieval tale 'Sigrid' won, marking the beginning of marmontelian stories in Danish.[5]

However, *Contes moraux*'s influence was not solely due to a top-down definition of taste but rather a result of a growing readership for Marmontel's works and prose fiction in general. The story of the agents involved in this process is less known: how and by whom did this work reach their readers, and who were they? Furthermore, how did publications and translations across different print media play out in the tales' reception?[6] In

---

[2]   'Préface' in J.-F. Marmontel, *Contes moraux* (The Hague [Paris?], 1761).

[3]   K. Astbury, *The Moral Tale in France and Germany 1750–1789* (Oxford, 2002), pp. 11–15, 36.

[4]   Advertisement in KA, 16 August 1771, p. 4 by Selskabet til de skiønne og nyttige Videnskabers Forfremmelse ('Det smagende Selskab'). Original title: 'Sigrid, eller Kierlighed Tapperhed's Belønning', in *Forsøg i de skiønne og nyttige Videnskaber*, vol. 10 (Copenhagen, 1772).

[5]   H. Stangerup, *Romanen i Danmark i det attende aarhundrede* (Copenhagen, 1936), pp. 279–85. The prize was for rhetoric ('Veltalenhed'). Suhm later wrote two similar stories: 'Euphron' (1774) and 'Signe og Habor' (1777).

[6]   Marmontel became the leading figure of *opera comique* in Denmark–Norway. That reception of the *Contes* goes beyond the scope here, while it certainly strengthened interest in the printed stories and vice versa.

Britain, Marmontel was the most frequently translated French author in magazines, with translations first appearing in serial form.[7] A similar and even more distinct pattern can be found in Denmark–Norway. Moreover, the *Contes* moved along trade networks of both imports and exports of French works to and from Denmark–Norway, modifying models of book diffusion or dissemination of prose fiction as one-way movements from centre to periphery into ones of entanglement, adaptation and circulation.[8] By examining the sociology (or even sociality) and geography of this work in its multiple material shapes on the fringes of Europe, the complexities of late eighteenth-century book trade and reading can be more fully understood and modified, even outside the region.[9] In order to map this out, this chapter will first apply a bibliographic analysis to argue the production of an unknown French volume edition of *Contes moraux* in Denmark before analysing the wider reception of the stories in terms of translation, criticism, readers and collections. Finally, the diffusion in Norway will serve as a case for arguing the diverging paths of a work depending on its language and format (volume or series).

STOLEN FRUIT: MARMONTEL'S *CONTES* ABROAD

The publication history of *Contes moraux* is complex, to say the least, and further complicated by the obfuscations and alterations of unauthorised editions. To untangle the work's publication history in Denmark–Norway, a short introduction to its early international publication history is necessary. Marmontel had fallen from royal grace in 1759 for reciting a satirical poem. When the encyclopaedist remerged from the Bastille in January 1760, stripped of his editorial post at the *Mercure*, he turned to collecting his tales. The author added a preface explaining the genre and his style along with three new stories and his well-received article 'Apologie du Théâtre'. Two small volumes of *Contes moraux* appeared in January 1761

---

[7]   R. D. Mayo, *The English Novel in the Magazines 1740–1815* (Evanston/London, 1962), pp. 372, 378. See also J. Grieder, *Translations of French Sentimental prose Fiction in Late Eighteenth-Century England* (Durham, NC, 1975), pp. 103–9.

[8]   F. Moretti, *Atlas of the European Novel 1800–1900* (London, 1998); S. Shep, 'Books in Global Perspectives', in L. Howsam (ed.), *The Cambridge Companion to The History of The Book* (Cambridge, 2015), pp. 53–70; M. Ogborn and C. Withers, *Geographies of the Book* (Farnham/Burlington, 2010).

[9]   D. Bellingradt and J. Salman, 'Chapter 1: Books and Book History in Motion: Materiality, Sociality and Spatiality', in D. Bellingradt and J. Salman (eds), *Books in Motion in Early Modern Europe* (Cham, 2017), pp. 1–11; D. F. McKenzie, *Bibliography and the Sociology of Texts* (Cambridge, 1999).

'À la Haye' [n The Hague], causing immediate success. However, they were probably printed semi-officially in Paris.[10] When a privileged edition by Lesclapart in Paris appeared a few months later, it was called new and revised, identical to one of the editions from The Hague.[11] This time, Marmontel had included three unpublished stories in the second volume, also sold separately as *Suite de Contes moraux*. According to the author, they were particularly well suited for theatre adaptations. Four years later, in the third edition, the author notes that his stories had appeared in several languages and on stages in Paris and London. This edition, published by J. Merlin in Paris, contains a further five new stories. The author altered the sequence of stories to vary the tone and create contrasts between stories.[12]

The illustrated and expensive Merlin edition (produced in two formats) aimed to outshine the numerous *éditions furtives*, some probably printed in France but many certainly abroad. Marmontel later described how during a visit to Liège in 1767 a printer-bookseller named Bassompierre informed him that his reprints were sold across the German states, including four editions of *Contes moraux* and three of the novel *Bélisaire* (1767). 'What!' Marmontel interrupted, 'you steal from me the fruit of my labour!' The printer responded that he had the right to print anything good – 'that is our trade' – as French privileges did not apply there, and that the editions printed in France were making the author quite rich enough.[13] French pirate editions of the *Contes moraux* appeared across Europe from 1761 onwards. As Bassompierre pointed out, the printers and publishers were

---

[10]   M. Freund, *Die moralischen Erzählungen Marmontels* (Halle 1904, pp. 82–3) lists three different 1761 editions (all 2 vols in duodecimo) with 'À La Haye' imprint and no publisher/printer. One is probably by Lesclapart in Paris (see below) and one a French pirate edition. In his *Memoires* Marmontel writes: 'the first editions of my Tales began to enrich me' (London, 1805), vol. 2, p. 220. At the time of this edition, books (often novels) with a so-called 'tacit permission' flourished. These were approved by a censor, but without a *privilège* and often with a false imprint indicating a city outside France (R. Darnton, *Pirating and Publishing* (Oxford, 2021), pp. 23, 54).

[11]   The copperplate signatures are difficult to make out but look identical. The privilege is dated 29 May and 11 July 1761 for *Contes moraux* and 22 September for the three new stories (reprinted in the Lesclapart edition, vol. 2, 1761). See also M. Freund 1904, pp. 7 and 82–3.

[12]   Marmontel, 'Préface', in his *Contes moraux* (Paris, 1765), vol. 1, p. XV. Adding and altering the content of books helped prolong the duration of the book's *privilège* (R. Darnton, *Pirating and Publishing*, p. 33).

[13]   Marmontel, *Memoirs*, vol. 3, pp. 94–5. Dating of the journey: D. Droixhe, "'Elle me coute dix milles écus'. La contrefaçon des œuvres de Molière offerte par l'imprimeur Bassompierre à Marmontel'", *Revue français d'histoire du livre*, No. 114–15 (2002), pp. 125–64. Freund (*Die moralischen Erzählungen Marmontels*, p. 84) only lists one Liège edition before 1767.

within their rights to do so, as were publishers of translations. In the 1760s there emerged French editions in The Hague, Amsterdam and Leipzig, cities that like Liège were known for their reprint industry.[14] Furthermore, the same decade saw translations into German, English, Swedish and Dutch in volume editions and periodicals – to say nothing of the countless 'moral tales' churned out by other authors.

Katherine Astbury depicts the development of the genre in France and Germany and demonstrates that it was adapted in terms of morality, politics and literary taste as it crossed linguistic and cultural borders.[15] The British seem to have preferred the stories in translation, or simply importing the French or Dutch editions. Robert L. Dawson argues that an edition *sans lieu* from 1768, made (according to the title page) 'Suivant l'Edition de Paris, chez Merlin' [after Merlin's Paris edition] must be the first French edition printed in Britain.[16] It turns out it is not. Rather it is a case of the periphery of European printing apparently being closer to the centre than we generally think.

Danish pears: *Contes moraux* in Copenhagen

Nimb did not specify which edition of the *Contes* the soldiers took. Catalogues from Copenhagen booksellers and newspaper advertisements of the 1760s and 1770s list several editions on offer, in French and German. They come from Amsterdam, Paris, Karlsruhe and Leipzig, in octavo and duodecimo formats, in two or three volumes and with or without illustrations – all well-known editions and translations.[17] However, what stands out is a French edition printed in Copenhagen in 1768 (3 volumes, octavo) which keeps reoccurring in the booksellers' lists. There is no such edition registered in any library catalogue today. Could there be a 'stolen fruit' in Copenhagen as well, as early as the 1760s?

[14] On the cities involved in the pirating industry of French books outside of France, see R. Darnton, *Publishing and Pirating*, particularly chapter 3.
[15] K. Astbury, *The Moral Tale*.
[16] R. L. Dawson, 'Marmontel Made in Britain', *Australian Journal of French Studies*, 38:1 (2001), 107–23.
[17] M. Freund, *Die moralischen Erzählungen Marmontels*, pp. 82–5; A. Martin *et al.*, *Bibliographie du genre romanesque français 1751–1800* (London/Paris, 1977), p. 61.12. (Freund (later cited in Martin *et al.*) lists a 1768-edition in French 'Suivant l'Edition de Paris, chez Merlin', but does not identify its origin.) Selected bookseller catalogues, 1761–89, from the companies Proft, Rothe, Mumme, Steinmann and Philibert (in the Gunnerus Library, Trondheim).

A court case from 1775 concerning German reprints made by the Copenhagen publisher Søren Gyldendal points a finger at the culprit: Claude Philibert (1709–76).[18] This printer had moved to Copenhagen in 1755 from his native Geneva and the top-of-the-line business he co-owned with the Cramer brothers. They were soon to win fame as Voltaire's publishers, while Philibert had fallen out with the *philosophe* over a pirate edition the year before his move. In Denmark, Philibert set up as an upmarket bookseller-printer while retaining a business in Geneva, now co-owned with and run by his brother Antoine. (Some books carry the imprint 'Copenhague et Genève'.) He mainly produced books and periodicals in French and a few titles in Danish, all high quality and expensive, earning him a good reputation in Denmark and beyond.[19] In addition, his bookshop offered imports particularly from Paris, Amsterdam, Leipzig and later Neuchatel.[20]

When the theatre-loving Christian VII opened the Court Theatre in Copenhagen in 1767, where French and Italian ensembles performed, Philibert acquired the privilege to (re)print the staged plays, 'Avec permission du Roi' [with the king's permission] printed on the title page. It often openly acknowledged the original edition, too, for instance 'Suivant la nouvelle edition de 1768' [after the new edition of 1768].[21] Several of these plays were adaptations of Marmontel's stories. As the defence pointed out in the case against Gyldendal (and as Bassompierre had reminded Marmontel), reprints

---

[18]   *Stevning [...] i Sagen imellem [...] Gyldendal og Schubothe* (Copenhagen, 1796), p. 15. It is noted that Philibert's reprints were supported (even financially) by the government. His *Contes moraux* edition is one of two editions specified (along with the bestselling Raynal's *Histoire philosophique* (1773–4, s.l.) among 'numerous other major French works printed in this way in Copenhagen'. See H. Horstbøll, 'En bogtrykker og boghandler i København', *Fund og forskning*, 51 (2012), 311–35, at p. 322.

[19]   Letters to Voltaire from the Cramer brothers and C. Philibert, both dated 15 April 1754 (Th. Besterman (ed.), *Correspondence and Related Documents*, vol. XV (Geneva, 1971), pp. 83–5). L. Bobé, 'Claude Philibert 1709–84. En Foregangsmand paa Boghaandværkets og Bogudbredelsens Omraade', *Nordisk Tidsskrift för Bok- och Bibliotekväsen*, vol. VII (1920), 14–18, at p. 16; 'Philibert, Claude' in *R.I.E.C.H. Inventory of Swiss printers and editors prior to 1850*, 2008/2017; J. R. Kleinschmidt, *Les imprimeurs et libraires de la république de Genève 1700–1798* (Geneva, 1948), pp. 92–5, 159–62. After Antoine's death in 1764 Claude Philibert partnered with B. Chirol in Geneva until 1775.

[20]   H. Ilsøe, *Bogtrykkerne i København og deres virksomhed ca. 1600–1810* (Copenhagen, 1992), pp. 153–5; L. Bobé, 'Claude Philibert 1709–84', pp. 15–17. *Contes moraux* does not figure on a (short) backlist of titles that Philibert provided the Royal Library with in 1780–1 under the new law on legal deposit (Royal Library, Copenhagen, KBs Arkiv (indtil 1943), Pligtaflevering, Ms E39, 1778–1784).

[21]   See for instance his collections of dramas, which includes long lists of titles on offer in his bookshop: *Theatre royal de Dannemarc* (1770–3, 5 vols).

of foreign books were common and legal, although frowned upon.[22] Rather, Philibert took part in an international, flourishing trade in unauthorised reprints and translations, of which the Danish contributions of 'numerous [...] major French works' remain to be studied in full.[23] Books forbidden in France, such as *Bélisaire*, were particularly attractive to reprint. Furthermore, Philibert's French titles from Copenhagen were potential objects of exchange with books from publishers abroad, as so-called 'change' rather than payments in cash was often preferred. For example, his pirate edition of Montesquieu's works (1759–65) found their way to his shop in Geneva and from there to Neuchatel – and from there, who knows where. Others, like his edition of Raynal's *Histoire philosophique* (1773–4), were considered a direct competition by pirate publishers abroad.[24]

Newspaper advertisements confirm that Philibert had offered *Contes moraux* at least from 1766. However, in May 1768 he announces that an edition of *Contes moraux* is currently in print, following other works by Marmontel all in octavo and printed 1767–8.[25] The others include *Fragmens de Philosophie Morale*, the 1767 novel *Bélisaire* (with the *Fragmens*) as well as an unattributed 'conte moral', 'L'Heureuse famille'. This confirms an unrecognised Danish 1768 edition. Does it still exist? Bibliographies of Marmontel's works list a 1768-edition in French (3 vols, octavo) with unknown place of publication. It is found in several Northern European libraries, where place of print is either given as unknown or as Paris due to a misreading of the title page: 'Suivant l'Edition de Paris, chez Merlin'

[22] See also R. Darnton, *Pirating and Publishing*, p. 2.
[23] *Stevning [...] i Sagen imellem [...] Gyldendal og Schubothe* (Copenhagen, 1796), p. 15 (cf. n. 18 above); H. Horstbøll, 'En bogtrykker og boghandler i København', pp. 322–3.
[24] H. Horstbøll, 'En bogtrykker og boghandler i København', pp. 319–20; A. Frøland, *Dansk boghandels historie 1482 til 1945* (Copenhagen, 1974), pp. 85, 88f, 119. Printing inexpensive books that were attractive abroad for 'change' was a difficult but necessary task for Danish booksellers. However, Philibert primarily had to rely on international payments through a financial agent, while his shop in Geneva more easily could engage in 'change'. S. Burrows' and M. Curran's The French Book Trade in Enlightenment Europe Database, 1769–94 (on the book trade to and from Société Typographique Neuchatel) lists Geneva as the top supplier of Montesquieu, but I have not found a list of specific editions (browse author: Montesquieu/supply origins).
[25] *Kiøbenhavnske Tidender* and KA, both 16 May 1768, p. 4. The first volume is finished, a second volume is due in June. The third (with *Nouveaux contes moraux*) is not mentioned here and no further advertisements are found until 9 November 1768 (KA) when 3 volumes in octavo (1768) are listed under 'Livres nouveaux chez Cl. Philibert'.

(referencing the 1765 Merlin edition).[26] So far, the wording echoes other reprints of Philibert's at the time, supported by a predominantly Scandinavian distribution.

The bibliographer Dawson gives a detailed description of the three volumes of this 1768 edition, arguing that certain printing features and paper qualities 'feels British'. If the edition is compared to Philibert's other Marmontel editions, however, it rather feels Danish. For instance, the layout and type of the title page of his *Bélisaire* (1767) is identical to *Contes moraux*', as are those of *Fragmens de Philosophie Morale* (1767), except for each work having different ornaments above the year of print. However, *Bélisaire* is embellished with the same ornament we find on the last page of *Contes moraux* (vol. 3). Furthermore, *Fragmens*' title page identifies Merlin's edition as its original with the same phrase as the *Contes*'. Bound between the copies of these editions in the Royal Library Copenhagen is Philibert's sales catalogue for August 1767, where *Bélisaire* is listed among his own publications. The reprint of *Bélisaire* in 1775, carrying the imprint 'A Copenhague, Chez Cl. Philibert', has a vignette of a bunch of pears and leaves on the title page and last page, identical to the vignette on the title page of *Contes moraux*. Philibert frequently used this vignette in his reprints of French drama 1769–70.[27] Again, the fonts, punctuation, the presentation of the author's name and title, and the use of single and double black lines are still exactly the same. While Philibert reprinted *Fragmens* and *Bélisaire* in 1775, he did not reprint the *Contes*.

Finally, a near mistake by Philibert laid out in his foreword to *L'Heureuse famille* (1768) confirms that *Contes moraux* was indeed published by him in 1768. The moral tale had previously been added to the Leipzig edition of *Bélisaire* (1767) and an Amsterdam edition of the *Contes*, mistaking the tale for Marmontel's and not (as was the case) by one of his many imitators, Lezay-Marnézia in Geneva.[28] Evidently Philibert had been made

---

[26] M. Freund (*Die moralischen Erzählungen Marmontels*, p. 84) and A. Martin *et al.* (*Bibliographie*, p. 61.12). Copies of this edition are owned by the University Library, Oslo, the library of Oslo Cathedral School, the royal libraries of Copenhagen and Stockholm, Staatsbibliothek Berlin and the British Library (the latter two list '[The Hague?]' as place of origin). R. Dawson ('Marmontel Made in Britain', p. 122) describes it as a 'rare book' as he is only aware of one or two copies. The provenance of the copy in Copenhagen (along with other works of Marmontel printed by Philibert) is diplomat and counsellor to the Dano-Norwegian king, Count Haxthausen (1733–1802).

[27] R. Dawson ('Marmontel Made in Britain', p. 111) describes the ornaments as 'enigmatic to [me]', but as having a 'British look'.

[28] Philibert adds that the story was included in an Amsterdam edition of *Contes moraux*, too, which I have not found. The original appeared in Geneva in 1766.

CONTES
MORAUX,

Par Mr. MARMONTEL,

DE L'ACADEMIE FRANÇOISE.

TOME PREMIER.

Suivant l'Edition de PARIS, chez MERLIN.

===

MDCC LXVIII.

PLATE 7.1. The 'pirate' edition of Marmontel's *Contes moraux*, published by Claude Philibert in Copenhagen, 1768.

aware of this mistake during printing, so he explains to the reader why the pagination of the story starts on page 49: it was supposed to follow *Fragmens* and precede *Contes moraux*.

Indirectly, we here learn that Philibert had consulted an Amsterdam edition of *Contes moraux*. Apparently, it contradicts the reference to the Merlin edition, but it could be the case that he consulted both. The Amsterdam edition opens with Marmontel's poem *Les Charmes de l'Etude* (1760).[29] So does the 1768 edition, with an added footnote that this text is not found in the Paris edition but in the one from Amsterdam.[30] More importantly, the 1768 edition has all the new stories from the Paris edition, although it rearranges their sequence (compared to both the Paris and Amsterdam editions) throughout the three volumes, thus altering the author's careful organisation and potentially the readers' reception of them. However, by combining textual and material elements to create a distinctly new edition, Philibert could more easily defend his publication if international trade partners should complain of his competition in the reprint market.[31]

In other words, Nimb and his fellow readers visiting Copenhagen bookshops would have had a range of editions in French to choose from, including one printed locally, for the Danish and Scandinavian markets and beyond. It would have been one of the earliest French editions of the *Contes moraux* outside France and the capitals of European reprints, preceding a Swedish edition by seventeen years. Furthermore, it would mean that no French edition was published in Britain.[32] Moreover, Philibert's active production of reprints over two decades in Copenhagen adds to Darnton's recent mapping of the European pirating industry of French books in this period.[33] However, Marmontel's tales were to reach far beyond Copenhagen and those fluent in French, or even readers of long volumes. The tales found their early and wide readership in Denmark–Norway by assuming their original form: as pieces in periodicals, only now in translation.

[29] Published by 'la Compagnie' (1761/62; several reprints before 1768).
[30] 'Cette pièce n'est pas dans l'édition de Paris, mais d'Amsterdam' (Marmontel, *Contes moraux* ([Copenhagen], 1768), p. [19]).
[31] See H. Horstbøll, 'En bogtrykker og boghandler i København', p. 322.
[32] According to R. Dawson ('Marmontel Made in Britain', p. 110), there are three French editions with a London imprint (1771, 1780 and 1795), all of which are fake.
[33] Darnton focuses on 'The Fertile Crescent' of printers in cities along France's borders while briefly referencing studies of Britain and Germany, but not beyond (*Pirating and Publishing*, p. 5).

'Moralske Fortællinger' – Dano-Norwegian translations

The first translation of one of Marmontel's stories is traditionally referred to as 'Den lykkelige Familie' [The happy family], published in the periodical *Fruentimmer- og Mandfolke-Tidenden* [Journal for Women and Men] in 1769.[34] The translator for this moral weekly had evidently not read Philibert's edition of 'L'heureuse famille', or he would not have given it the subtitle 'A story by Mr. Marmontel'.[35] Apparently, the imitators had overtaken the original in reaching readers in Danish. Either way, this was not the first translation of a Marmontel story into Danish. The first appeared in Norway, in a newspaper, but with no mention of the author.

'Fortællelse om en sig selv kaldende Philosophus' is an abridged version of 'The Pretended Philosopher', originally from *Mercure de France* (1759), published on 12 October 1767 in a recently established newspaper in Bergen, Norway's largest town at the time. As regular *news*papers were only allowed for publication in Copenhagen, the first Norwegian papers, *Norske Intelligenz-Sedler* (Christiania [Oslo] from 1763) and *Efterretninger Fra Addresse-Contoiret i Bergen i Norge* (Bergen from 1765), were so-called *adresseaviser* (from French *feuilles du bureau d'adresse*; German: *Intelligenz-Blätter*). These small weeklies peddled local advertisements and official announcements, filling the remaining space of their four pages with fables, stories and poems, letters to the editor or practical advice. The editor in Bergen, Ole Brose, could boast a significant private library of books in several languages, including *Contes moraux* in French.[36] He might have produced this translation, which provides no context such as the author's name or origin, as was often the case in these papers.

This story of the self-declared unworldly philosopher whose hypocrisy is unmasked and ridiculed in the manner of a traditional comedy was originally aimed at Rousseau following Marmontel's dispute with him over the moral use of theatre (and comedy in particular).[37] While this subtext was most probably lost on the readers in Bergen, the tale had acquired new topicality.[38] In the imported newspapers, readers in Bergen could follow the

---

[34] H. Stangerup, *Romanen i Danmark*, pp. 230–1.

[35] 'Den lykkelige Familie. (En Fortælling af Hr. Marmontel)', in *Fruentimmer- og Mandfolke-Tidenden*, no. 11–12 (1769). It might have been a Leipzig edition reprint (with *Bélisaire*, 1768), where we find the same error in a footnote as in the Danish (the year 1665 for 1765), which is correct in Philibert's edition.

[36] Inventory of his estate in 1784 includes *Contes moraux* in 3 vols (The Regional State Archive in Bergen, 'Skifteakter for Ole Brose').

[37] K. Astbury, *The Moral Tale*, p. 29.

[38] On fiction published in Norwegian papers in the 1760s, see A. Nøding, 'Vittige kameleoner: Litterære tekster i norske adresseaviser, 1763–1769' (PhD thesis Oslo, 2007).

developments of the censorship case against *Bélisaire* in Paris. Particularly the chapter that advocates tolerance and claims the salvation of honourable heathens created heated debate in the twin kingdom as it did on the continent. By printing a story well-read readers would recognise, and others would laugh at for its portrayal of a self-proclaimed expert on good and evil, the text could be read as a subtle contribution to the ongoing debate. It would be very typical of how these pre-censored papers applied literary texts. In addition, good texts sold papers.

This first translation points to three typical features of the following Dano-Norwegian translations of the *Contes*: they are printed in a periodical publication, they are addressed to a potentially wide (or widening) readership and they take advantage of Marmontel's fame following the publication of *Bélisaire* and later by its ban in France in early 1768.[39] (The Danish translation, *Belisarius*, appeared the same year.[40]) By the summer of 1768 bookseller Schiønning in Copenhagen invited subscriptions to a translation of 'Mr. Marmontel's Moral Tales or Contes moraux in Danish', but none appeared.[41] A second attempt at a translation of the entire work points directly to the success of the *Bélisaire* translation as an encouragement. The unknown translator ('F. v. Q.') announced a monthly publication of the tales (in random order) under the title *Moraliske Fortælninger*. In October 1773 the first tale 'Alcibiade eller mig' [Alcibiade, or myself] appeared in Copenhagen. The literary critics judged he should not continue until he mastered both French and Danish and, furthermore, choose stories that could be called 'moral' in a stricter sense. No new translations followed, and soon a hawker of carded flax sold 'Alcibiade' at his stall – 11 copies for the price of 10.[42] Again, the potential readership for the stories had widened substantially, if not successfully. There were to be no Danish translations of *Contes moraux* in volume form.

SERIAL STORIES FOR CHILDREN AND SENTIMENTAL READERS

Translations in periodicals met with much greater success, albeit not initially. Again, Philibert opens the ball as publisher. The story of 'The Good Mother' (*Suite*, 1761) is the first complete translation of a Marmontel story into Danish. It was presented in 1770 to readers of *Den danske Oversættere*,

---

[39]   *Bélisaire* was published in December 1766 or early 1767 (A. Martin *et al., Bibliographie*, p. 120).

[40]   Marmontel, *Belisarius* [trans. A. P. Bartholin] (Copenhagen, 1768).

[41]   'Hr. Marmontels Moralske Fortælninger eller Contes moraux i Dansk', KA 5 July 1768, p. 4.

[42]   *Nye kritisk Journal* (NKJ), No. 19 (1774), pp. 164–5; KA 2 March 1774.

eller Samling af valgte moralske Afhandlinger, oversat af fremmede Sprog
[The Danish translator, or collection of selected moral essays, translated
from foreign languages], a periodical for young people. The essays and stories came predominately from English and German moral weeklies. The
second issue provides 'Den gode Moder, En Fortælning. Contes moraux de
Marmontel' to an exclusive circle of readers. The list of subscribers never
surpassed 54, most of whom belonged to the upper social circles of Copenhagen. As always with Philibert, it is an expensive publication in roman
type. He soon had to reduce the price following complaints.[43]

The periodical ends after five months with the editor/translator Carl
Fr. Hellfriedt musing over its lack of success: is Danish taste less polished
than abroad, or do Danes prefer the original in order to learn languages?
Do young people not have fifteen minutes for morals, only masquerades?
Whatever the readers might have replied, Hellfriedt certainly was ahead of
his time in specifically adapting Marmontel's stories to their future readers:
the young. The entire industry of moral tales for children, which flourished
for generations to come, were indebted to *Contes moraux*, and the collection itself was increasingly marketed to children. Moreover, periodicals
were to be the only media for *Contes moraux* in Danish, returning to a
Mercure de France mode of reception, disconnected from the context and
sequence of the later *oeuvre*. Instead, the stories are juxtaposed with their
literary 'ancestors', the moral tales of weeklies in the *Spectator* tradition.

During the 1770s the serial publication continues, but still mainly
addressed to a general reading public rather than youth in particular. In
1773 'Annete and Lubin' (1761) found its way to *Kiøbenhavns Aften-Post*
[Copenhagen evening post], perhaps the most popular weekly in every
stratum of society. The story was known from Favart's *opera-comique*
adaptation, performed in French at The Court Theatre in Copenhagen in
1767.[44] In addition, a translation of the 'Shepherdess of the Alps' (1759) was
reportedly printed in a periodical before 1774, but it has not been found.[45]
However, 1774 saw the beginning of a series of *Contes* in the Danish serial
publication for short fiction, *Det nye Magazin, indeholdende Fortællinger
af adskillige berømte Forfattere* [The new magazine, containing stories by
several famous authors]. While published serially, it is a multi-volume collection rather than a periodical. Its first title, *Nye historiske Magazin* [New

---

[43]   Note at the end of no. 7 of *Den danske Oversættere* (1770), p. 112. List of subscribers
bound after the title page. Issue no. 2 is dated 5 May 1770.

[44]   P. Schiønning, *Dagbog*, 21 March and 25 April 1767. C. Philibert published a French
edition (1766) in Copenhagen aimed at theatre audiences (cf. his advertisement in
the collection *Théatre royal de Dannemarc*, vol. 1, 1770).

[45]   According to a critic in *Kritisk Tilskuer*, no. 7 (1776).

historical magazine], labelled the content as 'histories', which readers found confusing as 'history' implied non-fiction. The title is a nod to a now forgotten periodical, *Det historiske Magazin* (1758–62), which printed 'adventures and stories', some apparently in the moral and sentimental vein.[46] Short prose fiction still remained somewhat unfamiliar, existing outside the classic labels and hierarchies of genres. Interestingly, the editor included some stories in verse, too.[47]

The editor and main translator, the theologian Hans Birch, had established himself as a translator in Copenhagen while he waited for a position as a vicar. During his time with *Det nye Magazin* he became a respected literary critic at *Nye Kritisk Tilskuer* [New critical spectator] and translated sentimental and moral prose including Gellert, Sterne's *A Sentimental Journey* and Miller's *Siegwart* before his posting as a provincial vicar in late 1778. In addition to several of the *Contes*, *Det nye Magazin* presents stories by Gellert, d'Arnaud, Wieland, Rowe, Diderot, idylls by Gessner as well as Fielding's novel *Tom Jones*. The latest fashion of sentimental prose had eclipsed the didactic tales of old moral weeklies in the children's magazines or the topical genres of a newspaper, providing a completely new literary environment for Marmontel's texts in Danish. Birch also claimed that earlier translations had been ephemera, badly translated and soon forgotten.[48] Regarding readership, he imagines them as leisure readers vacationing in country houses. The questionable status of prose fiction prompts him to assure them of the virtuous intent and artistic quality of the texts.[49] By 1778 Birch turns the *Det nye Magazin* into a proper monthly periodical and changes its name to *Det nyeste Magazin af Fortællinger, eller Samling af moralske, rørende og moersomme Romaner og Historier* [The newest magazine of stories, or collection of moral, touching, and amusing novels and histories], adding that they are in Danish.[50]

---

[46] *Det historiske Magazin*, (6 vols, Copenhagen, 1758–62). No copy has been found but lists of content and even summaries of stories can be found in Holck's paper KA following the publication of each issue. The editor/author is unknown.

[47] *Det nye Magazin*, Birch's preface to vol. 1, no. 2 (1774); NKJ, no. 25 (1774), p. 214; *Lærde Efterretninger* (LE) no. 16 (1776), p. 244.

[48] In vol.1, no. 3, pp. 1–43 and 44–68. NKJ (no. 25, 1774, p. 214) called for Birch to include stories by Marmontel to discourage the translator of 'Alcibiade' from continuing his work.

[49] Preface to *Det nye Magazin* vol. 1, no. 3 (1775) and preface to *Det nyeste Magazin*, vol. 1 (1778). A critic, L. Sahl, labels the magazine's readers 'youth' ('Ungdom', *Min Kritiske Læsning*, no. 1 [178?], p. 64).

[50] Preface to *Det nyeste Magazin*, vol. 1 (1778). The lack of good short prose fiction is the reason he gives for introducing novels and continuing with stories in verse. The

The magazines combined were to include the most comprehensive translation of the *Contes* in Danish or Norwegian to this day, with 10 (of 23) stories published between 1774 and 1779.[51] The first issue in 1774 begins with 'The School of Fathers' (*Suite*, 1761). It is soon followed by 'The Shepherdess of the Alps' (1759) and 'The Two Unfortunates' (1758) in the third issue.[52] The next two appear in 1776 (vol. 2, nos 1 and 2): 'Soliman II' (1756) and 'Lausus and Lydia' (1758). The critics were unanimously positive towards Birch's magazines, his translations and these stories in particular: '[Sufficient praise is] they are written by Marmontel and chosen and translated by Birch.'[53] When the magazine was relaunched in 1778 the *Contes* continued to appear regularly: 'The Bad Mother' (1759) in the first issue is contrasted with 'The Good Mother' in the second. 'Friendship Put to the Test' (1765), which originally preceded *Bélisaire* as an argument for religious tolerance, follows later the same year. All three stories emphasise the importance of love and virtue within a wider context of family and society.

In the preface to the May issue 1779, Birch says goodbye to his around 200 subscribers in five towns.[54] He concludes: 'May Taste, Virtue and Religion reign in Denmark and Norway!' (While no Norwegians appear on the list, they clearly read the periodical (see below).) These values are reflected in his selection from the *Contes*, as he mostly leaves out the earliest stories from *Mercure*.[55] Marmontel scholars have pointed to a noticeable development from the satirical and frivolous love entanglements of the earliest stories to a concern for morals in a more social and political sense in the later ones, fully realised in *Bélisaire*.[56] The new editor, H. C. Amberg, followed suit by presenting two of the later love stories: the Clarissa-like story

---

critic in LE (no. 33, 1779, p. 513) calls it 'this periodical collection' ('denne periodiske Samling').

[51] Birch translated seven stories published 1774–8, H. W. Riber one in 1776 and H. C. Amberg two in 1779.

[52] Titles in the magazine: 'Fædrenes Skoele', 'Hyrdinden paa Alperne', 'De to ulykkelige', 'Soliman den Anden', 'Lausus og Lydie'.

[53] *Kritisk Tilskuer*, no. 7 (1776); *Kritisk Journal* no. 29 (1773), NKJ no. 25 (1774), no. 46 (1775) and no. 27 (1776). Quote from NKJ no. 46 (1775), p. 365: '[...] til hvis Roes vi ikke behøve at sige andet, end at de ere forfattede af Marmontel, og valgte og oversatte af Birch'.

[54] Subscription list for 1778–9 counts 195 people (including 16 women) in six locations in Denmark and two in Norway.

[55] Exceptions include 'Alcibiade' from the attempted translation of the entire work and 'Soliman II', which was immensely popular on the Copenhagen stage from 1770, cf. NKJ, no. 26 (1776).

[56] J. Renwick, 'Jean François Marmontel: The Formative Years 1753–1765', *SVEC* no. 76 (Geneva, 1970), p. 191; K. Astbury, *The Moral Tale*, pp. 33–6.

of 'Laurette' (1765) and 'the true story' of first cousins 'Annete and Lubin' (1761). While the latter questions both the laws of society and nature, the first links love to happy family life in the virtuous countryside. There are no new translations of the *Contes* for the next five years in Denmark, but Bergen and Norway are to see their second.

FAME AND IMITATION

One of Birch's co-critics in *Nye Kritisk Tilskuer* was the Norwegian Claus F. Fasting (1746–91), who upon his return to his hometown Bergen in 1777 started what was to become the country's first quality periodical: *Provinzialblade* (1778–81). The weekly magazine provided his subscribers in Southern Norway and Copenhagen with translations of stories, historical anecdotes, essays on art and philosophy, news of scientific inventions and the editor's own poetry. While catering to a variety of readers, his aim was to 'make the useful less tedious, and the pleasant more useful'.[57] To Fasting, the useful *and* pleasant primarily meant French literature and philosophy by Montesquieu, Voltaire and Rousseau, while his readers often disagreed. His women readers wanted short stories, particularly those by Marmontel and d'Arnaud, 'which are more famous than the most learned works *in Folio*'. 'That is exactly why there is no need to reprint them', Fasting replied.[58] However, towards the end of his last volume (1781) he ran a translation of 'The Connoisseur' (*Suite*, 1761), which carries some similarities to the editor's own difficulties in literary circles.[59] The story of the celebrated literary critic who fails miserably as a playwright echoes Fasting's own situation at the time.

Fasting advocated sensibility in literature and politics. Richardson's *Clarissa* and Sterne's *Sentimental Journey* were among his favourite novels. Empathy and compassion were key arguments in his continued fight against slavery, particularly in the Danish West Indies. There is a parallel call for sensibility and anti-slavery in the next periodical to pick up *Contes moraux*, namely *Bibliothek for det smukke Kiøn* ([Library for the fair sex]; published by Gyldendal, Copenhagen 1784–90). Again, women make up the targeted readership. The periodical boasted around three hundred subscribers across Denmark and Norway in the first two years, of whom nearly half were women of all ages. Even for a women's periodical, that figure is

[57]   *Provinzialblade* no. 52 (1778).
[58]   *Provinzialblade* no. 39 (1780). In no. 31 (1780) he had published a translation of a story by d'Arnaud, commenting that many in France and elsewhere preferred his stories to Marmontel's, 'perhaps rightly so'.
[59]   'Kienderen', *Provinzialblade*, nos 39–46 (1781).

remarkably large.[60] Leading Danish women writers are among the contributors, too. The first volume opens with a sequel to Richardson's *Clarissa*, written by Charlotte Baden, while the playwright and author of moral tales Charlotta D. Biehl provides a story in the marmontelian tradition in a later issue. As in *Provinzialblade*, the sensibility extends to a strong anti-slavery appeal, addressed to the women of Danish West Indies.[61]

It is within this context of virtue and sentiment that we find 'By Good Luck' (1758), an amusing story of how a woman's virtue is repeatedly saved from men with dubious intentions. The story is printed anonymously (as are the other stories), something one critic finds curious as Marmontel's name would add to the text's value.[62] The anonymous editors continued this practice, but it changed with volume 4 (1786) and the new editors K. L. Rahbek and J. Kjerulf. They belonged to the prominent literary circle of their day, as did probably their predecessors and several contributors. Among Rahbek's enormous literary production, this volume remained a particular pride and joy to him.[63] His translation of 'The Good Husband' (*Suite*, 1761), a more sober story of how female virtue and family happiness results from a combination of reason and a mother's love, comes with the author's name. The story was probably familiar to Rahbek and his readers in the form of Charlotta D. Biehl's comedy *The Loving Husband* (1764), too.[64] The play and its popularity on the Copenhagen stage were certainly known to the playwright Rahbek and his readers.

Women readers as the *Contes'* main public is cemented in the last translation of the century, that of 'The Sylph Husband' (*Nouveaux*, 1765) published as part of a 'New Year's Gift for Women' in 1796 (by Poulsen, Copenhagen). Again, there is no mention of the author as the story appears alongside five others by anonymous authors (and an essay on female vanity).[65] Books as New Year's gifts from the head of the household to his wife, children, staff etc. had become a booming business and a genre in its own right, with S.

---

[60] Subscribers are 284 in total, including 126 women, for vols 1–2. Normally a subscription list for a periodical would have less than 10 per cent women. Outside Copenhagen the periodical had readers in six to seven Danish towns and in Norway Christiania, Christiansand and the rural districts of Gudbrandsdalen and Rakkestad.
[61] Vol. 1, no. 2 (1784). The anonymous author is the vicar Peder Paludan (1755–99) in Holbæk, Denmark.
[62] LE no. 35 (1784), pp. 585–6.
[63] K. L. Rahbek, *Erindringer af mit Liv* (Copenhagen, 1825), p. 261.
[64] LE no. 52 (1764), p. 527 and *Dramatisk Journal*, no. 26, 12 and 16 January 1772.
[65] *Zulma, Sylphen, [...] Sex Fortællinger, tilligemed en lille Afhandling om Forskiønnelses-Driften hos det smukke Kiøn* (Copenhagen, 1796). One story is by Madame de Staël.

Poulsen as its main representative.[66] The leading critical journal, (for short known as) *Lærde Efterretninger*, was dismissive of the collection, adding that 'The Sylph Husband' is as 'banal and un-psychological as can be'.[67] The *Contes moraux* had travelled far in the northern literary market, from the high mark of taste and academic debate to proponents of moral and sentiment finally to anonymous entertainment in bad taste.

Overall, between 1767 and 1796, 16 of the 23 *Contes moraux* had been translated and only one (or perhaps two) in two different translations. Although the stories may appear randomly over almost three decades, combined they amount to a collective effort of translating the collection. In 1790, in the wake of the political and social turmoil of the Revolution, Marmontel returned to the genre and the *Mercure* with instalments of *Nouveaux contes moraux*. They soon reached Denmark–Norway and appeared in translation in periodicals as well as in a volume (five stories translated by K. L. Rahbek, *Nyeste Fortællinger*, 1794). By now the genre had several local exponents, notably Rahbek himself (collected in *Samlede Fortællinger*, 4 vols, 1804–14) and Charlotta D. Biehl (*Moralske Fortællinger*, 4 vols, 1781–82). Biehl wrote them explicitly for girls inexperienced in the matters of the heart, underlining a general tendency for the genre.[68]

READERS AND COLLECTIONS IN NORWAY

The history of *Contes moraux*'s publication and translation in Denmark–Norway points to some significant aspects of text distribution and reading. The stories are only printed in volume form in French, for a bourgeois and aristocratic readership at home as well as for international trade and distribution. Furthermore, translations in Danish appear exclusively in serial publications, mainly alongside a variety of other texts spanning from advertisements and essays to political statements and fiction. The serial publications invite a broader audience of readers socially while often addressing specific groups such as women or children. Publications centred on to cities: Copenhagen and Bergen. Copenhagen being the centre of print, book trade and publications by authors from both kingdoms and Bergen being Norway's largest city, that is hardly surprising. However, by

[66]   A. B. Rønning, 'Til 'Qvindernes Forædling'. Mary Wollstonecraft for danske lesere i 1800', in Bjørkøy *et al.* (eds), *Litterære verdensborgere* (Oslo, 2019), pp. 290–309; H. Ilsøe, 'Godt Nytår! Nytårshilsener fra 2-300 år siden', *Magasin Fra Det Kongelige Bibliotek*, 7:3 (1992), 3–22 <https://doi.org/10.7146/mag.v7i3.66302>.

[67]   LE no.7 (1796), p. 107: 'saa flau og upsychologisk som mueligt'.

[68]   C. Biehl's afterword, 'Til Læseren!', in her *Moralske Fortællinger*, vol. 4 (Copenhagen, 1782).

tracing some roads of dissemination for *Contes moraux* in Norway, we get a more nuanced picture of the reception of these stories – both 'stolen' and 'legitimate' fruit – at the periphery of Europe. Important sources of information include catalogues of book auctions, lending libraries and private collections, advertisements in newspapers, holdings in museums as well as the above-mentioned subscription lists for periodicals.

Book editions of *Contes moraux* (in French and translation, imported and local) are regularly advertised in the Copenhagen press and bookshop catalogues from around 1766 onwards, notably sold alongside *Bélisaire* in the following years. By the late 1790s it appears on a list of books suitable as textbooks/readers for students of foreign languages, pointing to a new status as a literary classic for the young (in French).[69] Copenhagen and Altona booksellers served readers in Norway as well, either by orders from individual readers, by sending agents or sales catalogues to the main cities (including from Gyldendal and Philibert), or by employing local commissionaires to provide books from their private homes. Furthermore, some readers ordered books directly from abroad or brought them back from their travels.[70]

It is difficult to determine which editions readers owned in Norway. Of a selection of more than 70 private book auction catalogues between 1766 and 1896, 12 included volumes of *Contes moraux*, all in French from the 1760s and 1770s (most s.a.), including one Paris and one Amsterdam edition. Interestingly, there are no German translations, even though they were available from the Copenhagen bookshops, too.[71] If we look at library catalogues from eighteenth-century Norway, there is only one edition in German (part of *Marmontels Werke*), available in Bergen's Reading Society for Foreign Literature (1796–1800). However, we find Philibert's 1768 edition at the Cathedral School library in Christiania (Oslo).[72] The volumes are

---

[69]   KA 15 May 1797.

[70]   H. L. Tveterås, *Den norske bokhandels historie*, vol. I (Oslo, 1987), pp. 98, 114, 124–9. On German agents in Norway (selling books in several languages): *Norske Intelligenz-Sedler* (NIS) 12 July 1775 (Altona) and *Efterretninger Fra Addresse-Contoiret i Bergen i Norge* (EAB) 21 August 1784. Books from Philibert: EAB 6 April 1772.

[71]   A selection of catalogues owned by the National Library of Norway, of which many are digitised. A search of all known catalogues across institutions could alter the percentage and geographical distribution of *Contes moraux* appearing in the catalogues. Also included is a list of books in the estate of Ole Brose, Bergen (d. 1784; Regional State Archive, Bergen, 'Skifteakter for Ole Brose'). A study of estates (predominantly of clergymen) in the second half of the 1700s found works by Marmontel in ten out of *c.* 130 book collections but does not name which ones (F. Bull, *Fra Holberg til Nordal Brun* (Kristiania, 1916), p. 235).

[72]   Online catalogue by K. Kukkonen and M. Sjelmo, *Literary Fiction in Norwegian Lending Libraries in the 18th Century* <www.nb.no/forskning/

evenly distributed between Christiania and Trondheim, with only a couple in Bergen.[73]

Marmontel's readership in Norway tended to be from the upper strata of society, often reading the stories in the original French or to some extent in translations in periodicals. Tellingly, a study of books owned by provincial farmers before 1840 shows no trace of Marmontel, except perhaps as locally written moral tales for children in the early 1800s.[74] As there was no nobility in the country, the owners of *Contes moraux* tend to belong to the 'economic aristocracy' of landowners, industrial magnates and leading officials of the crown. They are present in the subscription lists of the Danish and Norwegian periodicals that carried the translations, too. The same class of readers would adorn their houses with engravings picturing scenes from these stories, making them artefacts of taste on display.[75]

The periodicals and translations substantially widened the readership for the texts both demographically and geographically. While there are no advertisements for *Contes moraux* in volume form in Norwegian papers and bookshops, there are quite a few for periodicals carrying translations of the stories, including *Den danske Oversættere, Bibliothek for det smukke Kiøn*, and *Det nye Magazin* (both issues and volumes).[76] Language is key. Texts in foreign languages had a limited and often well-read readership, thus regarded by authorities as less liable to pose a threat to the public of dubious imported morals or ideas.[77] The selected translations in periodicals reached a variety of readers, including clergymen, teachers, doctors and lower officials.[78] One noteworthy recipient is 'Rechestad Læseselskab', a reading society in rural South-Eastern Norway, which subscribed to two

skjonnlitteratur-i-norske-bibliotek-pa-1700-tallet> (2019). Date of acquisition of the Philibert edition unknown.

[73]   The lack of editions in Bergen is partly due to the few Bergen catalogues available for this study.

[74]   J. Fet, *Lesande bønder* (Oslo, 1995), p. 177.

[75]   See for instance an engraving by J. R. Smith of Bélise from 'The Scruple' at the manor house Ulefoss in Telemark (<www.digitaltmuseum.no>).

[76]   See for instance EAB 6 April 1772 (catalogue of books from Philibert, including *Den danske Oversættere*), *Norske Intelligenz-Sedler* 16 June 1779 and 1 December 1784 and *Christiansandske Ugeblade* 12 November 1785 (Birch's magazines in volumes).

[77]   See for instance the Danish theologian Nannestad on the dangers posed to commoners by the translation of *Bélisaire* in 1768 (N. E. Nannestad, *Afhandling om dydige Hedningers Salighed* (Sorøe, 1768), pp. 4–5).

[78]   Subscription lists for *Bibliothek for det smukke Kiøn*, vols 1 and 2. *Provinzialblade* only refers to its readers in the periodical itself and in addition to those mentioned above includes farmers, military and tradesmen, as well as women and children (A. Nøding, *Claus Fasting* (Oslo, 2018), p. 215). Birch's *Magazin* lists two subscribers in Norway (1778–9).

sets of the *Bibliothek* for women. Its existence was previously unknown, but it is probably an initiative by Rakkestad's local vicar, Hans Hammond, who was very well read and connected in literary circles. In letters to P. F. Suhm he complains about the deplorable state of reading and knowledge among the local farmers, with faint hopes of improving the situation.[79]

Moving morals

The publisher of *Bibliothek for det smukke Kiøn*, Søren Gyldendal, issued a translation of d'Arnaud's stories in 1780. He advertised them to be more virtuous than 'the other so-called *Contes Moraux*'.[80] Gyldendal echoes a much-repeated criticism of the *Contes* from their first publication under this title in France. A Danish critic (1776) summed up the sentiment in his characterization of 'Soliman II': 'This story is, like most marmontelian ones, rich in invention and well-formed characters, but does otherwise not serve to improve morals'.[81] According to Astbury, this criticism dominated in the German states, where new *moralische Erzählungen* were given a more pronounced moral of virtuous individuals, rather than in the sense of *mœurs* or social norms. While this 'German' tendency in the Dano-Norwegian reception is reflected in the preference for translating the later and most 'moral' stories of the collection, the distribution of the French volume editions points to a parallel set of literary 'morals' for privileged readers of foreign languages. Regardless of language, however, many readers of these stories took part in a transnational practice of both reading to be entertained and reading to become a better citizen – in love, marriage, society and, not least, in the republic of fiction. While the ways these texts reach these readers sometimes remained morally contested themselves, the agents in the closely-knit European book market ensured that readers from Paris to Bergen could take part in literary sensations, adapt them locally, and sometimes send some new fruits in return. The story of Philibert's work is a reminder of the importance of re-evaluating the binary centre–periphery view of the European book market and consider a larger network of entangled literary citizens.

[79] Letters from the 1780s in P. F. Suhm, *Samlede Skrifter*, vol. 15 (Copenhagen, 1798), pp. 373, 381; 385–90.
[80] LE, 29 September 1780, p. 624: 'At enhver Fortælling sigter til at befordre Dyd i den egentligste Forstand, er et Fortrin, som overgaaer alle de andre, og mere end de andre saa kaldte *Contes moraux* kan rose sig af.'
[81] NKJ no. 27 (1776), p. 210: 'Denne Fortælning er, som de fleste marmontelske, rig paa Opfindelse og vel udførte Caracterer; men skal for Resten ikke tiene til at forbedre Sæderne.'

8

Secret Springs and Naked Truths: Scandalous Political Literature in Eighteenth-Century Denmark–Norway

Ellen Krefting

THE PRIVATE LIVES OF living as well as long dead kings, queens and courtiers entertain millions of readers and series viewers across the world. Disclosure of the hidden (and mostly unverifiable) sides of past and present royals, and especially the royal bodies, intrigues us to the point of becoming a compulsive obsession, novelist and essayist Hilary Mantel noted some years ago. She herself achieved huge literary success by digging up some of the royal bodies buried long ago.[1] Scandals involving secret affairs of the still living, however, saturate today's entire media ecology. Defamatory revelations sell because they appeal to voyeurism, but they also form public opinion concerning members of the elite, and occasionally they end up having legal or political consequences. Yet, most of us probably do not think of royal scandals or rumour-based revelations about people in power as a political literary genre, or as being part of a proper political discourse.

When we turn to the absolutist kingdoms of the eighteenth century such as Denmark–Norway, however, their political implications are undeniable. Personal, absolute, hereditary rule based on secrecy as a principle of government made stories about what goes on off stage, beyond the public gaze, especially in royal beds, not only popular and controversial but also

---

[1] See in particular her essay 'Royal Bodies', written for the *London Review of Books* in 2013, republished in H. Mantel, *Mantel Pieces. Royal Bodies and Other Writing from the London Review of Books* (London, 2020), pp. 269–87.

fundamentally political. Narratives about the secret appetites and hidden affairs of the political elite, circulating by word of mouth or in print, often mixed scandal with detailed accounts of contemporary history and politics. These could prove to be important agents in opinion formation. Moreover, scandalous stories could support Enlightenment ideas of political accountability, transparency and ultimately political alternatives to absolutism. Hence the importance of considering their role in the political culture of pre-democratic states. If books on sex and power did not necessarily cause revolutions, they still contributed to a widely diffused awareness of – and potential critical attitude to – the hidden structures of power and authority among broader groups of subjects.[2] They formed a hybrid kind of literature that sold well and surely appealed to many readers' curiosity while also playing a part in the formation of their burgeoning identities as citizens, in the sense of conceiving themselves as active members of a larger, political community and with the capacity to influence their betterment.

This chapter investigates the presence, popularity and potential impact on political awareness and engagement of the hybrid (semi-historical, semi-fictional) genres of anecdotes, private lives and secret histories in Denmark–Norway during the late eighteenth century. After sketching out this transnational current of literature, I will focus on the library catalogues of two important, but very different, reading institutions situated in the two main cities of the twin kingdom: the library of Drejer's club in Copenhagen (1792) and Diurendahl's lending library in Christiania (1797). While the two book collections vary in size and readerships, they both include a number of titles referring to anecdotes, private lives or secret information or histories. The last part of the chapter will show how the reading of these pan-European genres of 'chronique scandaleuse' and more particularly of 'secret history' influenced the writings of two major Dano-Norwegian intellectuals of the late eighteenth century: Charlotta Dorothea Biehl's 'historical letters' and Peter Frederik Suhm's 'Secret histories of the Danish kings after sovereignty'. Not surprisingly given the censorship conditions, neither of these manuscripts appeared in print during the era of absolutism. Nevertheless, I will argue that they both attest to the impact on political thinking, awareness and culture under absolutism of these specific genres of 'scandalous' literature, which claimed to reveal the 'hidden springs' of political history and the naked truths of statecraft.

---

[2]   On political culture and the importance of print for increasing political awareness among subjects during the Early Modern period, see T. Munck, *Conflict and Enlightenment. Print and Political Culture in Europe 1635–1795* (Cambridge, 2019), p. 5.

Gossip, print and politics

The political significance in pre-revolutionary France of slanderous gossip, seditious accounts of contemporary history and libellous biographies of people in power, circulating from mouth to mouth as well as in manuscript and print, is now well known. Darnton's list of the top forbidden bestsellers in pre-revolutionary France includes several titles of the kind, many of them substantial works in several volumes.[3] They appealed to hungry readers because, as Darnton notes, they were very good reading, but also because they offered an insight into politics and current events that licit literature could not. Slander, immorality, politics and contemporary history were the main targets of censorship regulations, in France as well as in Denmark–Norway. Nevertheless, Darnton shows how pieces of information that often began as oral gossip in the circuit of communication could travel on 'scraps of paper' before they ended up in more or less coherent printed narratives that represented public affairs as the product of private lives. As such, they became central in practices of unmasking politics. 'Anecdotes', 'chronique scandaleuse', 'vie privée', 'mémoires secrètes' were part of an underground literature that nurtured suspicion about the motives and capabilities of those in power. In pre-revolutionary France, by lifting the veil of secrecy in particular ways, they contributed to creating a new public sphere, eroded authority under absolute monarchy and became absorbed in a republican political culture.[4]

Darnton is not alone in pointing out how this current of literature drew on a long history of scandal in print and on techniques developed by earlier authors, such as the late antique Byzantine historian Procopius. His *Anecdota* presented the hitherto 'unknown' and 'unofficial' history of the reign of Emperor Justinian and Empress Theodora and claimed to expose the true, secret, private springs of their public actions. Behind their great public esteem was hidden immoral behaviour and scandalous relations. Over the last three decades scholars have demonstrated how the translations of Procopius' *Anecdota* into French in 1660 and English in 1674 (as *Histoire secrète* and *Secret history*) sparked a stream of 'secret histories' and 'anecdotes' in the fast-growing market of print, adapting the procopian model to various past as well as present European contexts.[5]

---

[3]   R. Darnton, *Forbidden Best-Sellers in Pre-Revolutionary France* (New York, 1996).

[4]   R. Darnton, *The Devil in the Holy Water, or the Art of Slander from Louis XIV to Napoleon* (Philadelphia, 2010), pp. 6–7. See also A. Farge, *Subversive Words. Public Opinion in Eighteenth Century France* (Philadelphia, 1995).

[5]   For instance, E. Tavor Bannet, '"Secret History": Or, Talebearing inside and outside the Secretoire', *Huntington Library Quarterly*, 68/1–2 (2005), 375–96; R. Bullard, *The*

Most of these adaptations promised to present the unofficial side of things, revealing the hidden, secret 'truth' about powerful institutions and people in Europe, past and present. They usually made the claim that the information they conveyed was authentic, based on insiders' eyewitnesses and trustworthy sources, and they frequently reported occurrences of scandalous nature involving sex and abuse of power. In his *Cyclopædia* (1728) Ephraim Chambers notes that 'Anecdotes' is a term used 'by some authors, for the titles of Secret Histories; that is, of such as relate the secret affairs and transactions of princes; speaking with too much freedom, or too much sincerity, of the manner and conduct of persons in authority, to allow of being made public'. He traces the term to Procopius, who 'seems to be the only person among the ancients, who has represented princes, such as they are in their domestic relations'.[6] Throughout the eighteenth century these kinds of representations proliferated across Europe, where they hid under a cover of anonymity and circulated more or less clandestinely, despite continuing danger of prosecution and persecution.

Darnton categorises the French anecdotes, private lives and secret histories as libels, and in the French context, they indeed were.[7] However, as they crossed borders as they increasingly did, whether in original language or in translation, in entire volumes or in bits and pieces, their categorisation and legal status changed. Denmark–Norway had its own local libels, however. Despite the laws that strictly prohibited libel and slander (called *smædeskrifter* or *paskviller*), which made them a main target for censorship restrictions, a rich platter of popular manuscript libels as well as erotic, scandalising literature circulated during the eighteenth century. Christina Holst Færch has shown how this 'unpublishable' literature became more radical after the introduction of absolutism in 1660. She sees the manuscript libels as a profoundly political weapon targeting the Dano-Norwegian elite and suggests that they resulted from the 'information vacuum' caused by the centralisation and secrecy of power. She also points to their importance for the growing political awareness in Denmark–Norway during the eighteenth century.[8]

The political implications of the printed anecdotes, private lives and secret histories imported from abroad were less obvious, however. By the

---

Politics of Disclosure 1674–1725 (London, 2009), and P. Burke, 'Publicizing the Private. The Rise of "Secret History"', in C. J. Emden and D. Midgley (eds), *Changing Perceptions of the Public Sphere* (New York, 2012).

6   E. Chambers, *Cyclopædia* (London, 1728), vol. 1, 'Anecdotes'.

7   R. Darnton, *The Devil*, pp. 266–7.

8   See C. Holst Færch, *Smædeskrifter, sladder og erotiske vers i 1700-tallet. Hans Nordrups forfatterskab* (Copenhagen, 2019), pp. 113, 141, 149.

latter half of the eighteenth century, 'anecdote' had become a versatile label referring to all sorts of short, illustrative accounts. Alongside moral tales and other short prose fiction, newspapers and journals in Denmark–Norway carried historical anecdotes in large numbers, mainly centring on foreign rulers and courts.[9] Anecdotes of even the semi-scandalous and semi-fictitious kinds were commonly ascribed didactic as well as moral functions as historical 'examples'. Intrigues and shady episodes from the private lives of the great past and present could go as moral illustrations, exemplary lessons or warnings from which readers could learn and be amused at the same time.[10] In 1793 the local Jutland magazine *Ribe Stifts Ugeblad* [The Diocese of Ribe's Weekly] addressed the common use and abuse of historical anecdotes in a piece translated from German entitled 'Om Anekdoter især vor Tids' [On anecdotes especially in our time].[11] According to the author, the Hamburg mathematician and publicist J. G. Büsch, anecdotes convey historical information that is not 'commonly known' and they mainly serve as 'bait' and 'spice' for broader readerships who find conventional political history dry and tedious. The noblest kind of anecdotes, however, are those revealing the character or state of mind of historical agents and thereby give access to the hidden springs behind important historical events, Büsch notes. He explicitly connects anecdotes to the genre of 'secret histories' from Procopius.[12] Hence, anecdotes and secret histories were more than didactic examples. According to the essay in the Danish weekly, the most important of them disclosed the deepest truths about history and politics.

As Brian Cowan has recently noted, there are two distinct approaches in scholarship devoted to the growth and significance in Europe of this

---

[9]   On moral tales in periodicals, see A. Nøding's chapter in this book. Claus Fasting's weekly *Provinzialblade* (1778–81) offers a substantial number of historical anecdotes cut and translated from various continental sources alongside short fiction, essays and poems, see A. Nøding, *Claus Fasting. Dikter, journalist og opplysningspioner* (Oslo, 2018).

[10]   What R. Koselleck in *Futures Past: On the Semantics of Historical Time* (Cambridge MA, 1985) coined the *historia magistra vitae* paradigm characterises not only historical writing but saturates the entire printed public sphere in late eighteenth-century Denmark–Norway. For the *historia magistra vitae*-topos in the Dano-Norwegian context, see for instance A. Eriksen, *Livets læremester. Historiske kunnskapstradisjoner i Norge 1650–1840* (Oslo, 2020) and also E. N. Johnsen, 'I Klios forgård. Forfatterroller, offentlighet og politisk evaluering i Niels Ditlev Riegels' (1755–1802) historieskriving', PhD thesis (Oslo, 2019).

[11]   The piece was originally published in *Niederelbischen Magazin*, 1787.

[12]   *Ribe Stifts Ugeblad*, 19 juli (1793), p. 2.

current of literature focusing on the hidden, private lives of people in power.[13] While literary scholars highlight the coherence and self-conscious use of the semi-historical and semi-literary genre of 'secret history', the historical approach has placed the publications in a wider history of writings involved in the 'politics of disclosure', which is seen as responding to the secrecy of politics during the Early Modern period.[14] In the following I will draw on both these approaches when I trace the presence of anecdotes, private lives and secret histories in the two libraries in late eighteenth-century Denmark–Norway and the ways in which Biehl and Suhm demonstrate a self-conscious awareness of the genres in their unpublished writings.

THE LIBRARY OF DREJER'S CLUB IN COPENHAGEN

The late eighteenth century saw the rise of privately or locally organised 'patriotic' societies and clubs all over Europe, focusing on a range of topics of public and 'patriotic' interest.[15] Drejer's club was one of the first and most prominent private literary clubs in Denmark–Norway. Established in Copenhagen in 1775 with regular meetings at the premises of Jacob Drejer, it soon turned into a hub for the intellectual bourgeois elite, gathering writers and literates, philosophers, actors, editors and printers and other defenders of 'Enlightenment' with the common aim of raising awareness of art and social improvement through constructive debate and self-education.[16] During the 1780s the club gained a more political profile, with increased attention to social reforms and issues of practical and political concern. The new liberal regency government established in 1784, lasting right through to the late 1790s, inspired this development. An enlightened

---

[13]   B. Cowan, 'The History of Secret Histories', *Huntington Library Quarterly*, 81/1 (Spring 2018), pp. 121–51.

[14]   The general obsession with secrets and secrecy inside as well as outside the state administration during the early modern period is well documented. See for instance J. Van Horn Melton, *The Rise of the Public in Enlightenment Europe* (Cambridge, 2001). Typically, Geheimeraad, Gehejmekonseil and Geheijmeexpeditionssekretær were titles for the king's closest councilors in Denmark–Norway during the eighteenth century, the period that also saw the rise of Freemasonry and other kinds of secret societies.

[15]   T. Munck, *Conflict and Enlightenment*, p. 254.

[16]   See P.M. Mitchell, 'Biblioteket i Drejers Klub', *Fund og Forskning* 7 (1/1960), 85–99. For the emergence and significance of 'patriotic societies' in Denmark–Norway, see J. Engelhardt, *Borgerskab og fællesskab: de patriotiske selskaber i den danske helstat 1769–1814* (Copenhagen, 2010). A number of clubs emerged across the country based on the model of Drejer's club, including 'Den borgerlige club' in Trondheim in 1783.

PLATE 8.1. Drawing of Drejer's Club in Copenhagen by F. L. Bernth, 1817.

team of ministers (most importantly Reventlow and Bernstorff) initiated
a moderate but wide-ranging reform programme, actively encouraging public discussions and proposals by private individuals.[17] One of the
prominent members of Drejer's club, literary critic and translator Knud
Lyne Rahbek, who was also co-editor of the moderate reformist monthly
journal *Minerva* (1785–1807), notes in his later memoires of the gatherings
at Drejer's how interest in 'public matters' and expectations for the future
developed in the club in this period. To him, the club's significance in the
new, emerging political culture was undeniable: 'the public opinion visited
us willingly and frequently, often raised its voice among our midst, and
developed from there'.[18]

---

[17] T. Munck, 'The Danish Reformers', in *Enlightened Absolutism. Reform and Reformers in Later Eighteenth Century Europe*, ed. H. M. Scott (London, 1990), pp. 245–63,
and T. Munck, *Conflict and Enlightenment*, pp. 277–8.

[18] 'Den almene Mening giæstede os ofte og gierne, ikke sielden opløftede sin Stemme i
vor Midie, og udgik herfra'. Rahbek in *Erindringer af mit Liv*, III (Copenhagen, 1825),
p. 37. All translations in this chapter by me, if not otherwise stated.

Typically, the activities of Drejer's club were explicitly formulated in bylaws ['lover'], which served as a marker of the club's independence and self-organisation as a kind of cultural and even political community.[19] The publication of the bylaws in 1780 demonstrates the importance of print and literary activities. Half of the eighty-eight paragraphs were devoted to the club's library, or 'reading society' as it was called, and its administration. In addition to prescribing the members' access to newspapers and journals, the book collection was supposed to include: 'fine arts and sciences ['de skiønne Videnskaber'], universal history, history of the fatherland, and eventually one or maximum two classical works on each of the other reign's history, the history of man, culture, arts and sciences, as well as popular philosophy. As regards languages of publication, they were restricted to Danish, Swedish, German, French and English'.[20] The collection was divided into an *in situ* and an ambulant part. Auctions were held twice a year where members could buy books from the ambulant part, and the income from the auction was, together with a monthly membership fee, used to acquire new books. The laws also included detailed prescriptions for the administration of storage, cataloguing and lending. When the library catalogue of Drejer's club appears in print in 1792 (entitled *Bogsamling i klubben opprettet i november 1775*), however, it does not bear marks of clear principles of classification. Nevertheless, the collection of 1,837 volumes reveals some interesting characteristics, demonstrating for instance a surprisingly multilingual and international literary orientation, mainly towards the contemporary world, which mirrors some general European trends in the late eighteenth-century book market.[21]

The majority of the titles are from the second half of the eighteenth century, and almost 500 of them from the 20 years prior to the catalogue's publication. German titles dominate, 327 compared with 232 Danish titles and 69 French. Only ten titles are English, a single one in Latin. The books bear witness to the up-to-date tastes and elite bourgeois interests of the club members, who preferred contemporary authors and topics to the classics, enlightenment to erudition. There is a striking lack of theology and religious works. Significant titles from the French, English and German Enlightenments (including an edition of *L'Encyclopédie*) are listed. Among the Danish titles, there is a substantial number of translations (22 from German, 12 from French, 12 from English and 8 from Latin). Literary works of various

[19] For the possible political dimensions of institutions such as libraries, see discussion by M. Towsey and K. Roberts in their 'Introduction', *Before the Public Library* (Leiden, 2018), p. 19.
[20] Quoted from P. Mitchell, 'Biblioteket', p. 87.
[21] See G. Dahl, *Books in Early Modern Norway* (Leiden, 2011), p. 9.

sorts dominate together with 'historical books'. In eighteenth-century Den-mark–Norway, this large category included a range of different 'histories told' about individuals, peoples, places, artefacts and events. Biographies, topographical descriptions as well as travel literature belonged to 'history', besides the various accounts of the past in works by proper 'historians', such as Ludvig Holberg. Often, even pure fiction could appear under the general label 'history', such as in Caspar Herman von Storm's book collec-tion, which went on auction in Christiania in 1772.[22] Anecdotes, private lives and secret histories certainly belong to the composite category of history, and we should not be surprised to find them included in the collec-tion of Drejer's club in Copenhagen. This hybrid category of semi-fictional, semi-historical literature would fit with the members' appetite for prose fiction, history writing as well as news and current affairs in Europe, even in the form of slanderous biographies and scandalous political narratives.

The catalogue includes at least six titles that connect to the pan-Euro-pean current of literature focusing on the hidden, private lives of powerful public personages.[23] Another two entries include the key word 'anecdotes' in their title. The first, *Journal et anecdotes intéressantes du Voyage de Mr. le Comte de Falckenstein, par Mr. l'Abbé Duval Pyrau* (1777) appears to be quite a conventional travel report, lacking focus on the hidden, private world of politics. The other, *En reisende Russers Anecdoter over de danskes Statsforfatning, Sæder og Skikke* (A Travelling Russian's Anecdotes of the Danish Government, Manners and Customs), published in Copenhagen in 1771, contains critical observations on the commerce, the laws, the state of learning, the hankering after rank and the position of women, among other things, in Denmark–Norway, all quite typical for the period of the free-dom of the press 1770–3. A more noticeable entry in the library of Drejer's club is *Vie privée de Louis XV. Ou principaux évènements, particularités et anecdotes de son règne*, probably by Moufle d'Angerville, one of the forbid-den bestsellers in Europe in the period.[24] It came in several editions from

[22]   G. Dahl, *Books*, pp. 176–77. On the category of 'history' in book collections, see also
        G. Dahl, *Libraries and Enlightenment. Eighteenth Century Norway and the Outer
        World*, (Aarhus, 2014).
[23]   I have focused on titles that include the words anecdote, private or secret and refer
        to the political elite.
[24]   According to Darnton's estimations, fifteen of the top hundred works on the STN
        bestseller list were *libelles* or *chroniques scandaleuses*, with *Vie privée* in 32nd place.
        R. Darnton, *The Forbidden Best-Sellers*, p. 138. See also his 'Mlle Bonnafon and "La
        vie privée de Louis XV"', *Dix-huitième Siècle* 35 (2003), p. 369. The STN online da-
        tabase (by Burrows and Curran) gives a hint of the broad distribution across Europe
        of this four-volume work.

1781 and gave a detailed, amusing and seemingly authoritative account of French political history from 1715 to 1774 through an extraordinary unveiling of the domestic world of the French king. The printer's preface places the work within the genre of contemporary history, presenting for the first time 'the entire life of a prince', painted 'in natural', based on collected pieces of eyewitness testimony.[25] The narrative includes details about his genital abnormality, numerous mistresses (such as the famous Mme de Pompadour and La comtesse du Barry) and various scandalous incidents, demonstrating how the monarchy had been degenerating since the time of Louis XIV. According to Darnton, *Vie privée de Louis XV* supplied 'a master narrative for contemporary history' that fuelled new waves of political slander and anti-ministerial pamphleteering during the very last years of Bourbon absolutism in France.[26] Exactly how it was read and potentially discussed in Drejer's club or elsewhere we cannot not know for sure, but the book was advertised in 1782 in *Kiøbenhavns Adresse-Contoirs Efterretninger*, the most important newspaper at the time (of the *feuilles du bureau d'adresse* kind), together with other French titles sold at 'Pierre Steinmann, vis-à-vis L'Eglise de la Garnison'.[27]

It is the secret affairs and hidden, private worlds of foreign kings and courts that appear among the entries in Drejer's club's catalogue. It includes *Anecdoter om Kongen av Preussens private liv* (Anecdotes of the King of Prussia's private life), translated into Danish and printed in Copenhagen in 1778, and *Geheime Geschichte des Berliner Hofes*, 1789, in two volumes. This is most probably the German translation of the French *Histoire secrète de la cour de Berlin, ou Correspondance d'un voyageur François depuis le mois de Juillet 1786 jusqu'au 19 Janvier 1787*, originally published anonymously as 'Ouvrage posthume' without place of publication in 1789, but easily attributed to the famous Honoré-Gabriel de Riquetti de Mirabeau. *Characters and Anecdotes of the Court of Sweden*, in two volumes in English from 1790, is also listed in a German translation published the same year. The most interesting and surprising entry given the official censorship regulation is the one of *Geheime Hof. U. Staatsgeschichte des Königreichs Dänemark, v. Marquv. L. D'Yves* from 1790, which offers a veritable 'secret history' of the recent political history of Denmark–Norway, in German. 'Germanien' is the place of publication given on the title page, commonly used as a cover for Osiander publishing house in Tübingen. Marquis d'Yves was a

[25]   *Vie privée de Louis XV. Ou principaux évènements, particularités et anecdotes de son règne* (London, 1784), 'Avertissement du libraire', vol. 1, pp. 2–3.
[26]   R. Darnton, *The Forbidden Best-Sellers*, pp. 78–9.
[27]   *Kiøbenhavns Adresse-Contoirs Efterretninger* (KA), 16 January 1782, p. 7.

pseudonym used by Friedrich Buchwald, who had served in a prominent role at the Danish court after the fall of Struensee. The tiny book, 117 pages long, centres on the political history of Denmark–Norway 'after the revolution of Struensee', as indicated in the subtitle. Struensee was the royal physician to Christian VII who during an intense sixteen months from 1770 to 1772 gained control over the political machine in Denmark–Norway, introducing a large number of political reforms inspired by Enlightenment ideas. *Geheime Hof und Staats-Geschichte* starts out pointing to a 'huge secret of the state' concerning the extremely delicate question of succession to the throne after the fall of Struensee.[28] Struensee's 'revolution' was made possible by Christian VII's mental illness, and the pamphlet reveals the hidden battles over succession in the case of the premature death of the king. Christian's heir was only four years old in 1772, when the Dowager Queen Juliana Maria and her son and Christian VII's half-brother, Hereditary Prince Frederick, led the coup against Struensee. Apparently, the question of succession was still relevant at the time of publication of Buchwald's pamphlet in 1790, although Christian VII's son Frederick had served as 'crown prince regent' since 1784. The book even discusses the healthy princess Louise Augusta (by Queen Caroline Mathilde, whose father was probably Struensee) as a rightful heir to the throne. While the critical review in the German *Allgemeine Literatur-Zeitung* shows more interest in commercial and military aspects of the account, it definitely takes it seriously as historical writing.[29] The readers in Drejer's club would probably be more attentive to the politically sensitive topic of succession. Either way, the book proves to what extent contemporary, political history could traverse linguistic and geographical borders, and probably speak differently to readers of various nationalities. It also proves that 'secret history' could be more than 'good reading'. The account of hidden events and eventualities relating to the future of the Dano-Norwegian kingdom in *Geheime Hof und Staats-Geschichte* was literature of a decidedly political character that somehow had circumnavigated censorship regulations, and which we must assume played a part in the rise of political awareness and discussions among the members of Drejer's club.

---

[28] *Geheime Hof und Staats-Geschichte des Königreichs Dänemark, Von dem Marquis Ludwig d'Yves. Zeiten nach der Struenseeischen Revolution* (Germanien, 1790), p. 1.

[29] *Allgemeine Literatur-Zeitung*, no. 28, January (1791), pp. 20–4.

DIURENDAHL'S LENDING LIBRARY CATALOGUE

Diurendahl's lending library in Christiania, the unofficial capital of the Norwegian realm, was a completely different reading institution compared to Drejer's club in Copenhagen. The commercial lending library grew out of Andreas Diurendahl's bookseller business in 1785.[30] Christiania readers could borrow books from Diurendahl against a fee, the size of which varied according to the title. During the eighteenth century, private and public book collections were made accessible to a range of different readers in various ways across Norway. From 1785 Christiania readers could borrow books from Carl Deichman's private library. Deichman's collection was much larger, it was free of charge, but it also had a more learned and exclusive profile than Diurendahl's library. As a commercial lending library, Diurendahl's selection of titles was certainly more adapted to the interests and tastes of a broader, bourgeois readership, and the more extensive opening hours (12 hours a day) contributed to the success of the library.

A catalogue of Diurendahl's lending library was published in 1797, as an advertisement, and included the lending conditions.[31] It contains 241 titles, of which some had several volumes and others were books that assembled several individual titles, ordered alphabetically. The lack of conventional religious or edifying books is striking, light entertaining prose genres dominate (novels and gallant novellas, collections of moral tales and traditional legends, exotic travel narratives and various kinds of history books, including biographical literature), and the focus on women, practical education and domestic life in quite a number of titles indicate a substantial female readership.[32] With very few exceptions, the books are in Danish, many of them translations of important foreign literary works, especially novels (*Pamela, Anti-Pamela, Don Quixote* for instance). Most interesting in our

[30] Diurendahl's was probably the first successful public lending library in Norway. The number of lending libraries and private reading societies in Norway increased decisively from the early nineteenth century. See E. S. Eide, 'Reading Societies and Lending Libraries in Nineteenth-Century Norway', *Library and Information History* 26:2 (2010), 121–38. See also K. Kukkonen's chapter in this volume and M. Björkman, 'Läsarnas nöje. Kommersiella lånbibliotek i Stockholm 1783–1809', PhD thesis (Uppsala, 1992), concerning Sweden.

[31] A. Diurendahl, *Fortegnelse over Endeel indbundne Bøger, Som ere til Leje hos Boghandler Diurendahl i Christiania, paa efterstaaende Conditioner* (Christiania, 1797).

[32] The turn from edifying literature to worldly practical advice books and all kinds of history in women's reading in late eighteenth-century Scandinavia is demonstrated by L. Byberg, '"Jeg gik i ingen Skole, jeg havde min Frihed hele Dagen og Nøglen til hans Bogskab". Kvinners lesning på 1700-tallet', *Historisk tidsskrift*, 90:2 (2011), 159–88, and M. Björkman, 'Läsernas nöje'.

context, however, is the supply of titles belonging to the current of hybrid political-historical literature. Diurendahl's lending library holds a number of anecdotes, private lives and secret histories from courts across Europe. Thus, it provides the readers with peepholes into the world of European politics and contemporary history from a perspective that the authors pretended to convey the secret, inside version of events, which could not be found in conventional accounts.

The sixth entry in Diurendahl's catalogue is *Anecdoter om Peter den store* [Anecdotes of Peter the Great], which is probably identical to *Original-Anekdoter om Peter den Store. Samlede af Anseelige Personers mundtlige Fortællinger i Moskau og Petersborg, og opbevarede for Efterslægten, af Jacob von Stählin*, translated into Danish by a Christian Dreyer in 1793. Stählin presents the curious and entertaining stories from the Russian court as authentic and partly initiated by the tsar himself.[33] The following catalogue entry is a collection that includes several titles, listed as follows: *Anecdoter og Efterretninger om Gustav den 3die, samt om hans Brødre og Søn* [Anecdotes and Histories of Gustav III and his Brothers and Son]; 2) *Hemmelige Efterretninger fra Satans Hof* [Secret histories of the court of Satan]; 3) *Campes Advarsel for den mandlige Ungdom* [Warning for the male youth by Campe]; 4) *Henzes opdagede Hemmelighed ved Børneavlinger* [The secret of procreation discovered by Henze], etc., etc. The first is probably an abridged Danish translation from *Characters and Anecdotes of the Court of Sweden* by the proliferous Swedish literate Adolf Fredrik Ristell, published in English in London in 1790. While the Swedish translation of these supposedly trustworthy anecdotes and secret histories from the hidden, private world of Gustav III and his brothers did not appear until 1820, the Danish translation is from 1792. Gustav III had seized power from the government in a coup d'état in 1772 and restored absolutism in Sweden. He was assassinated by a gunshot during a masked ball in 1772, a dramatic incident that gave rise to the Danish translation, whose precise title is 'Anecdotes and relations of the recently killed Gustav III.'[34] The second text that figures in the collection of 'secrets' in the seventh entry is the satirical

---

33 The German historian, writer on music and fireworks designer Jacob Stählin held several positions at the imperial court in St Peterburg from 1735. The Danish translation was advertised repeatedly in KA (including, on 21 May 1793, a note on how the anecdotes are amusing and useful/instructive at the same time). It was also advertised in *Norske Intelligenz-Sedler* (NIS) in Christiania.

34 The book is advertised for sale at Diurendahl's bookshop several times in the local Christiania newspaper NIS (6 June and 13 June 1792 and again on 28 January 1795). Also advertised in KA (27 April 1792, 27 April and 7 May 1796). It is briefly reviewed in Tode's Copenhagen review journal *Kritik og Antikritik* in 1792 (pp. 114–15).

'Secret histories of the court of Satan, with an introduction' by Anton Franz Just, published in the Danish town of Viborg in 1794.[35] This pure satirical use of the 'secret history' shows the extent to which the genre had developed a recognisable identity, open to mock versions, even in Denmark–Norway.

Diurendahl's lending library also holds *Geheime Beretning om Kong Georg den førstes Gemahlinde, hendes ulykkelige Historie* (Secret account of the wife of King George I, her sad story), whose full title is *Geheime Beretning om Danmarks og Norges Rigers Dronning Caroline Mathildes Frue Olde-Moder, Kong Georg den Førstes af Stor-Britannien Gemahlinde: denne ulykkelige Printsesses vanheldige Skiebne, hendes Fengsel paa Slottet Ahlen, samt hendes geheime Underhandlinger med Greven af Kønigsmark, som mistænkt blev myrdet.* This 'secret history' of the great-grandmother of Queen Caroline Mathilde was published in Viborg in 1773, shortly after the queen's exile following the Struensee affair.[36] The library also offers *Anecdoter om Friederich den 2den, Konge i Preussen* [Anecdotes of Frederick II, King of Prussia], which is probably identical to the *Anecdoter om Kongen av Preussens private Liv* in the library of Drejer's club, by the German musician Johann Adolph Schribe and translated into Danish anonymously as *Nyeste Anekdoter om Kongen av Preuszens Privat-levnet, tilligemed Anmerkninger over de Preusiske Armeers Krigs-forfatning* and published in Copenhagen in 1778 (by Christian Gottlob Proft). Also listed is the *Hemmelige Efterretninger om det Berlinske Hof* [Secret histories of the court of Berlin], a Danish translation by J. H. Meier from 1790 of the same controversial book by Mirabeau (*Histoire secrète de la cour de Berlin, ou correspondance d'un voyageur français*) that we find in a German version in the library of Drejer's club. Diurendahl's also includes *Baron Trencks politiske undersøgelse af samme* [Count Trenck's political investigation of the same] in Danish translation from 1790. Mirabeau's unscrupulous use of information that he had gathered on his secret mission in Berlin to disclose the amorous and political intrigues of the Prussian court caused a diplomatic scandal in France, and the book was banned shortly before the outbreak of the revolution in 1789. The ban apparently fuelled its popularity, and Friederich von der Trenck, who had served under Frederick the Great, took on the job of refuting Mirabeau's scandalous accounts. In his *Examen politique d'un ouvrage intitule Histoire secrète de la cour de Berlin* (1790) the author claims to establish the genuine and reliable truth about 'the Prussian court

---

[35] *Hemmelige Efterretninger fra Satans Hof* was advertised in NIS (9 September 1795).
[36] *Geheime beretning* was advertised repeatedly in NIS (14 October 1789, 5 May 1790, 13 April 1791, 18 July 1792).

and the springs of the Prussian machine.'[37] Diurendahl's library offers the readers both versions of the state of affairs in the absolute monarchy of Frederick II's Prussia.

The stock of anecdotes, private lives and secret histories in Diurendahl's commercial lending library gives a good indication of the relatively broad popularity of this current of literature in Christiania during the 1790s. As with the books in Drejer's club, we cannot know for certain how the readers responded to them. They must have appealed to the readers' appetite for entertaining, piquant narratives and to a genuine interest in current affairs in Europe. Many of the titles held by the two libraries, both original and in Danish translations, were widely advertised in newspapers and weeklies among other light entertaining books as well as more prominent enlightenment publications. When the Danish translations of Mirabeau and Trenck are reviewed in the major learned journal *Lærde Efterretninger*, the books are taken as signs of a general appetite for 'the scandalous and the critical' as well as for 'libels' (*paskviller*) and their refutations among the reading public. However, both reviewers side with Mirabeau in his 'secret' accounts of Prussian politics.[38] The readings by the borrowers from Diurendahl's more popular library probably varied from the naïve and curious to the more sophisticated and critical. These books can have been read as pure entertainment or as a kind of moral lessons in line with the *historia magistra vitae* paradigm, but they still provided a certain kind of insight into contemporary history and the political worlds and mechanisms in Europe at the time. Titles in Diurendahl's such as *Secret histories from the court of Satan* show that the readers were even offered self-conscious, playful versions of this particular genre of historical writing, which is often claimed to be based on truthful facts but not always meant to be taken literally.

Satirical or historical, fictitious or not, anecdotes and secret histories of the kind we find in Diurendahl's library nevertheless expose – even for

---

[37] *Trenk contra Mirabeau, eller Politisk og Kritisk Undersøgelse af Skriftet: Hemmelige Efterretninger om det Berlinske Hof, eller en reisende Franskmands Brevvexling* (Copenhagen, 1790), p. 4.

[38] The Danish translation of Mirabeau's secret histories was advertised in KA 2 December 1789. The advertisement also refers to the forthcoming *Trenk contra Mirabeau* by the same translator. *Trenk contra Mirabeau* was also advertised several times in NIS during 1791 and 1792. Mirabeau's text in Danish was reviewed in the Copenhagen journal *Lærde Efterretninger* (1790, pp. 185–90) and very briefly in Tode's *Kritik og Antikritik* (1790, p. 109). *Trenk contra Mirabeau* was reviewed, probably by the same reviewer, in *Lærde Efterretninger* in 1791 (pp. 13–15) and extensively in Tode's *Kritik og Antikritik*. While the reviewer questions Trenck's refusal of Mirabeau's revelations, he recommends the book to both 'the thoughtful as well as the purely curious reader' (vol. 7, p. 187).

broader readerships of both sexes in the provincial town of Christiania – a hidden side of statecraft and contemporary history. Most of them do convey a general impression of decadence and despotism. Moreover, while all the titles in Diurendahl's catalogue focus on foreign rulers and courts, we can assume that readers would be able to relate the hidden affairs and mechanisms as well as the politics of disclosure itself to the Dano-Norwegian context. Here, politics was still officially defined as the private business of sovereigns and banned from the public discourse in most forms.

BIEHL'S 'CHRONIQUE SCANDALEUSE' AND SUHM'S 'SECRET HISTORY'

Given the censorship regulations in Denmark–Norway under absolutism, which also targeted the import of foreign literature, the very presence of this current of underground literature in the two different library catalogues is noteworthy. A more liberal view on print and political debate by the government during the period 1785 to 1799, the moral didactic potential of anecdotes and 'histories' and the often playful tone and ambiguous status of this literature as something that should not be taken too seriously neither by authorities nor readers may be part of the explanation. However, to publish or offer anecdotes or secret histories of what happened in the inner cabinet or court of the contemporary Dano-Norwegian monarchy, in Danish, for Danish and Norwegian readers, would probably not be possible without persecution. Nonetheless, we do know that two of the most prominent enlightenment intellectuals at the time, Charlotta Dorothea Biehl (1731–88) and Peter Frederik Suhm (1728–98), were not only among the sophisticated readers of this current of literature but even took inspiration from the hybrid genres in their own, unpublished writings.

Biehl was raised in the outer circles of the Danish court, and through self-study she became an important intellectual in Copenhagen. She was renowned for her epistolary novel, poems, moral tales and comedies as well as her translations from English, French, Italian and Spanish, of which her most famous is *Don Quixote* (1776–7). In 1784 Biehl was encouraged by her intimate friend at the court Johan Bülow to write him letters on the contemporary political history of Denmark–Norway. Bülow is the chamberlain of Crown Prince Frederik (later Frederick VI), and he provides her with important source material, especially on the very latest happenings at court. The result is a series of 'historical letters' where Biehl presents and analyses the human characters, physical and moral deficits, indecent relations and secret motives that are deemed the true driving forces behind the reigns of Frederick IV, Christian VI, Frederick V and Christian VII, the

Struensee period and the coup by Crown Prince Frederick in 1784. In what she herself calls 'a sketch of the recent Danish history' she describes, in great detail, sicknesses, births and sexual excesses at court and how domestic life and bodily lusts and insufficiencies affect public decisions and the course of events. Anne-Marie Mai has called the letters 'the history of sexuality during the reigns of Christian VI, Frederick V and Christian VII' in which Biehl traces the springs of all the problems and bad decision back to the relations between the sexes and ruthless education.[39] Biehl herself, however, explicitly attaches her accounts to a particular genre of political historical writing, the 'chronique scandaleuse': 'I have wanted to convey to you the *Histoire Scandaleuse* in one unbroken chain', she tells Bülow in one of the letters.[40]

'Histoire' or 'chronique scandaleuse' is probably the most openly provocative of the key words used in titles belonging to this current of literature involved in the 'politics of disclosure' in early modern Europe. A descendant of French heroic romance, the 'chroniques scandaleuse' in various formats had gained success in the underground market of print in France as well as in England during the latter part of the seventeenth century. The genre's popularity reached a climax in pre-revolutionary France, first with *Le Gazetier cuirassé, ou anecdotes scandaleuses de la cour de France* (by Charles Thévenau de Morandes, anonymously published) appearing in 1771, at the height of the greatest political crisis during the reign of Louis XV. It contains endless anecdotes about prostitutes and their aristocratic clients, venereal diseases and other slanderous episodes, targeting the leading figures in the French government, recounted in an open mixture of fact and fiction that left it to the readers to sift the truth from the rumours, as a kind of game.[41] More publications of a similar kind followed, most famously *La Chronique scandaleuse, ou Mémoires pour server à l'histoire de la génération présente, contenant les anecdotes et pièces fugitives les plus piquantes que l'histoire secrète des sociétés a offertes pendant ces dernières années* (1783–8), which conspicuously includes all the attractively ambiguous key words in an elaborate subtitle. Biehl was apparently well acquainted with the genre of 'histoire scandaleuse' even before this last publication

---

[39] A.-M. Mai, 'Historien som scene hos Ludvig Holberg og Charlotta Dorothea Biehl', *Sjuttonhundratal*, 8 (2011), p. 203.

[40] 'Da jeg har vildet meddele Dem *L'Histoire Scandaleuse* i en uafbrudt Kiede, saa nödes jeg nu at gaae langt tilbake i Tiiden'. 'Charlotta Dorothea Biehls Historiske breve', *Historisk tidsskrift*, vol. 3, række 4 (Copenhagen, 1865–6), p. 266.

[41] R. Darnton, *The Devil*, pp. 17, 21. We know that the pamphlet was read in Copenhagen during the Struensee period by Luxdorph, see H. Horstbøll *et al.*, *Grov Konfækt*, I (Copenhagen, 2020), p. 39.

appeared in France, although her own 'historical letters' uses the scandalous, private details from the Danish court in a more analytical and compassionate way than most of the French libels. Rather than try to denounce ministerial despotism in the Dano-Norwegian monarchy, Biehl seems to want to explain the political problems by pointing to the all too human side of royals. Moreover, her letters are not written in order to shock and amuse a broad reading public hungry for scandals. As Sebastian Olden-Jørgensen argues, their content may have been intended as a record of contemporary history for use and interpretation by future historians, according to the ancient Greek Lucian's distinction between histories of the past and those of the contemporary world.[42] In any case, the letters remained unpublished until 1865, when they appeared in the Danish scholarly journal *Historisk tidsskrift* as 'Charlotte Dorothea Biehls historiske Breve (meddelte af J. H. Bang efter Originalerne, som findes i Sorø Academis Manuskriptsamling Nr. 71, 20)'.

Like Biehl, Peter Frederik Suhm also left an unpublished manuscript on the 'unofficial' political history of the recent past of the Dano-Norwegian monarchy. Suhm was a high-profile intellectual, renowned historian and an extraordinarily prolific writer who published in many learned as well as more popularising genres. He was a member of Drejer's club in Copenhagen for several years. He developed radical political ideas, some of which he tried to make public in different ways, with varying success *vis-à-vis* the censorship authorities.[43] During his years in Trondheim in Norway he co-founded the Royal Norwegian Society of Sciences and Letters (1760). This is also where he started spending his considerable fortune on collecting books. The book collection came to comprise around 100,000 volumes, and he opened it to public use in Copenhagen in 1775. Unfortunately, there is no existing catalogue of this collection, which was purchased by the Royal Library in 1797. In 1811 the doublets were offered to the new Norwegian University Library in Christiania, which is why we find many eighteenth-century books carrying Suhm's signature or ex libris in today's National Library of Norway.[44]

When the publication of Suhm's complete works in sixteen volumes was completed (posthumously) in 1799 it contained several of his most

[42]   S. Olden-Jørgensen, 'En fortidshistoriker og en samtidshistoriker. Ludvig Holberg og Charlotta Dorothea Biehl', *Temp. Tidsskrift for historie*, 17 (2018), pp. 54–6.

[43]   See E. Krefting, 'De usminkede sannhetenes forsvar. Peter Frederik Suhms publikasjonsstrategier og offentlighetsidealer under det dansk-norske eneveldet', in A. M. B. Bjørkøy *et al.* (eds), *Litterære verdensborgere: Transnasjonale perspektiver på norsk bokhistorie 1519–1850* (Oslo, 2019), pp. 332–76.

[44]   See E. Eide, 'Reading Societies'.

controversial manuscripts and works, some of which had never been published before. One manuscript that remained excluded, however, was his 'Hemmelige efterretninger om de danske konger efter soveraineteten' [Secret histories of the Danish Kings after Sovereignty]. It was not published until 1918, more than half a century after the publication of Biehl's 'histoires scandaleuses'.

Suhm's manuscript gives a dense and concise account of the political history of Denmark–Norway from the introduction of absolutism in 1660 until the death of Queen Caroline Mathilde in 1775, three years after the fall of her lover, Struensee. The text was probably conceived in this latter period. Like Biehl's historical letters, it may have been intended for the use of future historians. No more than 80 pages long, it begins with well-known accounts of the legitimate introduction of absolutism in 1660, when the assembly of the four estates freely transferred all power to the hereditary throne. The narrative then turns to the hidden aspects of the history, recounting how the ambitious Queen Sophie Amalie to Frederick III played a crucial part in the introduction of absolutism, which 'for the time present liberated the country from the chains of the aristocracy' but soon degraded into a series of despotic acts based on the highly affective personalities of the royals.[45] Suhm sums up the different characters and mental dispositions of the succeeding kings and the people in their surroundings that influence the execution of power. Like Biehl, he traces the 'secret springs' of their actions back to moral deficiencies, bodily lusts and shortcomings and the relation between the sexes at court. The narrative reaches its apex in the accounts of Christian VII and the Struensee period, with all its physical and moral excesses. Suhm describes how 'the king was skinny and weak. The queen strong and fat, and he only preferred skinny women of a good *taille*; sufficient reason for disagreement. Therefore, they did not have sex for months'.[46] Struensee, however, took advantage of the queen's voluptuousness, which resulted in a 'bastard', Suhm notes.

Not only does the manuscript's title attest to Suhm's familiarity with the genre of secret history; early in the text he explains why his accounts are entitled 'secret histories'. Actively deploying the procopian *anekdota* motive, he declares that he narrates 'things that are not to be found in printed books and that cannot be found there, at least not in books printed

---

[45] 'befriede landet for nærværende tid fra adelens haarde slag'. P. F. Suhm, *Hemmelige efterretninger: om de danske konger efter souveraineteten*, meddelte ved Julius Clausen (Copenhagen, 1918), p. 7.

[46] 'kongen var smækker og svag. Dronningen sterk og feed og han kunde ei lide uden smækre Fruentimmer og af god taille; Leilighed nok til Uenighed. De laae derfor i hele Maaneder ei sammen'. P. Suhm, *Hemmelige efterretninger*, p. 49.

in this country, and therefore with time would be forgotten.'[47] He presents the unofficial, hitherto unknown history of the Dano-Norwegian absolute monarchy. Suhm also insists, like nearly every secret history before his, on the factual liability of his accounts by claiming that the information relies on trustworthy persons' 'eyewitness' testimonies (including his father's) and even on his own, personal observations. Last but not the least, his 'secrets' refer to a specific kind of historical causality, pointing to the deep, hidden springs of politics and therefore also the true mechanisms of history. Behind the public chain of events there are always the private, domestic, intimate, bodily worlds of the people in power. The real and true causes of the degeneration of the monarchy of Denmark–Norway after 1660 are to be found behind the curtains, in royal beds.

Suhm's secret histories remained secrets and did not appear in print until long after the end of absolutism. We can easily understand why. His narrative does not present itself as an entertaining, piquant, playful piece of text, thriving on the blurred boundaries between fact and fiction, history and allegory. The text shows the extent to which this kind of writing of contemporary history was not only frivolous, but also deeply political. Suhm was probably one of the most radical critics of absolutist hereditary monarchy as a political system in eighteenth century Denmark–Norway. His 'rules of government', suggested in an appendix to a privately distributed edition of his political novel *Euphron* in 1774, attest to this.[48] Yet nowhere is his critique of absolutism demonstrated more empathically than in the 'secret histories of the Danish Kings after Sovereignty', where he reveals why states should be ruled by laws, and not people above them.

CONCLUSION

The presence of anecdotes, private lives and secret histories in the two very different libraries, as well as the clear traces of the genres in the unpublished writings of Biehl and Suhm, show how this pan-European current of literature reached readerships of different kinds in Denmark–Norway during the latter part of the eighteenth century. The popularity of the texts revealing the hidden sides of politics and contemporary history spanned from the intellectual elite in Copenhagen to the broader, bourgeois book

---

[47]   'Ting, som ei findes i trykte Bøger og som til dels ei kan findes der, i det mindste i saadanne, som trykkes heri Landet, og hvilke derover vilde med Tiden komme i Forglemmelse'. P. Suhm, *Hemmelige efterretninger*, p. 7.

[48]   The version of *Euphron* including the suggestion of a new form of government, in effect a constitutional monarchy, was published posthumously in 1799 in vol. 16 of his 'collected writings' (*Suhms Samlede Skrifter*), pp. 29–36.

consumers, including women, in Christiania. The two libraries share an astonishing international outlook and interest in current affairs of Europe, while Drejer's club also confirms the multilingual characteristic of Scandinavian literary culture in the late eighteenth century.[49] However, Diurendahl's shows that anecdotes, private lives and secret histories were not only imported and read in foreign languages. Many of the 'secret' accounts from foreign courts, even the Swedish court of Gustav III, were translated into Danish, which indicates that translators and booksellers saw the commercial potential in this hybrid literature, appearing enticingly at the boundaries between fact and fiction, public and private worlds, entertainment, moral instruction and politics. In the news press the translations were advertised among titles of a more political kind as well as among light entertaining fiction or didactic books, many of them specifically addressing female readers such as the popular genre of 'New Year's gifts'.

How the different titles in foreign languages and Danish translations were actually read and potentially discussed among the users of the two libraries, we cannot know. I have not tried to broach the complicated task of tracing individual readers' reactions or discussions in this chapter. We might, however, assume that they influenced political awareness and discussion among the consumers at some level. Given what Færch has argued about the impact on political awareness and public opinion of manuscript libels with slanderous and erotic content involving people in power, the potential impact of the printed anecdotes, private lives and secret histories on the individual as well as the collective attentiveness to the hidden structures of power and authority is considerable – despite the fact that the majority of the available titles mainly centred on foreign politics and contemporary history. The German account in Drejer's club of the secrets of the Danish court 'after the revolution of Struensee' is the exception. This *Geheime Hof und Staats-Geschichte* was undeniably a text of high political significance, and its very presence in a Danish collection raises intriguing questions. Moreover, together with the anecdotes from the Swedish court this publication also demonstrates how accounts of this kind not only travelled from Europe to Scandinavia, but even from Sweden and Denmark–Norway to the continent, and back again.

The unpublished manuscripts of Charlotta Dorothea Biehl and Peter Frederik Suhm are the most explicit witnesses of a sophisticated familiarity with the scandalous and critical genres of anecdotes, private lives and secret histories in Denmark–Norway. The texts by these two literary citizens of the world do not only attest to a deeply political reading and

---

[49]   See M. Björkman, 'Läsernas nöje', p. 336.

understanding of this European current of literature. Their careful adaptations of the transnational genres of 'chroniques scandaleuses' and 'secret history' in a contemporary, Dano-Norwegian political setting also demonstrate how these genres held the potential of a deep political critique of absolute, hereditary monarchic rule. The potential political effects of this kind of 'politics of disclosure' explain why the two texts remained 'unpublishable' until long after the end of absolutism in Norway and Denmark.

9

From the Dictated Lecture to the Printed Textbook: The Circulation of Notes in the Teaching of Philosophy in Denmark–Norway, 1790–1850

Thor Inge Rørvik

THIS CHAPTER WILL TAKE a closer look at an activity that, together with the disputation, has characterised European universities since the Middle Ages, namely the academic lecture. This way of teaching has not only survived all forms of criticism and attempts to modernise the institution, but it has also remained somewhat the same up until the present day, despite the abundance of digital aids at our disposal. This makes it all the more striking that the academic lecture seems to have received little attention from university historians, who rather focus on how a small number of well-known professors at a given institution have contributed to the scientific progress. Their role as teachers or, for that matter, the role of the university itself as an institution where knowledge is disseminated and transmitted to generations of students, thereby introducing them to an academic literary citizenship, has, among most scholars, simply not been regarded as a particularly interesting topic.[1]

---

[1] There are, of course, exceptions to the rule. See for instance J. McLeish, *The Lecture Method* (Cambridge, 1968), although the historical references here are sparse. More thorough is A. Bruter, 'Le cours magistral comme objet d'histoire', *Histoire de l'éducation*, 120:4 (2008) [Special issue: Le cours magistral XVe–XXe siècles] and B. Lindberg's studies of the history of the lecture in a national context: 'The Academic Lecture. A Genre in Between', *LIR Journal* I (2011), 38–48 and *Den akademiska läxan. Om föreläsningens historia* (Stockholm, 2017).

Far from arguing that academic lectures in themselves should be of inter-est to anyone occupied with the writing of university history, this chapter will suggest that there are nevertheless ways in which to treat this topic that justify its historical role and status without paying too much attention to its often-trivial content. One such approach could be book historical, in terms of investigating the 'sociology of the texts'. However, the intention is not simply to replace one approach with another; that is, to replace university history with book history, because the latter does not seem to have been interested in the academic lecture either. What it nevertheless provides us with is the concept of circulation – or, rather, a circulatory model in which the interaction of text and society takes place. This model not only points to the social realities of print media (and other media of textual transmis-sion). In the words of D. F. McKenzie, we can say that the academic lecture 'also directs us to consider the human motives and interactions which texts involve at every stage of their production, transmission, and consumption. It alerts us to the roles of institutions, and their own complex structures, in affecting the forms of social discourse, past and present.'[2] Without entering into the finer details of production and dissemination, the book historical approach enlightens the historical role of the academic lecture and pro-vides a starting point for further analysis. First and foremost, it can con-tribute to a shift of focus from the content of the individual lecture to its general function as a disseminator of knowledge.[3] Whether this process is based on a printed textbook or a written manuscript is, in this context, less important than the indisputable fact that any lecture will contain an oral component and that even the process of note-taking by students 'consti-tutes a central but often hidden phase in the transmission of knowledge.'[4]

---

[2]   D. F. McKenzie: *Bibliography and the Sociology of Texts* (Cambridge, 1999), p. 15. On the concept of a circulatory model in book history, see also R. Darnton: 'What is the History of Books', *Daedalus* 111 (1982), 65–83 and '"What is the History of Books?" Revisited', *Modern Intellectual History* 4 (2007), 495–508.

[3]   There will of course be examples of lectures where the content itself is of central im-portance. It should suffice to recall that several significant works in the European in-tellectual tradition such as Kant's *Anthropologie* or Hegel's *Vorlesungen über Ästhe-tik* are in fact based on student notes and not on a single authoritative manuscript by the lecturer. This in turn generates a set of issues that will not necessarily be relevant for a study of the history of the lecture, such as whether the notes represent a true reproduction of the lecturer's words. See i.a. W. Stark: 'Kritische Fragen und An-merkungen zu einem neuen Band der Akademie-Ausgabe von Kant's Vorlesungen', *Zeitschrift für philosophische Forschung* 38 (1984), 292–310, and 'Historical Notes and Interpretive Questions about Kant's Lectures on Anthropology', in B. Jacobs and P. Kain (eds): *Essays on Kant's Anthropology* (Cambridge, 2003), pp. 15–37.

[4]   A. Blair, 'Note Taking as an Art of Transmission', *Critical Inquiry*, 31 (2004), 85.

Regarded as a tool of transmission or dissemination there is in principle no significant difference between the lecture and the academic textbook. They both remain anchored in a tradition that must be accounted for in order to understand their content. What they often have in common is a lack of originality that is all the more interesting as it reveals something about the type of knowledge that the university conveys to their students in order to initiate them into an academic literary citizenship.

However, this does not mean that the relationship between the lecture and the textbook – or between orality, note-taking and print – is unproblematic. Precisely during the period here in question, i.e. the late eighteenth and early nineteenth century, there occurred a strong criticism of the traditional university and its role. This criticism, which was first voiced by German academics, soon also spread in a short time also to Denmark–Norway. A significant part of the critique, as well as the attempts to counter it, circled around the relationship between the spoken and the written word or – more precisely – between the academic lecture and the textbook and the question of which of these was the most appropriate means of transferring knowledge. Whereas the lecture had until then been seen as a natural part of the university's activities and its presence too obvious for words, one now had to start justifying it.

THE GENERAL AND THE LOCAL

An attempt to write about the academic lecture must take into account that the supply of sources is vast and almost unmanageable. But this should not be regarded as a problem, because focusing on a more restricted context – be it national or limited to a specific institution – will simply be a way of reducing the sources to a more manageable size. And the lecture itself is, after all, rooted in a transnational academic culture.[5] Although one might find some national or local peculiarities here, this material will also be relevant in a wider context. There is thus every reason to draw lessons from book history, where most of the analyses are concrete in the sense that they are anchored in an empirical source material. But before we move on to the Dano-Norwegian source material to be examined in this chapter, a word or two must be said about what characterises an academic lecture as such.

Although there are several types of academic lectures, what they all have in common is that they constitute a specific rhetorical situation where a qualified and certified lecturer speaks to an assembly of listeners who are students. The difference between them lies in how much the audience

---

[5]   B. Lindberg, *Den akademiska läxan*, p. 11.

already knows and the consequences this will have for the presentation of the content itself. How does one, as a lecturer, approach students who already are in possession of a certain amount of knowledge compared to students who can and know very little? Questions of this kind, interesting as they might be for an attempt to understand the academic lecture in a historical perspective, do seem to have been passed over in silence prior to the mid-eighteenth century, however. And although lectures and the art of lecturing are of course treated in the rich humanistic literature, it is far more difficult to find the academic lecture discussed or reflected on in more bureaucratic prose like manuals, bureaucratic provisions or regulations.

> It is striking how little attention the lecture attracted as a mode of communication. There was no room for it in the handbooks of classical rhetoric, since it did not fit into any of the three rhetorical genera, the deliberative, the judicial, and the demonstrative. There was more discussion of the disputation, i.e. the public defence of a thesis or dissertation, which was the most typical and conspicuous scholarly performance in the university tradition; *de arte disputandi*, 'how to discuss a thesis', was a rather frequent topic in academic self-reflexion. Very little was said about the lecture.[6]

Although the lecture was not perceived as a separate rhetorical genre, it is still not difficult to relate it to some of the basic concepts of the classical art of speech. In a rhetorical sense, the academic lecture will most often be designed in the so-called 'plain style' (genus *subtile*). This level of style does not aim to excite the listeners (*flectere*) but to teach them by arguing that so-and-so is the case and so-and-so is not: 'this is true, this is not true'! In line with the usual division of the rhetorical situation as such into speaker (*ethos*), message (*logos*) and audience (*pathos*), the emphasis is on *logos*. It is the message, not the speaker, which ought to be the object of the audience's attention. Finally, the classical rhetoric also contains a well-prepared doctrine of *aptum*, which includes reflections on what kind of audience the speaker is addressing and how he in a given case should and should not express himself.

The obvious lack of sources that could have shed light on the role and purpose of the lecture on the part of the institution need thus not constitute a serious obstacle. These questions will mainly be linked to 'the professorial voice' as part of the wider process of transmision of knowledge.[7] In

---

[6]   B. Lindberg, 'The Academic Lecture', p. 40.

[7]   See W. Clark, 'The Professorial Voice', *Science in Context* 16 (2003), 43–57, and *Academic Charisma and the Origins of the Research University* (Chicago, 2006).

any case, in order to understand not what the lecture was supposed to be, but what it really was, there are a multitude of sources available to us in the form of the notes that the students themselves put down in their lecture booklets, preserving the content of the lecture for a posterity in which the professorial voice has long since fallen silent.

Benefiting from the perspectives of book history mentioned above as well as supplied by the framework of university history, in what follows this chapter will turn its focus towards a limited period in the history of the academic lecture and a special type of lecture. The period is the late eighteenth century and early nineteenth century, and the lecture is the introductory course in philosophy often referred to as *examen philosophicum*. In a geographical sense, it will restrict itself to the University of Copenhagen and, after 1813, also the University of Christiania (Oslo). In order to illustrate how the academic lecture at these institutions was part of a transnational system, a small detour to Germany will however be necessary. The reason for choosing the introductory lecture is due to two factors, firstly that these lectures served as an introduction to what we might call academic literary citizenship and secondly because they bear the mark of being dictated by the lecturer. The primary sources that will be examined are all taken from the collection of manuscripts and student notes at the National Library of Norway in Oslo.

A BRIEF GERMAN DETOUR

In the spring of 1792 the readers of one of Denmark's most important periodicals noticed an anonymous proposal to abolish the University of Copenhagen 'as being a foundation far too expensive for the state and, in addition, completely unnecessary and useless.'[8] Whereas such criticism was not uncommon, it generally appeared in a somewhat milder form. As early as in 1744 Ludvig Holberg (1684–1754), professor at the university and probably the foremost representative of Dano-Norwegian Enlightenment, had declared that lectures were meaningless and that most students showed up only to be noticed by the teachers and not to be taught.

> Moreover, in such places they do not hear what they most demand to know, but rather what pleases the lecturer to recite. Not to mention that nowadays countless books have been written on all subjects, so that young people can read such books, which have been prepared

---

[8]   *Den danske Tilskuer* (Copenhagen, 1792), nr. 29.

diligently, with greater benefit than to hear what has been hastily compiled and read.[9]

Whereas it is not clear whether his reluctance applies to the topics treated or the lectures as such, Holberg's reasoning nevertheless testifies that doubts regarding the appropriateness of lectures had begun to arise, including among the university's own teachers. In this regard, it is also worth mentioning that the great Swedish commission for upbringing (*Uppfostrings-kommissionen*), which was appointed in 1745, also raised objections to the usefulness of the lecture in its present form.[10] The Scandinavian critique of the university, and in particular of the lecture, was nevertheless relatively modest compared with the exchange of words that took place in Germany, where a larger and more expanding book market had led many to question the role of the university as such. Although textbooks had been used at universities in some way or another since the Middle Ages, they had nevertheless been rare because they were often expensive or difficult to obtain, and they had never been perceived as viable alternatives to the academic lecture, but this was about to change as access to relevant knowledge and information through the medium of print had become far greater and much easier. That there were now alternative ways of acquiring knowledge was clearly expressed through the ever-decreasing number of students at German universities in the last decades of the eighteenth century.[11]

The question to be asked was why the university's traditional way of teaching had come into disrepute. As long as the institution had existed, the method of knowledge transfer had been the same – and this had proved to work in line with the university's objective, although this objective had not always been explicitly stated: the professor stood at his lectern and read from a manuscript, while the audience put what they heard down on paper – that is, if they were able to write fast enough, for it was not always a pure dictation where the lecturer adjusted the pace of his lecture to the students' skills in noting. It is probably fair to say that the increasing access to other sources of knowledge and information had created a change in mentality: why attend a lecture when one can just as easily acquire the same knowledge by sitting in one's armchair reading a book? Whereas this initially seems to be a rather innocent question about preferences, there was a further issue lurking just around the corner – namely why one should

---

[9]   L. Holberg, *Moralske Tanker* (Copenhagen, 1744), II, p. 485.
[10] B. Lindberg, *Den akademiska läxan*, pp. 123–31.
[11] For a more thorough presentation of the German debate on the relationship between the lecture and the textbook, see P. Josephson, 'Böcker eller universitet? Om ett tema i tysk utbildningspolitisk debatt kring 1800', *Lychnos* (2009), 177–208.

waste time attending a lecture when the professor has already made it clear that he did not intend to lecture on a topic that one has read about and found interesting.

This is not to say that the increasing access to knowledge and information necessarily developed into an interest in heterodox opinions. It was rather a general fascination with the new and contemporary in itself that helped to put the university in a bad light. The university was, after all, a conservative institution and it would remain so for a foreseeable future. To expect that a lecturer would offer something new and exciting, as well as the subsequent disappointment when this was not the case, was, according to the scholar Johann David Michaelis (1717–91), based on the prejudice that professors by virtue of their position were 'discoverers of new truths' (*Erfinder neuer Wahrheiten*).[12] But the fact is that until it transformed itself into a modern research institution during the late nineteenth century, the university rested on the assumption that the truth was already known and that its most important task was to administer this truth as a possession and, in time, pass it on to new generations. This view was also shared by the philosopher Niels Treschow (1751–1833), professor in Copenhagen from 1803 to 1813, who told his students that there were no more discoveries to be made in philosophy: 'Thus, when metaphysical opinions are presented as new truths, we must always expect that as soon as we have stripped them of the foreign costume in which they are made, they are either long known, or manifestly false.'[13] Treschow was not opposed to textbooks, however, and played a crucial role in the Danish book market with several publications, but as will be shown below, there is still a number of examples of him dictating his lectures. The dictation was, after all, an appropriate way to convey knowledge, given the premise that the truth was already known, even though this in no way precluded other forms of presentation. It is also obvious that the dictation would hardly be appropriate if the lecture had been a more tentative presentation of knowledge that was not yet considered definitive. However, the lecture was not yet regarded as a way of arriving at the truth but a way to convey a truth that had already been found.

Many of those who at the end of the eighteenth century advocated a thorough reform of the German university agreed that the expanding book market challenged the traditional form of university teaching, but few still wanted to turn their backs on the lecture. As long as the book and the lecture undoubtedly competed for the same territory, i.e., the transfer of

---

[12]   J. D. Michaelis, *Raisonnement über die protestantischen Universitäten in Deutschland. Zweiter Theil* (Frankfurt and Leipzig, 1770), p. 134.
[13]   N. Treschow, *Philosophiske Forsøg* (Copenhagen, 1805), p. 6.

knowledge, it had to be possible to divide the territory between them in a way that gave each of them a rightful place. One possible argument was to admit that the book was an important transmitter of knowledge but at the same time emphasise that it did not make the lecture superfluous. As the writer and official Ernst Brandes (1758–1810) argued, it would seem a serious mistake to think that one could get acquainted with science on one's own and only with the help of books.

> Good books that to a certain extent will be able to replace the university's teaching are not lacking, but what is remarkably lacking is the correct use of these books, and it is only the university that to a certain extent seems to be able to maintain a thorough study of the sciences.[14]

A medium of the kind that Brandes had found lacking was, however, already in existence, i.e. the meta-literature that flourished at the time and which dealt with the art of reading books. One such book, penned by the philosopher and publicist Johann Adam Bergk (1769–1834), contained i.a. chapters with titles such as 'What is the purpose of reading philosophical books and how should they be read?' and 'In what way and in what order should one study Kant's writings?'.[15] This was obviously advices to readers who wanted to study on their own, independent of the university, but such publications also had their parallel in the academic world in that textbooks on logic had long included so-called 'practical logic'. This sub-discipline had traditionally dealt with problems related to interpretation, the reliability of witnesses, historical vs. philosophical knowledge, etc. and were often rounded off with a description of how to defend one's position in a disputation. But as the disputation lost its general significance as something more than a final exam in the taking of an academic degree, this topic was replaced by practical questions such as how one should organise one's library, etc. In Niels Treschow's textbook on logic, published in 1813, a chapter that dealt with the role of the lecture was also introduced, i.e. precisely the issue that, as mentioned above, had until then rarely been addressed by the university itself.

> In scholarly teaching, the matter is explained thoroughly, in detail, and in a systematic context in a strictly logical or schooled manner (...). This kind of lecture is suitable only for educated listeners who can both

---

[14]   E. Brandes, *Ueber den gegenwärtigen Zustand der Universität Göttingen* (Göttingen, 1802), p. 153.
[15]   J. A. Bergk, *Die Kunst, Bücher zu lesen. Nebst Bemerkungen über Schriften und Schriftsteller* (München-Pullach, 1799), pp. 335, 355.

grasp it and whose attention does not need to be aroused or supported by repeated questions. But it is also less necessary than the ordinary kind arranged for the uneducated; since these can mostly firmly learn the same thing from Books. Those persons who, for this reason or for lack of opportunity, have learned any science by themselves, are called self-taught –*autodidaktoi* (...). Admittedly, these self-taughts are generally very thoughtful. But since people who read rather than hear seldom have the patience to go through whole systematic works in due order, or any part of such works with equal diligence, and rather indulge in a scattered reading in various, preferably pleasing, writings; then their knowledge becomes incomplete and disorderly.[16]

What the academic lecture could offer was precisely what the autodidact lacked during the acquisition of knowledge, namely the transmitter's *presence*, whereas for the self-taught, the author of the book would remain absent in the sense that he could not provide him with help in any other way than through the text he had once written. The lecturer, on the other hand, was present, not only as the professorial voice but as a physical person which embodied the techniques that according to classical rhetoric belonged to the doctrine of *actio*. As a result, 'the oral lecture has the general advantage of the written word that it attaches itself deeper into the mind.'[17] This, in turn, may also explain the fascination with the university lecturers from their own youth that is a recurrent topic among the authors of early nineteenth-century memoir literature as well as the fact that the then current interest in rhetorical declamation also found a place for the academic lecture.[18] It is important to keep this in mind now that the atten-

[16]   N. Treschow, *Almindelig Logik* (Copenhagen, 1813), pp. 298–9.
[17]   *Ibid.*, p. 299. It is worth noting that the philosopher Johann Gottfried Herder (1744–1803), who attended Kant's lectures in the 1760s, drew the same conclusion. It was, according to Herder, 'difficult to understand lecture notes when reading them after the lecture has ended. He argued that it was only by hearing the words from Kant himself that he managed to digest them.' J. Eriksson: 'Lecture-notes and Common-places. Reading and Writing about Experience in Late Eighteenth Century Prussia', *Lýchnos* (2009), p. 155.
[18]   Although professor of pedagogy at the University of Copenhagen Levin Sander (1756–1819) admitted that 'logical declamation does not really belong to the art of rhetorical emphasis in the strict sense of the word', he still made the following rhetorical demand on the lecturer: 'From the lecturer is noticeably required pleasance, but not the strongest and most lively speech. This would even be inappropriate, as it cannot be accompanied by the full use of the language of declamation. Whether the lecturer is now sitting or standing, he can really suggest something by glances, by gestures, by movements with one hand, by changed positions, and thus accompany his declamation. However, he is always restricted, and cannot act and gesticulate

tion shifted from thoughts about the lecture to the lecture as it is preserved in student notebooks.

THE MANUSCRIPTS AND THE LECTURE NOTES

Academic circles in Denmark–Norway were well aware of the discussion about the role of the textbook and the lecture in university teaching that flourished in Germany around 1800. Both the university in Copenhagen and Dano-Norwegian intellectual life in general were strongly influenced by German currents, and a number of philosophical textbooks had been translated from German since the mid-eighteenth century and Danish textbooks were also published according to a German pattern.[19] The fact that there were now textbooks in circulation did not mean that all students also had access to a copy; but it is beyond doubt that lecturers often used them in the preparation of their lecture manuscripts. Some lecturers, such as Professor Børge Riisbrigh (1731–1809), who during the 1790s lectured in Danish with constant references to his Latin textbooks, assumed that the students had access to it, however. This access tended to make pure dictation superfluous, for what the students then actually wrote down were the oral additions to the lecturer's more or less dogmatic presentation.[20] But where no references to a textbook were made, or where a textbook was not used as a basis for the lecture, the transfer of knowledge took place through pure dictation, which is easily to determine in cases where both the professor's manuscript and the students' notes have been preserved for posterity.[21] This traditional way of lecturing was thus retained both in

---

with Fineness: neither should he, as he is simply imagining a reader i.e. the poet's audible organ.' L. C. Sander, *Svada: eller theoretisk og practisk Veiledning til Betoningskunsten* (Copenhagen, 1814), p. 55; see also *Odeum: eller, Declamerekunstens Theorie, praktisk forklaret* (Copenhagen, 1819), p. 70.

[19] Among German textbooks translated into Danish were C. Wolff, *Vernünftige Gedancken von der Menschen Thun und Lassen* (Halle, 1720) and J. C. Gottsched, *Erste Gründe der gesamten Weltweisheit* (Leipzig, 1734). Latin textbooks were also used in teaching at the university, but unlike German textbooks, they were not translated into Danish.

[20] Ms. lecture No. 29 in the manuscript collection of the National Library of Norway (NBO), 'Prof Riisbrighs Forelæsninger over Philosophien'. The textbook in question was his own *Praenotiones philosophicae* (Copenhagen, 1783).

[21] Examples of this are Treschow's lectures on metaphysics (NBO Ms. forelesn. 694), originally held in Copenhagen in 1808, where there are student notes (privately owned) from 1815, and his lectures on the general encyclopaedia (NBO Ms. 4to 2302), originally held in Copenhagen in 1811, and where there are student notes from 1813 (NBO Ms. forelesn. 232). In both cases there is a close correspondence between the lecture manuscript and the student notes.

Copenhagen and, after 1813, in Christiania (Oslo), while in Germany at that time restrictions had been introduced against it, and in Prussia dictations had already been forbidden by a decree of 31 March 1781.[22]

The complete absence of textbooks on the teaching of philosophy at the new University of Christiania, which was established in 1811, was due not only to the passive continuation of a practice that had been dominant in Copenhagen but also to the fact that the production of textbooks in Norway at this time was virtually non-existent. There were also political reasons for this. In a pamphlet aimed at proving the harmfulness of the importation of foreign goods, written by the industrialist Hovel Helset (1779–1865), it was admittedly stated that 'books are the guidance of literature, and as such free',[23] but during a debate about the higher education system in parliament in 1818 one of the participants warned against initiating a domestic production of textbooks, and among the arguments he put forward was that it would be almost impossible to profit from such a project, even if one succeeded in finding a Norwegian author.

> Publishers, even of the most excellent scientific works, will find no author here, but these had to be sought in Copenhagen, and one would thereby support Danish printing companies and contribute to science in Denmark, but for such a purpose it would be unwise to spend any sum in our possession.[24]

Most student notes from lectures in philosophy, preserved at the National Library of Norway in Oslo, are from the 1830s and 1840s, and they all stem from the university's *examen philosophicum*, a one-year course of study that had been introduced in Copenhagen as early as 1675 and was compulsory for all new students. Until 1905 this course included not only philosophy but also a number of other subjects that did not fall under the traditional 'professional' studies (that is, theology, law and medicine). This means that the lectures in question were not held for students who studied philosophy exclusively or, for that matter, wanted to study philosophy at a more advanced level. It is also important to emphasise that the students were not presented with a specified syllabus at the beginning of the semester. The syllabus was simply the notes they themselves wrote down according to the lecturer's dictation, and these notes were what they would be tested in at the final oral examination. So in short: sloppy notes were not an option.

---

[22] W. Clark, *Academic Charisma*, p. 85.
[23] H. Helset, *Den lille Tarif. Et Forsøg paa at bevise Skadeligheden ved Indførselen af atskillige fremmede Varer i Norge* (Christiania, 1820), p. 10.
[24] *Storthings-Efterretninger 1814–1833* (Christiania, 1874), vol. I, p. 624.

The teaching of philosophy included four sub-disciplines: logic, meta-physics, psychology and ethics. What the students were offered under these headings was, in terms of content, an anonymous body of knowledge – anonymous in the sense that it could not be traced back to a particular philosopher or philosophical school. It consisted rather of what one might call the common ground of philosophy. This body of knowledge was in itself an expression of the aforementioned opinion that the truth was already known and that the university's task was to convey this to the students. That the teaching material was not linked to a specific philosophical position and, consequently, not to the person lecturing on it meant that in practice the lecturers could also borrow manuscripts from each other, and this was done on several occasions. When F. P. J. Dahl (1788–1864) arrived in Christiania in 1815 to take over as philosophy teacher after Treschow's resignation, Treschow put several of his lecture manuscripts at his successor's disposal; and when Poul Martin Møller (1794–1838) in 1828 joined as professor of philosophy in Christiania, Treschow made him the same offer. But Møller, who had already got a taste for German idealism, soon realised that he could not use these manuscripts and instead wrote to his mentor in Copenhagen, Professor Frederik Christian Sibbern (1785–1872), to get a copy of *his* manuscript on metaphysics. What Møller received from Sibbern was, however, far too strongly influenced by his mentor's own philosophical position, and as a result Møller had to write his own manuscript, based on what his predecessors had presented to their students. The result was a manuscript that any lecturer could have prepared and then used.[25]

Two of the booklets with lecture notes found in the manuscript collection at the National Library of Norway are particularly interesting because they illustrate parts of what has been referred to above as a system of circulation. This system includes the knowledge transfer which took place during the actual lecture, where the oral words were taken down, but an equally important part of it was the circulation of notes that obviously took place subsequently. The precondition for such circulation was, of course, that the content of the lectures was almost identical from year to year – and that the notes could thus be sold to, or copied by, new students. The fact that NBO Ms. forelesn. [lecture] 398 is a copy of an original note is clear from the first page of the booklet, where it is written: 'Lectures on moral philosophy by councillor Treschow held at the Norwegian University in its first semester. Copied in the summer of 1816 by Niels Schydtz.'

---

[25]   This manuscript, which is dated February 1828, can be found at the Royal Library in Copenhagen (The manuscript collection, Collin 377 4to).

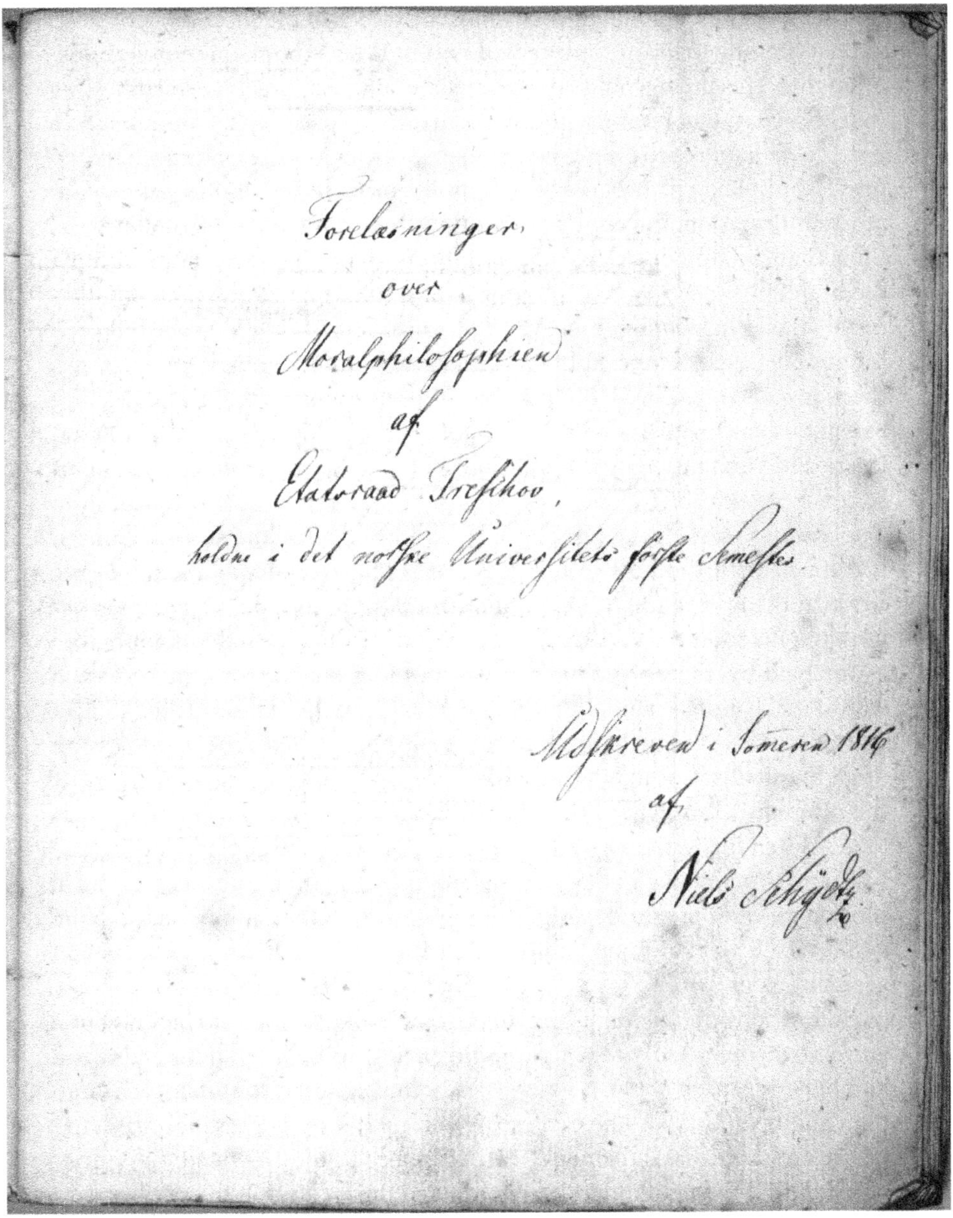

Forelæsninger

over

Moralphilosophien

af

Etatsraad Treschow,

holdne i det norske Universitets første Semester.

Udskreven i Someren 1816

af

Niels Schjødt

PLATE 9.1. Student notes from Professor Niels Treschow's lectures on moral philosophy.

That the copy is reliable is beyond doubt, since much of its content is almost literally the same as one will find in the textbook on moral philosophy that Treschow would later publish.[26] Furthermore, it is worth noting that the copy has retained the wide margins, which were often used to note down some of the more comprehensive parts of the lecture where the professor quickly elaborated on his points or provided additional explanatory information. The copy also contains many of the standard abbreviations that the students made use of in order to be able to keep up with the dictation.

On closer inspection, however, there are signs to suggest that the copy is not only based on one, but two earlier sets of student notes. For example, there is a discrepancy in the number of paragraphs as well as an attempt to establish a concordance by giving some paragraphs two numbers. What this second text might be is highly uncertain. It could of course be a manuscript from one of the lectures Treschow had given during his time in Copenhagen, but it may just as well be additions that the student himself had made with the help of a somewhat shadowy figure in the academic world at the time, namely the *manuductor*. Unlike a modern seminar assistant, the manuductor (litr: 'one who leads by the hand') was not appointed by, or paid by, the university. He was an older student who had found a way to make money, namely by teaching and rehearsing the current subject matter for new students. This meant that he himself had to be in possession of a complete set of lecture notes written down during lectures given by the same professor whom the new students later would meet at the exam table. When this system – in which student notes were copied, bought and sold, and in which the manuductor played an important role – did not pose the same threat to the lecture as the textbook, it was simply because the system itself was informal and in practice required personal contacts and acquaintances.

Before considering the second of the two booklets, it would be appropriate to take a quick look at the figure who during the debate mentioned above had been regarded as the one who made the lecture into something more than the textbook, i.e. the professor who by his mere presence attracted the attention of the audience. Few professors at the University of Christiania during the 1820s and 1830s embodied the lecturer in the same way as Professor Georg Sverdrup (1770–1850), and the attraction he exercised on his audience has been well documented. In his memoirs one of his former students emphasises 'Sverdrup's impressive personality (he resembled Goethe), his deep and sonorous voice and the nimbus that still stood about

---

[26]   N. Treschow, *Den philosophiske Sædelæres første Grunde* (Christiania, 1824).

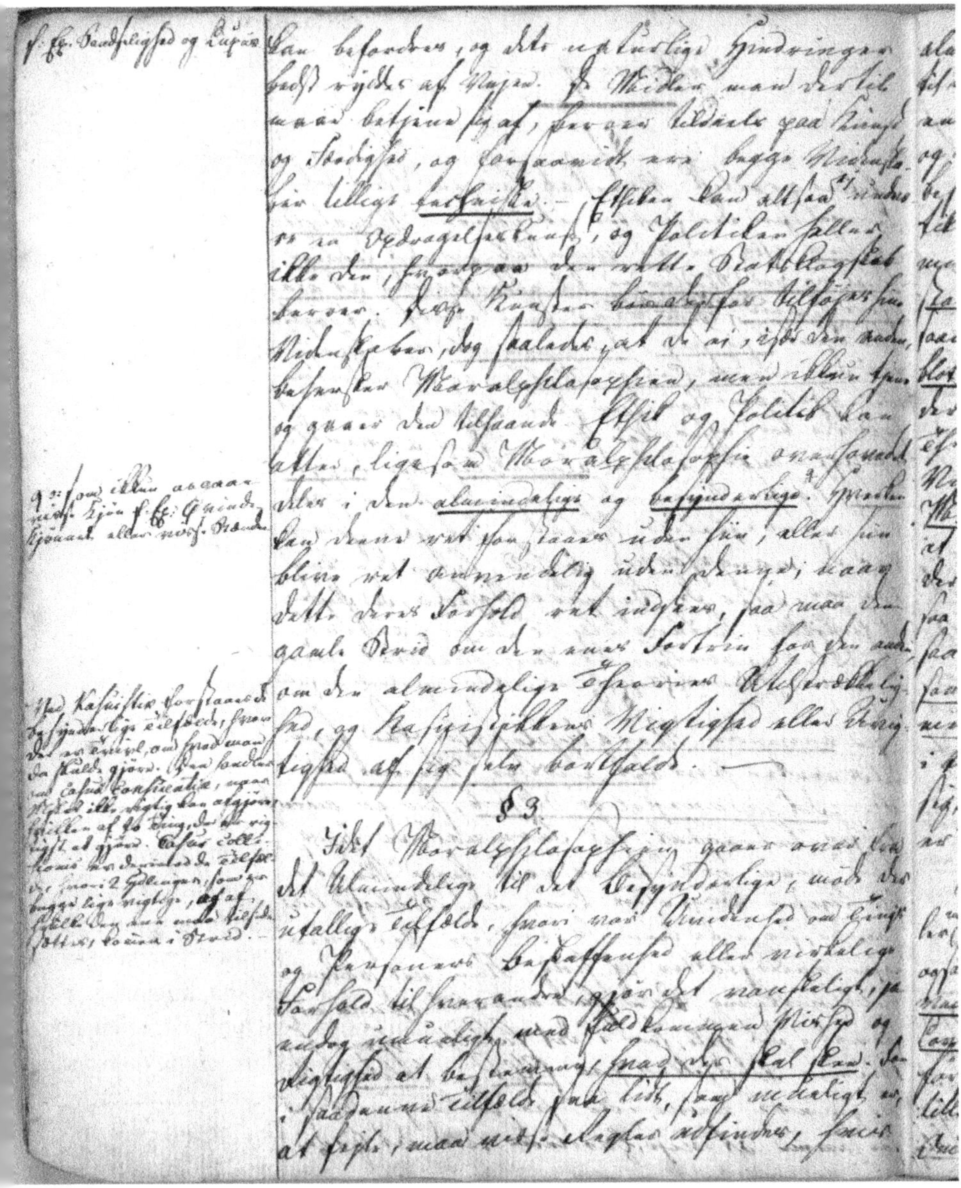

PLATE 9.2. Student notes from Professor Niels Treschow's lectures on moral philosophy.

him from his significant participation in my fatherland's new political life also helped to elevate the impression his lectures exerted on me as on all his other listeners'; another former student recalls 'the excellent lectures I heard from this so highly gifted man with the manly, impressive exterior and the powerful, deep voice,'[27] while a third gives the following description of Sverdrup's entrance into the lecture hall:

> Now an enormous number of people crowded together, so that the room became stuffed; by the benches and on the stools it was impossible to find a place; many had to stand. All this then heralded something strange. After a short while Professor Sverdrup moved through the masses with much difficulty; but now he ascended to the lectern and there was silence in the hall. Everyone stood in silent expectation. He began a truly delightful introductory speech to philosophy; he spoke all the time without stuttering or repeating; his lovely lectures and majestic exterior made a deep impression on all; his deep strong bass easily penetrated the whole hall to everyone's ear, and what he said with regard to us went to the heart. Much, of course, must be obscured to us of the philosophical.[28]

NBO Ms Lecture 377 (from the manuscript collection of the National Library of Norway) contains the dictated text from Sverdrup's lectures on psychology in the spring semester of 1832.

These lectures took place Monday to Saturday between 1 and 2 pm throughout the semester, and the number of listeners was just over 100. Originally, Sverdrup was also supposed to lecture on moral philosophy this semester, but according to the report which he himself submitted to the faculty, he had realised that he had to 'proceed so slowly that his audience, who come from the schools to the university without prior knowledge in any philosophical discipline, could still be able to understand some of what he said.'[29] A quick glance at this student note clearly reveals that it is not made on site. Although it still contains the standard abbreviations that characterise most dictated notes, it is a 150 pages long clean copy, meticulously calligraphed and bound in hard cover. The amount of work that is put into it also suggests that it was not meant for sale. In short, it is a manuscript turned into a book that is meant to remain in the owner's

---

[27] A. Munch, *Barndoms- og Ungdoms-Minder* (Christiania, 1874), p. 194, and S. B. Bugge: 'Autobiografiske Optegnelser', *Skilling-Magazin* (Copenhagen, 1881), p. 85.

[28] P. J. Collett, *Studenteraar. Oplevelser og refleksjoner 1831–1838* (Oslo, 1934), p. 28.

[29] *Departements-Tidende* (1833), no. 47.

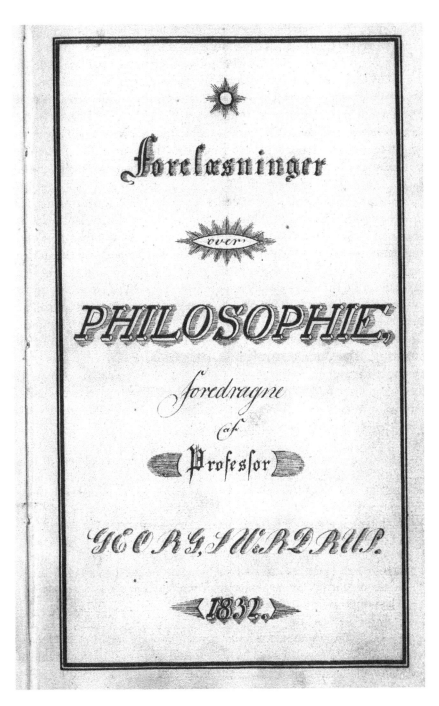

PLATE 9.3. Student notes from Professor Georg Sverdrup's lectures on psychology: Front page.

possession, and it even includes something that one will not normally find even in printed textbooks at the time: a register of items.

As such, it clearly testifies to what some students were willing to do with the notes they had once had dictated in the auditorium. Unlike Professor Sverdrup himself, who had all his own manuscripts burned after his death, it is obvious that a number of students wanted to keep and preserve their lecture notes, and these are thus available for posterity as an invaluable source material and, not least, as monuments to a dying form of teaching.

In the 1840s the dictation of lectures began to approach its end. As early as 1836 William Sverdrup (1809–72), the son of Professor Sverdrup, published a textbook on logic with the intention of documenting his qualifications with a view to a future position at the university, and his father also used this as a basis for his lectures with the result that the scope of the student notes decreased significantly. He simply assumed that the students themselves were in possession of the printed textbook and that in many cases he could therefore simply refer to it. Soon, critical voices outside the university also began to appear. In the spring of 1841 readers of Christiania's largest newspaper found in print a comprehensive critique of the university as a whole which also addressed the way in which the institution had hitherto carried out its task of transferring knowledge. Here it was stated, among other things, that whereas a school teacher could be compared to the merchant who resold the raw materials he had imported in unchanged form, a university teacher ideally resembled a merchant who processed his goods before putting them up for sale.

> [S]ince knowledge is valued everywhere, as much as possible of it must therefore be packed together for the benefit of the alumni, who are thus also troubled, and whose time is uselessly occupied with the truly spiritless dictation; everything must be dictated, the listener is nothing but a passive receiver and a copyist – and yet the demands of the office would be far better fulfilled when all dictation, with the exception of a schema, is abolished; from the lively lecture, on the other hand, a picture, a clear visual thought, should appear before the audience, and in a moment illuminate their interior more clearly than a laborious dictation of many hours.[30]

Several of the university's younger teachers were far from unreceptive to this critique. When Marcus Jacob Monrad (1816–97) in 1849 published his philosophical propaedeutic – the first textbook to be used on a large scale at the university – his explicit purpose was 'to give my contribution to

---

[30]   'Vort Universitets Aand og Fremtid', *Morgenbladet* (1841), no. 262.

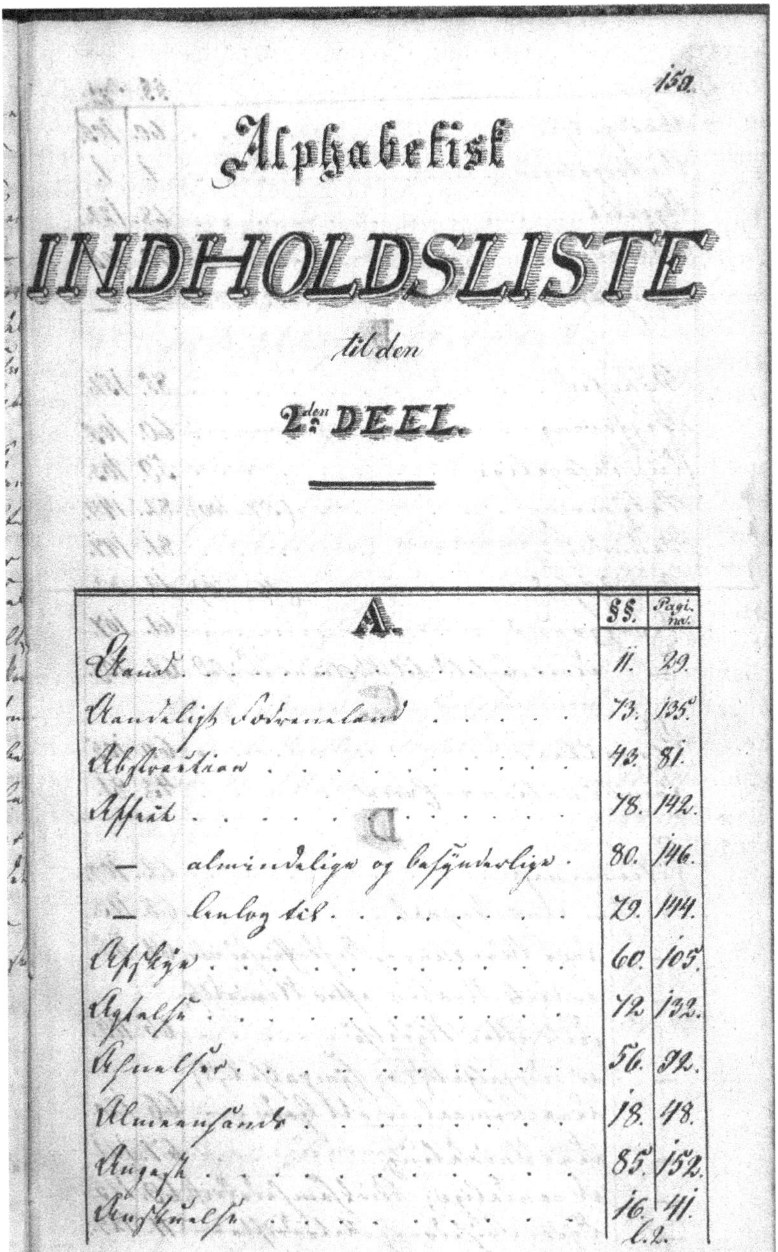

Alphabetisk

INDHOLDSLISTE

til den

2^{den} DEEL.

PLATE 9.4. Student notes from Professor Georg Sverdrup's lectures on psychology: Register of items.

the restriction of dictation at the University.'[31] He could further assure the students that his colleague would also make use of this textbook in order to promote a unity in the elementary teaching of philosophy. Although the introduction of textbooks made both the dictation and the process of circulation described above superfluous, it did not mean the end of the lecture's significant role in university teaching. On the contrary: now that all students had equal access to an authorised text that contained everything they needed for their forthcoming exam, they also had the opportunity to prepare themselves for the lectures which from now on, ideally speaking, would focus on the freer oral explanation of the content of the course.

Whereas it would be beyond the scope of this chapter to trace the occasionally tense relationship between the spoken and the written word in university teaching up until the present day, suffice it to say that this tension has still not been brought to rest. The students' introduction to an academic literary citizenship takes place, now as before, through the spoken words of the lecture and with the help of the textbook, although the circulatory process described above does not have the same significance as during the heyday of dictation – and it is highly uncertain to what extent today's students preserve their notes for posterity. Regarding the relationship between the oral, the note-taking and the printed book, a new component has undoubtedly been added in recent times, namely the pre-recorded lecture. A book-historical analysis of today's lecture will therefore have to take into account the fact that the tension does now not only lie between the spoken and the written word but also between the living voice in the lecture hall and the impersonal voice of the recording.

---

[31] M. J. Monrad, *Philosophisk Propædeutik. Grundrids til Brug ved Forelæsninger* (Christiania, 1849), 'Foreword'.

10

An Inspiring Model from the Periphery: The Transnational Circulation of the Norwegian 1814 Constitution

Ruth Hemstad

FEW PUBLICATIONS TRAVELLED FROM Norway to the broader literary world. Among those that did, and circulating Europe-wide, is the country's legal founding document, its constitution of 1814, thus connecting the politically re-established autonomous state to broader European political currents. The transnational print history of the Norwegian constitution reveals the heightened interest in all things constitutional in the wake of the American and French revolutions as well as the emergent transnational and transmedial character of the public sphere and print culture. Although coming from the periphery, from the 'distant rocky country' of Norway,[1] the Eidsvold constitution, regularly referred to as the most democratic constitution of the time, became a point of reference in the European constitutional discourse during the first half of the nineteenth century.

The Norwegian constitution was a result of a combination of external and internal constellations during a few hectic months in 1814. During this remarkable year in Norwegian history Norway was transformed from a subordinated province within the Dano-Norwegian dual monarchy at the

---

[1] The Austrian newspaper *Die Presse* referred in 1848 to Norway in this way and as 'the only democracy in Europe' in a series of articles on the Norwegian constitution. Quoted after K. Gammelgaard, 'Constitutions as a Transnational Genre. Norway 1814 and the Habsburg Empire 1848–1849', in K. Gammelgaard and E. Holmøyvik (eds), *Writing Democracy: The Norwegian Constitution 1814–2014* (New York, Oxford, 2014), p. 96.

beginning of the year to an autonomous part of the Swedish-Norwegian personal union at the end of it. The Treaty of Kiel, concluded on 14 January 1814, transferred Norway from the Danish to the Swedish king – like a herd of cattle, as it was said – stirring national protests in Norway.[2] While the Swedish Crown Prince Charles John and the Swedish army were still occupied with the ongoing Napoleonic Wars on the continent, the Norwegians, led by the Danish successor to the crown, Prince Christian Frederik, seized the moment and gave itself a constitution at Eidsvold Manor and elected Christian Frederik king of Norway on 17 May. During the summer, however, Charles John returned to Sweden and attacked Norway. After a short war, a Convention was agreed on in August, based on the acceptance of the new constitution. By 4 November the Swedish King Charles XIII was elected as Norwegian king, and the constitution was slightly revised. It was to become a national bulwark against Swedish efforts to strengthen the union, which was eventually dissolved in 1905. In this context the translations and publications of the Norwegian constitution directed at a foreign readership played a specific role, and it became an argument in a transnational war of opinion around 1814.

The wide transnational circulation of the revolutionary constitution from the Northern periphery, originating in a country hardly known to an international readership until the early nineteenth century, helped to place Norway on the European political and cultural map. The printed and published Eidsvold constitution – still in force today as the oldest one in Europe – became the most famous and broadly distributed Norwegian print of all during most of the century. The aim of this chapter is to examine the variety of translations and international publications of the Norwegian constitution from the beginning; the first full version of 17 May 1814 and the slightly revised one of 4 November the same year, and throughout the century until 1905, by applying a bibliographical book historical approach. This entails identifying and examining closely all recorded instances of translations, editions and transnational distribution of the Norwegian constitution; the whole text or parts of it, as well as central interrelated publications, seen as parts of intertextual political discourse.[3] By focusing on the transnational dimension, understood as the 'dynamics and movements between, within,

---

[2]   R. Hemstad, *Propagandakrig. Kampen om Norge i Norden og Europa 1812–1814* (Oslo, 2014).

[3]   On this approach used in the transnational debate on the 'Norwegian question' around 1814, see R. Hemstad, *Propagandakrig*; R. Hemstad (ed.), *'Like a Herd of Cattle.' Parliamentary and Public Debates Regarding the Cession of Norway, 1813–1814* (Oslo, 2014).

across, or above particular nations and cultures,'[4] new light may be shed on interconnections between Norwegian and European print cultures and the crucial role of translations.

The key to understanding the broad dissemination and transnational impact of this constitutional text is the flow of translations and reprints of it in a variety of formats and in different contexts. Like several other constitutional documents at this time, it was a very well-travelled text, and the many translations provided access to broader reading communities. James Brophy underlines that the 'scale and scope of transnational print circuits quickened in the late eighteenth century', with translation playing an increasingly larger role in mediating cultural transfer.[5] The impact of translation and transfer thus deserves greater emphasis in the study of transnational discourse and transmission of political knowledge during the 'age of democratic revolution'. In the expanding world of popular print, different forms of print are of relevance and should be included in measuring the 'acquisition of political competencies' in citizenship and participatory politics[6] and in examining and understanding the broadening of political engagement and literary citizenship.

By mapping the transnational circuits of the printed Norwegian constitution and tracing its appearances in different textual and political contexts, this chapter demonstrates how political ideas, also when coming from the periphery and in the form of a legal text, could travel far and wide, across boundaries and time.[7] The transnational exchange and reception of this key text reveal close entanglements and interconnections between centre and periphery; between European and Norwegian political and constitutional discourses in the nineteenth century. Copious new translations of the Norwegian constitution in several European countries and cities, especially until the 1850s, reflect political currents, an emerging political literacy and an expanding public and politicised sphere. The transnational print culture

[4]   W. Boutcher, 'Intertraffic: Transnational Literatures and Languages in Late Renaissance England and Europe', in M. McLean and S. Barker (eds), *International Exchange in the Early Modern Book World* (Leiden, Boston, 2016), pp. 353–73, at p. 353.
[5]   J. M. Brophy, 'The Second Wave: Franco-German Translation and the Transfer of Political Knowledge 1815–1850', *Archiv für Geschichte des Buchwesens*, 71 (2016), pp. 83, 94.
[6]   *Ibid.*, pp. 86, 94.
[7]   This chapter expands on and further develops, within the framework of print history, previous research conducted as part of the 200-year anniversary of the Norwegian constitution in 2014, at the National Library of Norway and the University of Oslo, of which one result is the retrospective *1814 Bibliography: Literature From and About 1812–1814* (<www.nb.no/bibliografi/1814>), developed in close cooperation with librarians at the National Library.

at the time offered a plethora of genres and formats directed at different segments of the population, thus contributing to the wide transmission of the Norwegian constitution. It served as an inspiring model and a political argument in ongoing political discourses in several countries and regions, not least in the German-speaking sphere but also in Great Britain.

QUANTITY, GENRE AND FORMATS

The Norwegian constitution is a relatively short legal text, consisting of 110/112 articles. The print history of the Norwegian constitution includes publications meant for a Norwegian – and Swedish – readership as well as a broader international audience. The translated published constitution, distributed immediately after it was framed and adopted in May 1814, was an argument towards the outside world, a declaration of Norwegian independence. Alongside providing translations of the Norwegian constitution, a main task for the framers of the constitution and later for the Norwegian authorities was to distribute the written and printed constitution to the Norwegian population. During the Norwegian-Swedish union (1814–1905), a rather loose state construction, it remained not only the legal foundation of the state and a bulwark of Norwegian independence and autonomy but also the main national symbol. The 'extraordinary symbolic power' of the constitution was strengthened by the annual celebration of it since early nineteenth century on Constitution Day 17 May[8] and by the extensive printing and distribution of the constitution directed at a popular readership. During the period 1814–1905 around sixty publications and editions were published in Norwegian[9] in all kinds of formats, ranging from miniatures as early as the 1830s to pictures on postcards, folios and posters.[10] Among the most popular versions from the 1830s onward was the constitution printed on a single sheet, which glazed and framed hang in ordinary people's living rooms. This popular dissemination and the strong position of the constitution among the Norwegian people attracted foreign interest and was emphasised in several travel accounts.[11] Before 1905 the Norwegian constitution was also published in several Swedish translations, as separate prints and in Swedish newspapers in 1814, later primarily as part of collections of Swedish and Norwegian fundamental laws.

---

[8]   W. B. Warner *et al.*, 'The Thing That Invented Norway', *Writing Democracy*, p. 36.
[9]   Norwegian written language during the first half of the nineteenth century was in effect Danish, inherited from the centuries of Danish rule of Norway.
[10]   Some of the editions are caused by amendments to the constitution.
[11]   See below on Laing and Latham's accounts.

Until recently a proper overview of Norwegian editions as well as the number of translations has been lacking. Most of these documents are now included in the online 1814 Bibliography, comprising literature from and about the period 1812–14, as well as in the national catalogue at the National Library of Norway.[12] The national print history of the constitution is not the topic of this chapter. Rather, it will study the translations and publications of the Norwegian constitution directed at a foreign readership during the period 1814 to 1905 with an emphasis on the years 1814 to 1850. The number of translations almost equals the number of Norwegian editions.

So far, around sixty translations, including different editions, of the Norwegian constitution have been identified for the period 1814–1905. Additionally, there were several translations into Swedish; at least twelve publications, some of them with many editions. The international circulation of the Norwegian constitution was most prominent during the first half of the nineteenth century, with forty translations in the first thirty-five years after its proclamation. The constitution – or parts of it – is translated into nine different languages, including English, German, French, Italian, Spanish, Czech, Hebrew, Danish and Swedish during this period, later also into Polish and Esperanto. The publication of translations saw certain peaks depending on shifting political contexts. The first of these is around the year of its adoption, in 1814, the next one in the 1840s and the third around 1905. Of the sixty translations up until 1905, the main languages are German (twenty-nine editions) and French (fourteen editions). Three of the French translations were published in Sweden using the international diplomatic language of the time. Out of eighteen translations from 1840 to 1850, as many as fifteen were translations in different German publications.

There are only six translations in English, three of which, including a second edition, are of the May constitution published in 1814 and 1816. The next one, and the first English translation of the November constitution, was published as part of a travel account in 1840. In 1895 an English translation was published in Chicago; another one in London in 1905.

As early as in 1820 the Norwegian constitution was translated into Italian, published as a separate print in Naples connected to the current constitutionalisation processes there.[13] During the last half of the century

[12] The numbers referred to in this chapter are based on the 1814 Bibliography and additional research literature (see enclosed bibliography): <www.nb.no/bibliografi/1814>. The bibliography comprises more than 4,000 references to books and articles in books and journals. Most of the publications mentioned in this chapter can be found in this database, many of them accessible in digitalised versions.

[13] *Constituzione di Norvegia del 1814 sotto Carlo XIII*. Trad. in italiano da Angelo Lanzellotto (Napoli, 1820).

it was translated into Spanish and Danish, and a Hebrew translation was published in Norway in 1904.

The published translations of the constitutional texts appeared in multiple formats and genres as part of a transnational discourse and targeting a broader readership. The present overview of translations thus includes publication of the constitution as a separate print, as a pamphlet or booklet, sometimes comparing different constitutions article by article, with or without editorial comments or explanations. In several instances the Norwegian Constitution – the whole text or parts of it – was translated and included in different kinds of publications. A new mode of publication from the early nineteenth century was the edited collection of constitutions, containing printed European or 'Modern' constitutions. Translations of the constitutions could also, as mentioned, be part of travel accounts, a genre that 'famously served as a medium for political reflection' where politics and history often intersected.[14] Other genres were political essays and treatises on constitutional law. Translations are also found – although not systematically collected in the overview – as parts of periodical literature and in encyclopaedias, both important genres and media for transmitting political and societal knowledge across national and linguistic borders. In addition, there were translations of the constitution in several newspapers as part of political reportage, of which are recorded translations in German and Swedish newspapers in 1814 and in a Czech newspaper in 1848.[15]

In the following sections I will examine some of the translations of the Norwegian constitution, focusing on the years around 1814, the 1840s and briefly the period around 1905. Whereas the first and third of these periods are characterised by published translations as part of more or less official diplomatic efforts, the second is part of a transnational constitutional discourse, which will be further discussed below.

'THE NORWEGIAN QUESTION':
PUBLIC DIPLOMACY AND TRANSLATIONS IN 1814

During 1813 and 1814 a considerable number of pamphlets circulated across Europe discussing the so called 'Norwegian question' concerning the transfer of Norway from the Danish to the Swedish king against the expressed will of the Norwegian people. In this debate Norway was for the first time discussed in the European public sphere in proclamations, bulletins and

---

[14]   J. Brophy, 'The Second Wave', pp. 89–90.
[15]   A Czech translation was printed in the Prague weekly *Kwěty a plody* 5 August 1848 (Gammelgaard, 'Constitutions as a Transnational Genre', p. 96).

tracts as well as in newspaper and journal articles. Almost 500 documents, including different editions and translations as well as handwritten pamphlets, circulated as part of this transnational propaganda war surrounding the cession of Norway to Sweden in 1814.[16]

The constitution itself played an important role in this war of opinion. As one of its last measures, the Constituent Assembly, gathered at Eidsvold Manor, chose an editorial board to publish in print its transactions, directed at the Norwegian as well as a foreign readership. The new constitution was adopted and signed on 17 May. The same day, the Danish Prince Christian Frederik, heir to the Danish and Norwegian throne and current governor of Norway, was elected king of Norway. By 31 May the constitution had been translated into French and English and published alongside the Norwegian versions. The editorial board ensured 'that this fundamental law of the Kingdom of Norway and the documents annexed to it, are, word for word, conformable to the chief records of the National Assembly.'[17] The English and French versions were printed by Jacob Lehmann, one of only three printers and publishers in the Norwegian capital of Christiania at that time.[18]

The writing, translation and printing of the new constitution, a revolutionary constitution based on the principle of popular sovereignty – although within a monarchical framework – were central parts of the struggle for national independence in a fundamentally unclear international situation. The constitution served as a declaration of independence, and the translations made the Norwegian policy known to a European public and may thus be seen as an effort of Norwegian *public diplomacy* at the time by 'engaging a foreign public through the explanation of policy.'[19] Additionally, at least four translations appeared during 1814, two of them by pro-Norwegian agents abroad. The first German translation of the May constitution, if only in part, was printed in Altona, at that time belonging to the Danish Empire, in June 1814. It was published as part of a propaganda

---

[16]   On the pamphlet war and the recorded publications, see R. Hemstad, *Propaganda-krig*; R. Hemstad (ed.), *'Like a Herd of Cattle'* and the 1814 Bibliography.

[17]   *The Constitution of the Kingdom of Norway* (Christiania, 1814); *Constitution du royaume de Norwège*. The other documents annexed to the constitution were an address from the assembly to the Prince Regent and the answer from Christian Frederik, accepting the election as king of Norway.

[18]   Lehmann also published three Norwegian editions in different formats, which could be bought in all post offices around the country. R. Anker Nilsen, *Hva fikk nordmennene å lese i 1814? En bibliografi* (Oslo, 1997), pp. 73–7.

[19]   N. J. Cull, 'A Region Speaks: Nordic Public Diplomacy in Historical Context', *Place Branding and Public Diplomacy*, 12:2–3 (2016), pp. 153.

tract defending Norway, comprising parts of the constitution alongside proclamations, letters, sermons and speeches.[20] A complete German translation was published later that year in *Politisches Journal* in Hamburg.[21] Another one followed in 1815 in the *Allgemeine Staats-Korrespondenz*.[22] The Norwegian constitution, or parts of it, was also published in the important German newspapers *Hamburgischen Unparteyischen Correspondenten, Augsburger Allgemeine Zeitung* and *Rheinischer Merkur*, thereby making it accessible to a broader German and international readership.[23]

The Norwegian resistance against Swedish power politics was met with acclamation from liberals, not least in Britain. The first English translation published in London was part of another propaganda publication, a travelogue dated August 1814 and published by Jens Wolff, an Englishman with strong Norwegian connections through his family and business relations. As an interesting example of politicised travel literature, this account comprised a comprehensive political appendix, reprinting a range of proclamations and other relevant Norwegian and British documents.[24] The helpful mediator in this process was Carsten Anker, the old Norwegian friend of Prince Christian Frederik and the owner of Eidsvold Manor. Anker had been sent to Great Britain in early 1814 in order to try to persuade the British government and to influence Parliament, the press and British opinion in general. The extensive publication used as its frontispiece a lithography showing Christian Frederik as 'King of Norway' – indeed the only one of its kind – and the book was dedicated to him. The translation of 'The New Constitution of Norway' is not identical to the official translation, indicating that this publication was not available to Anker and Wolff when editing the political appendix.

During the summer of 1814 the Swedish Crown Prince Charles John returned from the European battlefields and went to war against Norway. At the Convention at Moss of 14 August the Norwegians agreed to accept the union, and Charles John allowed the Norwegians to keep the new constitution with only minor changes. Christian Frederik had to abdicate, and

---

[20] 'Entwurf eines Grundgesetzes für das Königreich Norwegen', *Aktenstücke und Aufsätze die neueste Geschichte Norwegens betreffend* (Altona, 1814).

[21] *Politisches Journal nebst Anzeige von gelehrten und andern Sachen* 2:9 (1814), 778–86; 2:10 (1814), 880–92.

[22] 'Konstitutionen. Grundgesetz des Königreichs Norwegen', *Allgemeine Staats-Korrespondenz*, ed. Bauer, Behr and Schott 3:8–9 (1814–15), 128–39; 415–35.

[23] See S. Eisenträger, 'The European Press and the Question of Norwegian Independence', MA thesis, Norwegian University of Life Sciences (Ås, 2013).

[24] J. Wolff, *[A Northern Tour]: Sketches on a Tour to Copenhagen, through Norway and Sweden* (London, 1814), pp. cxi–cxxvi. Second edition 1816, reprinted 1820.

Christian Frederik.

KING of NORWAY.

Born 18th Sept 1786.

Elected 17th May 1814.

Published August 1, 1814. by Y Arliss York Street, Portman Square.

PLATE 10.1. The Norwegian constitution was translated into English and printed in a comprehensive political appendix in Jens Wolff's travel book, published August 1814 and dedicated to Christian Frederik as 'King of Norway' – the only known illustration of him during his few months in this position.

the recalled extraordinary Norwegian parliament revised and signed the constitution and elected the Swedish king, Charles XIII, as king of Norway on 4 November 1814.

The revised constitution of 4 November was published in four editions (one of those was suppressed due to a missing article) for a Norwegian readership.[25] It was not translated by the government, however – not in 1814, nor in the following years. It seems that there were no official translations of the November constitution until May 1905. The constitution was then, again, used in the renewed war of opinion against Swedish political claims. The first translated version of the revised constitution is tellingly in Swedish, published in Stockholm in December 1814.[26] During the year of its proclamation, the Norwegian constitution was thus published in fourteen different editions, half of them translations, six of those of the May constitution. In addition, the constitution was translated and published in newspapers connected to the diplomatic struggle on 'the Norwegian question'. The 1814 translations, and the range of translations that followed, made the constitution immediately known, or at least available, to a European public.

<h2 style="text-align:center">A WAVE OF CONSTITUTIONS</h2>

The period after 1815 is often described as a time of European reaction and restoration, an approach lately modified by, among others, Paul Schroeder.[27] The interest in translating, publishing and reading constitutional texts suggests a current liberal orientation among the population. One of these early constitutions, read and discussed after 1815 and to a certain degree being a point of reference, was the Eidsvold constitution of 1814. The wide transnational circulation of the Norwegian constitution is hence to be understood in the context of the modern constitutional movement, following the American and French revolutions. Evolving as a textual tradition since 1776, modern constitutional writing became a global practice.[28]

[25] A. Nilsen, *1814*, pp. 73–7, 162–70.
[26] *Konungariket Norriges Grundlag, gifven af Riksförsamlingen i Eidsvold den 17 Maj 1814, samt i anledning af Norriges och Sveriges förening, närmare bestämd på Norriges utomordentliga Storting i Christiania den 4 November 1814* (Stockholm, 1814). The May constitution, with suggested amendments, was published in *Allmänna Journalen*, 1–16 November 1814, the November constitution in *Göteborgs-Posten*, 27 December 1814 and following numbers.
[27] P. W. Schroeder, *The Transformation of European Politics 1763–1848* (Oxford, 1994). See also M. Broers and A. A. Caiani (eds), *A History of the European Restorations*, 2 vols (London, 2020).
[28] D. Michalsen, 'The Many Textual Identities of Constitutions', *Writing Democracy*, pp. 60–2.

Around 1814 Europe found itself, in Markus Prutsch's words, 'swept along by a wave of constitutionalisation'.[29] The Norwegian constitution was typical of its time, it was only one of many in this wave of modern written constitutions seen as the constitutive and normative foundation of the state's political organisation.[30]

Prescribing a political vision, the constitutions were not only national documents, the fundamental law governing a specific state, they were also connected with 'literally hundreds of similar constitutional texts across states', as Dag Michalsen points out.[31] A shared transnational genre, 'a category of texts similar in form, style, content, and the social actions they represent', guided the constitutional writings.[32] The new written and published constitutions were thus interconnected as parts of an intellectual exchange, an entangled transnational political discourse across borders. They served as transmitters of new ideas, as models and inspiration when drafting new constitutions and as arguments in political discourse. For the middle-class liberal movement in post-revolutionary Europe, the creation of a constitution became by far the most important concern, Fabian Rausch underlines; 'few subjects dominated political discourse as much [...] as the constitutions of the traditional and newly emerging states or political bodies'.[33]

This broad pan-European liberal discourse makes constitutional texts distinguished examples of a transnational print circuit across linguistic and national borders. Most of these new constitutions were short-lived, however. A central dimension making the Norwegian constitution of particular interest internationally as a possible point of reference was therefore not only its revolutionary, liberal and democratic character, but also its longevity.

This new constitutional discourse and the role of the public sphere are underlined in one of the first annotated collections of this kind, presented as a 'Handbook for present and future representatives', by Sebald Brendel, published in Bamberg and Leipzig in 1817. In the two-volume work the new political conditions and new modes of discussions among broader

---

[29]   M. J. Prutsch, *Making Sense of Constitutional Monarchism in Post-Napoleonic France and Germany* (London, 2012), p. 44.

[30]   E. Holmøyvik, 'The Changing Meaning of 'Constitution' in Norwegian Constitutional History', *Writing Democracy*, p. 46.

[31]   D. Michalsen, 'The Many Textual', p. 62.

[32]   K. Gammelgaard, 'Constitutions as a Transnational Genre', p. 92.

[33]   F. Rausch, '"Constitutional Fever"? Constitutional Integration in Post-Revolutionary France, Great Britain and Germany, 1814–c.1835', *Journal of Modern European History* 15:2 (2017), p. 221.

parts of the population, including demands for national parliaments, are clearly emphasised in the preface.[34] Brendel's work was one of two parallel publications of this kind, both containing a translation of the Norwegian constitution, Brendel's in an abridged version. *Die Constitutionen der europäischen Staaten zeit den letzten 25 Jahren* was published by Brockhaus in Leipzig and Altenburg from 1817 to 1825 and in an enlarged edition in 1832–3, naming Karl Heinrich Ludwig Pölitz as the editor.[35] In the preface the importance of knowledge about all the 'neueuropäischen Constitutionen' is underlined. The work, presented as new of its kind, was intended not only for 'Staatsmänner und Diplomaten' but for 'ein größeres Publicum' – anyone wanting historical knowledge of these constitutions, which were translated therefore into German and presented through historical introductions.[36]

Similar collections of constitutions became a popular publication form, with several mainly German and French collections during the nineteenth century and beyond, a couple of Spanish collections in the 1880s and 1890s and British and Irish publications in the early twentieth century and later.[37]

The Norwegian constitution and the German constitutional discourse of the 1840s

An early expression of the German interest in the Norwegian constitution after 1814 is the political pamphlet by Henrich Steffens, a Norwegian-born author and natural scientist connected to several German universities. His work on the Norwegian parliament, published in Berlin in 1825, contained a translation of the Norwegian constitution.[38] Whereas interest was somewhat limited during the first decades, the 1840s represented an upsurge of German translations of the Norwegian constitution. Fifteen of eighteen translations during this period were published in German states, reflecting the intensive domestic constitutional debates, culminating with the German revolution and the aborted National Assembly in Paulskirche in

---

[34] 'Vorrede', Sebald Brendel, *Die Geschichte, das Wesen und der Werth der National-al-Repräsentation oder vergleichende historisch-pragmatische Darstellung der Staaten der alten und neuen Welt*, 2 vols (Bamberg, Leipzig, 1817), p. [i].
[35] K. H. L. Pölitz, *Die europäischen Verfassungen seit dem Jahre 1789 bis auf die neueste Zeit: mit geschichtlichen Erläuterungen und Einleitungen*, 2nd edn (Leipzig, 1832–3). The Norwegian constitution was published in the second volume.
[36] *Ibid.*, p. ix.
[37] For references, see <www.nb.no/bibliografi/1814>.
[38] H. Steffens, *Der norwegische Storthing im Jahre 1824: geschichtliche Darstellung und Aktenstycke*, (Berlin, 1825), pp. 176–99.

Frankfurt 1848–9. In this context the Norwegian constitution served as a model and an inspiring example.[39]

In 1848–9 alone the Norwegian constitution appeared as separate prints or as part of political pamphlets comparing different constitutions in Stettin, Nuremberg, Erlangen, Stuttgart, Wesel and several in Berlin.[40] The harsh censorship regime in most of the German states at the time restricted the editorial comments to a minimum. However, the political message was suggested between the lines. The Stettin publication was 'dedicated to the free German nation.'[41] In the 1848 translation published in Nuremberg the title states that the Norwegian constitution is 'the most liberal constitutional-monarchic constitution in Europe.' The preface underlines that many people are pointing to the Norwegian constitution in the current turbulent times, and it is argued that there would be public interest in a separate publication of the constitution – not just printed as a part of a collection.[42]

In addition to the translations, with or mostly without comments, the Norwegian constitutional system was discussed in several German books and encyclopaedias: in Leipzig in 1847, in Halle in 1848 (with the following statement in the title: *Die Norwegische Verfassung: ein Vorbild für Preussen*), in Rotteck and Welcker's important multivolume work *Staats-Lexicon* (1841, 1847–8) and in the two-volume account *Das Königreich Norwegens, statistisch beschrieben*, written by the Norwegian author Gustav Peter Blom

---

[39] See also M. Löhnig, 'Die norwegische Verfassung von 1814 in der deutschen Verfassungspublizistik des 19. Jahrhunderts', *Journal on European History of Law* 10:1 (2019), 40–4.

[40] *Constitution des Königreichs Norwegen vom 17. Mai und 4. November 1814* (Stettin, 1848); F. W. Ghillany, *Die Verfassung des Königreichs Norwegen: Das freisinnigste constitutionell-monarchische Grundgesetz in Europa* (Nürnberg, 1848); A. Rauch, *Parlamentarisches Taschenbuch enthaltend die Verfassungen von Nordamerika, Norwegen, Neapel, Toscana, Sardinien, Rom, Oesterreich, Belgien, der Schweiz, England und den Entwurf einer deutschen Reichsverfassung* (Erlangen, 1848), vol. 1, pp. 27–57; T. Bromme, *Die Verfassungen der Vereinigten Staaten von Nord-Amerika, der Frei-Staaten Pennsylvania und Texas, der Königreiche Belgien und Norwegen, die Bundes-Verfassung der Schweiz und die Englische Staats-Verfassung Zur Beantwortung der Frage: Ob Republik, ob konstitutionelle Monarchie?* (Stuttgart, 1849); *Welche Verfassung ist die beste?* (Wesel, 1849); J. Horwitz, *Die Verfassungen der constitutionell-monarchischen und republikanischen Staaten der Gegenwart. Zweite Lieferung, Nord-America, Belgien, Norwegen* (Berlin, 1848); *Die Verfassungen der Vereinigten Staaten von Nord-Amerika, des Staates New-York, des Königreichs Norwegen und des Königreichs Belgien* (Berlin, 1848).

[41] All translations are by the author when not stated otherwise.

[42] F. Ghillany, *Die Verfassung*, p. 3.

and published in Leipzig in 1843.[43] Additionally four German translations
of the whole or parts of the constitution had been published between 1840
and 1844: by Ludolf Wienbarg in Altona in 1840, by August Theodor Brömel
(published in Bergen in Norway and commissioned in Leipzig and Hamburg in 1842), in a pamphlet in Königsberg in 1843 (where the translation is
introduced this way: 'Everyone recognises the importance the constitution
of the related people has for us Germans. – It is difficult to speak about it
publicly here, but hopefully that is also unnecessary') and as an appendix in
Theodor Mügge's travelogue *Reise durch Skandinavien* in 1844.[44]

In his seminal work on constitutional monarchism in post-Napoleonic
Europe, Prutsch states that even if foreign constitutions did assume the
role of a 'stockroom' of arguments for personal political purposes, the progressive Norwegian constitution did not become an 'immediate reference
point for Germans sceptical of "revolution" in any way, shape or form'.[45]
The main obstacle was that little was known about political developments
in Scandinavia. Prutsch refers to only one translation into German in 1815
(as we have seen, there were some more around 1814) and says that 'a critical analysis or debate of the Constitution did not ensue'.[46] The Norwegian
constitution was probably not a model in 1815, but it certainly became one
during the pre-March period, particularly as part of the German constitutional discourse of the late 1840s. The publication of numerous translations and reprints of the constitutional document itself as well as other
related kinds of publications on Norwegian political and constitutional life
reflected a growing interest among German readers in information on this

---

[43] *Parallele der Preussischen Verfassung vom 3. Februar 1847 mit den Verfassungen von
Churhessen, Norwegen und Belgie* (Leipzig, 1847); H. Hellmar, *Die Norwegische Verfassung: ein Vorbild für Preussen* (Halle, 1848); C. von Rottech and C. Welcker, *Das
Staats-Lexicon. Encyclopädie der sämmtlichen Staatswissenschaften für alle* Stände
11 (Altona, 1841), pp. 584–628; 2nd edn, 9 (Altona, 1847), pp. 764–86; *Supplemente
zur ersten* Auflage 4 (Altona, 1848), pp. 28–57; G. P. Blom, *Das Königreich Norwegens,
statistisch beschrieben*, 2 vol. (Leipzig, 1843). In his publication, Blom comments on
the lack of knowledge about Norway and about the real relationship between Norway and Sweden among Germans, even though, as he points out, the constitution
was known to the German readership through several translations (vol. 1, p. xi; vol.
2, p. 2).

[44] L. Wienbarg, *Geist der Norwegischen Verfassung, Quadriga. Vermischte Schriften*,
vol. 1 (Altona, 1840), pp. 127–246; A. T. Brömel, *Die freie Verfassung Norwegens in
ihrer geschichtlichen Entstehung und weiterer Entwicklung, ihrem Wesen und ihren
Folgen* (Bergen, 1842), pp. 297–322; *Grundgesetz des Königreichs Norwegen* (Königsberg, 1843), p. 3; T. Mügge, *Reise durch Skandinavien. Skizzen aus dem Norden*, 2 vol.
(Hannover, 1844), pp. 426–51.

[45] M. Prutsch, *Making Sense of*, pp. 72, 52.

[46] *Ibid.*, p. 53.

peripheral political entity and its constitutional system, which became a point of reference and a source of inspiration.[47]

BRITISH TRANSLATIONS, TRAVEL ACCOUNTS AS POLITICAL
LITERATURE AND TRANSLATIONS AROUND 1905

The Norwegian constitution served as an argument, an example and a model not only within a German constitutional discourse but also within a British nineteenth-century context, with the Chartist movement and later the Irish Repeal and Home Rule movements of clear relevance. The first English translation of the Norwegian November constitution was as part of a travelogue, confirming the socio-political dimension of the genre.[48] British travel accounts from Norway flourished during the first half of the nineteenth century, depicting Norway as an utopian model.[49] Among the most politicised of those, and with a transnational impact, was Samuel Laing's *Journal of a Residence in Norway*, published 1836, where the Norwegian constitution and liberal political system are highly praised, not least compared to his account of a despotic government in Sweden.[50] The political background for Laing's descriptions was the controversial British policy towards Norway around 1814, when Great Britain supported Sweden in forcing the Norwegians into the union. Laing calls it 'the foulest blot, perhaps, in British history', and argues that 'Norway has a claim morally and politically upon the British nation.'[51] Laing presents the Norwegian constitution as a model but does not include the constitutional text as such. His contemporary Robert Gordon Latham, who travelled in Norway in the mid-1830s, includes a translation of the whole constitution, which

[47] See also M. Löhnig, 'Die norwegische Verfassung', pp. 40–4.
[48] A French translation of the constitution was a part of *British and Foreign State Papers*, 1814, intended for the government and the diplomacy. In 1841 this series was republished to make it accessible to the common reader. *British and Foreign State Papers* 1: II (1812–1814), (London, 1841), pp. 926–41.
[49] P. Fjågesund and R. A. Symes, *The Northern Utopia. British Perceptions of Norway in the Nineteenth Century* (Amsterdam, New York, 2003), p. 99–101.
[50] S. Laing, *Journal of a Residence in Norway During the Years 1834, 1835, & 1836: Made with a View to Enquire Into the Moral and Political Economy of that Country, and the Condition of Its Inhabitants* (London, 1836, with several later editions). His critique of Sweden, expanded on in a separate account, was met by a counter-publication by the Swedish politician Magnus Björnstjerna. Laing's travel accounts from Norway and Sweden were also translated into German and his Swedish account into Norwegian. See also B. Porter, 'Virtue and Vice in the North. The Scandinavian Writings of Samuel Laing', *Scandinavian Journal of History*, 23 (1998), 3–4.
[51] S. Laing, *Journal*, iv.

he terms 'the most democratic constitution in Europe', in his two-volume account *Norway and the Norwegians,* published in 1840.[52] After reprinting and commenting on the constitution Latham enthusiastically underlines the prominent position the constitution had among ordinary people, not least through different printed formats:

> Such is the Norwegian Constitution, of which every man, woman, and child in the country knows the import and the value ... The whole Constitution is printed upon a single sheet. I never went into a farmhouse of the better, and rarely into one of the humbler sort, without seeing it glazed and framed, hanging against the wall like an ordnance map, or a family picture at home.[53]

Along with these poster versions there were also smaller mobile formats, Latham notes: 'Happy too are the children of the North! that have a Constitution as portable as a pocket-handkerchief.'[54]

The next translations into English, it seems, came around the turn of the century, connected to the emerging political crisis leading to the dissolution of the Norwegian-Swedish union during the second half of 1905. The first of these, published 1895, is probably also the first translation published in the United States. It was translated and published by the Norwegian-American Knute Nelson after his election as the first Scandinavian-born American to the United States Senate and before the Congress convened at the end of that year. There is no introduction to this translation.[55] The next one, however, published in London in April 1905 by the Norwegian journalist and later vice consul in London, Hans Lien Brækstad, does include a 'historical and political survey'.[56] *The Constitution of the Kingdom of Norway* was distributed, like the pamphlets in 1814, to politicians and editors as a public diplomacy measure with the aim of improving the knowledge of the constitution abroad and influence British opinion. The introduction refers to the lack of available translations abroad:

---

[52] R. G. Latham, *Norway and the Norwegians* (London, 1840), vol. 1, p. 3. The constitution is reprinted in vol. 2, pp. 61–100.

[53] R. Latham, vol. 2, p. 102.

[54] *Ibid.*

[55] *The Constitution of the Kingdom of Norway: adopted by the Convention at Eidsvold on the 17th day of May, 1814, and amended and ratified by the Storthing on the 4th day of November, 1814, with all subsequent amendments incorporated,* translated from the Norwegian by K. Nelson (Chicago, 1895), republished 1899.

[56] H. L. Brækstad, *The Constitution of the Kingdom of Norway: an Historical and Political Survey: with a complete translation of the Norwegian constitution and the act of union between Norway and Sweden* (London, 1905).

PLATE 10.2. In his travel account after visiting Norway in the 1830s, Robert G. Latham described the prominent position of the Norwegian constitution of 1814, also among ordinary people, as it was common to have an affiche of it hanging on the wall at home. Several different constitution posters were produced after the mid-1830s ('Grunnlovsplakat' (constitution poster), 1836, by J. C. Walter).

During the last twenty-five years, whenever the many conflicts between the Norwegians and the Swedes have attracted attention in the English and in the Continental press, it has been only too apparent from the articles that have appeared on the subject that the writers, for the most part, have been unacquainted with the Norwegian Constitution and with the Act of Union between Norway and Sweden. Nor is this to be wondered at, as the text of these important documents has not been accessible to English readers.

Samuel Laing's praise of the Norwegian constitution in his travel account serves as an additional argument for publishing a translation of this constitution in 1905, as 'the most liberal of constitutions, one of which any modern nation might boast'.[57]

In addition to Brækstad's translation, which seemingly served as a semi-official publication, the Norwegian constitution was translated into French and German and published in Norway during the spring and the ongoing political conflict with Sweden.[58] The updated translations comprised amendments made to the constitution until 25 May 1905. On 7 June the Norwegian parliament unilaterally declared the union dissolved, followed by negotiations with Sweden. On 26 October both parliaments sanctioned the results of the negotiation, hence securing a peaceful solution. The only Norwegian constitution published this autumn was a photo-lithography of the original handwritten document of 17 May 1814, kept in the Parliamentary archive.[59] On 18 November 1905 the original first article of the constitution was reinstated, proclaiming Norway, again, as a 'free, independent and indivisible Realm'.

CONCLUSION

The transnational print history of the Norwegian constitution is a history of Norwegian public diplomacy on the one hand and of the utilisation of this constitution as an argument, an example and a model in constitutional discourses in several European countries on the other. Translations published in Norway, provided by the Norwegian authorities, played an

---

[57]   *Ibid.*, p. viii.

[58]   *Staats-Grundgesetz des Königreichs Norwegen gegeben am 17. Mai 1814: mit späteren Änderungen bis zum 25. Mai 1905: nebst der Reichsakte vom 6. August 1815* (Kristiania, 1905); *Constitution du royaume de Norvège adoptée le 17. Mai 1814: Avec les changements et additions y apportés jusqu'au 25 Mai 1905: Suivie de l'acte d'union du 6 aout 1815* (Kristiania, 1905).

[59]   *Fotolitografisk Gjengivelse af det i Storthingets Arkiv opbevarede Original-Haandskrift af Kongeriget Norges Grundlov af 17:de Mai 1814* (Kristiania, 1905).

important role in the political conflicts with Sweden in 1814 and 1905, closely connected to the establishment and dissolution of the union on the Scandinavian Peninsula. Around the turn of the century, as part of the conflict leading to the dissolution of the union with Sweden in 1905, new translations of the constitution were published in order to promote the Norwegian case.

The Eidsvold constitution was – and still is – of extraordinary symbolic importance in Norway. Less known is its international dimension, both as a declaration of the independence of the re-established state in 1814 and in making Norwegian policy known internationally as regards the dissolution of the Norwegian-Swedish union in 1905, but also as a vital part of the transnational circuits of constitutions in the nineteenth century. The mapping of the transnational print history of the Norwegian 1814 constitution illuminates a circulation of prints not only within but also outside Norway, despite the peripheral geographical, political and cultural position of the country. Numerous translations in a variety of different publication formats helped to disseminate political knowledge and Norwegian experiences to broader European reading communities. The liberal Norwegian constitution thus served as an argument, an example and a model in the transnational constitutional discourse that flourished in post-Napoleonic Europe, with the German-speaking sphere as a pertinent example. Transnational and transmedial print history of different kinds of publications – even short constitutional texts originated in the periphery of Europe – may open new perspectives on the role of translations and circulation in expanding political literacy and empowering citizens by promoting a politically engaged literary citizenship.

No. 1.　　　　　　Januar 1868.　　　　1. Aargang

Børnevennen

Missionsblad for Børn

Kom over og hjælp os! Ap. Gj. 16, 9.

PLATE 11.1. *Børnevennen*, January 1868.

11

Heavenly Citizens of the World: Child Readers and the Missionary Cause

Janicke S. Kaasa

THE WOODCUT THAT FEATURES regularly on the cover of the monthly missionary children's magazine *Børnevennen* (The Children's Friend, 1868–86) shows six men placed in a landscape. Each of them seems to represent a heathen culture, and all of them are either reading or appear to be listening to those who are reading from what most probably are bibles. The cross figures prominently in the middle, placed against a background of water, mountains and a rising or possibly setting sun, enveloped in a radiant light that falls upon the group. Spruce and birch tower on the left, their roots intertwined with the palm trees on the right, stretching upwards to the banner on which the magazine title is written. Below the woodcut are the words from the Acts of the Apostles 16:9, 'Come over and help us!',[1] referring to Paul's vision of a Macedonian man begging for help and his interpretation of this vision as a call from God to go and preach the gospel. Both the woodcut and the quotation anticipate the magazine's emphasis on pagan people in faraway countries and on missionary work and suggest the importance of the written word in that context. What is more, the cover seems to establish the active role of the reader through the call from the heathens, implying his or her responsibility to come over and help, or at least to preach the gospel.

The first magazines aimed at child readers in Europe were published during the latter half of the eighteenth century. Briton John Newbery's

---

[1] 'Kom over og hjælp os!' (*Børnevennen. Missionsblad for Børn*, December 1868). All translations are by me, unless otherwise stated.

The Lilliputian Magazine, published in 1751, is considered the very first, but both the Swedish *Wecko-Blad til Barns Nytta och Nöje*, published by Samuel Hasselberg in 1766, and the Dano-Norwegian *Ungdommens Ven*, published in 1770, are early examples of European children's magazines.[2] Although relatively short-lived, and without a large readership, these early children's magazines illustrate the important changes in European eighteenth-century print culture, of which periodicals were a driving force.[3] These developments in the production and spread of children's periodical literature continued into the next century, and by the time the Norwegian missionary children's magazine *Børnevennen* was established in 1868, there had been a slow but steady increase in the number of magazines of general interest aimed at Norwegian children, leading up to a significant growth of new periodicals in the 1870s.[4]

The first attempts to establish specialised missionary magazines for children in Norway, however, appeared some thirty years earlier, in the late 1840s, and thus correspond with the growth in religious children's magazines elsewhere in Europe. These periodicals came about in a larger flora of religious literature aimed specifically at children, such as books with religious content, Bible editions, catechisms and psalm books (see Haarberg's chapter in this book).[5] In the 1840s and 1850s, when the children's magazine became an increasingly important genre in Norway, there were also attempts to establish general-interest children's magazines, such as Niels Andreas Biørn's successful weekly *Børnevennen* (1843–50) in addition to more ephemeral endeavours like *Huusvennen* (1847) and *Illustreret Børneven* (1856).[6] Evidently, like their predecessors, these publications also featured religious materials, and their editors were often, like Biørn,

[2]   S. Svensson, *Barnavänner och skolkamrater. Svenska barn- och ungdomstidningar 1766–1900 sedda mot en internationell bakgrund* (Stockholm, 2018), p. 93; N. Shine, 'Børneblade i Danmark fra 1770–1900', *Børn og Bøger*, 4 (1971), 91–8, at p. 91. It should be noted that many of these early periodicals also catered to adults, and Nina Christensen argues that *Ungdommens Ven* was aimed at young girls as well as their mothers and aunts (N. Christensen, *Videbegær – Oplysning, børnelitteratur, dannelse* (Aarhus, 2012), p. 178).

[3]   E. Krefting et al., *En pokkers skrivesyge. 1700-tallets dansk-norske tidsskrifter mellom sensur og ytringsfrihet* (Oslo, 2014), pp. 25–6. See also E. Krefting et al., 'Introduction', in E. Krefting et al. (eds), *Eighteenth-Century Periodicals as Agents of Change: Perspectives on Northern Enlightenment* (Leiden, Boston, 2015), pp. 1–13.

[4]   E. Økland, 'Norske barneblad', in T. Ørjasæter et al., *Den norske barnelitteraturen gjennom 200 år: Lesebøker, barneblad, bøker og tegneserier* (Oslo, 1981), p. 103.

[5]   S. Hagemann, *Barnelitteratur i Norge inntil 1850* (Oslo, 1965), p. 248; E. Økland, 'Norske barneblad', p. 100.

[6]   E. Økland, 'Norske barneblad', p. 99.

priests. Both the general-interest magazines and those that were more specifically dedicated to religious content, including missionary magazines, contributed to widening the scope of religious reading materials for children as well as the contexts for this reading beyond school and beyond the catechism.[7] Certainly, these developments are not unique to Norway. Yet the missionary magazines aimed at Norwegian children offer a useful vantage point for considering the staging of eighteenth-century child readers as well as the transnational contexts for the periodical literature that was made available to them.

Like so many of these early periodicals, the first missionary magazines were neither numerous, widely read nor long lived and could be considered marginal and of minor importance. Nonetheless, they possibly paved the way for later and more prolific publications, and they testify to the range of reading materials that were available in the early stages of Norwegian printed children's literature. They also offer valuable insight into the various roles the child readers were ascribed in children's magazines generally and in the missionary magazines specifically: as citizens of the world and of the heavens, and as potential future missionaries.

In the following I examine the staging of the child reader in the early Norwegian children's magazines that were issued by or affiliated with missionary movements, with particular emphasis on the very first children's missionary magazine in Norway, *Missionsblad for Børn* (Missionary Magazine for Children, 1847–8). The chapter argues that the Norwegian missionary magazines are important to be able to understand the ways in which the Norwegian child was staged as an active participant in religious life and, as such, in print culture. Furthermore, by tracing the foreign models from which these publications drew both inspiration and actual material, the chapter investigates some of the transnational networks of and contexts for these magazines.

CHRISTIAN CITIZENS IN TRAINING: RELIGIOUS CHILDREN'S MAGAZINES

Reading religious periodicals from the nineteenth century requires 'careful and ongoing methodological reflection', Mark Knight notes, pointing to the complexities of the term 'religion' and of interpreting theological material from earlier periods and of often little-known religious groups.[8] Similarly,

---

[7] E. Krefting *et al.*, *En pokkers skrivesyge*, p. 185.
[8] M. Knight, 'Periodicals and Religion', in A. King *et al.* (eds), *The Routledge Handbook to Nineteenth-Century British Periodicals and Newspapers* (London, 2016), p. 356.

Felicity Jensz and Hanna Acke remind us how missionary periodicals 'can inform us of historical events, actors, and places, but must all be read cautiously, and with an awareness of missionary biases', and how these biases were often political as much as religious.[9] These remarks are also valid for the study of the early religious magazines that were aimed at Norwegian children, many of which were affiliated to *Brødrevennene*,[10] the Norwegian branch of the evangelical Moravian Church with strong ties to Germany and Denmark.[11] Indeed, several of the early Norwegian missionary magazines for children were published in the south-western town of Stavanger, where the Moravian Church played a significant role in Christian life from the 1820s until the turn of the century.[12] In this chapter, however, I am less concerned with the theological contents of the magazines as such, and more interested in how the missionary cause had an impact on the staging of the child reader, and how we through these publications may gain a broader understanding of the ways in which the child reader was cast by writers, editors and publishers in mid-nineteenth-century print culture.[13]

Missionary magazines have mainly been approached 'as sources of information on religious, imperial, and cultural history. As historical documents, these often well-indexed and increasingly accessible publications have provided a treasure trove of information.'[14] In the case of missionary magazines for children, academic interest in them as either sources or primary texts has been limited, and due to an apparent lack of literary value, missionary publications are often left out of general historical overviews of children's literature.[15] Another aspect concerns the scarcity of mate-

[9] F. Jensz and H. Acke, 'Introduction', in F. Jensz and H. Acke (eds), *Missions and Media: The Politics of Missionary Periodicals in the Long Nineteenth Century* (Stuttgart, 2013), p. 10.

[10] *Herrnhuter Brüdergemeine* in German.

[11] L. Harberg, *Hundre år for barnet: Norsk Søndagsskoleforbund 1889–1989* (Oslo, 1989), p. 13; I. Sagvaag, *Søndagsskulebarnet i Søndagsskulebladet. Utgreiing om Børnebibliotheket/Barnas Søndagsblad* (Bergen, 1999), p. 12.

[12] P. Øverland, *Kortere avhandlinger om Brødremenigheten i Norge* (Trondheim, 1987), pp. 10, 40. Also significant is that the School of Mission and Theology was founded in Stavanger in 1843 by the Norwegian Mission Society.

[13] For child-centred approaches to children's literature, see for example Ch. Appel and N. Christensen, 'Follow the Child, Follow the Books – Cross-Disciplinary Approaches to a Child-Centred History of Danish Children's Literature 1790–1850', *International Research in Children's Literature*, 10:2 (2017), 194–212; M. O. Grenby, *The Child Reader, 1700–1840* (Cambridge, 2011).

[14] A. King *et al.* (eds), *The Routledge Handbook to Nineteenth-Century British Periodicals and Newspapers* (London, 2016), p. 159.

[15] Sagvaag, *Søndagsskulebarnet i Søndagsskulebladet*, p. 36. For instance, they are omitted from the major historical overviews of Norwegian (T. Birkeland *et al.* (eds),

rials: these first missionary magazines for children were often small and unassuming, printed on cheap paper and with inexpensive binding. Consequently, many copies have been lost. Nevertheless, the materials we *do* have access to in the libraries and archives shed light on the early children's missionary magazines and invite us to approach them not merely as historical or theological sources, but as texts worthy of study in their own right. As Anja Müller points out in her discussion of eighteenth-century English periodicals and prints, 'it is high time that these texts were considered in their function as printed mass media for the construction of childhood'.[16] No doubt, this applies to nineteenth-century missionary children's magazines, too.

In his study of the religious periodical and newspaper press in England during the late eighteenth century and into the nineteenth century, Louis Billington identifies a growth of specialised religious magazines in the period between 1790 and 1840 in which journals promoting foreign missions played a pioneering role.[17] Between the 1820s and 1840s this growth became especially noticeable in the increase of religious children's magazines, which were usually small, with brief texts and a few simple illustrations.[18] *The Child's Companion; or, Sunday Scholars Reward* (1824–1932), issued by the Religious Tract Society, *The Children's Friend* (1824–1930) and the Wesleyan *Child's Magazine* (1824–45) are early examples of successful and long-lived publications, whereas later examples include the *Church Missionary Juvenile Instructor* (1844–90), the London Missionary Society's *Juvenile Missionary Magazine* (1844–66) and the *Juvenile Missionary Herald* (1845–1905).[19] In Germany important publications were

Norsk barnelitteraturhistorie (Oslo, 2018); Hagemann, *Barnelitteratur i Norge inntil 1850*; T. Ørjasæter et al., *Den norske barnelitteraturen gjennom 200 år: Lesebøker, barneblad, bøker og tegneserier* (Oslo, 1981)), Swedish (G. Klingberg, *Svensk barn- och ungdomslitteratur 1591–1839* (Stockholm, 1964); Svensson, *Barnavänner och skolkamrater*) and Danish children's literature (I. Simonsen, *Den danske børnebog i det 19. aarhundrede* (Copenhagen, 1966); T. Weinreich, *Historien om børnelitteratur – dansk børnelitteratur gennem 400 år* (Copenhagen, 2006)).

16   A. Müller, *Framing Childhood in Eighteenth-Century English Periodicals and Prints, 1689–1789* (London, New York, 2009), p. 6.

17   L. Billington, 'The Religious Periodical and Newspaper Press, 1770–1870', in M. Harris and A. Lee (eds), *The Press in English Society from the Seventeenth to Nineteenth Centuries* (Rutherford, London, Toronto, 1986), p. 119.

18   *Ibid.*, p. 121.

19   *Ibid.*, pp. 120–1; K. Drotner, *English Children and their Magazines, 1751–1945* (New Haven and London, 1988), p. 25; Svensson, *Barnavänner och skolkamrater*, pp. 48–9. Even earlier examples include *Katholischer Kinderfreund* (Vienna, 1785) and *The Youth's Magazine or Evangelical Miscellany* (London, 1805–67) (Svensson, *Barnavänner och skolkamrater*, pp. 48–50).

Jugendblättern (1836–1916) and the *Die Sonntagsschule* (1863–c. 1925), and among the most popular examples of such magazines in the Scandinavian countries – influenced by the publications in England and Germany – were the Swedish *Dufwo-rösten* and *Christlig Barntidning* (1848–61), the Danish *Børnenes Blad* (1877–98) and the Norwegian *Børnenes Søndagsblad* (1874–99).[20]

As some of these magazine titles indicate, many of the publications were affiliated to the Sunday school movements, which were hugely influential in distributing religious texts to children.[21] In England, Robert Raikes' Sunday schools in 1780 mark the beginning of the organised Sunday school, whereas the first Sunday school in Germany can be dated to 1824.[22] In Norway early variants of Sunday schools date back to 1734 and to Sunday gatherings for children organised by Brødrevennene. In the 1750s these became more organised, not least with the Haugean movement at the turn of the century, and gradually took the form of Sunday schools. There was a significant increase in the 1870s, concurrent with the development towards a civil public school,[23] but the very first official Sunday school in Norway was the Stavanger Søndagsskole started on 10 March 1844, inspired by and financially supported by the Religious Tract Society (1799) in England.[24] In addition, tract societies had been established in Bergen, Christiania and Stavanger (1832) and had begun publishing texts, mostly translations from English, German and Swedish.[25] This, and the Sunday school movement, certainly played a major role in the development of religious magazines for children in Norway, including those focusing on the missionary cause.

Søndagsblad for Børn (Sunday Magazine for Children) appeared only as a trial issue on 7 July 1844 and is possibly the first Sunday school magazine for children in Norway. The issue is an eight-page leaflet, edited by Erik Nicolai Saxild and published in Christiania (today's Oslo).[26] Clearly,

---

[20]   S. Svensson, *Barnavänner och skolkamrater*, pp. 49–50.
[21]   C. S. Hannabuss, 'Nineteenth-century Religious Periodicals for Children', *British Journal of Religious Education*, 6:1 (1983), 20–40, at p. 21; S. Svensson, *Barnavänner och skolkamrater*, p. 49.
[22]   The first Sunday school in Sweden was organised in the 1850s, and in Finland in 1870 (I. Sagvaag, *Søndagsskulebarnet i Søndagsskulebladet*, p. 21).
[23]   A. Danbolt, 'Den kristelige søndagsskolen – et middel i Lutherstiftelsens kamp for luthersk kristendom. Søndagsskolen og indremisjonen i 1870-årene', *Tidsskrift for Teologi og Kirke*, 79:1 (2008), 48–65.
[24]   I. Hagen, *Barnet i norsk kristenliv: søndagsskolen i Norge gjennom 100 år* (Oslo, 1947), p. 36.
[25]   E. Molland, *Norges kirkehistorie i det 19. århundre*, vol. 1 (Oslo, 1979), p. 164.
[26]   Saxild (1787–1846) was a former teacher, co-director and inspector at the Christiania Sunday school, and a key figure in the establishment of the city's first child

Søndagsblad for Børn was not a successful endeavour. In the postscript dated 29 June 1844 it becomes clear that Saxild, having invited subscribers in January earlier that year, has not yet gathered enough subscribers to cover the costs of the magazine. He once again encourages parents and teachers in and outside the city to subscribe but admits that the magazine's future is uncertain.[27] The magazine explicitly addresses children aged between five and twelve but was intended as a Sunday read for the whole family to facilitate an appropriate marking of the Sabbath. The materials that would provide such an appropriate marking, based on the first and only issue, were religious stories, questions on the scripture, hymns and poetry in the form of an excerpt from the prominent author Henrik Wergeland's poem *Aftenbøn*. The postscript also tells us something about the magazine's over-all purpose: *Søndagsblad for Børn*, Saxild hopes, will enable children's faith to bear fruit for a happy childhood and youth, for the fatherland, and finally for 'the eternal Sabbath, the divine, eternal home!'[28] Thus, it shares with the missionary magazines the function of preparing the child for the divine afterlife and of promoting the idea of the child as what D. J. Konz refers to as 'a pious, responsible Christian citizen in-training'.[29]

The first missionary children's magazines in Norway

The first two examples of children's magazines that were affiliated to the missionary movement in Norway, *For Ungdommen* (For the Youth, 1846–9) and the previously mentioned *Missionsblad for Børn* (1847–8), were both established and edited by Johan Christian Johnsen.[30] A newspaperman and politician, Johnsen (1815–98) is today mostly known for his efforts to

---

asylums in 1839. He published several texts for children, and his attempt to establish *Søndagsblad for Børn* rather late in his life must be seen in context with his longtime engagement in children's welfare in the city.

[27] In an announcement in the later *Børnevennen*, the magazine's future seems to de-pend more on divine intervention than on financial circumstances: "'The Children's Friend", God willing, is to be published next year in the same way and on the same terms as this year' ('"Børnevennen" udkommer, om Gud vil, næste Aar paa same Maade og same Betingelser som iaar'): (*Børnevennen*, December 1868, p. 16).

[28] 'den evige Sabbat, det himmelske, evige hjem!' (*Søndagsblad for Børn*, 1844, p. 8).

[29] D. J. Konz, 'The Many and the One: Theology, Mission and Child in Historical Per-spective', in B. Prevette et al. (eds), *Theology, Mission and Child: Global Perspectives* (Oxford, 2014), pp. 23–46, at p. 32.

[30] K. Aukrust, *Menighetsblad og andre religiøse og kirkelige tidsskrifter i Norge: en foreløpig oversikt* (Oslo, 1991), p. 14; J. B. Halvorsen, *Norsk Forfatter-Lexikon 1814– 1880: paa Grundlag af J.E. Krafts og Chr. Langes 'Norsk Forfatter-Lexikon 1814–1856'*, vol. 3: I–L. (Kristiania, 1892), p. 164.

promote general knowledge and education. He initiated and established several periodicals, his most successful by far being the illustrated and widely read weekly *Almuevennen* (The Friend of the Common People), which he edited from 1848 until 1893.[31]

For Ungdommen was published in Stavanger and anticipates *Almuevennen* in that it features assorted texts on various topics that all qualify as general knowledge.[32] The religious and edifying purpose of the magazine, however, is clear from the very beginning: in the first issue of July 1846 Johnsen invites his readers to join him on a journey, more specifically 'the life journey': 'I have already told you what I consider to be the destination of my life journey, namely Heaven, and it would be dear to me if you agree: because only if this is so, could we travel together.'[33] Later the magazine is presented as the very means to help prepare the young readers for such a journey – 'to look towards the eternal life, that will be the task of this magazine'[34] – to guide them towards Heaven, and to make sure that their role as divine citizens does not yield to that of world citizens. This life journey, then, makes up the framework for the magazine's miscellaneous contents with stories on topics such as zoology, history, geology and geography as well as fables, poetry and biographical texts. Knowledge of the human world, Johnsen explains, makes for a better world, but more importantly it prepares the young reader for the journey towards their heavenly home. In this way, the staging of the child reader as a world citizen is made subordinate and preparatory to what Johnsen considers to be the child's main role, namely that of the heavenly citizen.

[31]　Johnsen also issued a Norwegian translation of Harriet Beecher Stowe's *Uncle Tom's Cabin* in 1861–2 (*Onkel Toms Hytte eller Negerlivet i de amerikanske Slavestater*). Although not credited, it is possible that Johnsen himself translated the text: a decade earlier he had written a series of articles in the weekly *Morgenbladet* entitled 'Nord-Amerika, dets Folk og Institutioner' (North America, its People and Institutions, 1852–3).

[32]　As such, the magazine is comparable to *Billed-Magazin for Børn* (Picture Magazine for Children, 1838–9), the first children's magazine in Norway (see J. S. Kaasa, '"Saavel fra fjerne Lande som fra vort eget Hjem". Importert materiale i *Billed-Magazin for Børn*', in A. M. B. Bjørkøy et al. (eds), *Litterære verdensborgere: Transnasjonale perspektiver på norsk bokhistorie 1519–1850* (Oslo, 2019), pp. 310–29).

[33]　'Jeg har allerede ovenfor sagt eder, hvad jeg anseer som min Livsreises Maal, nemlig Himmelen; og det skulde være mig kjært, hvis I deri være enige med mig: thi kun I dette Tilfælde kunde vi reise med hinanden' ('Livsreisen', *For Ungdommen*, July 1846, pp. 1–2).

[34]　'at rette Blikket mod det evige Liv, – det vil være dette Skrifts Opgave' (*For Ungdommen*, July 1846, p. 8).

The magazine's evangelical tone and emphasis on the child's journey towards eternal life are recognisable in many of the religious children's magazines and in the missionary magazines particularly. However, *For Ungdommen* does not associate with the missionary cause until it returns after a halt in publication with a third volume in 1849 by an unknown editor.[35] Now the magazine's subtitle has been somewhat altered and mentions the missionary cause explicitly: *Et Maanedsskrift for opbyggelig og underholdende Læsning, med særdeles hensyn paa Missionssagen* (A monthly for edifying and entertaining reading, with particular regard to the missionary cause). The change is also noticeable in the magazine's contents, with several of the stories now describing the works of missionaries in various parts of the world. Early in the next year, in January 1850, however, the subtitle is changed back to *Et Maanedsskrift til Befordring af sand Dannelse* (A monthly for promotion of true education), again leaving out any reference to the missionary cause. Still, the magazine keeps a certain emphasis on missionary work in its contents.

Given the fact that *For Ungdommen* did not underline its missionary aspects until, and only in, 1849, Johnsen's *Missionsblad for Børn* is probably Norway's very first missionary magazine for children. The magazine was issued monthly in 1847 and 1848, and in 1849 under the title of *Missionsblad for Ungdommen* (Missionary Magazine for the Youth).[36] Like *For Ungdommen*, it was printed in Stavanger and appeared as twelve-page leaflets in the duodecimo format, featuring usually one or two woodcuts in each issue. The preface to the trial issue of January 1847, which unfortunately has been cut mid-sentence due to the joint binding of several issues, presents *Missionsblad for Børn* as a translation of the German *Missionsblatt für Kinder* (1842–1918) by Christian Gottlob Barth (1799–1862), who was a prominent figure in the hugely successful evangelical press and missionary society in the southern region of Württemberg.[37] Comparing the issues of *Missionsblad for Børn* from January to July 1847 to the German issues from January to July 1842, it becomes clear that texts and illustrations in the Norwegian

---

[35] Aukrust, *Menighetsblad og andre religiøse og kirkelige tidsskrifter i Norge*, p. 14; Økland, 'Norske barneblad', p. 99.

[36] H. L. Tveterås, *Norske tidsskrifter. Bibliografi over periodiske skrifter i Norge inntil 1920* (Oslo, 1940), p. 91. Unfortunately, the holdings of *Missionsblad for Børn* at the National Library of Norway, the University of Oslo Library and NTNU University Library are incomplete and consist only of the issues from January to July 1847 (bound together) and from February to March 1848 (single issues). I have not been able to locate any copies of *Missionsblad for Ungdommen*.

[37] N. Hope, *German and Scandinavian Protestantism 1700–1918*, in H. and O. Chadwick (eds), *Oxford History of the Christian Church* (Oxford, 1995).

magazine have all been taken and translated from the German publication. In this way, the first Norwegian missionary children's magazine, like so many other early publications for children in Norway, is not Norwegian at all in the sense that there is no original material here, only translated texts and imported illustrations.[38] However, the German publication also seems to have foreign models: in his introduction rendered in the translation, Barth writes about how he in the making of the magazine was presented with examples from England, 'where specific missionary magazines for children are issued, and where there are even missionary associations consisting only of children.'[39] As such, *Missionsblad for Børn* illustrates the transnational contexts for early printed children's literature in general and its exchanges across linguistic and cultural borders.

DYING CHILDREN, THE MISSIONARY CAUSE AND CIRCULATING TEXTS

Missionsblad for Børn features various types of texts, ranging from songs and letters to brief biographies such as the eulogy of David Brainerd who missioned in North America and, not least, stories from missionary stations around the world. All are edifying and relate to missionary life and work, and several are, to use Billington's words, 'morbidly pious.'[40] In this, they are representative of the many texts about dead and dying children in eighteenth- and nineteenth-century children's literature. As Merethe Roos has pointed out in her discussion of dead and dying children in one of the first Dano-Norwegian children's periodicals, these texts take on various forms, appearing as 'stories from the sick bed, death notices, obituaries, or didactic texts aimed at children.'[41] What they have in common is that they depict idealised deaths, where the dying child is noble and at peace with God, honourable and strong until the very end.

Several of the stories in *Missionsblad for Børn*, however, are morbid in ways that do not so much idealise children's deaths and prepare them for their heavenly journey as insist on the importance of and need for missionary work. In one story the little Indian boy Orta tells 'with his own

---

[38]   See J. S. Kaasa, '"Saavel fra fjerne Lande som fra vort eget Hjem"', pp. 310–29.

[39]   'Man har anført mig Englands Exempler, hvor der ogsaa udkommer særskilte Missionsblade for Børn, og hvor der endog gives Missionsforeninger, der bestaa blot af Børn' (*Missionsblad for Børn*, January 1847, p. 3).

[40]   Billington, 'The Religious Periodical and Newspaper Press, 1770–1870', p. 121.

[41]   M. Roos, 'Children, Dying, and Death: Views from an Eighteenth-Century Periodical for Children', in R. Aasgard *et al.* (eds), *Nordic Childhoods 1700–1960: From Folk Beliefs to Pippi Longstocking* (New York, London, 2018), pp. 241–53, at p. 242.

words' of how his father and oldest brother disappear during a storm, never to be seen again, whereas his mother and his baby brother soon after are snatched and eaten by a tiger.[42] Orta and his elder brother survive and are sent to a children's home, but the brother dies three months later and leaves Orta as the only surviving member of the family. It is a story about suffering, but with a hopeful message, ending with a reflection on Orta's joy over living with the missionaries, but also on how he at times is struck by sadness over the fact that his family never got to know Christ.

The text entitled 'Børnene i Hedningeland' (The Children in the Hea-then Lands) narrates the deaths of numerous children, giving detailed and gruesome descriptions of a child having been buried alive, of the killing of female babies and of a Rajah's beheading of his 11-year-old daughter, of child offerings and cholera and of the rescue of an eight-day-old infant who had been abandoned by his 'unnatural mother'.[43] The piece paints a sinister and morbid picture of the lives of the heathen children, underlining the importance of and need for the missionaries' work, not least emphasised by the fact that the surviving children are raised by missionary families or in children's homes run by the local missions. The text 'Den døende Hotten-totdreng' (The Dying Hottentot Boy), too, is representative of the deathbed story but has been adapted to a missionary setting. It tells of ten-year-old Frederik Roode in Pacaltsdorp in what is now South Africa. Realising that he will not recover from an inflammatory infection, the boy summons Mr Anderson of the London Missionary Society, who is stationed in Pacalts-dorp, to bid him farewell before he dies blissfully.

The Frederik Roode story furthermore exemplifies how materials in early printed children's literature in general and in this magazine in par-ticular circulated through import and translation. Not surprisingly, the story as it appears in Missionsblad for Børn seems to be a direct translation from 'Der sterbende Hottentottenknabe' in Barth's Missionsblatt für Kinder of February 1842. Looking at the English missionary children's magazines, which Barth mentions explicitly as models, the story seems to have been first published in the British Missionary Magazine in September 1836 under the title 'The Dying Hottentot Boy'.[44] Likewise, the accompanying woodcut with the scene where Frederik lays his head on Mr Anderson's knee first appears in the Missionary Magazine, then in Missionsblatt für Kinder, and finally in Missionsblad for Børn.

[42] 'med hans egne Ord': (Missionsblad for Børn, February 1847, p. 23).
[43] 'unaturlige Moder' (Missionsblad for Børn, July 1847, p. 79).
[44] It appears in the Ohio-based Gambier Observer on 16 November 1836 and in the London-based The Missionary Register in February 1837, with minor variations and entitled 'Frederick Roode, A Hottentot Youth'.

Whereas the texts in this publication are generally translated more or less verbatim from the German, the text on Greenlandic children has been adapted so that it relates the narrated events to Norwegian children and to missionary work in Norway, and in Stavanger specifically. After a letter written by Josva in Lichtenau (today's Alluitsoq) to a group of German children, editor Johnsen inserts a note on how children in Stavanger have also sent gifts and letters to the children of Greenland and how they too have received letters of thanks in return. *Missionsblad for Børn* renders one of these letters, written by 13-year-old Christian on behalf of the children in Nyhernhut (New Herrnhut, today's Nuuk) to '[y]ou, who live over there in Europe and have written to us, you, who are in the land called Norway, we here answer your writing and greet you all.'[45] In this way, Johnsen brings the translated piece about Greenland closer to home; to the children in Stavanger and to Norwegian readers at the same time as he promotes the work in Norwegian foreign missions. This is, however, the only example of such adaptation and domestication in *Missionsblad for Børn*.

From child to child: letters from the missions

Missionsblad for Børn portrays children as central characters in the various texts but also stages children as active voices by letting the children themselves narrate their experiences, often in the form of letters. In the afore-mentioned Fredrik Roode story, for example, the missionary framing of the death bed scene asserts itself at the narrative level from the very beginning and introduces the daughter of a missionary as the narrator: 'This time I first let a child relate. It is the daughter of missionary Anderson in Pacalts-dorp in South Africa, who in a letter describes the event here depicted. She writes thus:'[46] In the letter, Anderson's daughter tells of how the boy called for her father – '"Frederik," said my father, "why have you sent for me?" –

---

[45] 'I, som bo derover i Europa og have skrevet os til, I, som ere i det Land, som kaldes Norge, vi besvare herved eders Skrivelse og hilse eder alle': ('Børnene i Grønland', *Missionsblad for Børn*, March 1847, p. 32). The letter is dated 7 April 1845.

[46] 'Dennegang lader jeg først et Barn fortælle. Det er Datter af Missionær Anderson i Pacaltsdorp i Sydafrika, hvilken i et Brev skildrer det Optrin, som her er afbildet. Hun skriver saaledes:' (*Missionsblad for Børn*, February 1847, p. 15). This sentence is almost verbatim to the German text. In the earlier English versions, however, this is not the first sentence in the text, nor is it identical: 'The following incident, communicated by one of Mr. Anderson's daughters, will be regarded with peculiar feelings by the friends of missions' (*The Missionary Magazine*, 1836, p. 419; *The Gambier Observer*, 16 November 1836); 'One of the daughters of Mr. Anderson, of the London Missionary Society, communicates the following particulars of the death of this particular Youth, at Pacaltsdorp' (*The Missionary Register*, February 1837, p. 105).

and later his school-fellows, sisters and parents, urging them, to lead lives without sin and to seek the Lord while you are healthy and wholesome'.[47] She then goes on to depict Frederik Roode's final moment: 'These were his last words, he died without great death struggle. The patience and compo-sure, with which he bore his painful affliction, both surprised and edified those around him, and they have thus learnt something, which I hope, they will not easily forget'.[48]

The letters from the Greenlandic children, too, are examples of how communication between children is made manifest in the magazine. More-over, they give a glimpse into the lives of the children and how they have been affected by the missionaries: expressing gratitude for the gifts they have been sent and for having been introduced to Christ, they also hint to the difficulties of combining traditional ways of life with new beliefs. In good weather, Josva writes, he often has to go seal hunting instead of attending school. This, he relates, is slowing down his way towards the ideals he is presented with by the missionaries:

> [W]e found a lot of pleasure in writing, and wanted to do this, to learn
> and in following the word of the Saviour always be more like the youth
> in the East (Europe). We often hear how hard-working the children
> of the East are in this. We too wanted to be like them and always be
> prepared to praise the Lord and to thank him.[49]

[47] '"Frederik," sagde min Fader, "hvorfor har du sendt Bud efter mig?"'; 'søger Herren medens I ere friske og sunde!' (*Missionsblad for Børn*, February 1847, pp. 15, 17).

[48] 'Dette var hans sidste Ord, han døde uden stor Dødskamp. Den Taalmodighed og Fatning, hvormed han bar sin smertelige Sygdom, var for de Omkringstaaende lige-saa forunderlig som opbyggelig, og de have derved lært noget, som de, hvilket jeg haaber, ikke saa let ville glemme' (*Missionsblad for Børn*, February 1847, p. 17). In *The Missionary Magazine* (1836, p. 420): 'He died without a struggle. The patience and composure, with which he bore the painful affliction allotted to him, at once surprised and edified those who witnessed it; and afforded to them a lesson, which, it is to be hoped, will not be lost'.

[49] ': thi vi fandt megen Fornøielse i at Skrive, og hadde Lyst dertil, for at lære det, og ogsaa heri, og i at følge Frelserens Bud stedse blive Ungdommen i Østen (i Europa) mere lige. Vi høre oftere, hvor flittige Børnene i Østen heri ere: ogsaa vi ønskede at ligne dem, og stedse være beredte til at prise Frelseren og at takke Ham' (*Mis-sionsblad for Børn*, March 1847, p. 31). Christian, in his letter, is less concerned with Christ and more detailed in his descriptions of Greenlandic daily life, writing about how they are often out in their kayaks in dangerous waters when they train to use their weapons. Like Josva, though, he too notes the challenges of combining a no-madic life with schooling. The text concludes with two sentences in Greenlandic in Latin letters, so that the readers may have an 'understanding of the Greenlandic lan-guage, whose words are as long as a prayer' ('et Begreb om det grønlandske Sprog, der har saa lange Ord som en Bønnestal' (*Missionsblad for Børn*, March 1847, p. 33).

There are also several other examples of children's letters in *Missionsblad for Børn*, such as 'To Breve fra Hedningebørn' (Two Letters from Heathen Children). Again, the communication is between Christian and heathen children, this time between children in England and South Africa. The first letter is written by the children at a school in Bersaba in today's South Africa, thanking the children in England for the clothing and gifts they have sent. The letter ends with a request for more: 'We are happy on Sundays, because then we wear the small dresses you have sent us: we are so many and therefore not all could have a dress, and those who did not get one, cried. ... Would you not send us some more pieces of clothing?'[50]

The second letter is from Amy, 'a small girl of about nine years; my father was a slave, but there are no more slaves now.'[51] In her brief note she gives thanks for the aprons, working skirts and thimbles they have received and goes on, like the writers of the previous letter, to describe the Sundays: 'On Sundays, the small children come to the missionary's house; they are clean and in their nice dresses, they are quietly seated. When the horn blows, they go to church; they sing Heir kniel ik vol van droefheid; but that you cannot understand.'[52] In all these letters the communication is staged as being directly from child to child. Thus, the children are cast as readers and writers, which to a certain degree promotes their agency, even though it is located within the framework of the power imbalance between adults and children that characterises children's literature as such.[53]

The letter is indeed a familiar genre in early printed children's literature (as it is in eighteenth-century literature generally), and scholars have shown how for example eighteenth-century Dano-Norwegian children's magazines stage children, and girls in particular, as letter writers.[54] Even though

[50] 'Vi ere glade om Søndagen, thi da have vi de smaa Kjoler paa, som I have sendt os: vi ere så mange og derfor kunne ikke alle faa en Kjole, og de, som ingen faa, græde da. ... Vilde I ikke sende os endnu nogle Klædningsstykker?' (*Missionsblad for Børn*, March 1847, p. 11).

[51] 'Jeg er Amy, an liden Pige paa omtrent ni Aar; min Fader var en Slave, men der gives nu ingen Slaver mere' (*Missionsblad for Børn*, March 1847, p. 11).

[52] 'Om Søndagen komme de smaa Børn i Missionærens hus; de ere renlige, de trække fine kjoler paa, de sætte sig rolige ned. Naar der bliver blæst i Hornet, drage de til Kirken; de synge Heir kniel ik vol van droefheid*); med det forstaa I ikke': (*Missionsblad for Børn*, March 1847, p. 12). In a note the editor translates the song title to 'Here I kneel full of affliction' ('Her knæler jeg fuld af Bedrøvelse').

[53] See M. Nikolajeva, *Power, Voice and Subjectivity in Literature for Young Readers* (New York, London, 2010).

[54] H. Bache-Wiig, 'Avis for Børn' (1779–1782): Lesestykker om "Ungdommens Tilbøielighed til Dyden eller Lasten" – et monotont repertoar?', in E. Tjønneland (ed.), *Kritikk før 1814. 1700-tallets politiske og litterære offentlighet* (Oslo, 2014); N. Christensen, 'Lust for Reading and Thirst for Knowledge: Fictive Letters in a Danish

these letters were most probably fictional, they convey an understanding of the child as an independent and reflective individual in possession of humour and irony.[55] Moreover, eighteenth-century children's magazines in Denmark–Norway and Sweden, for instance, staged children as readers and consumers, signalling their increasingly important role in print culture.[56] Surely, these roles are somewhat different in the missionary magazines discussed in this chapter. Yet the children are staged as active participants in the missionary endeavour as well as in the magazine through the letters ascribed to them.

There is no way to prove these letters' authenticity and that they were actually written by the children in question, although it is not unlikely. For instance, William Anderson was indeed a missionary in Pacaltsdorp and he did indeed have daughters, and there were German and Norwegian missionary stations in Greenland at the time the letters by Josva and Christian were supposedly written.[57] Regardless of their potential factuality or fictionality, we should approach these letters as *mediated* letters that were shaped by the missionary contexts from and in which they were written and published. More important than the question of their authenticity is the fact that the letters are *presented* as being written by children. Although the letters to different degrees have been shaped by adult actors, they seem to want to give the impression of a more or less direct relation between the child writer and the child reader. The presence of adult actors, be they missionaries or magazine editors, remains secondary here, leaving room for the children's voices. In this way, the magazine represents the children in what appears to be their own words, staging them as letter writers and readers, albeit within the context of the missionary cause.

LITERARY CITIZENS?

'The great demands of Eternity on your hearts must not be forgotten in favour of the many demands that education of life in the world puts into force, the purpose of being a heavenly citizen not being set back by the call

---

Children's Magazine of 1770', *The Lion and the Unicorn*, 2 (2009); N. Christensen, *Videbegær*.

[55]   N. Christensen, *Videbegær*, p. 180.

[56]   See J. S. Kaasa, 'Hvordan bli en tidsskriftleser? Medieoppdragelse i 1700-tallets barnemagasiner', *Arr – Idéhistorisk tidsskrift*, 31:4 (2019), 21–31; J. S. Kaasa, 'Å gi sin daler med glede: Barn som forbrukere i *Ungdommens Ven* (1770)', *Barnboken*, 42 (2019), 1–18.

[57]   For more background on these missions, see for example C. Larsen *et al.*, *Da skolen tog form. 1780–1850* (Aarhus, 2013), pp. 279–89.

of the world citizen', is the message in *For Ungdommen*.[58] The passage casts the child as both world and heavenly citizen, with a light warning against letting the first take precedence over the latter. Rather, world citizenship seems to mainly serve the function of preparing the child – as a Christian citizen in training – for his or her heavenly citizenship. An important part of this world citizenship, it seems, is the role of the child in missionary work, and we find in these magazines the staging of the child as a future missionary, or at least that of an active participant in religious life.

Missionsblad for Børn is quite explicit in this regard, such as in the self-reproachful text entitled 'Hjælp dog de arme Hedninger!' (Help the Poor Heathens!): 'Every day fifty to sixty thousand unconverted heathens die. And it is our fault! Had we brought them the Gospel, they there would have found light and support, and could have wandered on the road of salvation.'[59] The text goes on to present various ways in which the child reader may support the missionary cause, ranging from prayer – 'If it be so, that they could not do anything but pray for the missionaries and their work, this is still indeed the most important one can do for them'[60] – to donations: 'But children could also do more, if they wanted to, you have perhaps a money box from where you could take a small trifle for the missionary cause and place it in the missionary box.'[61] In this way, the text encourages the child to be an active participant in missionary work in various ways, to be like the boy who prays to God to make him a missionary or, at the very least, to ask: 'What can I do for the poor Heathens?'[62] The child saviour motif, which we usually think of in terms of Romantic symbolism,[63] here takes on a much more pragmatic role as future helpers in the lands of the

---

[58]   'Det store krav, som Evigheden gjør paa eders Hjerte, maa ikke forglemmes over de mange Fordringer, som Dannelsen for Livet I Verden gjør gjældende, Bestemmelsen til Himmelborger ikke sættes tilbage for Verdensborgerens Kald' (*For Ungdommen*, July 1846, p. 8).

[59]   'Enhver Dag dør femti til sextitusinde uomvendte Hedninger. Og det er vor Skyld! Havde vi bragt dem Evangelium, saa haavde de deri fundet Lys og Støtte, og havde kunnet vandre paa Salighedens Vei' (*Missionsblad for Børn*, February 1848, p. 14).

[60]   'Sæt endog, at de ikke kunne andet end bede for Missionærerne og deres Arbeide, saa er dog dette netop det Vigtigste, som man kan gjøre for dem' (*Missionsblad for Børn*, February 1848, pp. 15–16).

[61]   'Men Børn kunne ogsaa gjøre noget Mere, hvis de ville, De have maaske en Spare-bøsse, hvoraf de kunne tage en liden Skjærv for Missionssagen og lægge den i Missionskassen' (*Missionsblad for Børn*, February 1848, p. 16).

[62]   'Hva kan da jeg gjøre for de arme Hedninger?': (*Missionsblad for Børn*, February 1848, p. 17).

[63]   A. Byrnes, 'The Child Saviour: A Literary Motif', in *The Child: An Archetypal Symbol in Literature for Children and Adults* (New York, 1995), pp. 7–32. See also R. C. Kuhn, *Corruption in Paradise: The Child in Western Literature* (London, 1982).

heathens. In all of these examples the child's agency, which also involves responsibility and blame, is tightly connected to the missionary cause and seems to answer to the words from the Acts of the Apostles that reverberate throughout these magazines, calling for the child reader to come over and help.

The idea of children as future citizens and as active participants in society is certainly in tune with Lutheran notions of the child. In the missionary magazines I have studied in this chapter this citizenship and participation relates first and foremost to religious life and missionary work but also makes itself manifest in the children's ascribed roles as (letter) readers and writers. As such, the notion of the child as a *Christian* citizen in training seems to be intertwined with another training, namely that of a *literary* citizen in training, preparing the child to become a participant in print culture, which through the import of foreign materials and the international geography of the missionary work is also fundamentally transnational. Literary citizenship in these first missionary magazines, then, although concentrating on the missionary cause, encompasses at least the possibility of a range of different citizenships and roles for the child: as world citizen, heavenly citizen, and literary citizen.

12

Diffusing Useful Knowledge: *Skilling-Magazin*, Transnational Images and Local Communities

Iver Tangen Stensrud

AROUND 180 PRINTERS, BOOKSELLERS, writers and other interested people gathered on 24 June 1840 for a grand celebration in the Norwegian capital Christiania, now Oslo.[1] The occasion was the four-hundredth anniversary of the invention of the art of printing. Celebrations such as these had been held on every anniversary in Germany and in centres of printing in Europe and were important in cementing Gutenberg as the inventor of printing.[2] This, however, was the first time such a celebration had been held in Norway. The initiative came from an article in the *Morgenbladet* newspaper signed 'a printer'. While the celebration in Norway may be insignificant compared to festivals held in other countries, 'I do not in any way doubt' the printer stated, 'that every printer in the country would see it as appropriate that Norway, the freest country in Europe' would join the celebrations.[3]

---

[1]   This chapter is based on my PhD thesis: 'The Magazine and the City: Architecture, Urban Life and the Illustrated Press in Nineteenth-Century Christiania' (PhD thesis, Oslo School of Architecture and Design, 2018), <http://hdl.handle.net/11250/2501383>.

[2]   In Europe the 1840 celebrations had a more radical edge than earlier celebrations. Especially in French and German regions calls for press freedom served as a prelude to the revolutions of 1848. See: E. Eisenstein, *Divine Art, Infernal Machine: The Reception of Printing in the West from First Impressions to the Sense of an Ending* (Philadelphia, 2011), pp. 170–8.

[3]   Quoted from *Morgenbladet*, 12 May 1840. Unless otherwise noted, all translations from Norwegian to English are my own. See also: *Beretning om Sekularfesten i Christiania den 24. Juni 1840 i Anledning af Bogtrykkerkunstens Opfindelse* (Christiania,

In 1814 Norway had passed a new democratic constitution (see Hem-stad's chapter in this book). Article 100 of the constitution stated that 'there shall be freedom of expression.'[4] As Norwegian historian Francis Sejersted has pointed out, this article, together with article 85 (today 84) which stated that the Parliament 'shall meet in open session, and its proceedings shall be published in print,'[5] established a principle of openness, publicity and transparency in the political system. This showed the commitment of the constitutional founders to the idea of what Jürgen Habermas called the public sphere.[6]

Norway was one of the last countries in Europe in which the art of print-ing had been introduced, yet now the development of the art went hand in hand with 'the free progressive life which now moves all around the coun-try', editor and publisher of *Skilling-Magazin* Carl August Guldberg wrote in his history of printing published for the Gutenberg quatercentenary.[7] The author Henrik Wergeland's cantata *Vord lys!* [Be Light!] was performed at the mass held in the Church of Our Saviour in the main square in Chris-tiania. Wergeland here depicted the printing press as a light that would diffuse knowledge and education to all classes of society. In his sermon for the occasion, the local bishop mostly agreed with Wergeland: Gutenberg's art was given to mankind to drive out darkness, to promote enlightenment, truth and brotherly love. But the bishop also provided some warnings. The most dangerous products of the press were 'those publications that endanger innocence and morality', he argued. Mainly 'the countless army of novels, many of which must be understood to be a terrible nuisance, as their reading leads to reverie and a distaste for useful activities, fills the brain with overwrought ideas and opens the heart to dangerous temptation.'[8]

1840); O. A. Øverland, *Den Norske bogtrykkerforening 1884–1909: med træk af boghaandverkets historie og arbeidskaar i Norge* (Kristiania, 1909), p. 54ff.

[4]   Quoted from the English translation on the Norwegian parliament's website: 'The Constitution, as Laid down on 17 May 1814 by the Constituent Assembly at Eidsvoll and Subsequently Amended, Most Recently in May 2018', <www.stortinget.no/glo-balassets/pdf/english/constitutionenglish.pdf> [accessed 3 November 2021].

[5]   'The Constitution, as Laid down on 17 May 1814'.

[6]   F. Sejersted, *Norsk Idyll?* (Oslo, 2000), pp. 62, 75–6; J. Habermas, *The Structural Transformation of the Public Sphere: An Inquiry Into a Category of Bourgeois Society* (Cambridge, MA, 1989).

[7]   C. A. Guldberg, *Historisk Udsigt over Bogtrykkerkonsten fra dens Begyndelse til nærværende Tid: et Indbydelsesskrift til Sekularfesten i Christiania d. 24 Juni 1840* (Christiania, 1840), p. 24.

[8]   Bishop Christian Sørensen's sermon is quoted in Øverland, *Den Norske bogtryk-kerforening 1884–1909*, p. 62. 'Langt farligere have ufeilbar de Skrifter været, som have været til Skade for Uskyld og Sædelighed, den talløse Hær af Romaner nemlig,

The celebrations expressed a general belief in the power of the printing press to change society. However, as the bishop reminded the printers and booksellers gathered in the church that day, not all products of the press were useful or morally edifying. One way to combat the reading of immoral novels or dangerous political texts was to provide the public with useful, entertaining knowledge.

The Gutenberg quatercentenary is connected to the aforementioned Norwegian illustrated periodical *Skilling-Magazin* (published from 1835 to 1891) in many ways. Its editor-publisher were one of the driving forces behind the celebrations. The celebrations also show the belief in the early nineteenth century in the printing press to change society and echo the motivation behind creating an illustrated educational magazine such as *Skilling-Magazin*. Moreover, just as the Gutenberg centennial was inspired by similar celebrations in cities across Europe, *Skilling-Magazin* took inspiration from the British educational *Penny Magazine* and similar periodicals. *Skilling-Magazin* was a node in a transnational network of magazines that not only shared the same form and general purpose, forming recognisable 'brands' in the eyes of their readers and publishers, but also engaged in a lively exchange of texts and images. However, like the Norwegian Gutenberg centennial, *Skilling-Magazin* also needs to be understood in its local context, as a part of a local community of publishers, writers and readers.

The publishers and readers of *Skilling-Magazin* were literary citizens. They took part in a transnational literary community of publishers, writers, editors, engravers, draftsmen and readers. *Skilling-Magazin* and other educational periodicals were transnational products. The transnational context of the illustrated press shaped the format of the periodicals, the techniques used to make the images and the discourse around these periodicals.[9] Audiences from all over the world not only expected the images from these illustrated periodicals to look a certain way, but also to a large extent looked at the same images.[10] *Skilling-Magazin* also shared the ethos of other illustrated educational magazines, namely to diffuse useful knowledge; to educate and enlighten the common man.

---

hvoraf mange maa ansees som en frygtelig Plage, da deres Læsning forvilder Forstanden, leder til Sværmeri og Afsmag for gavnlig Virksommhed, fylder Hjernen med overspændte Ideer, ophidser Indbildningskraften og aabner Hjertet for farlige fristelser'.

9   T. Smits, *The European Illustrated Press and the Emergence of a Transnational Visual Culture of the News, 1842–1870* (London, 2019); I. Stensrud, 'The Magazine and the City'.

10   T. Smits, *The European Illustrated Press*, p. 19.

However, *Skilling-Magazin* was also part of a local community of printers, publishers, writers and readers with different organisational and technical resources to those we find in the centres of printing in England, Germany or France. The magazine's educational efforts were also connected to a state-supported enlightenment drive in nineteenth-century Norway. In the scholarly literature, illustrated educational magazines of the 1830s are most often placed in the context of a burgeoning mass market for periodicals and the beginning of popular magazine publishing in the nineteenth century.[11] In this chapter I argue that we can place *Skilling-Magazin* at a historical and geographical crossroads, between the Northern Enlightenment and nineteenth-century mass publishing.

PENNY MAGAZINE, 'THE MARCH OF MIND' AND THE ILLUSTRATION REVOLUTION

The first issue of *Skilling-Magazin* was published on 9 May 1835, its front page showing an engraving of Benjamin Franklin (Plate 12.1). The magazine was published almost every Saturday until 1891, and in it the interested reader could find illustrated educational articles on a large variety of topics from animals, biographical and topographical descriptions to prison systems and steam engines. When the first issue was published, the magazine had already acquired more than two thousand subscribers. This was considered an extraordinary success, and it was stated that so many subscribers 'perhaps never in such a short time had been reached by any other publication in this country'.[12] However, publishing the magazine in a small peripheral country had not been easy. As editor Carl August Guldberg explained in an address to the reader in the first issue, the lack of 'artistic establishments' in Christiania meant they had difficulties publishing the magazine with wood-engraved images – in what Guldberg called a 'form suitable to the times'.[13] To achieve this more suitable form, Guldberg drew on the transnational network of educational illustrated magazines and contacted Charles Knight in London to source some stereotyped wood engravings for the magazine.

Skilling-Magazin was not only inspired by the *Penny Magazine* (Plate 12.2) and similar magazines across Europe, but it would also rely heavily on both images and texts from English, German and French magazines.

---

[11] See e.g. P. J. Anderson, *The Printed Image and the Transformation of Popular Culture, 1790–1860* (Oxford, 1991).
[12] 'Til Læseren', *Skilling-Magazin* no. 1, 9 May 1835, p. 1.
[13] *Ibid.*

Skilling-Magazin
til Udbredelse af almeennyttige Kundskaber.

1.]   Udkommer hver Løverdag   [Mai 9, 1835.

Til Læseren.

I det Skilling-Magazinet endelig træder frem for Lyset, skeer dette ikke uden Frygt for alt for meget at have trættet vore Subscribenters Taalmodighed, og Red. troer derfor at skylde Læseren nogen Oplysning om de Aarsager, der hidtil have forhindret Skriftets Udgivelse. Uden at ville give nogen detailleret Fremstilling, der her neppe vilde være passende, ville vi kun anføre, at uagtet de Hindringer, der fra Begyndelsen mødte Foretagendet, saavel i pecuniær Henseende, som fordi Mangelen paa gode artistiske Anstalter gjorde det umuligt for Red. at faae Bladet nogenledes taaleligt udstyret, opgav man dog ikke Haabet om engang at kunne udgive Magazinet i en efter Tidens Fordringer mere passende Form, end den, det udkomne Prøveblad havde. I den Anledning foretog den daværende Forlægger en Reise til Kjøbenhavn og Hamburg, for at erholde Afbildningerne trykte, og Red. nærede Haab om at kunne udgive Bladet i Juli Maaned forrige Aar, da Forlæggerens pludselige Afreise til Udlandet paa ngang standsede det temmelig vidtskredne Foretagende. Forend han forlod Norge, havde han imidlertid overdraget Forlagsretten til de nærværende Udgivere, der ogsaa strax gjorde Foranstaltninger til Bladets hurtige Udgivelse.

Man henvendte sig desaarsag til Udgiveren af et engelsk Magazin for at erholde de nødvendige Plader, hvilke ogsaa under visse Betingelser bleve tilsaaede, Red. seer sig altsaa nu istand til at lade Magazinet udkomme regelmæssig og uafbrudt, saalænge den tør nære Haab om at Nationen selv ikke unddrager den sin Gunst. Paa den beroer det, om vore Anstrængelser og vor Møie skal bære Frugter, om vort Haab og vor Tillid ei skal skuffes. Med Glæde maae vi tilstaae, at den Deeltagelse, vi have nydt fra saa mange Sider, have været os ligesaa kjær, som overraskende. Subscribenternes Antal udgjorde allerede ved forrige Aars Udløb henimod 2000, — Noget, som maaskee neppe i saa kort Tid er bleven noget andet Skrift til Deel her i Landet. Dette er nu meget mere forbausende, som det udkomne Prøvenummer i flere Henseender lod Meget tilbage at ønske, og vi maae saaledes antage, at den blotte Idee om ort Foretagendes Værd og gavnlige Indflydelse paa Folkets Dannelse, har været Aarsag til en saa gunstig Modtagelse. Uagtet enhver Læser, ved at sammenholde nærværende Nummer med det først udkomne Prøveblad, sikkert, som vi haabe, vil tilstaae at vi have holdt Mere, end vi havde lovet, er det dog mgtfra at vi ansee vort Arbeide fuldkomment; tvertnod vil vor bestandige Bestræbelse gaae ud paa, saavel i Form som Materie at udstyre det alt bedre og bedre. Men for at denne vor Bestræbelse kan lykkes,

maae vi ogsaa kunne gjøre Regning paa Nationens Understøttelse. Et Skrift som dette, der skal leveres til en saa lav Priis, kan ei bestaae uden et forholdsmæssigt stort Antal Kjøbere. Enhver, der interesserer sig for Oplysningens Fremme i vort Land, vil derfor sikkert, som vi haabe, bidrage Sit til at vort Foretagende maa have Fremgang og bære de Frugter, som vi vente os deraf, at det ei, som saa mange andre skal døe i Fødselen. Vi opfordre ogsaa Alle og Enhver, som besidde Kundskaber og Evne til at virke paa Folkets Dannelse, og som ei nægte at Oplysning og Kultur er et Gode, der bør vorde Alle til Deel, baade Høie og Lave, Rige og Fattige, at skjænke os deres Bistand. Ethvert Bidrag, der omfatter dette Maal, vil af os vorde modtaget med Taknemmelighed. — Saaledes lade vi da vort Magazin drage ud blandt Folket med de bedste Ønsker for dets Held. Maatte det stifte den Nytte, som vi haabe; maatte det vorde en Hjælp for den fattige, men videbegjerlige Læser; maatte det skjænke dem en gavnlig Adspredelse, som af Kjøbsomhed og Tiden med unyttige eller sønderlige Beskjæftigelser; maatte det vorde til Held og Velsignelse for Enhver, som tager det ihaand — og vor Møie er rigeligen lønnet.

Benjamin Franklin.

THE PENNY MAGAZINE

OF THE

Society for the Diffusion of Useful Knowledge.

52.]   PUBLISHED EVERY SATURDAY.   [JANUARY 26, 1833.

COLOGNE.

[Church of St. Martin, Cologne.]

COLOGNE, called by the Germans Cöln, is situated in a district of the same name, which is one of the two divisions of the Prussian province of Jülich-Cleve-Berg, so called from its containing the three old duchies of Jülich or Juliers, Cleve, and Berg. Cologne is the capital of the whole province, and stands on the left or west bank of the Rhine, N. L. 50° 55′, E. L. 6° 45′, forming a kind of semicircle. The city is fortified, and with its numerous spires and large buildings makes a good show from the opposite side of the river. It is about one hundred and seven miles east by north from Brussels. Cologne was an old Roman station often mentioned in Tacitus, and took its name of Colonia Claudia Agrippinensis, or " the Colony of Claudius and Agrippina," from Agrippina the

VOL. II.   E

PLATE 12.2. Front page of *Penny Magazine* 26 January 1833 with an engraving of the Church of St Martin, Cologne.

While there were local and national variations, the beginnings of what we could call the illustrated educational magazine can be traced to Charles Knight and the *Penny Magazine*. Charles Knight was a prominent member of the Society for the Diffusion of Useful Knowledge and the editor of the *Penny Magazine* throughout its existence from 1832 to 1845.[14] The periodical combined new wood engraving techniques with cylinder presses and stereotype techniques. Moreover, Charles Knight built up a large network of distributers all over the British Isles. The magazine reached a circulation of 200,000 within its first year of publication, and the magazine was one of the first examples of what one might call a mass market publication.

The *Penny Magazine* and the other publications of the Society for the Diffusion of Useful Knowledge was part of a movement that has been characterised as 'the march of intellect', or the 'march of mind', which became a rallying cry for the technologically and scientifically optimistic reform movement in early nineteenth-century Britain. In the words of Alice Jenkins, this represented the 'extraordinary conjunction of enormous elite scientific progress and convulsive movements towards mass education'.[15] This was part of a scientific and utilitarian spirit which made its mark on British intellectual life in the early nineteenth century. However, as Elisabeth L. Eisenstein argues, the Society for the Diffusion of Useful Knowledge has 'become celebrated less for its virtuous intentions than for the satire it inspired'.[16]

The founder of the Society for the Diffusion of Useful Knowledge, Henry Brougham, and his followers possessed an almost religious faith in the economic and social laws formulated by utilitarian thinkers such as Adam Smith, David Ricardo, Thomas Malthus, Jeremy Bentham and John Stuart Mill. 'Useful knowledge' was the good, solid, employable facts of mechanics and chemistry, metallurgy and hydraulics, facts that could be applied in the workshop and on the railway line, to produce goods cheaply and efficiently, to communicate and transport more swiftly.[17]

As the title of the society that published it implies, the content of the *Penny Magazine* was largely educational. Its content was described as being 'all ramble-scramble', but as Knight explained, 'it was meant to be

---

[14] In 1846 a periodical called *Knight's Penny Magazine* appeared, but it only lasted about 6 months.

[15] A. Jenkins, *Space and the 'March of Mind': Literature and the Physical Sciences in Britain 1815–1850* (Oxford, 2007), p. 9. See also A. Rauch, *Useful Knowledge: The Victorians, Morality, and the March of Intellect* (Durham, 2001).

[16] Eisenstein, *Divine Art, Infernal Machine*, p. 188.

[17] R. D. Altick, *English Common Reader: A Social History of the Mass Reading Public, 1800–1900*, 2nd edn (Columbus, 1998), pp. 130–1.

so – to touch rapidly and lightly upon many subjects'.[18] It contained articles and illustrations on a whole range of subjects: architecture, modern and ancient history, biographies, travel, topography of cities and rural landscapes, technology, science and the arts, with no special emphasis on any of those topics.[19] Much like the British Spectator journals of the eighteenth century, the success of the *Penny Magazine* encouraged imitators all over Europe. These include periodicals such as its Anglican rival *The Saturday Magazine* (1832–44), the French *Magazin Pittoresque* (1833–1938), the German *Pfenning Magazin* (1833–55) and *Heller Magazin* (1834–45), the Swedish *Lördags-Magasin* (1836–8) and the Danish *Dansk Penning Magazin* (first published in 1834) to name just a few.

Illustrated periodicals that used wood-engraved images were a vital part of what the historian of printing Michael Twyman has called the illustration revolution of the nineteenth century.[20] One of the earliest illustrated magazines, the *Mirror of Literature* founded in 1822, was published for many years with only one wood engraving on the front page of its sixteen octavo pages. Ten years later the *Penny Magazine* and similar magazines had wood engravings scattered throughout its eight pages, its quarto format being twice as large as the *Mirror of Literature*. Ten years later again, the *Illustrated London News* and similar magazines had wood engravings of different shapes and sizes throughout their sixteen folio pages and a format that was double that of the *Penny Magazine*.[21]

Important to this illustration revolution was the development of wood engraving. The most important figure in the development of wood engraving was the Newcastle engraver Thomas Bewick (1753–1828). Traditionally, woodcuts were cut by knife on the side of a softwood board. Bewick's innovation was to apply sharp tools, like those used in metal engraving, on the end grain of hardwood blocks, preferably boxwood.[22] The compact end grain allowed the engraver to cut very fine lines, producing work with far

[18] C. Knight, *Passages of a Working Life during Half a Century: With a Prelude of Early Reminiscences* (3 vols, London, 1864), vol. 2, p. 182.
[19] See S. Bennett, 'The Editorial Character and Readership of "The Penny Magazine": An Analysis', *Victorian Periodicals Review*, 17:4 (1984), 127–41.
[20] M. Twyman, 'The Illustration Revolution', in D. McKitterick (ed.), *The Cambridge History of the Book in Britain*, vol. 6, *1830–1914* (Cambridge, 2009), pp. 117–43.
[21] *Ibid.* p. 118. For a discussion of the early illustrated magazines, see also: B. Maidment, 'Dinners or Desserts?': Miscellaneity, Illustration, and the Periodical Press 1820–1840', *Victorian Periodicals Review*, 43:4 (2011).
[22] According to Mason Jackson, what was called 'Turkey-boxwood' growing in the forests of the Caucasus was the preferred kind, see M. Jackson, *The Pictorial Press: Its Origin and Progress* (London, 1885), p. 315. On Bewick, see e.g. J. Uglow, *Nature's Engraver: A Life of Thomas Bewick* (Chicago, 2009).

greater detail than traditional woodcuts.²³ Wood engravings were cheaper, easier and faster to produce than copper or steel engravings and could provide more elaborate images than traditional woodcuts. Like woodcuts, they could also be printed along with the text.

The success of wood engraving relied, to a large extent, on technologies for casting copies of printing plates – stereotyping. It was the *Penny Magazine* that tied stereotyping to wood engraving. Stereotyping allowed the *Penny Magazine* to use several presses simultaneously and protected the woodblocks from wear. A bonus of stereotyping was that it allowed the magazine to sell engravings across Europe and the USA, prompting a vigorous international circulation of images. 'The art of wood engraving is imperfectly understood in France and Germany,' proclaimed Charles Knight. Selling wood engraving casts 'at a tenth of the price of having them re-engraved' could therefore assist 'foreign nations in the production of "Penny Magazines".²⁴ The trade in wood engravings was important not least to the establishment of illustrated magazines in places – like Norway – that could not support a large wood engraving trade.

With mechanical presses, large circulations and extensive use of illustrations, the *Penny Magazine* and its imitators have largely been seen in the context of an emerging modern mass culture in the nineteenth century. As Patricia Anderson has argued, the *Penny Magazine* and its imitators depended upon and fostered new technology, commercialised their operation, continually augmented the amount and range of their written and pictorial content, and persistently reached and communicated with an ever-widening socially and geographically diverse body of readers and viewers. In this way, Anderson argues, these periodicals 'accommodated all the necessary preconditions for the development of the twentieth-century mass media'.²⁵ But investigating the *Skilling-Magazin*, a small and peripheral magazine, can provide us with a different picture. *Skilling-Magazin* shows us that this genre of periodicals must not only be understood as an

---

²³ A. Griffiths, *Prints and Printmaking: An Introduction to the History and Techniques* (Berkeley, 1996), pp. 22ff. The techniques of wood engraving are also explained in a number of treatises published during the nineteenth century, the most extensive of which is J. Jackson, *A Treatise on Wood Engraving: Historical and Practical* (London, 1839). Compared to lithography, relatively few treatises on wood engraving were published, this indicates that the trade of wood engraving was generally learnt by apprenticeship.

²⁴ 'The Commercial History of a Penny Magazine', *Penny Magazine*, 30 September 1833.

²⁵ P. Anderson, *The Printed Image*, p. 198.

early predecessor of mass media but can also be placed in a continuum with earlier forms of publishing.

GULDBERG & DZWONKOWSKI AND THE
CHRISTIANIA PUBLISHING BUSINESS

This connection to earlier forms of publishing becomes more evident when we look more closely at the publishers and printers of the *Skilling-Magazin* and at the local context in which the periodical was published and produced. The *Skilling-Magazin* was the result of an unusual partnership between the Swedish-born priest Carl August Guldberg and the allusive Polish refugee Adam Alexander Dzwonkowski. Born in the Swedish border town of Strömstad, Guldberg had grown up in the Norwegian town of Fredrikstad and came to Christiania to study in 1829.[26] Dzwonkowski came from a Polish noble family and participated in the Polish uprisings against Russia in 1832. He was forced to flee, first to Prussia and then to Copenhagen. To cut a long story short, he ended up in Christiania, where he married the daughter of a French consul and partnered with Guldberg to start a bookshop, publishing house and printing house.[27]

Guldberg & Dzwonkowski quickly expanded their business, becoming one of the most active printers and publishers in Christiania between 1835 and 1844. Their publishing business had an emphasis on similar content to the *Skilling-Magazin*. They published mostly educational literature, schoolbooks, books and periodicals for children, illustrated works and practical guides in addition to some historical, legal and medical literature.[28]

Guldberg & Dzwonkowski was part of a relatively substantial printing and publishing industry that had developed in Christiania by the end of

[26] J. G. Tanum, 'Guldberg, Carl August', in E. Bull *et al.* (eds), *Norsk Biografisk Leksikon* (Oslo, 1931).

[27] According to August Mortensen, Dzwonkowski had originally planned to go to South America after encountering Guldberg in Copenhagen. His ship called at Larvik, where he on Guldberg's recommendation sought out the local vicar. The vicar convinced him to stay in Norway over the winter, and on 31 October 1834 he arrived in Christiania. Dzwonkowski is on the list of arrivals in Christiania for 31 October in *Morgenbladet*, 2 November 1834. See A. Mortensen, 'Boktrykkerkunstens Indførelse i Norge: Kritiske bemerkninger væsentlig paa grundlag av bibliotekar J. C. Tellefsens efterladte manuskripter', in *Mindeskrift i anledning Fabritius' boktrykkeris 75-aars jubilæum 1844 – 1. januar – 1919* (Kristiania, 1919), pp. 9–26.

[28] Numerous advertisements for the firm can be found in newspapers as well as in *Skilling-Magazin*, e.g. *Tillæg til Skilling-Magazinet no. 4*, 24 January 1837. See also H. L. Tveterås, 'Norsk bokhandel gjennom 100 år', in C. Just (ed.), *N.W. Damm & søn 1843–1943: et firmas historie* (Oslo, 1947), p. 105.

the 1830s. Christiania became the capital of Norway after Denmark ceded Norway to Sweden in 1814. In 1814 it was a small town with some 14,000 residents. The city grew quickly, however, reaching around 34,000 inhabitants by 1845. Christiania was in 1819, according to a topographic-statistic description of Norway from 1840, home to five printers with nine presses, employing 35 workers. In 1839 the number of printers had increased to fifteen, with 35 presses, employing 91 workers.[29] The growth in the number of periodicals and books published reflected the increased activity in the printing trades.[30]

This increased activity also reflected a better political climate for newspapers and periodicals in Norway. While the Norwegian constitution of 1814 had established freedom of the press, this newfound freedom of the press was not embraced by everyone. The foremost sceptic was Charles John (1763–1844), the new king of Sweden and Norway. When he witnessed how the press used its freedom, he was seriously worried by the destabilising effect some of the utterances might have. The king's policies to stifle press freedom in Norway were successful and very effective for short periods of time, but they ultimately failed on a general level. In combination with the growing belief in the great advantages of the freedom of the press, the king's failure gradually led to better terms for newspapers and periodicals in the decades following 1814.[31]

While the decades following the emancipation from the Danish crown saw a substantial rise in the Norwegian and Christiania book and periodical trade, it took time for the local printing and publishing trade to develop into what we can recognise as a modern publishing business. The publisher, by the early nineteenth century, had become a specialised part of the book trade in many places in Europe. In Norway, long into the 1850s, there were no clear boundaries between being a printer, bookseller and publisher. As Guldberg & Dzwonkowski was an example of, the printer, publisher and the establishment that sold you a book or periodical would,

---

[29] In 1839 there were also three lithographic presses and one 'copper press' in Christiania, see: J. Kraft, *Topographisk-statistisk Beskrivelse over Kongeriget Norge*, 2nd edn, (4 vols, Christiania, 1838–42), vol. 1, p. 140.

[30] In 1814 there were six newspapers in the entire country, three of them coming out in Christiania. By 1848, forty newspapers were published in Norway, five of them in Christiania: H. L. Tverås, *Norske tidsskrifter: bibliografi over periodiske skrifter i Norge inntil 1920*, Kronologisk utg. (Oslo, 1984); H. L. Tverås, *Den norske bokhandels historie: Forlag og bokhandel inntil 1850* (Oslo, 1950), vol. 1, pp. 179–84.

[31] K. Nymark, 'Kampen om trykkefriheten. Karl Johan og den norske presse 1814–1844' (PhD thesis, University of South-East Norway, 2020), <https://openarchive.usn.no/usn-xmlui/handle/11250/2681517>.

in many cases, be one and the same. The function of a publisher was not yet established as a specialised part of the book trade, and printers, book-sellers, bookbinders and in many cases the author would often be listed as the publisher of a work.[32]

The *Penny Magazine* and its imitators were central in the transforma-tion of the printing and publishing industry in the nineteenth century. On the surface, *Skilling-Magazin* looked like the *Penny Magazine* and similar illustrated magazines, many of its texts and images even came directly from those periodicals. However, while periodicals and newspapers in Europe were beginning to employ more efficient iron presses and steam-driven cylindrical presses in specially built premises from the 1820s, printers in Norway continued to use wooden hand presses far into the mid-century.[33] It took around 30 years from the first usable cylinder presses were sold in England until the technology was applied in Norway. Yet the volume of newspapers, periodicals and books published in Norway and Christiania grew significantly during these three decades. More important than the availability of technology, however, was a market that was large enough to justify the significant investments in mechanised presses. Until the mid-nineteenth century, hardly any Norwegian publications achieved a circulation that could not be met by employing an extra hand press or two. As such, wooden hand presses were not a hindrance to the printers in Christiania, but a useful tool.

STATE-SUPPORTED ENLIGHTENMENT

The subtitle of the *Skilling-Magazin* was *til utbredelse av almennyttige kunnskaper.* This was a translation of the phrase 'for diffusion of useful knowledge' found in the society that published the *Penny Magazine.* But in Norwegian it could have other implications as well. The term *almennyttig* is today used with reference to companies or causes that are non-profit or for public benefit. At the time it could also denote the intended readership of the magazine. It was primarily aimed at what in Norway during the nine-teenth century was called *allmuen,* the common people.

What Henrik Wergeland called 'the cultivation of the masses' was an important project in the period.[34] It was argued that the common people,

---

[32]   H. Tveterås, *Den norske bokhandel,* 1, pp. 221–2.
[33]   On technologies of printing in nineteenth-century Norway, see T. A. Johansen, *Trangen til læsning stiger, selv oppe i Ultima Thule': aviser, ekspansjon og teknologisk endring ca. 1763–1880,* Pressehistoriske skrifter 7 (Oslo, 2006), pp. 65ff.
[34]   'Massens kultiveren' in Norwegian. See F. Sejersted, *Den vanskelige frihet: 1814–1851* (Oslo, 1978), pp. 317ff.

to be able to participate in the new democratic society, needed to raise their levels of knowledge and education. As the future Norwegian prime minister Frederik Stang put it in 1835, 'the will of the common people, chastened and moderated, should be the driving force of the workings of the state'.³⁵ Disseminating knowledge about history, science, technology, the arts, moral and religious texts was seen as key to building the new nation.

The connections between the *Skilling-Magazin* and these Enlightenment ideals become evident when we look more closely at the printers of *Skilling-Magazin*. *Skilling-Magazin* was first printed at a printing house started by Professor of Economics Gregers Fougner Lundh. Lundh was an important figure in public education, and as secretary (from 1822) and later literary director he was one of the driving forces behind *Selskabet for Norges Vel* (Society for the Good of Norway), established in 1809.³⁶ The society was an important agent in the fight for Norwegian rights within the union between Denmark and Norway and one of the most important campaigners for establishing the first Norwegian university, Det Kongelige Frederiks Universitet in Christiania in 1811. In 1810 the society started a publishing house to print and promote its own material, and in the 1820s and 1830s the printing house was used to promote public education. The society also acted as a patent office, and while it was not a part of the Norwegian state, it had an official character.³⁷

In his application to establish a printing house, Lundh justified his reasons for going into the printing trade. He believed printing played an important role in the intellectual and political education of the nation and therefore thought that it would be of the utmost importance to the government that their literary productions were not left to 'the often one-sided and greedy arbitrariness' of industry and trade. His printing house, he stated, would combine 'cheap services' with an 'interest in something other than mere monetary gain'.³⁸ By 1835 Guldberg & Dzwonkowski had also applied to the king to start their own printing house. In their application

³⁵ The quote is from a tract published in 1835. Here quoted from R. Slagstad, *De nasjonale strateger* (Oslo, 1998), p. 33. 'Almeenviljen, lutret og modereret [...] skal være den bevægende Kraft i alle Statsorganismens Retninger'.
³⁶ A. Fr. Andresen, 'Gregers Lundh', in *Norsk biografisk leksikon*, 13 February 2009, <http://nbl.snl.no/Gregers_Lundh>; Tveterås, *Den norske bokhandel*, 1, pp. 241–2.
³⁷ J. P. Collett and E. Bjerke (eds), *Vekst gjennom kunnskap: Det kongelige selskap for Norges vel 1809–1814* (Oslo, 2009).
³⁸ H. Tveterås, *Den norske bokhandel*, 1, p. 241.

they also stressed the mission of the magazine 'to diffuse enlightenment to the middle and lower classes'.[39]

Like many enlightenment projects in Norway at the time, *Skilling-Magazin* was closely connected to the state. This connection is apparent when we look at the financing of the images. As mentioned above, many of the images in *Skiling-Magazin* were stereotyped wood engravings bought from magazines such as the *Penny Magazine*, its rival *The Saturday Magazine*, the German *Heller Magasin*, the French *Magasin Pittoresque* or other publications. This made *Skilling Magazin* a part of a transnational network of educational illustrated magazines. But Guldberg & Dzwonkowski also made efforts to incorporate more original material in the first years of publication. They promised, when summing up the first five years of publishing in 1839, more Norwegian material for the 1840 volume. They mention a description of Norwegian fisheries, several descriptions of Norwegian towns and places, and portraits of the family of the Crown Prince. These images were not made in Norway, however; the illustrations had already been cut in wood especially for the magazine by the Parisian wood engravers Andrew, Best and Leloir.[40] In addition to the Parisian firm, some of the images in *Skilling-Magazin* were cut especially for the magazine in London, and some by the Danish engraver A. C. F. Finch.[41]

It was expensive to have images cut in wood abroad, and the editors of *Skilling-Magazin* received support from the highest levels of the state.[42] Charles John offered in some cases direct help to the *Skilling-Magazin* to have images of events or public buildings cut in wood abroad (e.g., Plate 12.3).[43] The man responsible for these royal commissions was probably the

---

[39] The application was transcribed for the 100-year anniversary of the Fabritius & Co printing and publishing house and can be found the Fabritius archives: National Archives of Norway, Fabritius og sønner – SAO/PAO-0050 Z-Lo011, Forlagskontrakter.

[40] 'Til Læseren', *Skilling-Magazin* no. 47, 28 December 1839.

[41] I. Stensrud, 'The Magazine and the City', pp. 101–2.

[42] Answering complaints in a newspaper article about the lack of Norwegian scenes in the *Skilling-Magazin*, the editors mentioned that 800 subscribers were needed to pay for a single series of engravings, 1,400 if the cost of paper, printing and office hours were accounted for. 'Svar fra Skilling-Magazinets Redaction til Indsenderen i Morgenbladet No. 295', *Tillægg til Morgenbladet no. 23*, 23 January 1839.

[43] One was of a new road in Verdal, the so-called Karl Johan Road, which the king contributed 50 speciedaler to have cut in wood. Charles John contributed the same amount for an engraving of the parliament chambers. See: E. H. Edvardsen, 'Den tidligste ukepresse i Norge', in E. H. Edvardsen (ed.), *Gammelt nytt i våre tidligste ukeblader: aktstykker om folketro og sagn i Illustreret Nyhedsblad og Norsk Folkeblad* (Oslo, 1997), p. 10.

Kong Carl Johans Indtog i Christiania den 21 December 1838.

PLATE 12.3. King Charles John's arrival in Christiania 21 December 1838. Wood engraving by 'one of the best engravers in London' after drawing by J. Flintoe. *Skilling-Magazin* 10 August 1839.

chamberlain Christian Holst. In addition to being the royal chamberlain, Holst was secretary of Det Kongelige Frederiks Universitet and took a keen interest in promoting Norwegian culture. Holst continued to fund engravings of Norwegian scenes, illustrations of antiquarian objects and illustrations of national paintings that could be used by the illustrated press with government funds well into the 1870s.[44]

The connections between the government and the *Skilling-Magazin* are evident in other ways than direct financing. *Skilling-Magazin* was granted reduced postage from the beginning, something that was afforded by the king to publications of an especially useful character.[45] In addition, the Storting decided that 97 volumes every year should be distributed to particularly gifted students in the common schools at the government's expense.[46]

Skilling-Magazin, like the *Penny Magazine*, was a part of an enlightenment project. However, unlike in England and many other places in Europe, in Norway this was a project that was closely connected to the state. For *Skilling-Magazin* this meant that many of the images printed in the magazine were not only directly financed by the king, but the magazine also received several benefits such as reduced postage and distribution to particularly gifted students. This state-supported enlightenment can be seen as a continuation of the particular character of the Enlightenment movement in Scandinavia. One of the things that characterised the Northern Enlightenment was the movement's close ties to the state administration, the Church, universities and local governments.[47] *Skilling-Magazin* must be seen as a continuation of this project, a part of a state-driven effort to educate the common people. But how successful was this state-driven enlightenment effort? To find out, it will be useful to look more closely at the magazine's reception and readers.

[44] *Ibid.*
[45] F. E. Johannessen, *Alltid underveis: Postverkets historie gjennom 350 år*, vol. 1, 1647–1920 (Oslo, 1997), pp. 152–6. Postage exemption (*portofrihet*) was granted to letters from state and public institutions, schools, and the poor relief system. Reduced postage (*portomoderasjon*) was granted to newspapers and magazines of an especially useful character. The new postage act of 1837 transferred the task to grant reduced postage to newspapers and magazines from the king to parliament and *Skilling-Magazin* was the first publication to be granted reduced postage by parliament.
[46] A. Mortensen, 'Boktrykkerkunstens representanter i Norge XLIII', *Nordisk trykkeritidende: organ for de grafiske fag og papirindustrien*, XVI, no. 5 (May 1907), pp. 47–8.
[47] E. Krefting *et al.* (eds), *Eighteenth-Century Periodicals as Agents of Change: Perspectives on Northern Enlightenment* (Leiden, Boston, 2015).

A HOUSE LIBRARY?

As we saw at the beginning of this chapter, the belief in the power of the printing press to diffuse knowledge was widespread among the elites of nineteenth-century Norway. One of the most eager supporters of the *Skilling-Magazin* and these enlightenment efforts was Henrik Wergeland. Wergeland was one of the period's most prolific, influential and controversial writers. He wrote not only tributes to the art of printing but also published his own educational journals *For Almuen* [For the Common Man] and *For Arbeidsklassen* [For the working classes] in the 1830s and early 1840s. In the future, Wergeland argued, *Skilling-Magazin* had the potential to become a 'house library', a 'comfort for the peasant to take up and read out loud in the winter nights when he comes home from work'. *Skilling-Magazin* would be 'ranked only after the Bible and the Psalm book and could be put beside Snorro since its usefulness in daily life will always be felt'.[48] Wergeland expressed lofty beliefs about the importance of the *Skilling-Magazin* and the enlightenment efforts more generally. But how widespread was *Skilling-Magazin*? And who were its readers?

As no subscription lists survive, it is hard to say anything definitive about circulation numbers or who actually read the *Skilling-Magazin*. As we have seen, *Skilling-Magazin* was initially considered a success, boasting two thousand subscribers in 1835. This was a substantial number for Norway at the time, a country of around 1.2 million inhabitants of whom only around 130,000 lived in urban areas.[49] In comparison, the leading daily newspaper *Morgenbladet* had around 850 subscribers in the early 1830s, reaching 1,500 in the 1840s.[50] However, it seems that the initial novelty of the *Skilling-Magazin* soon faded. The number of subscribers probably decreased slowly, to somewhere between 1,500 and 1,600 in 1838.[51] By the

---

[48]   H. Wergeland, 'Om Skilling-Magazinet (Indsendt)', *Statsborgeren*, 25 October 1835, in H. Jæger and D. Arup Seip, *Samlede skrifter: trykt og utrykt*, vol. 3, b. 2, *Artikler og småstykker: polemiske og andre 1833–1836* (Oslo, 1933), pp. 246–7. '[...] bliver [Skilling-Magazinet] og eengang i Tiden, eftersom det gaaer fremad et Huusbibliothek, der bliver en Vederqvægelse for Bonden at tage for sig og læse høit af i Vinterqvellene, naar han kommer ind fra sit Arbeide, og det kan blive en nyttig Haandbog, hvori han kan kaste op om nyttige Tings Tilberedelse o.s v. Skillings-magazinet faaer altsaa Rang efter Bibelen og Psalmebogen, og kan lægges ved Siden af Snorro, da Nytten af Skillingen i daglig Liv altid føles'. Snorro refers to the Icelandic historian, poet and author of the history of Norwegian kings, Snorri Sturluson.

[49]   'Hjemmehørende Folkemengde', Statistisk sentralbyrå, <www.ssb.no/a/kortnavn/hist_tab/3-1.html> [accessed 29 September 2021].

[50]   Y. Hauge, *Morgenbladets historie*, vol. 1, *1819–1854* (Oslo, 1963).

[51]   This figure is mentioned by Guldberg & Dzwonkowski in an article in *Morgenbladet*. 'Svar fra Skilling-Magazinets Redaction til Indsenderen i Morgenbladet No.

early 1860s the number of subscribers had increased again, probably to well over 2,000.[52]

Subscriptions were important, but the number of subscribers does not tell the whole story about who had access to the magazine. There was a widespread practice of sharing subscriptions, within a single household and between several households.[53] *Skilling-Magazin* could also be read in Christiania and across the country at reading clubs and commercial lending libraries or in book collections.[54] Wergeland played an important role in establishing book collections aimed at common people around the country from the 1840s, and *Skilling-Magazin* became a favoured item.[55]

As for who the readers were, there are some indications that subscribers to the magazine in the 1830s and 1840s were a mix of educated craftsmen, middle class merchants and more educated people of the 'upper classes'.[56] The editors of *Skilling-Magazin* stated in 1838 that it was a common misconception among the public that the main target for the magazine was the peasant population. It was rather aimed at all who wanted to obtain useful knowledge, 'whether peasant or bourgeois'. In fact, they argued, most of the people who subscribed to the magazine were people of the 'so-called middle classes'.[57] While the magazine clearly aimed to foster an educated common man, it seems that the magazine was just as popular among the wealthier, already book-buying public. A review in the *Morgenbladet* newspaper in 1835 confirms this. It states that 'the goodwill with which several

---

295', *Tillægg til Morgenbladet no. 23*, 23 January 1839.

[52] In 1863 and 1866 around 2,000 subscriptions of *Skilling-Magazin* were sent by post, half of them to the eastern part of Norway. Probably, the actual circulation figures were higher, as many would subscribe within the city of Christiania or its immediate surroundings. The figures are from B. J. Langseth, 'Christian Johnsens "Almuevennen": en analyse av ukebladets innholds- og utbredelsesstruktur i tidsrommet 1849–1873' (MA thesis, Oslo, 1975), pp. 144–6.

[53] Hauge, *Morgenbladets historie*, vol. 1, p. 136.

[54] See e.g. E. S. Eide, *Bøker i Norge: boksamlinger, leseselskap og bibliotek på 1800-tallet* (Oslo, 2013); E. S. Eide, 'Reading Societies and Lending Libraries in Nineteenth-Century Norway', *Library & Information History*, 26:2 (June 2010), 121–38.

[55] In 33 of the 88 book collections Eilert Sundt investigated in the 1860s, *Skilling-Magazin* and *Almuevennen* were the most loaned out items. See A. Arnesen, 'Eilert Sundt', in *Fire foregangsmænd: Peder Hansen, Henrik Wergeland, Eilert Sundt, H. Tambs Lyche*, Norsk bibliotekforenings småskrifter, 3 (Kristiania, 1917), p. 52.

[56] See I. Stensrud, 'The Magazine and the City', p. 113. From his meticulous diaries we also know that the linguist Ivar Aasen read *Skilling-Magazin* in the 1830s and was a subscriber in the 1860s. I. Aasen, *Brev og dagbøker*, vol. 3, *Dagbøker 1830–1896*, ed. R. Djupedal (Oslo, 1960).

[57] 'Svar fra Skilling-Magazinets Redaction til Indsenderen i Morgenbladet No. 295', *Tillægg til Morgenbladet no. 23*, 23 January 1839.

of Christiania's better citizens have met this beneficent endeavour deserves the nation's highest gratitude'.[58] It seems that at least some of the initial support for the *Skilling-Magazin* was as much a support for the cause of diffusing useful knowledge to the common man as it was a genuine interest in the magazine's content.

Skilling-Magazin, like *Penny Magazine* and other illustrated educational magazines, must be seen as a part of and a continuation of an enlightenment project. As French theorist Michel de Certeau has argued, the ideology of enlightenment claimed that printed texts could 'transform manners and costumes, that an elite's products could, if they were sufficiently widespread, remodel a whole nation'.[59] As we saw above, this sentiment was also clearly a part of the Norwegian state-supported enlightenment project at the time. However, in the case of the *Skilling-Magazine* it is unclear how successful it was. The magazine certainly received support and many subscribers. But part of the support can no doubt be attributed to an elite supporting an elite project.

What set *Skilling-Magazin* apart from similar educational journals in Norway at the time – like those published by Henrik Wergeland – was its use of images. The images in *Skilling-Magazin* were no doubt seen partly as a way to 'lure the people in' and to make them interested. This extensive use of illustrations also implied a particular audience to the learned elite. As the writer Aasmund Olavsson Vinje put it, illustrations were mainly there for 'women and children', but he had to admit that portraits and technical illustrations could be useful 'for adults as well'.[60] But wood engravings could also be important for teaching the common people a sense of form and aesthetics. In an article on wood engraving as a tool of popular education, art historian Lorentz Dietrichson argued that the cold Norwegian climate meant that urban spaces were not as much used as in southern countries. Adornments on buildings and public spaces could therefore not play the same role in fostering an aesthetic sense among the public as they did in places such as Italy or southern Germany. This made wood engravings even more important in the Nordic countries, Dietrichson argued.[61]

---

[58] 'Skilling-Magazin (indsændt)', *Morgenbladet*, 4 June 1835.
[59] M. de Certeau, *The Practice of Everyday Life*, trans. S. F. Rendall (Berkeley, 1984), p. 166.
[60] A. O. Vinje, 'Bladsjaa', *Dølen. Eit Vikublad*, no. 8, 12 December 1858, p. 30. '[S]like Afskjeldringar ere for Kvennfolk, og Smaaborn, og mange, sosom Mannslik (Portræter) og Reidskaper, for vaxne Folk og.'
[61] L. Dietrichson, 'Træsnittets Betydning Som Folkedannelsesmiddel Med Specielt Hensyn Til de Nordiske Nationer', *Nordisk Tidskrift for Literatur og Kunst*, vol. 1 (1863), 309–16.

To Wergeland, as to Dietrichson, the images were not only a tool to get people to read the articles but played an important educational role in themselves. Wergeland argued that the images in *Skilling-Magazin* could give a 'new liveliness' to the imagination of the common people. As an example of this, Wergeland claimed to have witnessed a peasant attempt to draw a picture of a leopard he had seen in the first issue of *Skilling-Magazin*. In the end, the peasant could not finish the drawing, and his cat had to help him out. To Wergeland, this little story showed how the *Skilling-Magazin* could help foster imagination and fantasy, capacities that lay dormant in the minds of the common people.[62]

Wergeland's observations point us to the notion of reading as a creative practice. Regardless of their success, publications such as *Skilling-Magazin* can easily be discarded as attempts of the more powerful to impose their values and ideology on the less powerful. However, as de Certeau reminds us, the 'strategies' of those in power are met with the 'tactics' of those whom power is asserted upon. Readers are like travellers, de Certeau states, they 'move across lands belonging to someone else'.[63] In moving across those lands, they always reshape the landscape. This allows the reader freedom. The fleeting nature of reading also makes historical reading practices hard to capture.

While it is hard to know exactly how the *Skilling-Magazin* was read by individual readers, we can say something general about the reception of the magazine. The magazine was clearly at first seen as a success, but as the novelty disappeared it also lost some of its subscribers. However, the magazine proved long-lasting, ceasing publication in 1891. The fact that the magazine lasted can be attributed to its state support. But it could also be that it found its audience among the more affluent as well as the interested readers among the common people. In addition, its extensive use of images could be one of the reasons the magazine had a continued appeal. Lastly, *Skilling-Magazin* can represent the dual nature of the state-driven enlightenment project. It was an elite project intended to impose elite values and interests on the common people. At the same time, as both Wergeland and de Certeau remind us, printed texts and images can be appropriated and used in many ways.

[62] H. Wergeland 'Træk af den periodiske Litteraturs Indflytelse paa Almuesmand', *Morgenbladet*, 20 August 1835, in *Artikler og småstykker 1833–38*, pp. 232–3.
[63] M. de Certeau, *The Practice of Everyday Life*.

CONCLUSION

In this chapter I have placed *Skilling-Magazin* at a historical and geographical crossroads, between the Northern Enlightenment and nineteenth-century mass publishing. Like the Gutenberg centenary which opened this chapter, *Skilling-Magazin* contains both past and future, the local and the transnational.

The publishers and readers of *Skilling-Magazin* were literary citizens of Europe. *Skilling Magazin* was a part of a Europe-wide transnational literary network that shaped its content and its format. Its format mirrored the *Penny Magazine* and similar magazines across Europe, and many of the texts and images were brought in from these periodicals. In the 1830s and 1840s the magazine even ordered wood engravings from engravers in London and Paris. This transnational network extended to its readers as well. Readers of educational illustrated periodicals all over Europe not only expected the images from these illustrated periodicals to look a certain way but also to a large extent looked at the same images. In being part of this transnational network of editors, engravers, writers and readers, *Skilling-Magazin* can be seen as a part of an emerging modern mass culture in the nineteenth century.

At the same time, however, its local context and connection to a Norwegian state-supported enlightenment made the *Skilling-Magazin* a different kind of publication. *Penny Magazine* and its competitors were pioneers in applying new technology and organisation to increase circulation. *Skilling-Magazin*, meanwhile, was printed on simple wooden presses long into the 1850s. It was part of a Norwegian book and periodical business that looked more like what we associate with the eighteenth century than the nineteenth century. *Skilling-Magazin* was also connected to a state-supported enlightenment in nineteenth-century Norway. This can be seen as a continuation of particular aspects of the eighteenth-century Northern Enlightenment.

These enlightenment ideals were also expressed in the reception of the magazine. But while aspirations were high, there are indications that perhaps the magazine was not as popular among the intended audience – the common people – as the editors and had hoped. However, while it is easy to dismiss the *Skilling-Magazin* as an elite project, the fact that it proved long-lasting also points to a genuine appeal. In its reception we also find reminders that printed texts and images can be appropriated and used in many ways. *Skilling-Magazin* thus not only represents a historical and geographical crossroads but can also represent the dual nature of the enlightenment project.

Afterword

James Raven

L ITERARY CITIZENSHIP HAS BEEN variously defined as the act of promoting literature, literary community and literary culture, but this
volume has demonstrated how capacious and stimulating such concepts
can be. Not that the questions are settled. As a crucial aspect of the writing
life over many centuries, the scope of literary citizenship is wide and sometimes perilously elusive of variable, even capricious, concepts of identity,
engagement, participation and performance. All are subjects for consideration and debate.

Many contemporary college and university courses on 'literary citizenship' have examined in very particular ways the material and ideological
conditions that inform such activity, and given that most of today's writers
and artists receive training in state-funded institutions, those individual
citizens are unsurprisingly encouraged to reflect on their public and civic
roles and responsibilities.[1] For some critics, modern emphasis on volunta-
rism as being integral to literary citizenry also skews the debate towards
an acceptance by writers of unfairly penurious returns.[2] For other, more
optimistic critics, modern media expansion makes real a community
involvement that spans governmental institutions, literary festivals, reading series, coffee-serving bookshops, book clubs and online platforms such
as Wattpad and Goodreads. Such modern equivalence can indeed be sug-
gestive: it can foster awareness and promotion of the exotic and eccentric
as much as the mainstream and popular, of the political as much as the
social and cultural.

[1]   R. Martin, 'Artistic Citizenship: Introduction', in M. Schmidt Campbell and R. Mar-
      tin (eds), *Artistic Citizenship: A Public Voice for the Arts* (New York, 2006), p. 1.
[2]   See, for example B. Tuch, 'More Work, No Pay: Why I Detest "Literary Citizenship"',
      Salon (23 April 2014), <www.salon.com/2014/04/23/more_work_no_pay_why_i_
      detest_literary_citizenship> (accessed 23 February 2023).

Before Brexit I was a subject of the United Kingdom and a citizen of the European Union. Now I am back to being a subject of the British Crown although, confusingly since the 1948 Nationality Act, all British subjects can be known by the alternative title Commonwealth Citizen. At the same time, in both practice and legal definition, 'citizenship' has become the critical term, in Britain as elsewhere, for rights of abode (or 'settlement') and nationality. Such citizenship carries the legal status whereby a person has the right to live in a state. As a result, the state cannot refuse them entry or deport them. In Norway, as in most states, citizenship can be acquired by (and only by) fulfilling a particular set of requirements which depend largely on nationality and immigration status. Since January 2020, however, it is also possible to obtain Norwegian citizenship without having to renounce an existing citizenship (or nationality) of another country. Modern citizenship can thus overlap with other allegiances, much as in the past. Individuals, groups and communities might all hold diverse allegiances to different cultural and linguistic entities as well as to different political and religious authorities: familial, local, state and international.

Such presentist considerations of citizenship, and particularly in relation to subjecthood, are not inappropriate for interrogation of a past '*literary* citizenship', a term broadly accepted by all contributors to this volume to address recent understandings of diverse and changing literary involvement and engagement. Considerations of responsibility, of community and place, of material and ideological origination and movement, of overlapping and non-exclusive allegiances, and above all of what participation and commensurate rights actually mean are at the heart of the foregoing history of literariness. As this volume has also shown, the debate between citizenship and subjecthood remains very much alive: a debate that centres upon notions of civic engagement, participation and rights. Historically within most states, specific (but much debated) processes ensured that subjects of the Crown gradually became, as indeed Holberg put it, 'all the subjects in a State'. It was a transformation involving the accretion of very real testimonies of allegiance from taxation, voting and other concrete participatory activities which widened in scope and in legally enforceable authority over the centuries. And today, within a particular polity and as subject to the particular laws and practices of that polity, citizenship exists as a reciprocal relationship between the individual and the state to which the individual owes allegiance and, in turn, is entitled to that state's protection.

Beyond these relational considerations are issues of permanence and change, issues which also feature prominently in any analogous enquiry into literary citizenship. Legal citizenship may be conferred at birth, but also, at least in most states, obtained through naturalisation. Entitlement to authorship might seem a specious notion, but status at birth and connections of family have clearly assisted in literary endeavour. Citizenship within well-resourced and acquiescent states further involves, just as in literary realms, relational complexity between individuals, or citizens, given the supply of participatory rights. Where voting, education, welfare and healthcare (among other considerations) support such relational development in states, so contract, copyright, pre- and post-publication censorship and policing and restrictions on the number and sites of printing presses all feature within the elaboration of literary spheres. In return, the author, mediator and reader accept, consciously or not, self-censorship, market conditioning and a raft of activities and perceptions which constitute a sense of literary community and belonging. Citizenship and authorship, literary infrastructure and mediation, and readership and reception thus become intrinsically entangled with the nature of civil society, with questions of self and group identity, notions of belonging, and the acts and understanding of reciprocity and responsibility. Evidence for the valuation of citizenship is consequentially inherent to the larger history of 'literary citizenship'.

In adopting and elaborating such a richly analogous concept, this collection of essays has also offered further significant correlations. In initial terms at least, citizenship pivots on the individual, most obviously the writer but also the publisher-bookseller, other circulatory and editorial agents, and finally the reader. There are in fact many mediating agencies (including, as shown in the chapters above, media technology, transportation, critical intervention, and libraries and book clubs), but by adopting the perspective of the citizen, the individual actor is invariably given pre-eminence. This means that in considering *livres sans frontières* and the importance of crossing borders, itself another key aspect of citizenship and the boundaries of belonging and perception, that crossing is often chronicled as undertaken by human agents – by travellers, by merchants and factors, by clerics and subversives, all conclusively putting the individual first. It is a marked feature, for example, of many of the studies in this volume that individual writers, booksellers and printers are exceptionally well travelled. A characteristic of many northern European literary endeavours was to experience and connect with likeminded individuals and professionals in the towns and cities of the heartland of the continent. A recurrent focus is the conveyor as well as the originator and the receiver, rather than the cross-bordered text. The transnational practices explored in these essays are fundamentally personal, affecting individual lives and decisions as practices change and adapt.

Exploration of identity is the concomitant of this focus on the individual, while concentration on the personal and on identity heightens interest
in the 'vantage point'. The point of view, as we might also call it, was in
fact given linguistic prominence by Bergen bishop Erik Pontoppidan in
his mid-eighteenth-century personal and published writings. In Pontoppidan's 1752–3 *Det første Forsøg paa Norges naturlige Historie*, his (partly
posthumously published) 1763–7 *Den danske Atlas*, and frequently in his
private correspondence, the bishop savoured the combination of *hoved*
(main), *øye/øje* (eye) and *mærke* (mark/point) as *Hoved-Øyemærke* (*Hov-
ed-Øjemærke*).[3] This interest in the focal point of attention, the perspective
of the author, attests to growing rumination on what it meant to write and
be published both at home and abroad in what Pontoppidan himself called
the Enlightenment or *Oplysning* (the latter also translating as 'information',
'disclosure' and 'awareness'). As he wrote about his own literary citizenship,
he strove to

> become someone who might be called the first to attempt the Natural
> History of Norway and whose translation, in time, will usefully reveal
> unusual things for different Nations as well as for ourselves, particu-
> larly in this period of enquiry which has the close scrutiny of Nature[4]
> as its main focal point [*Hoved-Øyemærke*], although not always with
> the Creator's great knowledge and love in mind.[5]

Perspectives, of course, are not *sui generis* and derive in part from comparative social, economic and political advantage. Among many others
analysed in this volume, Valkendorf, Archbishop of Nidaros/Trondheim,
belonged to a noble Dano-German family. In successive centuries writers
of means and civic and clerical connections from Hans Poulsen Resen to
William Sverdrup and Carsten Anker exploited their status and privilege
to enable a confident and expansive 'citizenship', both intellectual and geographical. The much-travelled Valkendorf died in Rome in 1522. By contrast,
Peder Palladius was representative of more humble means and restricted
movement, but despite the ravages of the Thirty Years' War, new routes
and transportation methods allowed greater travel in the seventeenth
century. Increasingly during the eighteenth century gentlemen and nobles
from northern Europe undertook the Tours more commonly associated

---

[3] See *Ordbog over det danske Sprog*, <https://ordnet.dk/ods_en/>.
[4] 'Naturens Randsagning'; literally, the ransacking of Nature.
[5] Pontoppidan to Count Holstein, 29 December 1750, Pontoppidan Copybook of Letters, 1749–51, Regional State Archives, Bergen; also reproduced in Gina Dahl, *Biskop
Pontoppidans brevbok 1751–1753* (Bergen, 2019), p. 240.

with rich young men from the south and west. As part of this expanding reach, both visited and reported, the emergent production and circulation of periodical reviews, learned journals, essays and even novels (such as the translations of Marmontel and Richardson) were the domain of privileged readers – and usually privileged writers of comfortable means. At least until enterprises like the children's missionary magazines and, even more, the *Skilling-Magazin*, printing and illustration revolutions and attempts at the 'cultivation of the masses', readerships were notably restricted. Internationalism also cost: *livres sans frontières* were largely read by the well-to-do, while those individuals crossing borders for pleasure and education were likely to be very wealthy members of their population just as imported books were very expensive compared to their fuller literary cohort.

It would seem, therefore, that reciprocity involving the individual and his or her awareness of different mutualities is fundamental to this study, and yet also apparent are numerous tensions and paradoxes. Nationality, for example, can be both central but also tangential and contingent with citizenship in the sense that literary citizenship often embodied linguistic or national belonging but also bore a transgressive relationship with boundaries. This is particularly complex across the Nordic countries stretching from the Hanseatic and Germanic south to the northern Finnmark boundary of Christendom and to colonies from Greenland to Tranquebar. The subordination of Norway in union with Denmark and the nineteenth-century union of the Crown with Swedish realms also paradoxically demonstrate both the fragility and obduracy of boundaries as well as the sometimes surprising lack of exchange in experience and understanding. The latter includes, for example, the different paths to the greater freedom of the press taken in Sweden and Denmark–Norway described in Chapter 5 (Langen, Nordin and Stjernfelt). And as explored by Ellen Krefting in Chapter 8 and elaborated on by other contributors, nationalism does not simply equate to patriotism. 'Patria' extended to the sense of belonging to a place, of a rootedness that might also generate or release a certain romanticism and nostalgia, a literary longing and invention of the past for current reasons. Other tensions appear in the linguistic and philological where on the one hand elasticity between written and oral degrees of comprehension heightened interest in different literacies and dialects and the impeding of communication, but on the other hand, writing and interest in the vernacular promoted linguistic purification and standardisation akin to a reification of citizenship (as particularly explored in Chapter 4 by Bjerring-Hansen). As Chapters 6 (Kukkonen), 7 (Nøding) and later contributors remind us, the issue is one of different *literacies* informing different types and perceptions of citizenship – one size does not fit all.

Such differentials bring us back to parallels in present connotations of the word 'citizenship'. That denotation is usually associated with those guided by or acting with a sense of civic responsibility; this, however, can conflict with a 'citizenship' of the nation more associated with rights and privileges than with responsibilities and, moreover, as enforceably bounded by passports, customs controls, detention centres and deportations. Literary citizenship again embraces both broad-based participation and exclusive and excluding practices. Some concerned with modern citizenry have insisted on demarcation. As then British Prime Minister Theresa May protested after Brexit, 'if you believe you're a citizen of the world, you're a citizen of nowhere. You don't understand what the very word "citizenship" means'.[6] Belonging brings boundaries; the freedom to write and the freedom to believe that you are part of a community inevitably creates frontiers, exclusions, privileges, limitations. But also, as Anthony Appiah argued in contradicting at least part of the May contention, 'transnational institutions can stand alongside national ones. [...] You can feel a profound loyalty to a particular community and to humanity'.[7] In other words, the literary citizenship we are uncovering created boundaries but also multiple and overlapping and porous allegiances – some boundaries were more rigid, more permanent and, for that matter, more illusory than others.

The tensions are again particularly evinced in the sense of belonging. To varying degrees, citizenship embodies perceptions of allegiance, of being aware of participation in a community, but also widespread is the interplay between censorship and freedom, of expression and control. As Annabel Patterson put it, 'literature' in the Early Modern period was conceived in part as the way around censorship.[8] This, above all else, is what these essays describe: the understanding, often in the face of objection and interference, of a sense of shared literariness, shared literary participation and shared engagement. Such tensions are evidenced across different literary and media forms. A compelling range is analysed in this collection: bibles, catechisms and liturgical works, missionary tracts and religious textbooks, scandal sheets, illustrated books, periodicals and the multiple and faster-produced forms of the greater mechanised nineteenth century. Professionalisation increased, but standards were not always what we might expect. The quality of production often proved variable and the means by which

[6]   T. May, speech to the Conservative Party Annual Conference, 9 October 2016, <www.ukpol.co.uk/theresa-may-2016-speech-at-conservative-party-conference/> (accessed 23 February 2023).
[7]   K. A. Appiah, 'Mistaken Identities', The Reith Lectures, BBC Radio 4, 8 November 2016, <www.bbc.co.uk/programmes/b08otwcz> (accessed 23 February 2023).
[8]   Annabel M. Patterson, *Censorship and Interpretation* (Madison, WI, 1984).

works were written, printed and circulated often chaotic. Literary citizenship might have applied a certain formalism of operation and expectations across many genres, but the reality of creation, imposition, circulation and reception was sometimes unexpected, poor and disappointing.

Finally, as noted at the outset, many commentators on literary citizenship also emphasise the voluntary. Cathy Day and Lori A. May have emphasised the need for contemporary writers to be generous in their community involvements. Katey Schultz has argued that we should think not about 'literary citizenship' but about 'literary stewardship', a term that she sees as better placing an emphasis on 'contributing and collaborating, not taking and capitalizing'.[9] In fact, making money is not excluded from such consideration of citizenship: literary philanthropy balances literary entrepreneurship on literary citizenship courses (all related in different ways to courses in creative writing) at Ball State University, SUNY Oswego, the College of New Rochelle and the University of Chicago Graham School, Arizona State University, California Institute of the Arts, and the University of Central Arkansas (among others).[10] Robert McGill and André Babyn run a course in Literary Citizenship at the University of Toronto which majors in the interrogative:

> We ask questions such as: Who is most able to participate in literary citizenship, and why? Who benefits from various kinds of literary citizenship? Who gets excluded? What challenges are there in establishing literary journals, presses, reading series, and writing groups? How can such ventures be successful? Just as importantly, what should the criteria for success be?'[11] That last question is particularly pertinent to evaluating the *type* of profit gained by literary citizenship, not simply monetary, but also intellectual, social and religious benefit.

[9] K. Schultz, 'Literary Citizenship: Point and Counterpoint' *Kateyschultz.com* (n.d.), <www.kateyschultz.com/2017/10/literary-citizenship/> (accessed 23 February 2023); cf. D. Ebenbach, 'Literary Citizenship Does Not Mean "Gimme", *Medium* (28 April 2014), <https://medium.com/human-parts/literary-citizenship-does-not-mean-gimme-e7ac3f97b140> (accessed 23 February 2023).

[10] See C. E. Smitherman and S. Vanderslice, 'Service Learning, Literary Citizenship, and the Creative Writing Classroom', in A. Peary and T. C. Hunley (eds), *Creative Writing Pedagogies for the Twenty-First Century* (Carbondale, IL, 2015), pp. 153–68.

[11] R. McGill and A. Babyn, 'Teaching Critical Literary Citizenship', *The Writer's Notebook*, February 2019, <www.awpwriter.org/magazine_media/writers_notebook_view/311#NOTES> (accessed 23 February 2023); and see website, <literarycitizenshiptoronto.com>.

Nonetheless, contemporary courses teach students about the organisations and communities that make writing and publishing possible with critical thinking about assumptions, values and practices of literary citizenship which veer towards the unpaid and the socially responsible.[12] And the voluntary naturally invokes the poor return. Lori A. May argues that '[v]olunteering one's time is certainly the standard for offering something to the greater community',[13] and Donna Steiner has similarly emphasised the importance of reciprocity in literary citizenship, arguing for 'giving your time and expertise in return for what that community has given to you.'[14] Literary citizens are broadly identified as people interconnected 'by a love of writing and reading'[15] but also bound to the economics and demographics of the publishing industry, the roles of social media in literary culture, the uses of literature in promoting social justice, and the relationship between literary citizenship and other forms of citizenship. Rights, obligations and identities change and overlap, while a sense of community and belonging generally relate to specific locales. Literary citizenship remains both an open and an exclusionary term.

Such duality, drawing on contemporary parallels to the nature of citizenship today, extends perspectives in the meaning and intent of historical bibliography and the history of the book. Literary citizenship is revealed in this volume as the act of promoting literature, literary community and literary culture, and one with a range of settings, the most abiding of which are northern, certainly, but also continental European and with global networking. The new perspective incorporates both the material and the global turn that have been so important to recent developments in the history of the book, while the focus on equity also affords the opportunity to think about how gender inflected literary citizenship. Above all, the concept highlights a number of tensions and paradoxes that actually help us think through the way in which a bookish culture develops. In

---

[12]   R. Gay, 'The Eight Questions Writers Should Ask Themselves', *Awpwriter.org* (November 2015), <www.awpwriter.org/magazine_media/writers_notebook_view/5> (accessed 23 February 2023); and cf. C. Day, 'Cathy Day's Principles of Literary Citizenship', *Literarycitizenship.com* (24 September 2012), <https://literarycitizenship.com/?s=principles) (accessed 23 February 2023); and C. Morganti, 'Celebrating Literary Citizens', *My Two Cents* (15 August 2013), <https://charlottemorganti.com/?s=celebrating> (accessed 23 February 2023).

[13]   L. A. May, *The Write Crowd: Literary Citizenship and the Writing Life* (New York, 2015), p. 8.

[14]   D. Steiner, 'Literary Citizenship: How You Can Contribute to the Literary Community and Why You Should', in S. Vanderslice (ed.), *Studying Creative Writing Successfully* (Newmarket, 2016), p. 132.

[15]   D. Steiner, 'Literary Citizenship', p. 133.

twenty-first-century Scandinavia, along with many countries worldwide, entitlement to citizenship has become more exclusive in terms of residence and language requirements – all responses to globalisation and immigration and wider pressures to close down access as much as to open it up. That interplay between current citizenship definitions and the 'literary citizen' remains tense, unstable, unsettled and open to productive debate. The connotations of the scope of literary citizenship and its performance are wide-ranging. Windows are opened indeed.

Bibliography

PRIMARY SOURCES

MANUSCRIPT AND ARCHIVAL COLLECTIONS

Danish National Archives, Copenhagen

232. Danske Kancelli. Box C35: Bilag til jysk missive af 7. november 1696 ang. Kommissionen i den thistedske besættelsessag (1283 pages).
1790. Højesteret. Voteringsprotokol (1661–1939).
  Box 56: 1697 Protokol B (658 pages).
  Box 57: Appendix til høyesterets Protocoll af anno 1697 (250 folios).
Kabinetssekretariatet 1766–1771: Kgl. ordrer til kabinetssekretariatet

National Archives of Norway, Oslo

SAO/PAO-0050 Z-Lo011 Fabritius og sønner, Forlagskontrakter.

National Library of Norway, Oslo

Riisbrigh, Børge
Ms. foreles. 29: 4: 'Forelæsninger over Philosophien'. Referert av Søren B. Bugge.
Sverdrup, Georg
Ms. forelesn. 377: 'Forelæsninger over Philosophie. 2den Deel; Psychologie' (1832), (digitized edition at <http://urn.nb.no/URN:NBN:no-nb_digimanus_120093>.)
Treschow, Niels
Ms. 4to. 2302: 'Almindelig Encyclopædie'.
Ms forelesn. 232: 'Forelæsninger over en almindelig Encyclopædie' (1813).
Ms. forelesn. 398: 'Forelæsninger over Moralphilosophien [...] Udskreven i Sommeren 1816 af Niels Schydtz' (1816), (digitized edition at <http://urn.nb.no/URN:NBN:no-nb_digimanus_120458>.)
Ms. forelesn. 694: 'Metaphysik' (1809).

Regional State Archive, Bergen

A-3401/06 Byfogd og Byskriver i Bergen, Bergen skifterett, Skifteakter: 'Skifteakter for Ole Brose'

Royal Library, Copenhagen

KBs arkiv (indtil 1943), Pligtaflevering, Ms E 39: Fortegnelse over leverancer til bogbinderne, afleveringer fra bogtrykkerne samt bogkøb og gaver, 1778–84
Collin 377 4to. Poul Martin Møller: Forelesninger over filosofi (original manuskript).
Gammel Kongelige Samling (GKS) 3304 4to: Jens Bircherod: Til en Biskop i Jylland angaaende Besættelsen i Thisted, 1696.

Swedish National Archives, Stockholm

Börstorpsamlingen, E3011: Anders Nordencrantz' arkiv, koncept (tidiga)
Kanslikollegium E IV:17
Kanslikollegium A IIa:39
R 1207: Borgarståndets arkiv 1726–1727, vol. 5
R 3405: Tredje utskottet 1765–1766, protokoll och bilagor

PRINTED PRIMARY SOURCES

Contemporary books and articles

Angelus, Andreas, *Wider- Natur- und Wunder-Buch* (Frankfurt am Main, 1597).
[Anon.] 'Nordia', [Review] *Kiøbenhavnske lærde Efterretninger*, no. 9 (1795), 128–9.
[Anon.] 'Det nittende Aarhundrede. Subskriptions-Indbydelse', *Morgenbladet*, 21 October 1874.
Arnold, August, *Einleitung in die Staatslehre durch tabellarische und vergleichende Darstellung von sieben neuern Verfassungen* (Berlin, 1849).
Bárðarson, Ivar, *Det gamle Grønlands beskrivelse*, ed. Finnur Jónsson (Copenhagen, 1930).
Bartholin, Thomas, *Epistolarum Medicinalum: Centuria III* (Copenhagen, 1667).
Bekker, Balthasar, *Der betoverde Weereld*, vol. IV (Amsterdam, 1693).
Beretning om Sekularfesten i Christiania den 24. Juni 1840 i Anledning af Bogtrykkerkunstens Opfindelse (Christiania, 1840).
Bergk, Johann Adam, *Die Kunst, Bücher zu lesen. Nebst Bemerkungen über Schriften und Schriftsteller* (Jena, 1799).
Besterman, Theodore (ed.), *Correspondence and related documents*, vol. XV, *The Complete Works of Voltaire* (Geneva, 1971).
[Bie, Jacob Christian], *Philopatria's Remarks, I: On the dear Times, and Decay of Trade; II: On the Courts of Justice; III: On the Revenues of the Clergy* (St Croix, 1771).
Biehl, Charlotta D., *Moralske Fortællinger*, vol. 4 (Copenhagen, 1782).
—— 'Charlotta Dorothea Biehls Historiske breve', *Historisk tidsskrift*, 3:4 (Copenhagen, 1865–6) (Facsimile edition at <www.kb.dk>).

Blom, Gustav Peter, *Das Königreich Norwegens, statistisch beschrieben*, 2 vols (Leipzig, 1843).

Bobé, Louis (ed.), 'Aktstykker til oplysning om Grønlands Besejling 1521–1607', *Danske Magazin* 5th ser., 6 (1909), 303–24.

Bogsamling i Klubben opprettet i November 1775 (Copenhagen, 1792) (Facsimile edition at <www.kb.dk>).

Brækstad, H[ans] L[ien], *The Constitution of the Kingdom of Norway: an Historical and Political Survey: with a complete translation of the Norwegian constitution and the act of union between Norway and Sweden* (London, 1905).

Brandes, Ernst, *Ueber den gegenwärtigen Zustand der Universität Göttingen* (Göttingen, 1802).

Brendel, Sebald, *Die Geschichte, das Wesen und der Werth der National-Repräsentation oder vergleichende historisch-pragmatische Darstellung der Staaten der alten und neuen Welt, besonders der deutschen, in Beziehung auf die Entstehung, Ausbildung, Schicksale und Vorzüge der Volksvertretung oder der öffentlichen Theilname an der höchsten Staatsgewalt: nebst einem Anhage, die merkwürdigsten Verfassungsurkunden seit 1789 enthaltend: ein Handbuch für wirkliche oder künftige Volksvertreter*, 2 vols (Bamberg und Leipzig, 1817).

Breviarium Nidrosiense, ed. Erik Valkendorf (Paris, 1519). (Digital facsimile edition at <www.nb.no/items/URN:NBN:no-nb_digibok_2007092813001>).

Brömel, August Theodor, *Die freie Verfassung Norwegens: in ihrer geschichtlichen Entstehung und weiterer Entwicklung, ihrem Wesen und ihren Folgen, T. 1, Die freie Verfassung Norwegens in ihrer geschichtlichen Entstehung nebst einleitender Vorgeschichte* (Bergen, 1842).

Bromme, Traugott, *Die Verfassungen der Vereinigten Staaten von Nord-Amerika, der Frei-Staaten Pennsylvania und Texas, der Königreiche Belgien und Norwegen, die Bundes-Verfassung der Schweiz und die Englische Staats-Verfassung Zur Beantwortung der Frage: Ob Republik, ob konstutionelle Monarchie?*, 2nd edn (Stuttgart, 1849).

Brunsmand, Johan, *Das geängstigte Köge, oder Eine warhaffte und Denckwürdige Historie: von einer entsetzlichen Versuchung des leidigen Satans, Mit welcher Zu Köge in Seeland eines recht ehrlichen und auffrichtigen Bürgers gantze Familie einige Jahre lang sehr hart beleget* (Leipzig, 1696).

—— *Energumeni Coagienses Sive Admirabilis Historia, De Horrenda Cacodæmonis tentatione* (Amsterdam, 1693).

—— *Energumeni Coagienses Sive Admirabilis Historia, De Horrenda Cacodæmonis tentatione* (Leiden, 1693).

—— *Et forfærdeligt Huus-Kaars eller en sandfærdig Beretning om en gruelig Fristelse som tvende fromme Ægte-Folk i Kiøge for nogen rum Tid siden har været plagede med* (Copenhagen, 1691).

—— *Et forfærdeligt Huus-Kaars eller en sandfærdig Beretning om en gruelig Fristelse som tvende fromme Ægte-Folck i Kiøge for nogen rum Tid siden har været plagede med* (Copenhagen, 1700).

—— *Et forfærdeligt Huus-Kaars, eller en sandfærdig Beretning om en gruelig Fristelse, som tvende fromme Egte-Folk i Kiøge for nogen rum Tid siden har været plagede med*, ed. Louis Pio (Copenhagen, 1870).

—— *Et forfærdeligt Huus-Kaars, eller en sandfærdig Beretning om en gruelig Fristelse, som tvende fromme Egte-Folk i Kjøge, for nogen rum Tid siden, har været plaget med* (Copenhagen, 1757).

—— *Et forfærdeligt Huus-Kaars eller en sandferdig Beretning om en gruelig Fristelse aff Dieffvelen som tvende fromme oc gudfryctige Æcte-Folck i Kiøge for nogen rum Tid siden hafver været plagede med* (Copenhagen, 1684).

—— *Et forfærdeligt Huus-Kaars eller en sandferdig Beretning om en gruelig Fristelse aff Dieffvelen som tvende fromme oc gudfryctige Æcte-Folck i Kiøge for nogen rum Tid siden hafver været plagede med* (Copenhagen, 1710).

—— *Et forfærdeligt Huus-Kaars, eller en sandferdig Beretning om en gruelig Fristelse aff Dieffvelen som tvende Fromme oc Gudfryctige Ectefolck i Kiøge for nogen rum tid siden haffver været plagede med* (Copenhagen, 1674).

—— *Johannis Brunsmanni Energumeni Coagienses, sive Admirabilis Historia, De Horrenda Cacodæmonis tentatione* (Leipzig, 1695).

—— *Kiøge Huuskors en original dansk Folke-Roman i 8 Kapitler* (Copenhagen, 1820).

—— *Køge Huskors*, ed. Anders Bæksted (Copenhagen, 1953).

[Buchwald, Friedrich], *Geheime Hof und Staats-Geschichte des Königreichs Dänemark, Von dem Marquis Ludwig d'Yves. Zeiten nach der Struenseeischen Revolution* (Germanien, 1790).

Chambers, Ephraim, *Cyclopædia* (London, 1728), vol. 1, 'Anecdotes'.

Characters and Anecdotes of the Court of Sweden, vol. 2 (London, 1790).

Collett, Camilla, *Amtmandens Døttre (1854/1855)* (Oslo, 2013).

—— *The District Governor's Daughters*, trans. Kirsten Seaver (Norwich, 1991).

Constitution des Königreichs Norwegen vom 17. Mai und 4. November 1814, Aus dem Norwegischen übersetzt und der freien deutschen Nation gewidmet (Stettin, 1848).

Constitution du royaume de Norwège (Christiania, 1814).

Constitution du royaume de Norvège adoptée le 17. Mai 1814: Avec les changements et additions y apportés jusqu'au 25 Mai 1905: Suivie de l'acte d'union du 6 aout 1815 (Christiania, 1905).

'Constitution of the Kingdom of Norway', *British and Foreign State Papers* 1: II (1812–14) (London, 1841).

Constituzione di Norvegia del 1814 sotto Carlo XIII, Trad. in italiano da Angelo Lanzellotto (Napoli, 1820).

C.V.B. [= Carl von Bergen], 'Det nittende Aarhundrede', [review] *Stockholms Dagblad* (18 November 1874).

Dahl, Gina, *Biskop Pontoppidans brevbok 1751–1753* (Bergen, 2019).

Danmarks og Norgis Kirke-Ritual (Copenhagen, 1685).

Dass, Petter, *Katekismesanger. D. Mort: Luthers Lille Catechismus, Forfatted I beqvemme Sange, under føyelige Melodier*, critical edn by Jon Haarberg (Oslo, 2013). <www.bokselskap.no/boker/katekismesanger/tittelside>.

Die Verfassungen der Vereinigten Staaten von Nord-Amerika, des Staates New-York, des Königreichs Norwegen und des Königreichs Belgien. Als Anhang der Entwurf der neuen Preussischen Constitution, 5th edn. (Berlin, 1848).

Dietrichson, Lorentz, 'Træsnittets Betydning Som Folkedannelsesmiddel Med Specielt Hensyn Til de Nordiske Nationer', *Nordisk Tidskrift for Literatur og Kunst*, vol. 1, (1863), 309–16.

Diplomatarium Norvegicum 1–23, ed. Kjeldeskriftkommisjonene Riksarkivet (1847–2011). (Online edition at <dokpro.uio.no/dipl_norv/diplom_felt. html> [accessed 6 March 2022]).

Diurendahl, Andreas, *Fortegnelse over Endeel indbundne Bøger, Som ere til Leje hos Boghandler Diurendahl i Christiania, paa efterstaaende Conditioner* (Christiania, 1797).

En Kircke Ordinantz, hvor effter alle, Baade Geistlige oc Verdslige vdi Norgis Rige, skulle sig rette oc forholde, in Norsk historisk kjeldeskrift-institutt, *Kirkeordinansen av 1607 og Forordning om ekteskapssaker gitt 1582*, facsimile edition, Norsk historisk kjeldeskrift-institutt (Oslo, 1985 [1607]).

En reisende Russers Anecdoter over de danskes Statsforfatning, Sæder og Skikke, i Breve til sine Venner (Copenhagen, 1771) (Facsimile edition at <www.kb.dk>).

'Entwurf eines Grundgesetzes für das Königreich Norwegen', *Aktenstücke und Aufsätze die neueste Geschichte Norwegens betreffend* I. Im Juny 1814 (Altona, 1814).

Forsskål, Peter, *Thoughts on Civil Liberty: Translation of the Original Manuscript with background* (Stockholm, 2009).

Fotolitografisk Gjengivelse af det i Storthingets Arkiv opbevarede Original-Haandskrift af Kongeriget Norges Grundlov af 17:de Mai 1814 (Kristiania, 1905).

Gessner, Conrad, *Historia animalium* IV (Frankfurt, 1604; 1st edn, 1551–8).

Ghillany, F[riedrich]. W[ilhelm], *Die Verfassung des Königreichs Norwegen: Das freisinnigste constitutionell-monarchische Grundgesetz in Europa: unter den gegenwärtigen politischen Verhältnissen dem deutschen Publicum zur Kenntnißnahme vorgelegt* (Nürnberg, 1848).

Gottsched, Johann Christoph, *Erste Gründe der gesamten Weltweisheit* (Leipzig, 1734)

'Grundgesetz des Königreichs Norwegen', *Politisches Journal nebst Anzeige von gelehrten und andern Sachen*, herausgegeben von einer Gesellschaft von Gelehrten, Hamburg auf den Postämtern und in der Hoffmannschen Buchhandlung, 2:9 (1814), 778–86; 2:10 (1814), 880–92.

Grundgesetz des Königreichs Norwegen, Aus dem Norwegischen übersetz (Königsberg, 1843).

Guldberg, C. A., *Historisk Udsigt over Bogtrykkerkonsten fra dens Begyndelse til nærværende Tid: et Indbydelsesskrift til Sekularfesten i Christiania d. 24 Juni 1840* (Christiania, 1840).

Hellmar, H[ugo], *Die Norwegische Verfassung: ein Vorbild für Preussen. Gedanken über die indirekte Wahl, das Zweikammersystem und das suspensive Veto* (Halle, 1848).

Helset, Hovel, *Den lille Tarif. Et Forsøg paa at bevise Skadeligheden ved Indførselen af atskillige fremmede Varer i Norge* (Christiania, 1820).

'His Majesty's Gracious Ordinance Relating to Freedom of Writing and of the Press' (1766), transl. Peter Hogg, in *The World's First Freedom of Information Act Anders Chydenius' Legacy Today*, ed. Juha Mustonen (Kokkola, 2006).

Holberg, Ludvig, *Moralske Tanker*, vol. II (Copenhagen, 1744).

Hondorff, Andreas, *Promptuarium illustrium exemplorum* (Leipzig, 1582).

Horwitz, J., *Die Verfassungen der constitutionell-monarchischen und republikanischen Staaten der Gegenwart. Zweite Lieferung, Nord-America, Belgien, Norwegen: nach der Quellen Zusammengestellt erläuternden Anmerkungen versehen* (Berlin, 1848).

Høst, Jens Kragh, *Erindringer om mig og mine Samtidige* (Copenhagen, 1835).

——— 'Subskribtionsplan. Nordia', *Kiøbenhavnske lærde Efterretninger*, no. 3 (1795), 46–7.

Instruction For Degne, Klokkere Og Skoleholdere paa Landet i Norge, facsimile edn (Oslo, 1959 [23.01.1739]).

Jackson, John, *A Treatise on Wood Engraving: Historical and Practical* (London, 1839).

[Just, Anton Franz], *Hemmelige efterretninger fra Satans Hof* (Viborg, 1794) (Facsimile edition at <www.kb.dk>).

Kirkeordinansen av 1537: Reformasjonens kirkelov, trans. Terje Ellingsen (Oslo, 1990).

Knight, Charles, *Passages of a Working Life during Half a Century: With a Prelude of Early Reminiscences*, 3 vols (London, 1864).

Kong Christian Den Femtes Norske Lov 15de april 1687 (Oslo, 1982).

Kong Christian den Siettes II. Forordning, Angaaende den tilvoxende Ungdoms Confirmation og Bekræftelse udi deres Daabes Naade. [13 January] 1736. Diplomatic edn. Kirkehistorisk arkiv, Norsk Lærerakademi <www.fagsider.org/kirkehistorie/lover/1736_konf.htm>.

Kongl. Maj:ts Nådige Förordning, Til Befrämjande af Lagarnes behörige wärkställighet bland Rikets Ämbetsmän och öfrige undersåtare. Gifwen Stockholm i Råd-Cammaren then 12. Novemb. 1766 (Stockholm, 1766).

'Konstitutionen. Grundgesetz des Königreichs Norwegen', *Allgemeine Staats-Korrespondenz [als zeitgemässe Reihefolge der Zeitschrift der Rheinische Bund]*. 3:8–9 (1814–1815), 128–39; 415–35.

Konungariket Norriges Grundlag, gifven af Riksförsamlingen i Eidsvold den 17 Maj 1814, samt i anledning af Norriges och Sveriges förening, närmare bestämd på Norriges utomordentliga Storting i Christiania den 4 November 1814 (Stockholm, 1814).

Kraft, Jens, *Topographisk-statistisk Beskrivelse over Kongeriget Norge*. 2nd edn, 4 vols (Christiania, 1838–42).

Læreplanverket for den 10-årige grunnskolen (Oslo, 1996).

Laing, Samuel, *Journal of a Residence in Norway During the Years 1834, 1835, & 1836: Made with a View to Enquire Into the Moral and Political Economy of that Country, and the Condition of Its Inhabitants* (London, 1836).

Latham, Robert Gordon, *Norway and the Norwegians* (London, 1840).

[Lezay-Marnézia, Claude-François-Adrien], *L'Heureuse famille, conte moral* (Copenhagen, 1768).

—— 'L'Heureuse famille. Conte moral', in J.-F. Marmontel, *Bélisaire [...] augmenté de L'Heureuse famille. Conte moral, par le même* (Leipzig, 1768).

Luther, Martin, *Barn-lærddomen eller den litle katekjesen hans Morten Luther*, trans. O. J. Høyem (Nidaros, 1873).

—— *Der kleine Catechismus, fuer die gemeyne Pfarherr und Prediger* (Marpurg, 1529) (Facsimile edition at <www.zvdd.de/dms/load/met/?PPN=oai%3Adiglib.hab.de%3Appn_664786359>.

—— *Dr. Martin Luthers lille katekisme*, ed. A. Chr. Bang, 38th printing (Oslo, 1976).

—— *Kakjesboki eller Barnalærdomen vaar*. trans. S. Aarrestad (Stavanger, 1877).

—— *Small Catechism*, anon. trans. (Saint Louis, MO, 1986) <https://catechism.cph.org>.

Lyschander, Claus C., *C.C. Lyschander's Digtning*, eds Fl. Lundgreen-Nielsen and E. Petersen, Det Danske Sprog- og Litteraturselskab (2 vols, Copenhagen, 1989).

Magnus, Olaus, *Historia de gentibus septentrionalibus* (Rome, 1555).

Magnússon, Árni, *Kort og sandfærdig Beretning, om den viit-udraabte Besettelse udi Tistæd, til alles Efterretning af Original-Akter og troværdige Dokumenter uddragen og sammenskreven* (Copenhagen, 1699).

Mantel, Hilary, *Mantel Pieces. Royal Bodies and Other Writing from* the London Review of Books (London, 2020).

Marmontel, Jean-François, *Belisaire* ([Copenhagen], 1767).

—— *Belisarius, skreven i det Franske Sprog og nu i Dansk oversat*, trans. [A. P. Bartholin] (Copenhagen, 1768).

—— *Contes moraux* (The Hague [Paris?], 1761).

—— *Contes moraux* (Paris, 1761).

—— *Contes moraux* (Amsterdam, 1761/62).

—— *Contes moraux* (Paris, 1765).

—— *Contes moraux* ([Copenhagen], 1768).

—— *Memoirs of Marmontel, written by himself*, 4 vols (London, 1805).

—— *Nyeste Fortællinger*, trans. Knud Lyne Rahbek (Copenhagen, 1794).

May, Theresa, Speech to the Conservative Party Annual Conference, 9 October 2016,   <www.ukpol.co.uk/theresa-may-2016-speech-at-conservative-party-conference/> (accessed 23 February 2023).

Menneskeliga och medborgerliga Rättigheter [Copenhagen, 1792].

Michaelis, Johann David, *Raisonnement über die protestantischen Universitäten in Deutschland. Zweiter Theil* (Frankfurt, Leipzig, 1770).

[Mirabeau, Honoré-Gabriel de Riquetti de], *Hemmelige Efterretninger om det Berlinske Hof, eller en reisende Franskmands Brevvexling*, trans. [J. H. Meier] (Copenhagen, 1789).

Missale Nidrosiense, ed. Erik Valkendorf (Copenhagen, 1519). (Digital facsimile edition at <nb.no/items/URN:NBN:no-nb_digibok_2014081128001> [accessed 27 February 2022]).

[Moufle d'Angerville], *Vie privée de Louis XV. Ou principaux évènements, particularités et anecdotes de son règne* (London, 1784).

Mügge Theodor, *Reise durch Skandinavien. Skizzen aus dem Norden*, 2 vols (Hannover, 1844).

Nannestad, Nicolai E., *Afhandling om dydige Hedningers Salighed* (Sorøe, 1768).

Nelson, Knute, *The Constitution of the Kingdom of Norway: adopted by the Convention at Eidsvold on the 17th day of May, 1814, and amended and ratified by the Storthing on the 4th day of November, 1814, with all subsequent amendments incorporated*, translated from the Norwegian by Knute Nelson (Chicago, 1895, republished 1899).

Nordencrantz, Anders Bachmansson, *Arcana oeconomiæ et commercii, eller Handelens och hushåldnings-wärkets hemligheter: Undersökte och på det möjeligaste sätt utforskade, pröfwade och ändteligen framstälte uti åtskilliga capitel och materier* (Stockholm, 1730).

—— *Oförgripelige tankar, om frihet i bruk af förnuft, pennor och tryck, samt huru långt friheten derutinnan i et fritt samhälle sig sträcka bör, tillika med påfölgden deraf* (Stockholm, 1756).

—— *Tankar, om friheten i tryck, samt desz nytta och skada; hwilke år 1730 blifwit öfwersatte ifrån den engelska periodiska skriften, kallad Craftsman; men ej kunnat til trycket befordras, förrän riksens högloflige ständer dertil banat wägen fri, med förordningen af den 2 dec. 1766. Härwid bifogas jämwäl et kort företal, om tryck-frihetens rätta wärde och egenskap* (Stockholm, 1767).

Novellae Constitutiones, in Holger Rørdam (ed.), 'Aktstykker til Universitetets historie', *Danske Magazin*, 5:I (1887–9 [1621]), 37–47.

Nyerup, Rasmus (ed.), *Luxdorphiana, eller Bidrag til den danske Literairhistorie* (Copenhagen, 1791).

Original-Anekdoter om Peter den Store. Samlede af Anseelige Personers mundtlige Fortællinger i Moskau og Petersborg, og opbevarede for Efterslægten, af Jacob von Stählin (Copenhagen, 1793).

Ot. prp. nr. 12, Om utfærdigelse av en lov om konfirmantforberedelse og konfirmation (Oslo, 1911).

Parallele der Preussischen Verfassung vom 3. Februar 1847 mit den Verfassungen von Churhessen, Norwegen und Belgie (Leipzig, 1847).

Pölitz, Karl Heinrich Ludwig, *Die europäischen Verfassungen seit dem Jahre 1789 bis auf die neueste Zeit: mit geschichtlichen Erläuterungen und Einleitungen.* 2nd edn (Leipzig, 1832–3).

Prahl, Niels, *Greve Johan Friderich Struensee, forrige Kongelige Danske Geheime-CabinetsMinister og Maitre des Requettes, Hans Levnets-Beskrivelse og Skiebne udi de sidste Aaringer i Dannemark* (Copenhagen, 1772).

Pyrau, abbé Duval, *Journal et anecdotes interessantes de Mr Comte de Falckenstein* (Frankfurt, 1777).

Rahbek, Knut Lyne, *Erindringer af mit Liv*, vols 2 and 3 (Copenhagen, 1825).

—— *Samlede Fortællinger*, 4 vols (Copenhagen, 1804–14).

Rauch, A., *Parlamentarisches Taschenbuch enthaltend die Verfassungen von Nordamerika, Norwegen, Neapel, Toscana, Sardinien, Rom, Oesterreich, Belgien, der Schweiz, England und den Entwurf einer deutschen Reichsverfassung*, vol. 1, 2nd edn. (Erlangen, 1848).

'Rescr. (til Biskopperne i Norge og Danmark, samt Notits til General-Kirke-Inspections-Collegium), ang. en Forklaring over *Luthers Catechismus*, som skal bruges i alle Kirker og Skoler, samt ved privat Undervisning', (22 August 1738), in *Kongelige Rescripter, Resolutioner og Collegial-Breve for Norge i Tidsrummet 1660–1815*, ed. Fr. Aug. Wessel Berg, vol. 1 (1660–1746) (Christiania, 1841).

Rørdam, Holger Fr., *Breve fra Langebek* (Copenhagen, 1895).

[Rothe, Casper], *Geheime Beretning om Danmarks og Norges Rigers Dronning Caroline Mathildes Frue Olde-Moder, Kong Georg den Førstes af Stor-Britannien Gemahlinde: denne ulykkelige Printsesses vanheldige Skiebne, hendes Fengsel paa Slottet Ahlen, samt hendes geheime Underhandlinger med Greven af Kønigsmark, som mistænkt blev myrdet* (Viborg, 1773).

Rottech, Carl von and Carl Welcker, *Staats-Lexicon oder Encyclopädie der Staatswissenschaften, in Verbindung mit vielen der angesehensten Publicisten Deutschlands.* Vol. 11 (Altona, 1841); 2nd edn, vol. 9 (Altona, 1847); *Supplemente zur ersten Auflage des Staats-Lexicon oder der Encyclopädie der Staatswissenschaften*, vol. 4 (Altona, 1848).

Sander, Levin C., *Svada: eller theoretisk og practisk Veiledning til Betoningskunsten* (Copenhagen, 1814).

Sander, Levin C., *Odeum: eller, Declamerekunstens Theorie, praktisk forklaret* (Copenhagen, 1819).

Saxo Grammaticus, *Danorum regum heroumque historia*, ed. Christiern Pedersen (Paris, 1514).

[Schribe, Johann Adolph], *Nyeste Anekdoter om Kongen av Preussens Privat-levnet, tilligemed anmerkninger over de Preussiske Armeers Krigs-forfatning* trans. (Copenhagen, 1778) (Facsimile edition at <www.kb.dk>).

Secher, V. A. (ed.), *Forordninger, Recesser og andre kongelige Breve, Danmarks Lovgivning vedkommende 1558–1660* (Copenhagen, 1887–1918).

Staats-Grundgesetz des Königreichs Norwegen gegeben am 17. Mai 1814: mit späteren Änderungen bis zum 25. Mai 1905: nebst der Reichsakte vom 6. August 1815 (Christiania, 1905).

Staf, Nils (ed.) *Borgarståndets riksdagsprotkoll från frihetstidens början*, 3: 1726–1727 (Stockholm, 1956).

Steele, Richard, *Tatler* no. 1 (12 April 1709).

Steffens, Heinrich, *Der norwegische Storthing im Jahre 1824: geschichtliche Darstellung und Aktenstycke* (Berlin, 1825).

Stevning, Indlægge og Dom i Sagen imellem Boghandlerne Agent Gyldendal og Schubothe [...] 19de Sept. 1796 (Copenhagen, [1796]).

Suhm, Peter Frederik, *Hemmelige efterretninger: om de danske konger efter souveraineteten*, meddelte ved Julius Clausen (Copenhagen, 1918) (Facsimile edition at <www.kb.dk>).

—— *Samlede Skrifter*, vols 15 and 16 (Copenhagen, 1798–99).

—— 'Sigrid, eller Kierlighed Tapperhed's Belønning. En Fortælling som Priis-skrift i Veltalenhed', in *Forsøg i de skiønne og nyttige Videnskaber*, vol. 10 (Copenhagen, 1772).

Sveriges ridderskaps och adels riksdags-protokoll från och med år 1719, 11: 1738–1739. 3 (Stockholm, 1889).

'The Commercial History of a Penny Magazine', *Penny Magazine*, 30 September 1833.

The Constitution of the Kingdom of Norway, translated pursuant to order of Government (Christiania, 1814).

Théatre royal de Dannemarc ou Recueil des meilleures pièces dramatiques françoises, représentées sur le Théâtre de la Cour, depuis 1766 à 1769, vols 1–5 (Facsimile edition at <www.kb.dk>) (Copenhagen, 1770–3).

Trenk contra Mirabeau, eller Politisk og Kritisk Undersøgelse af Skriftet: Hemmelige Efterretninger om det Berlinske Hof, eller en reisende Franskmands Brevvexling (Copenhagen, 1790) (Facsimile edition at <www.kb.dk>).

Treschow, Niels, *Almindelig Logik* (Copenhagen, 1813).

—— *Den philosophiske Sædelæres første Grunde* (Christiania, 1824).

—— *Philosophiske Forsøg* (Copenhagen, 1805).

Valkendorf, Erik, *Breuis et summaria descriptio Nidrosiensis diocesis et special-iter cuiusdam ipsius partis, que Findmarkia dicitur, extrema aquilonaris christianitatis plaga*, ed. K. H. Karlsson and Gustav Storm, *Det Norske Geografiske Selskabs Aarbog* (Kristiania, 1901), pp. 1–24.

—— 'Om de af Erkebiskop Erik Walkendorf (henved 1516) samlede eller med-deelte Efterretninger om Grönland', *Grønlands historiske mindesmærker*, vol. 3, ed. Det Kgl. Nordiske Oldskrift-Selskab (Copenhagen, 1845), pp. 482–504.

Vinje, Aasmund Olavsson, 'Bladsjaa', *Dølen. Eit Vikublad* no. 8, 12 December 1858, p. 30.

Voltaire, *Œuvres de Voltaire*, ed. A. J. Q. Beuchot, vol. 13 (Paris, 1833).

Welche Verfassung ist die beste? Eine Frage, beantwortet durch eine übersicht-liche Zusammenstellung der Verfassungen fünf anderer Staaten (Belgien, Norwegen, England, Frankreich, New-York) mit der preussischen, nach den correspondirenden Paragraphen geordnet (Wesel, 1849).

Wienbarg, Ludolf, *Geist der Norwegischen Verfassung, Quadriga. Vermischte Schriften*, vol. 1 (Altona, 1840), pp. 127–246.

Wolff, Christian, *Vernünftige Gedancken von der Menschen Thun und Lassen* (Halle, 1720).

Wolff, Jens, *[A Northern Tour]: Sketches on a Tour to Copenhagen, through Norway and Sweden: interspersed with historical and other Anecdotes of public and private characters: to which is added a political Appendix rela-tive to the present political State of Norway* (London, 1814; 2nd edn, London, 1816).

Ziegler, Jacobus, 'Schondia' in *Quae intus continentur Syria, Palestina, Arabia, Aegyptus, Schondia, Holmiae* (Strasbourg, 1532).

Zulma, Sylphen, Matilda, Donna Eleonora og Don Juan eller Spansk Elskov, Ismael og Zora og Prøven, Sex Fortællinger, tilligemed en lille Afhandling om Forskiønnelses-Driften hos det smukke Kiøn. Ogsaa en Nytaarsgave for Damer (Copenhagen, 1796).

Newspapers and periodicals

Allgemeine Literatur-Zeitung (Jena, 1791).

Allmänna Journalen (Stockholm, 1814).

Bibliothek for det smukke Kiøn, [eds vol. 4: K. L. Rahbek and J. Kjerulf] (Copen-hagen, 1784–6) (vol. 1, facsimile edition at <www.kb.dk>).

Borger-Vennen (Copenhagen, 1788).

Børnevennen. Missionsblad for Børn, [ed. H. G. Heggtveit] (Christiania, Janu-ary 1868).

Christiansandske Ugeblade (Christiansand, 1785) (Facsimile edition at <www.nb.no>).

Den danske Oversættere, eller Samling af valgte moralske Afhandlinger, oversat af fremmede Sprog, [ed. C. F. Hellfriedt] (Copenhagen, 1770).

Departements-Tidende (Christiania, 1833) (Facsimile edition at <www.nb.no>).

Det nye Magazin, indeholdende Fortællinger af adskillige berømte Forfattere. Oversatte ved H. J. Birch (Copenhagen, 1774–7).

Det nyeste Magazin af Fortællinger eller Samling af moralske, rørende og moer-somme Romaner og Historier. Paa Dansk udg. ved H.J. Birch, [ed. from 1779: H. C. Amberg] (Copenhagen, 1778–9).

Dramatisk Journal, [ed. P. Rosenstand-Goiske] (Copenhagen, 1772).

EAB – *Efterretninger Fra Addresse-Contoiret i Bergen i Norge* (Bergen, 1767, 1772) (Facsimile edition at <www.nb.no>).

En fri swänsk (Stockholm, 1761).

For Ungdommen. Et Maanedsskrift til Befordring af sand Dannelse, [ed. Chr. Johnsen] (Stavanger, 1846, 1850).

For Ungdommen. Et Maanedsskrift for opbyggelig og underholdende Læsning, med særdeles hensyn paa Missionssagen [ed. Chr. Johnsen] (Stavanger, 1849).

Fruentimmer- og Mandfolke-Tidenden (Copenhagen, 1769).

[*Gazette de Leyde*]: *Nouvelles extraordinaires de divers endroits* (Leiden, 1766–7).

Göteborgs-Posten (Gothenburg, 1814).

KA – *Kiøbenhavns Adresse-Contoirs Efterretninger* (Copenhagen, 1758–62, 1768, 1771, 1774, 1781–2, 1789, 1795). (Facsimile edition at <www2.statsbiblioteket.dk/mediestream>).

Kiøbenhavns Aften-Post, [ed. E. Balling] (Copenhagen, 1773).

Kiøbenhavnske Danske Post-Tidender (1757).

Kiøbenhavnske Tidender (Copenhagen, 1768) (Facsimile edition at <www2.statsbiblioteket.dk/mediestream>).

Kritik og Antikritik (Copenhagen, 1792).

Kritisk Journal, [ed. W. Abrahamson, C. F. Fasting, J. C. Tode] (Copenhagen, 1773).

Kritisk Tilskuer, [ed. W. Abrahamson, C. F. Fasting, J. C. Tode] (Copenhagen, 1776).

LE – *Lærde Efterretninger* (Copenhagen); short for
   Kiøbenhavnske Nye Tidender om lærde Sager (1764).
   Kiøbenhavnske Efterretninger om lærde Sager (1776).
   Kiøbenhavnske Nye Efterretninger om lærde Sager (1780).
   Nyeste Kiøbenhavnske Efterretninger om lærde Sager (1784, 1790).
   Kiøbenhavnske lærde Efterretninger (1795, 1796).

Min Kritiske Læsning: en liden uskyldig Journal kan sagte gaa med, [ed. L. Sahl] (S. l., [178?]).

Missionsblad for Børn (Stavanger, 1847, 1848).

Missionsblatt für Kinder, [ed. C. B. Barth, vol. 1] (Calw, Stuttgart, 1842).

Morgenbladet (Christiania, 1834, 1835, 1839–41) (Facsimile edition at <www.nb.no>).

NIS – *Norske Intelligenz-Sedler* (Christiania, 1779, 1784, 1789–92, 1795) (Facsimile edition at <www.nb.no>).

Nova literaria Maris Balthici et Septentrionis, (Lübeck, 1698).

NKJ – *Nye Kritisk Journal,* [ed. J. Baden] (Copenhagen, 1774–6).

Provinzialblade, [ed. C. F. Fasting] (Bergen, 1778–81) (Facsimile edition at <www.nb.no>).

Ribe Stifts Ugeblad (Fredericia, 1793) (Facsimile edition at <www2.statsbiblioteket.dk/mediestream>).

Skilling-Magazin (Copenhagen, 1881).

Skilling-Magazin (Christiania, 1835, 1837, 1839).

Søndagsblad for Børn [ed. Erik Nicolai Saxild] (Christiania, 1844).

Storthings-Efterretninger 1814–1833 (Christiania, 1874). (Facsimile edition at <www.nb.no>).

SECONDARY SOURCES

Aasen, Ivar, *Brev og dagbøker*, vol. 3, *Dagbøker 1830–1896*, ed. Reidar Djupedal (Oslo, 1960).

Almond, Philip C., *Demonic Possession and Exorcism in Early Modern England: Contemporary Texts and Their Cultural Contexts* (New York, 2004).

Altick, Richard D., *English Common Reader: A Social History of the Mass Reading Public, 1800–1900*, 2nd edn (Columbus, 1998).

Andersen, Anette Storli, *Deus ex machina? Henrik Ibsen og teatret i norsk offentlighet, 1780–1864* (Oslo, 2010).

Andersen, Dan H., *Store Nordiske Krig*, vols 1–2 (Copenhagen, 2021).

Anderson, Benedict, *Imagined Communities*, 2nd edn (London, 2006 [1983]).

Anderson, Patricia J., *The Printed Image and the Transformation of Popular Culture, 1790–1860* (Oxford, 1991).

Appel, Charlotte, *Læsning og bogmarked i 1600-tallets Danmark*, 2 vols (Copenhagen, 2001).

Appel, Charlotte and Nina Christensen, 'Follow the Child, Follow the Books – Cross-Disciplinary Approaches to a Child-Centred History of Danish Children's Literature 1790–1850', *International Research in Children's Literature* 10:2 (2017), 194–212.

Appel, Charlotte and Ning de Coninck-Smith (eds), *Dansk skolehistorie*, vols 1 and 2 (Aarhus, 2013).

Appel, Charlotte and Morten Fink-Jensen, 'Introduction. Books, Literacy, and Religious Reading in the Lutheran North', in Charlotte Appel and Morten Fink-Jensen (eds), *Religious Reading in the Lutheran North* (Newcastle upon Tyne, 2011), pp. 1–14.

—— *Når det regner på præsten. En kulturhistorie om sognepræster og sognefolk. 1550–1750* (Højbjerg, 2009).

——, 'Præsten og de besatte. Ole Bjørn, præst i Thisted 1693–1698', in Charlotte Appel and Morten Fink-Jensen, *Når det regner på præsten. En kulturhistorie om sognepræster og sognefolk 1550–1750* (Højbjerg, 2009), pp. 195–232.

—— (eds), *Religious Reading in the Lutheran North* (Newcastle upon Tyne, 2011).

Appel, Charlotte and Karen Skovgaard-Petersen, 'The History of the Book in the Nordic Countries', in M. F. Suarez (ed.), *The Oxford Companion to the Book* (Oxford, 2010), pp. 240–7.

Arnesen, Arne, 'Eilert Sundt', in *Fire foregangsmænd: Peder Hansen, Henrik Wergeland, Eilert Sundt, H. Tambs Lyche*, Norsk bibliotekforenings småskrifter 3 (Kristiania, 1917), pp. 43–59.

Astbury, Katherine, *The Moral Tale in France and Germany 1750–1789*. SVEC, no. 7 (Oxford, 2002).

Aukrust, Knut, *Menighetsblad og andre religiøse og kirkelige tidsskrifter i Norge: en foreløpig oversikt* (Oslo, 1991).

Bache-Wiig, Harald, '*Avis for Børn* (1779–1782): Lesestykker om "Ungdommens Tilbøielighed til Dyden eller Lasten" – et monotont repertoar?', in

Eivind Tjønneland (ed.), *Kritikk før 1814. 1700-tallets politiske og litterære offentlighet* (Oslo, 2014), pp. 451–64.

Bæksted, Anders, *Besættelsen i Tisted 1696–98*, vols 1 and 2 (Copenhagen, 1959–60).

—— 'Indledning og noter', in Johan Brunsmand, *Køge Huskors*, ed. Anders Bæksted (Copenhagen, 1953).

Bannet, Eve Tavor, '"Secret History": Or, Talebearing Inside and Outside the Secretorie', *Huntington Library Quarterly*, 68:1–2 (2005), 375–96.

Barker, Hannah and Simon Burrows, *Press, Politics and the Public Sphere in Europe and North America, 1760–1820* (Cambridge, 2002).

Barnes, Sherman B., 'The Editing of Early Learned Journals', *Osiris*, 1 (January 1936), 155–72.

Beecroft, Alexander, 'World Literature Without a Hyphen', *New Left Review*, 54 (2008), 87–100.

Bellingradt, Daniel and Jerome Salman (eds), *Books in Motion in Early Modern Europe* (Cham, 2017).

—— 'Chapter 1: Books and Book History in Motion: Materiality, Sociality and Spatiality', in D. Bellingradt and J. Salman (eds), *Books in Motion in Early Modern Europe* (Cham, 2017), pp. 1–11.

Benjamin, Walter, 'Was die Deutschen lasen während sie ihre Klassiker schrieben', *Rundfunkarbeiten. Kritische Gesamtausgabe*, 9:1 (Frankfurt, 2017), pp. 7–19.

Bennett, Scott, 'The Editorial Character and Readership of "The Penny Magazine": An Analysis', *Victorian Periodicals Review*, 17:4 (1984), 127–41.

Berg, Ivar, 'Reformasjonen og norsk språkhistorie', *Teologisk tidsskrift*, 7 (2018), 167–76.

—— 'The Making of the Scandinavian Languages', in G. Rutten and K. Horner (eds), *Metalinguistic Perspectives on Germanic Languages. European Case Studies from Past to Present* (Oxford, 2016), pp. 35–55.

Berge, Kjell Lars, 'Developing a New Political Text Culture in Denmark-Norway 1770–1799', in Ellen Krefting, Aina Nøding and Mona Ringvej (eds), *Eighteenth-Century Periodicals as Agents of Change* (Leiden and Boston, 2015), pp. 172–84.

—— 'Noen tekstvitenskapelige betraktninger omkring studiet av tekster, kulturer og ideologier i dansk-norsk 1700-tall', *Arr: Idéhistorisk tidsskrift*, 4 (1999), pp. 72–80.

Billington, Louis, 'The Religious Periodical and Newspaper Press, 1770–1870', in Michael Harris and Alan Lee (eds), *The Press in English Society from the Seventeenth to Nineteenth Centuries* (Rutherford, Madison and Teaneck; London and Toronto, 1986), pp. 113–32.

Birkeland, Tone, Gunvor Risa and Karin Beate Vold, *Norsk barnelitteraturhistorie*, 3rd and rev. edn (Oslo, 2018).

Bjerke, Ernst, '"Prentet udi Christiania". Nye perspektiver på det første boktrykkeriet i Norge', in Tore Kr. Andersen, Øivind Berg and Torbjørn Eng (eds), *Bokhistorie. Bibliotekhistorie: En jubileumsantologi fra Norsk bok- og bibliotekhistorisk selskap* (Oslo, 2019), pp. 7–20.

Bjerring-Hansen, Jens, *Ludvig Holberg på bogmarkedet* (Copenhagen, 2015).

Bjerring-Hansen, Jens and Torben Jelsbak, *Boghistorie* (Aarhus, 2010).

Bjørkøy, Aasta M. B., Ruth Hemstad, Aina Nøding and Anne Birgitte Rønning (eds), *Litterære verdensborgere: Transnasjonale perspektiver på norsk bokhistorie 1519–1850* (Oslo, 2019).

Björne, Lars, 'Freedom of Expression in the Nordic Countries 1815–1914: Theory and Practice', *Scandinavica*, 58:2 (2019), 12–28.

Blair, Ann, 'Note Taking as an Art of Transmission', *Critical Inquiry*, 31 (2004), 85–107.

Bobé, Louis, 'Claude Philibert 1709–84. En Foregangsmand paa Boghaandværkets og Bogudbredelsens Omraade', *Nordisk Tidsskrift för Bok- och Bibliotekväsen*, vol. VII (1920), 14–18.

Boberg, Stig, *Gustav III och tryckfriheten, 1774–1787* (Stockholm, 1951).

Borregaard, Svend, *Danmarks og Norges kirkeritual af 1685* (Copenhagen, 1953).

Boutcher, Warren, 'Intertraffic: Transnational Literatures and Languages in Late Renaissance England and Europe', in Matthew McLean and Sara Barker (eds), *International Exchange in the Early Modern Book World* (Leiden, Boston, 2016), pp. 343–73.

Brake, Laurel, *Print in Transition 1850–1910: Studies in Book and Media History*, (Basingstoke, 2001).

Brandes, Georg, *Levned*, vols 1–3 (Copenhagen, 1905, 1907, 1908).

—— 'Nye skandinaviske Tidsskrifter', *Det nittende Aarhundrede* (April 1877), 72–82.

Brandtzæg, Siv Gøril, '"Jeg ridsede mit Navn paa Héloïses kolde Bryst": Camilla Colletts *Amtmandens Døttre* i lys av den europeiske sentimentale roman', *Edda*, 102:2 (3 June 2015), 94–109.

Brdr. Brandes Brevveksling med nordiske Forfattere, ed. Morten Borup et al., vol. IV (Copenhagen, 1940).

Briggs, Asa and Peter Burke, *A Social History of the Media: From Gutenberg to the Internet* (Cambridge, 2009).

Broers, Michael and Ambrogio A. Caiani (eds), *A History of the European Restorations*, 2 vols (London, 2020).

Brophy, James M., 'The Second Wave: Franco-German Translation and the Transfer of Political Knowledge 1815–1850', *Archiv für Geschichte des Buchwesens*, vol. 71 (Berlin, 2016), pp. 83–115.

Brusewitz, Axel, *Representationsfrågan vid 1809–10 års riksdag: En inledning till representationsreformens historia* (Uppsala, 1913).

Bruter, Annie, 'Le cours magistral comme objet d'histoire', *Histoire de l'éducation*, 120:4 (2008) [Special issue: Le cours magistral XVe–XXe siècles], 5–32.

Bugge, Søren Bruun, 'Autobiografiske Optegnelser', *Skilling-Magazin*, no. 6 (1881).

Bull, Francis, *Fra Holberg til Nordal Brun. Studier i norsk aandshistorie* (Kristiania, 1916).

Bullard, Rebecca, *The Politics of Disclosure, 1674–1725. Secret History Narratives* (London, 2009).

Burius, Anders, *Ömhet om friheten. Studier i frihetstidens censurpolitik* (Uppsala, 1984).

Burke, Peter, *Languages and Communities in Early Modern Europe* (Cambridge, 2004).

—— 'Publicizing the Private. The Rise of "Secret History"', in Christian J. Emden and David Midgley (eds), *Changing Perceptions of the Public Sphere* (New York, 2012), pp. 57–72.

Burrows, Simon, *The French Book Trade in Enlightenment Europe*, vol. 2: *Enlightenment Bestsellers* (New York/London, 2018).

Byberg, Lis, *Brukte bøker til bymann og bonde: bokauksjonen i den norske litterære offentligheten* (Oslo, 2007).

—— '"Jeg gik i ingen Skole, jeg havde min Frihed hele Dagen og Nøglen til hans Bogskab". Kvinners lesning på 1700-tallet', *Historisk tidsskrift*, 90:2 (2011), 159–88.

—— 'På sporet av 1700-tallets lesere', in Tore Rem (ed.) *Bokhistorie* (Oslo, 2003), pp. 82–101.

Byrnes, Alice, 'The Child Saviour: A Literary Motif', in *The Child: An Archetypal Symbol in Literature for Children and Adults* (New York, 1995), pp. 7–32.

Cambers, Andrew, 'Demonic Possession, Literacy and "Superstition" in Early Modern England', *Past and Present*, 202 (2009), 3–35.

Certeau, Michel de, *The Practice of Everyday Life*, trans. Steven F. Rendall (Berkeley, 1984).

Chartier, Roger, 'Reading Matter and "Popular" Reading: From the Renaissance to the Seventeenth Century', in Guiglielmo Cavallo and Roger Chartier (eds), *A History of Reading in the West* (Cambridge, 1999), pp. 269–83.

—— *The Cultural Origins of the French Revolution* (Durham, NC, and London, 1991).

—— *The Order of Books: Readers, Authors and Libraries in Europe between the 14th and 18th Centuries* (Stanford, 1994 [1992]).

Christensen, Christian Villads, and Frederik Hallager, 'Besættelsen På Rosborg', *Samlinger Til Jydsk Historie Og Topografi*, 3:2 (1900), 225–60.

Christensen, Nina, 'Lust for Reading and Thirst for Knowledge: Fictive Letters in a Danish Children's Magazine of 1770', *The Lion and the Unicorn*, 2 (2009), 189–201.

—— *Videbegær – Oplysning, børnelitteratur, dannelse* (Aarhus, 2012).

Clark, Stuart, *Thinking with Demons: The Idea of Witchcraft in Early Modern Europe* (Oxford, 1997).

Clark, William, *Academic Charisma and the Origins of the Research University* (Chicago and London, 2006).

—— 'The Professorial Voice', *Science in Context*, 16 (2003), 43–57.

Cohen, Matt, '"Between Friends and Enemies": Moving Books and Locating Native Critique in Early Colonial America', in Scott Richard Lyons (ed.), *The World, the Text, and the Indian: Global Dimensions of Native American Literature* (New York, 2017), pp. 103–28.

Collett, John Peter, and Ernst Bjerke (eds), *Vekst gjennom kunnskap: Det kongelige selskap for Norges vel 1809–1814* (Oslo, 2009).

Collett, Peter Jonas, *Studenteraar. Oplevelser og refleksjoner 1831–1838* (Oslo, 1934).

Cowan, Brian, 'The History of Secret Histories', *Huntington Library Quarterly*, 81:1 (Spring 2018), 121–51.

Cull, Nicholas J., 'A Region Speaks: Nordic Public Diplomacy in Historical Context', *Place Branding and Public Diplomacy*, 12:2–3 (2016), 152–9.

Dahl, Gina, *Books in Early Modern Norway* (Leiden, 2011).

—— *Libraries and Enlightenment: Eighteenth-Century Norway and the Outer World* (Aarhus, 2014).

Dahl, Helge, *Språkpolitikk og skolestell i Finnmark 1814–1905* (Oslo, 1957).

Danbolt, Alf, 'Den kristelige søndagsskolen – et middel i Lutherstiftelsens kamp for luthersk kristendom. Søndagsskolen og indremisjonen i 1870-årene', *Tidsskrift for Teologi og Kirke*, 79:1 (2008), 48–65.

Darnton, Robert, 'First Steps Towards a History of Reading', in J. L. Machor and Ph. Goldstein (eds), *Reception Study. From Literary Theory to Cultural Studies* (New York and London, 2001), pp. 160–79.

—— 'Mlle Bonnafon and "La vie privée de Louis XV"', *Dix-huitième Siècle*, 35 (2003), 369–91.

—— *Pirating and Publishing. The Book Trade in the Age of Enlightenment* (Oxford, 2021).

—— *The Devil in the Holy Water, or the Art of Slander from Louis XIV to Napoleon* (Philadelphia, 2010).

—— *The Forbidden Best-Sellers of Pre-Revolutionary France* (New York and London, 1996).

—— 'What is the History of Books', *Daedalus*, 111 (1982), 65–83.

—— 'What Is the History of Books?', in David Finkelstein and Alistair McCleery (eds), *The Book History Reader* (London, 2002 [1982/1990]), pp. 9–26.

—— '"What is the History of Books?" Revisited', *Modern Intellectual History*, 4 (2007), 495–508.

Dawson, Robert L., 'Marmontel Made in Britain', *Australian Journal of French Studies*, 38:1 (2001), 107–23.

Droixhe, D., '"Elle me coute dix milles écus". La contrefaçon des œuvres de Molière offerte par l'imprimeur Bassompierre à Marmontel', *Revue français d'histoire du livre*, No. 114–15 (2002), 125–65.

Drotner, Kirsten, *English Children and their Magazines, 1751–1945* (New Haven and London, 1988).

Dunker, Conradine, *Gamle dage. Erindringer og tidsbilleder* (Copenhagen, 1871).

Edvardsen, Erik Henning, 'Den tidligste ukepresse i Norge', in Erik Henning Edvardsen (ed.), *Gammelt nytt i våre tidligste ukeblader: aktstykker om folketro og sagn i Illustreret Nyhedsblad og Norsk Folkeblad* (Oslo, 1997), pp. 7–59.

Egeland, Marianne, '"De fleste Romaners Læsning er skadelig": Suhm, Snee-dorff og romanen', *Edda* 108:1 (3 March 2021), 8–21.

Eide, Elisabeth, *Bøker i Norge: boksamlinger, leseselskap og bibliotek på 1800-tallet* (Oslo, 2013).

—— 'Reading Society and Lending Libraries in Nineteenth-Century Norway', *Library and Information History*, 26:2 (June 2010), 121–38.

Eisenstein, Elisabeth, *Divine Art, Infernal Machine: The Reception of Printing in the West from First Impressions to the Sense of an Ending* (Philadelphia, 2011).

—— *The Printing Revolution in Early Modern Europe*, 2nd edn (Cambridge, 2005).

Ekman, Kari Haarder, *'Mitt hems gränser vidgades'. En studie i den kulturella skandinavismen under 1800-talet*. Centrum för Danmarksstudier 23 (Gothenburg, Stockholm, 2010).

Engelhardt, Juliane, *Borgerskab og fællesskab: de patriotiske selskaber i den danske helstat 1769–1814* (Copenhagen, 2010).

—— 'Patriotism, Nationalism and Modernity: The Patriotic Societies in the Danish Conglomerate State, 1769–1814', *Nations and Nationalism*, 13:2 (2007), 205–23.

Engelsing, Rolf, *Der Bürger als Leser: Lesergeschichte in Deutschland* (Stuttgart, 1974).

Eriksen, Anne, 'Fedrelandskjærlighet i oversettelse. Ove Mallings *Store og gode Handlinger af Danske, Norske og Holstenere*', in Aasta M. B. Bjørkøy, Ruth Hemstad, Aina Nøding and Anne Birgitte Rønning (eds), *Litterære verdensborgere* (Oslo, 2019), pp. 357–76.

—— *Livets læremester. Historiske kunnskapstradisjoner i Norge 1650–1840* (Oslo, 2020).

Eriksson, Jens, 'Lecture-notes and Common-places. Reading and Writing about Experience in Late Eighteenth-century Prussia', *Lýchnos: Årsbok för idé- och lärdomshistoria* (2009), 149–75.

Ertler, Klaus-Dieter, Elisabeth Hobisch and Ellen Krefting (eds), *La spectatrice danoise de La Beaumelle. Édition commentée* (Berlin, Bern, Brussels and New York, 2020).

Espagne, M. and M. Werner (eds), *Transferts: Les relations interculturelles dans l'espace franco-allemand (XVIIIe et XIXe siècle)* (Paris, 1988).

Etting, Vivian, 'The Rediscovery of Greenland During the Reign of Christian IV', *Journal of the North Atlantic*, 2 (2010), 151–60.

Evju, Håkon, *Ancient Constitutions and Modern Monarchy. Historical Writing and Enlightened Reform in Denmark–Norway 1730–1814* (Leiden, 2019).

Færch, Christina Holst, *Smædeskrifter, sladder og erotiske vers i 1700-tallet. Hans Nordrups forfatterskab* (Copenhagen, 2019).

Farge, Arlette, *Subversive Words. Public Opinion in Eighteenth Century France* (Philadelphia, 1995).

Febvre, Lucien and H.-J. Martin, *The Coming of the Book: The Impact of Printing 1450–1800* (London, 1997 [1958]).

Federhofer, Marie-Theres and Sabine Meyer (eds), *Mit dem Buch in der Hand. Beiträge zur deutsch-skandinavischen Buch- und Bibliotheksgeschichte/A Book in Hand. German-Scandinavian Book and Library History* (Berlin, 2022).

Feldbæk, Ole, 'Kærlighed til fædrelandet. 1700-tallets nationale selvforståelse', *Fortid og Nutid*, 31 (1984), 270–88.

Ferber, Sarah, *Demonic Possession and Exorcism in Early Modern France* (London, New York, 2004).

Fet, Jostein, *Lesande bønder: Litterær kultur i norske allmugesamfunn før 1840* (Oslo, 1995).

—— *Skrivande bønder. Skriftkultur på Nord-Vestlandet 1600–1850* (Oslo, 2003).

Fjågesund, Peter and Ruth A. Symes, *The Northern Utopia. British Perceptions of Norway in the Nineteenth century* (Amsterdam, New York, 2003).

Freedman, Jeffrey, *Books Without Borders in Enlightenment Europe: French Cosmopolitanism and German Literary Markets* (Philadelphia, 2012).

Freund, Max, *Die moralischen Erzählungen Marmontels* (Halle, 1904).

Friis-Jensen, Karsten, 'Humanism and Politics. The Paris Edition of Saxo Grammaticus's *Gesta Danorum* 1514', *Analecta Romana Instituti Danici*, 17–18 (Rome, 1988–89), 149–62.

Frøland, Alex, *Dansk boghandels historie 1482 til 1945* (Copenhagen, 1974).

Frost, Simon and Robert W. Rix, *Moveable Type, Mobile Nations: interactions in Transnational Book History* (Copenhagen, 2010).

Fulsås, Narve, 'Noreg som kulturell eksportnasjon', in Jan Eivind Myhre (ed.), *Myten om det fattige Norge. En misforståelse og dens historie* (Oslo, 2021), pp. 261–308.

Fulsås, Narve and Tore Rem, 'From Periphery to Center: The Origins and Worlding of Ibsen's Drama', in Marja Jalava, Stefan Nygård and Johan Strang (eds), *Decentering European Intellectual Space* (Leiden and Boston, 2018), pp. 43–64.

—— *Ibsen, Scandinavia and the Making of a World Drama* (Cambridge, 2018).

Gammelgaard, Karen, 'Constitutions as a Transnational Genre. Norway 1814 and the Habsburg Empire 1848-1849', in Karen Gammelgaard and Eirik Holmøyvik (eds), *Writing Democracy: The Norwegian Constitution 1814-2014* (New York and Oxford, 2014), pp. 92–197.

Gammelgaard, Karen and Eirik Holmøyvik (eds), *Writing Democracy: The Norwegian Constitution 1814–2014* (New York and Oxford, 2014).

Genette, Gérard, *Paratexts, Thresholds of Interpretation*, trans. Jane E. Lewin (Cambridge, 1997).

Gerven, Tim van, *Scandinavism. Overlapping and Competing Identities in the Nordic World 1770–1919* (Amsterdam, 2022).

Gibson, Marion, *Possession, Puritanism and Print: Darrell, Harsnett, Shakespeare and the Elizabethan Exorcism Controversy* (London, 2006).

Gjerløw, Lilli, 'The Breviarium and the Missale Nidrosiense (1519)', in H. Bekker-Nielsen, M. Borch and B. A. Sørensen (eds), *From Script to Book. A Symposium* (Odense, 1986), pp. 50–77.

Glenthøj, Rasmus, *Experiences of War and Nationality in Denmark and Norway 1807–1815*, (Basingstoke, 2014).

Gørlitz, Kim and Ole Hoffmann, *Djævlen i kroppen. Synden i hjertet* (Copenhagen, 1987).

Gregory, Brad S., *The Unintended Reformation: How a Religious Revolution Secularized Society* (Cambridge, 2012).

Grenby, M. O., *The Child Reader, 1700–1840* (Cambridge, 2011).

Grieder, Josephine, *Translations of French Sentimental Prose Fiction in Late Eighteenth-Century England* (Durham, NC, 1975).

Griffiths, Antony, *Prints and Printmaking: An Introduction to the History and Techniques* (Berkeley, 1996).

Haakonsen, Knut and Henrik Horstbøll (eds), *Northern Antiquities and National Identities. Perceptions of Denmark and the North in the Eighteenth Century* (Copenhagen, 2008).

Haarberg, Jon, 'Earways to Heaven: Singing the Catechism in Denmark–Norway, 1569–1756', in Charlotte Appel and Morten Fink-Jensen (eds), *Religious Reading in the Lutheran North: Studies in Early Modern Scandinavian Book Culture* (Newcastle, 2011), pp. 48–69.

Habermas, Jürgen, *The Structural Transformation of the Public Sphere: An Inquiry Into a Category of Bourgeois Society* (Cambridge, MA, 1989).

—— *The Structural Transformation of the Public Sphere* (Cambridge, 2014).

Hagemann, Sonja, *Barnelitteratur i Norge inntil 1850* (Oslo, 1965).

Hagen, Ingar, *Barnet i norsk kristenliv: søndagsskolen i Norge gjennom 100 år* (Oslo, 1947).

Hallager, Fr., *Magister Ole Bjørn og de besatte i Thisted* (Copenhagen, 1901).

Halvorsen, J. B., *Norsk Forfatter-Lexikon 1814–1880: paa Grundlag af J. E. Krafts og Chr. Langes 'Norsk Forfatter-Lexikon 1814–1856'*, vol. 3: I–L (Kristiania, 1892).

Hamlyn, Hilda H., 'Eighteenth-Century Circulating Libraries in England', *The Library*, 5th Series, 1 (1947), 197–222.

Hamre, Lars, *Erik Valkendorf. Trekk av hans liv og virke* (Bergen, 1943).

Hannabuss, C. Stuart, 'Nineteenth-century Religious Periodicals for Children', *British Journal of Religious Education*, 6:1 (1983), 20–40.

Hansen, Henning and Maria Simonsen (eds), *The Book in the Northern Countries. Mémoires du livre/Studies in Book History*, 13:1 (2022).

Hansen, Holger, *Kabinets-styrelsen i Danmark*, vol. 1 (Copenhagen, 1916).

Hansen, Peter, *Den danske Skueplads. Illustreret Theaterhistorie*, vol. 1 (Copenhagen, [1889]).

Hansen, Tor Ivar, 'Bøker og skandinavisk forbrødring. Et forsøk på en bokhistorisk tilnærming til skandinavismen', in Ruth Hemstad, Jes Fabricius Møller and Dag Thorkildsen (eds), *Skandinavismen. Vision og virkning* (Odense, 2018), pp. 163–86.

Harberg, Lars, *Hundre år for barnet: Norsk Søndagsskoleforbund 1889–1989* (Oslo, 1989).

Hauge, Yngvar, *Morgenbladets historie*, vol. 1, *1819–1854* (Oslo, 1963).

Heffermehl, A.V., *Folkeundervisningen i Norge indtil omkring Aar 1700* (Christiania, 1913).

Hemstad, Ruth (ed.), '"En skandinavisk Nationalitet" som litterært prosjekt: 1840-årenes transnasjonale offentlighet i Norden', in Anna Bohlin and Elin Stengrundet (eds), *Nation som kvalitet: Smak, offentligheter och folk i 1800-talets Norden* (Bergen, 2021), pp. 311–32.

—— 'I "Tidens Fylde". Panskandinaviske publisister og transnasjonale tidsskrifter', in Aasta M. B. Bjørkøy, Ruth Hemstad, Aina Nøding and Anne Birgitte Rønning (eds), *Litterære verdensborgere: Transnasjonale perspektiver på norsk bokhistorie 1519–1850* (Oslo, 2019), pp. 377–404.

—— *'Like a Herd of Cattle'. Parliamentary and Public Debates Regarding the Cession of Norway, 1813–1814* (Oslo, 2014).

—— *Propagandakrig. Kampen om Norge i Norden og Europa 1812–1814* (Oslo, 2014).

Hemstad, Ruth and Dag Michalsen (eds), *Frie ord i Norden? Offentlighet, ytringsfrihet og medborgerskap 1814–1914* (Oslo, 2019).

Henningsen, Gustav. 'Trolddom og hemmelige kunster', in Axel Steensberg (ed.), *Dagligliv i Danmark. I det syttende og attende århundrede* (Copenhagen, 1969), pp. 161–96.

Hermann, Pernille, 'Politiske og æstetiske aspekter i Rimkrøniken', *Historisk Tidsskrift* 107:2 (2007), 389–411.

Hoche, Johann Gottfried, *Des Amtmanns Tochter von Lüde. Eine Wertheriade* (Bremen, 1791).

Holberg-Ordbog. Ordbog over Ludvig Holbergs Sprog, ed. Aage Hansen, from 1957 with Sv. Eegholm-Pedersen. In collaboration with Christopher Maaløe, 5 vols (Copenhagen, Oslo, 1981–88), online edn <www.holbergordbog.dk>.

Holmøyvik, Eirik, 'The Changing Meaning of "Constitution" in Norwegian Constitutional History', in Karen Gammelgaard and Eirik Holmøyvik (eds), *Writing Democracy: The Norwegian Constitution 1814–2014* (New York, Oxford, 2014), pp. 43–59.

Hope, Nicholas, *German and Scandinavian Protestantism 1700–1918*, in Henry and Owen Chadwick (eds), *Oxford History of the Christian Church* (Oxford, 1995).

Horstbøll, Henrik, 'Bolle Luxdorphs samling af trykkefrihedskrifter 1770–1773', *Fund & Forskning*, 44 (2005), 371–414.

—— 'De "Små historier" og læserevolutionen i 1700-tallet', *Fund og Forskning i Det Kongelige Biblioteks Samlinger* 33 (1994), 77–99.

—— 'En bogtrykker og boghandler i København. Claude Philiberts forbindelse med Societé typographique de Neuchatel 1771–1783', *Fund og forskning*, 51 (2012), 311–35.

—— *Menigmands medie: Det folkelige bogtrykk i Danmark 1500–1840* (Copenhagen, 1999).

Horstbøll, Henrik, Ulrik Langen and Frederik Stjernfelt, *Grov konfækt. Tre vilde år med trykkefrihed, 1770–73* (Copenhagen, 2020).

Howsam, Leslie, 'The Study of Book History', in Leslie Howsam (ed.), *The Cambridge Companion to History of the Book* (Cambridge, 2015), pp. 1–13.

Huitfeldt-Kaas, H. J., *Christiania Theaterhistorie* (Oslo, 1876).

Ibsen, Henrik. *Henrik Ibsens Skrifter: Brev*, eds Narve Fulsås *et al.*, DOI: <https://www.ibsen.uio.no/BREV_1871-1879ht%7CB18740420GB.xhtml>.

Ihalainen, Pasi, Michael Bregnsbo, Karin Sennefelt and Patrick Winton (eds), *Scandinavia in the Age of Revolution. Nordic Political Cultures, 1740–1820* (Farnham, 2011).

Ilsøe, Harald, *Bogtrykkerne i København og deres virksomhed ca. 1660–1810* (Copenhagen, 1992).

—— 'Godt Nytår! Nytårshilsener fra 2-300 år siden', *Magasin Fra Det Kongelige Bibliotek*, 7:3 (1992), 3–22.

—— 'Peder Resens nordiske bibliotek', *Fund og Forskning*, 30 (1991), 27–50.

Israel, Jonathan, 'Northern Varieties: Contrasting the Dano-Norwegian and the Swedish-Finnish Enlightenments', in Ellen Krefting, Aina Nøding and Mona R. Ringvej (eds), *Eighteenth-Century Periodicals as Agents of Change* (Leiden, 2015), pp. 17–45.

Jackson, Mason, *The Pictorial Press: Its Origin and Progress* (London, 1885).

Jacobs, Edward, 'Eighteenth-Century British Circulating Libraries and Cultural Book History, *Book History*, 6 (2003), 1–22.

Jacobsen, J. C., *Besættelse og Trolddom i Nibe 1686* (Copenhagen, 1973).

Jakobsen, Jesper, *Uanstændige, utilladelige og unyttige skrifter: En undersøgelse af censuren i praksis 1746–1773* (Copenhagen, 2017).

Jenkins, Alice, *Space and the "March of Mind": Literature and the Physical Sciences in Britain 1815–1850* (Oxford, 2007).

Jensen, Janus Møller, *Denmark and the Crusades 1400–1650* (Leiden, 2007).

—— *Korstoget til Grønland. Danmark, korstogene og de store opdagelser i renæssancen 1400–1523* (Aarhus, 2022).

Jensz, Felicity and Hanna Acke, 'Introduction', in Felicity Jensz and Hanna Acke (eds), *Missions and Media: The Politics of Missionary Periodicals in the Long Nineteenth Century* (Stuttgart, 2013), pp. 9–15.

Johannessen, Finn Erhard, *Alltid underveis: Postverkets historie gjennom 350 år*, vol. 1, *1647–1920* (Oslo, 1997).

Johansen, Jens Christian V., *Da Djævelen var ude... Trolddom i det 17. århundredes Danmark* (Odense, 1991).

—— 'Denmark: The Sociology of Accusations', in Bengt Ankerloo and Gustav Henningsen (eds), *Early Modern European Witchcraft. Centres and Peripheries* (Oxford, 1990), pp. 339–65.

Johansen, Tor Are, *'Trangen til læsning stiger, selv oppe i Ultima Thule': aviser, ekspansjon og teknologisk endring ca. 1763–1880.* Pressehistoriske skrifter 7 (Oslo, 2006).

Johns, Adrian, *The Nature of the Book: Print and Knowledge in the Making* (Chicago, 1998).

Jørgensen, Harald, *Trykkefrihedsspørgsmaalet i Danmark 1799–1848: Et bidrag til en karakteristik af den danske enevælde i Frederik VI's og Christian VIII's tid* (Copenhagen, 1944).

Josephson, Peter, 'Böcker eller universitet? Om ett tema i tysk utbildningspolitisk debatt kring 1800', *Lychnos: Årsbok för idé- och lärdomshistoria* (2009), 177–208.

Kaasa, Janicke S., 'Å gi sin daler med glede: Barn som forbrukere i *Ungdommens Ven* (1770)', *Barnboken*, 42 (2019), 1–18.

—— 'Hvordan bli en tidsskriftleser? Medieoppdragelse i 1700-tallets barnemagasiner', *Arr, Idéhistorisk tidsskrift*, 31:4 (2019), 21–31.

—— ''Saavel fra fjerne Lande som fra vort eget Hjem.' Importert materiale i *Billed-Magazin for Børn*', in Aasta Marie Bjorvand Bjørkøy, Ruth Hemstad, Aina Nøding and Anne Birgitte Rønning (eds), *Litterære verdensborgere: Transnasjonale perspektiver på norsk bokhistorie 1519–1850* (Oslo, 2019), pp. 310–29.

Kallestrup, Louise Nyholm, *Agents of Witchcraft in Early Modern Italy and Denmark* (Houndmills, Basingstoke, Hampshire, 2015).

—— 'Knowing Satan from God: Demonic Possession, Witchcraft, and the Lutheran Orthodox Church in Early Modern Denmark', *Magic, Ritual, and Witchcraft*, 6:2 (2011), 163–82.

—— 'Women, Witches, and the Town Courts of Ribe: Ideas of the Gendered Witch in Early Modern Denmark', in Marianna G. Muravyeva and Raisa Maria Toivo (eds), *Gender in Late Medieval and Early Modern Europe* (New York, London, 2013), pp. 121–36.

Karlsen, Espen, 'Breviarium og Missale Nidrosiense – Om trykk og bokkultur i Nidaros før reformasjonen', *Det Norske Vitenskaps-Akademis Årbok* (Oslo, 2019), pp. 172–93.

Keymer, Thomas, Peter Sabor and John Mullan (eds), *The Pamela Controversy: Criticism and Adaptations of Samuel Richardson's Pamela, 1740–1750* (2 vols, London, 2001).

King, Andrew, Alexis Easley and John Morton (eds), *The Routledge Handbook to Nineteenth-Century British Periodicals and Newspapers* (London, 2016).

Kleinschmidt, J. R., *Les imprimeurs et libraires de la république de Genève 1700–1798* (Geneva, 1948).

Klemming, G. E., *Sveriges Äldre liturgiska literatur* (Stockholm, 1879).

Klingberg, Göte, *Svensk barn- och ungdomslitteratur 1591–1839* (Stockholm, 1964).

Knight, Mark, 'Periodicals and Religion', in Andrew King, Alexis Easley and John Morton (eds), *The Routledge Handbook to Nineteenth-Century British Periodicals and Newspapers* (London, 2016), pp. 355–65.

Konz, D. J., 'The Many and the One: Theology, Mission and Child in Historical Perspective', in Bill Prevette, Keith J. White, C. Rosalee Velloso Ewell and D. J. Konz (eds), *Theology, Mission and Child: Global Perspectives* (Oxford, 2014), pp. 23–46.

Koopmans, Joop W., 'Dutch Censorship in Relation to Foreign Contacts (1581–1795)', in Hanno Brand (ed.), *Trade, Diplomacy and Cultural Exchange: Continuity and change in the North Sea Area and the Baltic c. 1359–1750* (Hilversum, 2005).

Koselleck, Reinhard, *Futures Past: On the Semantics of Historical Time* (Cambridge, MA, 1985).

——*Kritik und Krise: Ein Beitrag zur Pathogenese der bürgerlichen Welt* (Alber, 1988).

Krefting, Ellen, 'De usminkede sannhetenes forsvar. Peter Frederik Suhms publikasjonsstrategier og offentlighetsidealer under det dansk-norske eneveldet', in Aasta M. B. Bjørkøy, Ruth Hemstad, Aina Nøding and Anne Birgitte Rønning (eds), *Litterære verdensborgere: Transnasjonale perspektiver på norsk bokhistorie 1519–1850* (Oslo, 2019), pp. 332–76.

—— 'News versus Opinion: The State, the Press, and the Northern Enlightenment, in Siv Gøril Brandtzæg, Paul Goring and Christine Watson (eds), *Travelling Chronicles: News and Newspapers from the Early Modern Period to the Eighteenth Century* (Leiden, 2018), pp. 299–318.

—— 'The Urge to Write: Spectator Journalists Negotiating Freedom of the Press in Denmark–Norway', in Ellen Krefting, Aina Nøding and Mona R. Ringvej (eds), *Eighteenth-Century Periodicals as Agents of Change* (Leiden and Boston, 2015), pp. 153–71.

Krefting, Ellen and Aina Nøding, 'The Spectatorial Press from the Kingdom of Denmark–Norway: General Survey', in Misia Sophia Doms (ed.), *Spectator-Type Periodicals in International Perspective. Enlightened Moral Journalism in Europe and North America* (Berlin, 2020), pp. 369–92.

Krefting, Ellen, Aina Nøding and Mona R. Ringvej (eds), *Eighteenth-Century Periodicals as Agents of Change. Perspectives on Northern Enlightenment* (Leiden and Boston, 2015).

—— *En pokkers skrivesyge. 1700-tallets dansk-norske tidsskrifter mellom sensur og ytringsfrihet* (Oslo, 2014).

—— 'Introduction', in Ellen Krefting, Aina Nøding and Mona Ringvej (eds), *Eighteenth-Century Periodicals as Agents of Change: Perspectives on Northern Enlightenment* (Leiden and Boston, 2015), pp. 1–13.

Kuhn, Reinhard Clifford, *Corruption in Paradise: The Child in Western Litera-ture* (London, 1982).

Lagerroth, Fredrik, *Frihetstidens författning: En studie i den svenska konstitu-tionalismens historia* (Stockholm, 1915).

Langen, Ulrik, 'Kragen ved nok hvad Soe den skal ride paa: Fruentimmer-Tidenden og trykkefrihedens første debat', *Temp: Tidsskrift for historie*, 9:17 (2018), 67–88.

—— 'Le roi et les philosophes: le séjour parisien de Christian VII de Danemark en 1768', *Revue d'Histoire, économie et Société*, 1 (2010), 5–21.

—— 'Raising a Crown Prince in the Age of Reason', in Veera Gancheva (ed.), *The 18th Century and Europe* (Sofia, 2013).

Langen, Ulrik and Frederik Stjernfelt, *The World's First Full Press Freedom. The Radical Experiment of Denmark–Norway 1770–73* (Berlin, 2022).

Larsen, Christian, Erik Nørr and Pernille Sonne, in Charlotte Appel and Ning de Coninck-Smith (eds), *Da skolen tog form. 1780–1850, Dansk skolehistorie*, vol. 2 (Aarhus, 2013).

Latham, Robert G., *Norway and the Norwegians*, vol. 1 (London, 1840).

Laursen, John Christian, 'David Hume and the Danish Debate about Freedom of the Press in the 1770s', *Journal of the History of Ideas*, 59 (1998), 167–72.

Lausten, Martin Schwartz, *Peder Palladius: Sjællands første lutherske biskop* (Copenhagen, 2006).

Lederer, David, *Madness, Religion and the State in Early Modern Europe: A Bavarian Beacon* (Cambridge, 2006).

Levack, Brian P., *The Devil Within: Possession and Exorcism in the Christian West* (New Haven, 2013).

Lindberg, Bo, *Den akademiska läxan. Om föreläsningens historia* (Stockholm, 2017).

—— 'The Academic Lecture. A Genre in Between', *LIR. Journal*, 1 (2011), 38–48.

Littau, Karin, *Theories of Reading: Books, Bodies and Bibliomania* (Cambridge, 2006).

Löhnig, Martin, 'Die norwegische Verfassung von 1814 in der deutschen Ver-fassungspublizistik des 19. Jahrhunderts', *Journal on European History of Law*, 10:1 (2019), 40–4.

Lundblad, Kristina and Henrik Horstbøll (eds), 'Bokhistoria', *Lychnos. Årsbok för idé och lärdomshistoria/Annual of the Swedish History of Science Society* (Uppsala, 2010).

Lyons, Martyn, *A History of Reading and Writing In the Western World* (Bas-ingstoke, New York, NY, 2010).

Magnusson, Lars, 'Anders Nordencrantz', in B. Wennberg and K. Örtenhed (eds), *Press Freedom 250 Year: Freedom of the Press and Public Access to Official Documents in Sweden and Finland – a Living Heritage from 1766s* (Stockholm, 2018), pp. 77–87.

Mai, Anne-Marie, 'Historien som scene hos Ludvig Holberg og Charlotta Dor-othea Biehl', *Sjuttonhundratal* 8 (2011), 197–208.

Maidment, Brian, 'Dinners or Desserts?: Miscellaneity, Illustration, and the Periodical Press 1820–1840'. *Victorian Periodicals Review*, 43:4 (14 January 2011), 353–87.

Martin, Angus, Vivienne G. Mylne and Richard Frautschi. *Bibliographie du genre romanesque français 1751–1800* (London, Paris, 1977).

Martin, Randy, 'Artistic Citizenship: Introduction', in Mary Schmidt Campbell and Randy Martin (eds), *Artistic Citizenship: A Public Voice for the Arts* (New York, 2006), pp. 1–22.

May, Lori A., *The Write Crowd. Literary Citizenship and the Writing Life* (New York, NY, London, 2015).

Mayo, Robert D., *The English Novel in the Magazines 1740–1815* (Evanston, London, 1962).

McDowell, Paula, 'Media and Mediation in the Eighteenth Century', *Oxford Handbooks* (2018). DOI: <10.1093/oxfordhb/9780199935338.013.46>.

McGann, Jerome, *The Textual Condition* (Princeton, 1991).

Mchangama, Jacob and Frederik Stjernfelt, *MEN: Ytringsfrihedens historie i Danmark* (Copenhagen, 2016).

McKenzie, D.F., *Bibliography and the Sociology of Texts* (Cambridge, 1999 [1984]).

McKillop, Alan. D., 'English Circulating Libraries, 1725–1750', *The Library*, 4th Series, 14 (1934), 477–85.

McLeish, J., *The Lecture Method* (Cambridge, 1968)

Melton, James van Horn, *The Rise of the Public in Enlightenment Europe* (Cambridge, 2001).

Metcalf, Michael F., 'Parliamentary Sovereignty and Royal Reaction, 1719–1809', in Herman Schück (ed.), *The Riksdag: A History of the Swedish Parliament* (New York, 1987), pp. 109–64.

Michalsen, Dag, 'The Many Textual Identities of Constitutions', in Karen Gammelgaard and Eirik Holmøyvik (eds), *Writing Democracy: The Norwegian Constitution 1814–2014* (New York, Oxford, 2014), pp. 60–74.

Midelfort, H. C. Erik, *A History of Madness in Sixteenth-Century Germany* (Stanford, 1999).

—— *Witchcraft, Madness, Society, and Religion in Early Modern Germany* (Farnham, Ashgate, 2013).

Milstein, B. M., *Eight Eighteenth-Century Reading Societies: A Sociological Contribution to the History of German Literature* (Bern and Frankfurt, 1972).

Mitchell, P. M., 'Biblioteket i Drejers Klub', *Fund og Forskning*, 7:1 (1960), 85–99.

Moe, Oscar, *Katechismus og Katechismusundervisningen fra Reformationen, især i Danmark og Norge* (Kristiania, 1889).

Molland, Einar, *Norges kirkehistorie i det 19. århundre*, vol. 1 (Oslo, 1979).

Monrad, Marcus Jacob, *Philosophisk Propædeutik. Grundrids til Brug ved Forelæsninger* (Christiania, 1849).

Moretti, Franco, *Atlas of the European Novel 1800–1900* (London, 1998).

Morrissey, Lee, *The Constitution of Literature. Literacy, Democracy, and Early English Literary Criticism* (Stanford, 2008).

Mortensen, August, 'Boktrykkerkunstens Indførelse i Norge: Kritiske bemerkninger væsentlig paa grundlag av bibliotekar J.C. Tellefsens efterladte manuskripter', in *Mindeskrift i anledning Fabritius' boktrykkeris 75-aars jubilæum 1844 – 1. januar – 1919*, pp. 9–26. (Kristiania, 1919).

—— 'Boktrykkerkunstens repræsentanter i Norge XLIII'. *Nordisk trykkeritidende: organ for de grafiske fag og papirindustrien*, 16:5 (May 1907), 47–8.

Müller, Anja, *Framing Childhood in Eighteenth-Century English Periodicals and Prints, 1689–1789* (London and New York, 2009).

Munch, Andreas, *Barndoms- og Ungdoms-Minder* (Christiania, 1874).

Munck, Thomas, *Conflict and Enlightenment. Print and Political Culture in Europe 1635–1795* (Cambridge, 2019).

—— 'Eighteenth-Century Review Journals and the Internationalization of the European Book Market', *The International History Review*, 32:3 (2010), 415–35.

—— 'Public Debate, Politics and Print. The Late Enlightenment in Copenhagen During the Years of the French Revolution 1786–1800', *Historisk Tidsskrift*, 114:2 (2014), pp. 323–51.

—— 'The Danish Reformers', in H. M. Scott (ed.), *Enlightened Absolutism. Reform and Reformers in Later Eighteenth Century Europe* (London, 1990), pp. 245–63.

Mynster, Jacob Peter, *Om de danske Udgaver af Luthers lille Katechismus*. 2nd edn (Copenhagen, 1837 [1835]).

Neiiendam, Michael, *Erik Pontoppidan*, 2 vols (Copenhagen, 1930–3).

Nesse, Agnete (ed.), *Norsk språkhistorie*, vol. 4, *Tidslinjer* (Oslo, 2018).

Nielsen, Lauritz, *Dansk bibliografi* (4 vols, Copenhagen, 1996, 1st edn, 1919–33).

Nikolajeva, Maria, *Power, Voice and Subjectivity in Literature for Young Readers* (New York and London, 2010).

Nilsen, Ragnar Anker, *Hva fikk nordmennene å lese i 1814? En bibliografi* (Oslo, 1997).

[Nilssøn, Jens], *Biskop Jens Nilssøns Visitatsbøger og Reiseoptegnelser 1574–1597*, ed. Yngvar Nielsen (Kristiania, 1885).

Nilzén, Göran, 'Anders Nordencrantz som konsul i Portugal. En studie över bitterhetens ideologiska följder', *Personhistorisk tidskrift*, 83 (1987), 38–49.

Nissen, Martinus, 'Statistisk Udsigt over den norske Litteratur fra 1814 til 1847'. *Norsk Tidsskrift for Videnskab og Litteratur*, 3 (1849), 177–224.

Nøding, Aina, 'Book History in Norway. From Peasant Readers to Reading Ibsen', in Sandra van Voorst *et al.* (eds), *Jaarboek voor Nederlandse boekgeschiedenies* (Nijmegen and Leiden, 2013), pp. 141–52.

—— *Claus Fasting. Dikter, journalist og opplysningspioner* (Oslo, 2018).

—— 'Hva er et 1700-tallstidskrift?', in Eivind Tjønneland (ed.), *Opplysningens tidsskrifter* (Bergen, 2008), pp. 3–14.

—— 'Periodical Fiction in Denmark and Norway Before 1900', *Oxford Research Encyclopaedia of Literature* (New York, 2017), DOI: <https://doi.org/10.1093/acrefore/9780190201098.013.293>.

—— 'Syndfloden kommer: redaktøren som internasjonal formidler' in Ellen Krefting, Aina Nøding and Mona R. Ringvej, *En pokkers skrivesyge* (Oslo, 2014), pp. 205–23.

—— 'The Editor as Scout: The Rapid Mediation of International Texts in Provincial Journals', in Ellen Krefting, Aina Nøding and Mona R. Ringvej (eds), *Eighteenth-Century Periodicals as Agents of Change* (Leiden, 2015), pp. 62–76.

Nordin, Jonas, 'En revolution i tryck: Tryckfrihet och tryckproduktion i Sverige 1766–1772 och däromkring', *Vetenskapssocieteten i Lund årsbok* (2020), pp. 87–112.

—— *Ett fattigt men fritt folk: Nationell och politisk självbild i Sverige från sen stormaktstid till slutet av frihetstiden* (Eslöv, 2000).

—— 'From Seemly Subjects to Enlightened Citizens', in B. Wennberg and K. Örtenhed (eds), *Press Freedom 250 Years* (Stockholm, 2018), pp. 27–59.

Nordin, Jonas and John Christian Laursen, 'Northern Declarations of Freedom of the Press: The Relative Importance of Philosophical Ideas and of Local Politics', *Journal of the History of Ideas*, 81 (2020), 217–37.

Nowakowska, Natalia, 'From Strassburg to Trent: Bishops, Printing and Liturgical Reform in the Fifteenth Century', *Past and Present*, 213 (2011), 3–31.

Nygren, Rolf, 'The Freedom of the Press Act of 1766 in its Historical and Legal Context', in B. Wennberg and K. Örtenhed (eds), *Press Freedom 250 Years* (Stockholm, 2018), pp. 167–205.

Nyman, Elmar, *Indragningsmakt och tryckfrihet 1785–1810* (Stockholm, 1963).

Ødemark, John, 'Djevelbesettelsen i Køge og ånden fra Thisted: bokhistorie, kulturelle skript og virkelighetsforståelse', in Bente Lavold and John Ødemark (eds), *Reformasjonstidens Religiøse Bokkultur. Tekst, visualitet og materialitet* (Oslo, 2017), pp. 71–109.

—— 'Inscribing Possession: Køge Huskors and Other Tales of Demonic Possession across Genres and Cultural Fields in Denmark–Norway (1647–1716)', *Ethnologia Scandinavica*, 47 (2017), 1–20.

Ogborn, M. and C. W. J. Withers (eds), *Geographies of the Book* (Farnham, 2013).

Ogilvie, Brian W., *The Science of Describing. Natural History in Renaissance Europe* (Chicago, 2006).

Økland, Einar, 'Norske barneblad', in Tordis Ørjasæter, Halldis Leirpoll, Jo Lie, Gunvor Risa and Einar Økland, *Den norske barnelitteraturen gjennom 200 år: Lesebøker, barneblad, bøker og tegneserier* (Oslo, 1981), pp. 86–134.

Olden-Jørgensen, Sebastian, 'En fortidshistoriker og en samtidshistoriker. Ludvig Holberg og Charlotta Dorothea Biehl', *Temp. Tidsskrift for historie*, 17 (2018), 50–66.

Olsen, Michel, 'La Recezione di Goldini in Danimarca', in Giuliano D'Amico and M.P. Muscarello (eds), *Terre Scandinave in Terre d'Asti* (Asti, 2009), pp. 37–49.

Ørjasæter, Tordis, Halldis Leirpoll, Jo Lie, Gunvor Risa and Einar Økland, *Den norske barnelitteraturen gjennom 200 år: Lesebøker, barneblad, bøker og tegneserier* (Oslo, 1981).

Oscarsson, Ingemar, 'En revolution i offentligheten: om lärda tidskrifter i Europa under tidigmodern tid och om hur svensk vetenskap representerades i dem', *Sjuttonhundratal* (2011), 93–115.

Øverland, O. A., *Den Norske bogtrykkerforening 1884–1909: med træk af boghaandverkets historie og arbeidskaar i Norge* (Kristiania, 1909).

Øverland, Per, *Kortere avhandlinger om Brødremenigheten i Norge* (Trondheim, 1987).

Patterson, Annabel M., *Censorship and Interpretation* (Madison, WI, 1984).

Pettegree, Andrew, *Brand Luther: 1517, Printing and the Making of the Reformation* (New York, 2016 [2015]).

—— *The Invention of News. How the World Came to Know About Itself* (New Haven, London, 2014).

Porter, Bernard, 'Virtue and Vice in the North. The Scandinavian Writings of Samuel Laing', *Scandinavian Journal of History*, 23:3 (1998), 153–72.

Powers, Elizabeth (ed.), *Freedom of Speech: The History of an Idea* (Lewisburg, 2011).

Price, Leah, *What We Talk About When We Talk About Books: The History and Future of Reading* (New York, 2019).

Prutsch, Markus J., *Making Sense of Constitutional Monarchism in Post-Napoleonic France* (London, 2012).

Putnam, Laura, 'The Transnational and the Text-Searchable: Digitized Sources and the Shadows They Cast', *The American Historical Review*, 121:2 (April 2016), 377–402.

Rambø, Gro-Renée, 'Det selvstendige Norge (1905–1945)', in A. Nesse (ed.), *Norsk språkhistorie*, vol. 4, *Tidslinjer* (Oslo, 2018), pp. 503–602.

Rauch, Alan, *Useful Knowledge: The Victorians, Morality, and the March of Intellect* (Durham, NC, 2001).

Rausch, Fabian, '"Constitutional Fever"? Constitutional Integration in Post-Revolutionary France, Great Britain and Germany, 1814–c.1835', *Journal of Modern European History* 15:2 (2017), 221–42.

Raven, James, *Bookscape: Geographies of Printing and Publishing in London before 1800* (Chicago, London, 2014).

—— 'Historical Introduction: The Novel Comes of Age', in James Raven and Antonia Forster, with Stephen Bending (eds), *The English Novel 1770–1829: A Bibliographical Survey of Prose Fiction Published in the British Isles. Vol 1: 1770–1799* (Oxford, 2000), pp. 15–121.

Reinert, Sophus A., 'Northern Lights: Political Economy and the Terroir of the Norwegian Enlightenment', *The Journal of Modern History*, 92 (March 2020), 76–115.

Rem, Tore (ed.), *Bokhistorie* (Oslo, 2003).

Renwick, John, 'Jean François Marmontel: The Formative Years 1753–1765', *SVEC*, no. 76 (Geneva, 1970).

Rian, Øystein, *Sensuren i Danmark–Norge: Vilkårene for offentlige ytringer 1536–1814* (Oslo, 2014).

Richter, Marco, *Die Diözese am Ende der Welt: Die Geschichte des Grönlandbistums Garðar* (München, 2017).

Ringdal, Nils Johan, *By, bok og bibliotek* (Oslo, 1985).

Roberts, Michael, *The Age of Liberty: Sweden 1719–1772* (Cambridge, 1986).

Rønning, Anne Birgitte, 'Til "Qvindernes Forædling". Mary Wollstonecraft for danske lesere i 1800'. In Aasta Marie Bjorvand Bjørkøy, Ruth Hemstad, Aina Nøding and Anne Birgitte Rønning (eds), *Litterære verdensborgere: Transnasjonale perspektiver på norsk bokhistorie, 1519–1850* (Oslo, 2019), pp. 290–309.

Roos, Merethe, 'Children, Dying, and Death: Views from an Eighteenth-Century Periodical for Children', in Reidar Aasgard, Marcia J. Bunge and Merethe Roos (eds), *Nordic Childhoods 1700–1960: From Folk Beliefs to Pippi Longstocking* (New York and London, 2018), pp. 241–53.

—— *Enlightened Preaching: Balthasar Münter's Authorship 1772–1793* (Leiden, 2013).

—— 'Struensee in Britain: The Interpretation of the Struensee Affair in British Periodicals, 1772', in Ellen Krefting, Aina Nøding and Mona R. Ringvej (eds), *Eighteenth-Century Periodicals as Agents of Change* (Leiden and Boston, 2015), pp. 77–92.

Rosenberg, Rainer, 'Eine verworrene Geschichte. Vorüberlegungen zu einer Biographie des Literaturbegriffs', *Zeitschrift für Literaturwissenschaft und Linguistik*, 77 (1990), 36–65.

Rydholm, Lena, 'China and the World's First Freedom of Information Act: The Swedish Freedom of the Press Act of 1766', *Javnost–The Public*, 20 (2013), 45–63.

Sagvaag, Inger, *Søndagsskulebarnet i Søndagsskulebladet. Utgreiing om Børnebibliotheket/Barnas Søndagsblad* (Bergen, 1999).

Sandmo, Erling, 'Circulation and Monstrosity. The Sea-pig and the Walrus as Objects of Knowledge in the Sixteenth Century', in Johan Östling *et al.* (eds), *Circulation of Knowledge: Explorations in the History of Knowledge* (Lund, 2018), pp. 175–96.

Santana, Mario, 'Mapping National Literatures: Some Observations on Contemporary Hispanism', in Brad Epps and Luis Fernándes Cifuentes (eds), *Spain Beyond Spain: Modernity, Literary History, and National Identity* (Cranbury, NJ, 2005), pp. 109–25.

Saxtorph, Peder, *Udtog af Doct. Erich Pontoppidans Forklaring, til De Enfoldiges Nytte Uddraget* (Copenhagen, 1771).

Schroeder, Paul W., *The Transformation of European Politics 1763-1848* (Oxford, 1994).

Schücking, Lewin, *The Sociology of Literary Taste* (Routledge, 1966).

Secord, James A., 'Knowledge in Transit', *Isis*, 95:4 (1 December 2004), 654–72.

Sejersted, Francis, *Den vanskelige frihet: 1814–1851* (Oslo, 1978).

—— *Norsk Idyll?* (Oslo, 2000).

Selboe, Tone, 'Camilla Collett (1813–1895)', in E. B. Hagen (ed.), *Den norske litterære kanon: 1700–1900*, (Oslo, 2009), pp. 66–74.

Selvik, Randi M., Ellen Karoline Gjervan and Svein Gladsø (eds), *Lidenskap eller Levebrød? Utøvende Kunst i endring rundt 1800* (Bergen, 2015).

Shep, Sydney, 'Books in Global Perspectives', in L. Howsam (ed.), *The Cambridge Companion to History of the Book* (Cambridge, 2015), pp. 53–70.

—— 'Books Without Borders: The Transnational Turn in Book History' in Robert Fraser and Mary Hammond (eds), *Books Without Borders*, vol. 1. *The Cross-National Dimension in Print Culture* (Basingstoke, 2008), pp. 13–37.

Shine, Norman, 'Børneblade i Danmark fra 1770–1900', *Børn og Bøger*, 4 (1971), 91–8.

Simonsen, Inger, *Den danske børnebog i det 19. Aarhundrede* (Copenhagen, 1966).

Siskin, C. and W. Warner, 'This Is Enlightenment. An Invitation in Form of an Argument', in C. Siskin and W. Warner (eds), *This Is Enlightenment* (Chicago, 2010), pp. 1–33.

Skautrup, Peter, *Det danske sprogs historie*, vol. 2, *Fra unionsbrevet til Danske lov* (Copenhagen, 1947).

Skjelbred, Dagrun, *Norske ABC-bøker 1777–1997* (Tønsberg, 2000).

Skuncke, Marie-Christine, 'Press Freedom in the Riksdag 1760-62 and 1765-66', in B. Wennberg and K. Örtenhed (eds), *Press Freedom 250 Years* (Stockholm, 2018), pp. 109–44.

Slagstad, Rune, *De nasjonale strateger* (Oslo, 1998).

Smitherman, Carey E. and Stephanie Vanderslice, 'Service Learning, Literary Citizenship, and the Creative Writing Classroom', in Alexandria Peary and Tom C. Hunley (eds), *Creative Writing Pedagogies for the Twenty-First Century* (Carbondale, IL, 2015): 153–68.

Smits, Thomas, *The European Illustrated Press and the Emergence of a Transnational Visual Culture of the News, 1842–1870* (London, 2019).

Stangerup, Hakon, *Romanen i Danmark i det attende aarhundrede: en komparativ Undersøgelse* (Copenhagen, 1936).

Stark, Werner, 'Historical Notes and Interpretive Questions about Kant's Lectures on Anthropology', in Brian Jacobs and Patrick Kain (eds), *Essays on Kant's Anthropology*, (Cambridge, 2003), 15–37.

—— 'Kritische Fragen und Anmerkungen zu einem neuen Band der Akademie-Ausgabe von Kant's Vorlesungen', *Zeitschrift für philosophische Forschung*, 38 (1984), 292–310.

Steiner, Donna, 'Literary Citizenship: How You Can Contribute to the Literary Community and Why You Should', in Stephanie Vanderslice (ed.), *Studying Creative Writing Successfully* (Newmarket, 2016).

Stolpe, P. M., *Dagspressen i Danmark, Dens Vilkaar og Personer indtil Midten af det attende Aarhundrede*, vol. 2 (Copenhagen, 1881).

Strauss, Gerald, 'Lutheranism and Literacy: A Reassessment', in Kaspar von Greyerz (ed.), *Religion and Society in Early Modern Europe 1500–1800* (London, 1984), pp. 109–23.

—— *Luther's House of Learning: Indoctrination of the Young in the German Reformation* (Baltimore, MD, 1978).

Svensson, Sonja, *Barnavänner och skolkamrater. Svenska barn- och ungdomstidningar 1766–1900 sedda mot en internationell bakgrund* (Stockholm, 2018).

Sylwan, Otto, *Svenska pressens historia till statshvälfningen 1772* (Lund, 1896).

Tanum, Johan Grundt, 'Guldberg, Carl August', in Edvard Bull, Anders Krogvig, and Gerhard Gran (eds), *Norsk Biografisk Leksikon*, vol. 5 (Oslo, 1931), pp. 72–4.

Taule, Liv, 'Norge – et sekulært samfunn', *Samfunnsspeilet*, 1 (2014) (Statistics Norway), <www.ssb.no/kultur-og-fritid/artikler-og-publikasjoner/norge-et-sekulaert-samfunn>.

Thanner, Lennart, *Revolutionen i Sverige efter Karl XII:s död: Den inrepolitiska maktkampen under tidigare delen av Ulrika Eleonora d.y:s regering* (Uppsala, 1953).

Thomas, Peter D. G., *John Wilkes: A Friend to Liberty* (Oxford, 1996).

Thomson, Ann, Simon Burrows and Edmond Dziembowski (eds), *Cultural Transfers: France and Britain in the Long Eighteenth Century*, SVEC, no. 4 (Oxford, 2010).

Tjønneland, Eivind (ed.), *Opplysningens tidsskrifter. Norske og Danske periodiske publikasjoner på 1700-tallet* (Bergen, 2008).

Toftgaard, Anders, 'Princely Libraries, the Readings of Common Man and the Entry of the Book Cover into Literary Studies. Trends in Book History Research in Denmark', in Sandra van Voorst *et al.* (eds), *Jaarboek voor Nederlandse boekgeschiedenis* (Nijmegen/Leiden, 2013), pp. 163–86.

Tønsberg, Niels Chr. (ed.), *Norske Folkelivsbilleder* (Christiania, 1854).

Torp, Arne, 'Talemål i Noreg på 1800-talet', in A. Nesse (ed.), *Norsk språkhistorie*, vol. 4, *Tidslinjer* (Oslo, 2018), pp. 435–48.

Tortarolo, Edoardo, 'La censure à Berlin au XVIIIe siècle', *La Lettre Clandestine*, 6 (1997), 253–62.

Towsey, Mark and Kyle B. Roberts (eds), 'Introduction', *Before the Public Library* (Leiden, 2018), pp. 1–30.

Tveterås, Harald L., *Den norske bokhandels historie*, vol. 1 (Oslo, 1950).

—— *Den norske bokhandels historie*, vol. 1, *Forlag og bokhandel inntil 1850* (2nd edn Oslo, 1987).

—— 'Norsk bokhandel gjennom 100 år', in Carl Just (ed.), *N.W. Damm & søn 1843–1943: et firmas historie* (Oslo, 1947), pp. 101–25.

—— *Norske tidsskrifter. Bibliografi over periodiske skrifter i Norge inntil 1920* (Oslo, 1940).

—— *Den norske bokhandels historie: Forlag og bokhandel inntil 1850* (Oslo, 1950).

—— *Norske tidsskrifter: bibliografi over periodiske skrifter i Norge inntil 1920* (2nd edn; Oslo, 1984).

Twyman, Michael, 'The Illustration Revolution', in David McKitterick (ed.), *The Cambridge History of the Book in Britain*, vol. 6, *1830–1914* (Cambridge, 2009), pp. 117–43.

Uglow, Jenny, *Nature's Engraver: A Life of Thomas Bewick* (Chicago, 2009).

Varey, Simon, 'The Craftsman', *Prose Studies*, 16 (1993), 58–77.

Vegesack, Thomas von, *Smak för frihet. Opinionsbildningen i Sverige 1755–1830* (Stockholm, 1995).

Voges, Michel, *Aufklärung und Geheimnis. Untersuchungen zur Vermittlung von Literatur- und Sozialgeschichte am Beispiel der Aneignung des Geheimbundmaterials im Roman des späten 18. Jahrhunderts* (Tübingen, 1987).

Vulpius, Christian August, *Rinaldo Rinaldini, der Räuberhauptmann: Eine Romantische Geschichte* (Berlin, 2016).

Wald, James, 'Periodicals and Periodicity', in S. Eliot and J. Rose (eds), *A Companion to the History of the Book*, 2nd edn (Hoboken, NJ, 2020), pp. 617–31.

Walker, D. P., *Unclean Spirits: Possession and Exorcism in France and England in the Late Sixteenth and Early Seventeenth Centuries* (Philadelphia, 1981).

Warner, William, *Licensing Entertainment: The Elevation of Novel Reading in Britain* (Berkeley, 1998).

Warner, William B., Eirik Holmøyvik, and Mona Ringvej, 'The Thing That Invented Norway', in Karen Gammelgaard and Eirik Holmøyvik (eds), *Writing Democracy: The Norwegian Constitution 1814–2014* (New York, Oxford, 2014), pp. 21–42.

Weinreich, Torben, *Historien om børnelitteratur – dansk børnelitteratur gennem 400 år* (Copenhagen, 2006).

Wennberg, Bertil and Kristina Örtenhed (eds), *Press Freedom 250 Years: Freedom of the Press and Public Access to Official Documents in Sweden and Finland – a Living Heritage from 1766* (Stockholm, 2018).

Wergeland, Henrik, *Samlede skrifter: trykt og utrykt*, vol. 3, b. 2, *Artikler og småstykker: polemiske og andre 1833–1836*, eds Herman Jæger and Didrik Arup Seip (Oslo, 1933).

Werner, Michael and Bénédicte Zimmermann, 'Beyond Comparison: Histoire Croisée and the Challenge of Reflexivity', *History and Theory*, 45:1 (February 2006), 30–50.

Wiesener, Anton Mohr and Hjalmar Christensen. *Et Bergensk Boktrykkeri gjennem 200 år* (Bergen, 1921).

Williams, Abigail, *The Social Life of Books: Reading Together in the Eighteenth-Century Home* (New Haven, 2018).

Wilster, C., *Digtninger* (Copenhagen, 1827).

Winge, Vibeke, 'Dansk og tysk 1790–1848', in Ole Feldbæk (ed.), *Dansk identitetshistorie*, vol. 2, (Copenhagen, 1991), pp. 110–49.

Wittmann, Reinhard, 'Was there a Reading Revolution at the End of the Eighteenth Century?', in Guglielmo Cavallo and Roger Chartier (eds), *A History of Reading in the West* (Cambridge, 1999), pp. 284–312.

Zerlang, Martin, 'Det moderne gennembrud 1870–1900: Presse og magasiner', The Royal Library (Copenhagen, 2010). <www2.kb.dk/elib/mss/dmg/presse/index.htm>.

Zuckerman, Phil, *Society without God: What the Least Religious Nations Can Tell Us About Contentment* (New York, 2008).

Unpublished theses

Björkman, Margaretha, 'Läsarnas nöje. Kommersiella lånbibliotek i Stockholm 1783–1809' (PhD thesis, Uppsala University, 1992).

Eisenträger, Stian, 'The European Press and the Question of Norwegian Independence' (MA thesis, Norwegian University of Life Science, Ås, 2013).

Engedalen, Lars T., 'Erik Valkendorf og grønlandsforskningen – fra middelalderen til moderne tid' (MA thesis, University of Oslo, 2010).

Jakobsen, Jesper, 'Uanstændige, utilladelige og unyttige skrifter: En undersøgelse af censuren i praksis 1746–1773' (PhD thesis, University of Copenhagen, 2017).

Johnsen, Emil Nichlas, 'I Klios forgård. Forfatterroller, offentlighet og politisk evaluering i Niels Ditlev Riegels' (1755–1802) historieskriving' (PhD thesis, University of Oslo, 2019).

Langseth, Bjørn Jarl, 'Christian Johnsens "Almuevennen": en analyse av ukebladets innholds- og utbredelsesstruktur i tidsrommet 1849–1873' (MA thesis, University of Oslo, 1975).

Maliks, Jacob, 'Vilkår for offentlighet. Sensur, økonomi og transformasjonen af det offentlige rom i Danmark-Norge 1730–1770' (PhD thesis, Norwegian University of Science and Technology, Trondheim, 2011).

Nøding, Aina, 'Vittige kameleoner: Litterære tekster i norske adresseaviser, 1763–1769' (PhD thesis, University of Oslo, 2007).

Nymark, Kristian, 'Kampen om trykkefriheten. Karl Johan og den norske presse 1814–1844' (PhD thesis, University of South-East Norway, 2020) <https://openarchive.usn.no/usn-xmlui/handle/11250/2681517>.

Ommundsen, Åslaug, 'Books, Scribes and Sequences in Medieval Norway' (PhD thesis, University of Bergen, 2007).

Skjelbred, Dagrun, '"... de umistelige Bøger": En studie av den tidlige norske abc-tradisjonen' (PhD thesis, University of Oslo, 1998).

Stensrud, Iver Tangen, 'The Magazine and the City: Architecture, Urban Life and the Illustrated Press in Nineteenth-Century Christiania' (PhD thesis, Oslo School of Architecture and Design) (<http://hdl.handle.net/11250/2501383>).

Thomsen, Jonas Thorup, 'Besat af Djævelen: Djævlebesættelserne i Thisted 1696–98 og fænomenets kulturelle ophav' (MA thesis, Aarhus, 2018).

ONLINE SOURCES

1814 Bibliography: Literature From and About 1814 (<www.nb.no/bibliografi/1814>).

Andresen, Anton Fr., 'Gregers Lundh', in *Norsk biografisk leksikon*, 13 February 2009 <http://nbl.snl.no/Gregers_Lundh>.

Appiah, Kwame Anthony, 'Mistaken Identities', The Reith Lectures, BBC Radio 4, 8 November 2016, <www.bbc.co.uk/programmes/b080twcz> (accessed 23 February 2023).

Breviarium Nidrosiense, ed. Ingrid Sperber with an introduction by Espen Karlsen and Sigurd Hareide (Oslo, 2019) (<bokselskap.no/boker/breviarium/titlepage> [accessed 27 February 2022]).

Burrows, Simon and Mark Curran, The French Book Trade in Enlightenment Europe Database, 1769–1794, (<fbtee.uws.edu.au/stn/interface>, accessed 6 January 2021).

Day, Cathy, 'Cathy Day's Principles of Literary Citizenship', *Literarycitizenship.com* (24 September 2012), < https://literarycitizenship.com/?s=principles> (accessed 23 February 2023).

Ebenbach, David, 'Literary Citizenship Does Not Mean "Gimme"', *Medium* (28 April 2014), <https://medium.com/human-parts/literary-citizenship-does-not-mean-gimme-e7ac3f97b140> (accessed 23 February 2023).

Gay, Roxane, 'The Eight Questions Writers Should Ask Themselves', *Awpwriter.org* (November 2015), <www.awpwriter.org/magazine_media/writers_notebook_view/5> (accessed 23 February 2023).

Holberg, Ludvig, *Danmarks Riges Historie*, eds Nina M. Evensen and Eiliv Vinje, *Ludvig Holbergs Skrifter* (2015 [1st edn, Copenhagen, 1732–5]) (<holbergsskrifter.no>).

Kukkonen, Karin and Marit Sjelmo, *Literary Fiction in Norwegian Lending Libraries in the 18th Century*, (open access database, <www.nb.no/forskning/skjonnlitteratur-i-norske-bibliotek-pa-1700-tallet> (2019)).

McGill, Robert and André Babyn, 'Teaching Critical Literary Citizenship', *The Writer's Notebook* (February 2019), <www.awpwriter.org/magazine_media/writers_notebook_view/311> (accessed 23 February 2023).

Missale Nidrosiense, ed. Ingrid Sperber with an introduction by Espen Karlsen and Sigurd Hareide, bokselskap.no (Oslo, 2019) (<bokselskap.no/boker/missale/part1> [accessed 27 February 2022]).

Morganti, Charlotte, 'Celebrating Literary Citizens', *My Two Cents* (15 August 2013), <https://charlottemorganti.com/?s=celebrating> (accessed 23 February 2023).

R.I.E.C.H. Inventory of Swiss printers and editors prior to 1850, 2008/2017. Bibliothèque Cantonal et Universitaire BCU Lausanne, database: <www.db-prod-bcul.unil.ch/riech> [accessed 11 August 2021].

Schiønning, Peter, *Dagbog*, (online edition, <www.natmus.dk>) ([1732–1812]).

Schultz, Katey, 'Literary Citizenship: Point and Counterpoint', *Kateyschultz. com*(n.d.),<www.kateyschultz.com/2017/10/literary-citizenship/>(accessed 23 February 2023).

Statistisk sentralbyrå, 'Hjemmehørende Folkemengde' <www.ssb.no/a/kortnavn/hist_tab/3-1.html> [accessed 29 September 2021].

'The Constitution, as Laid down on 17 May 1814 by the Constituent Assembly at Eidsvoll and Subsequently Amended, Most Recently in May 2018', Stortinget.no, <https://www.stortinget.no/globalassets/pdf/english/constitutionenglish.pdf> [accessed 3 November 2021].

Tuch, Becky, 'More Work, No Pay: Why I Detest 'Literary Citizenship'', *Salon* (23 April 2014), <www.salon.com/2014/04/23/more_work_no_pay_why_i_detest_literary_citizenship> (accessed 23 February 2023).

OTHER RECOMMENDED ONLINE RESOURCES (SELECTED)

Det danske sprog-og litteraturselskab [repository of critical editions of Danish classics and historical dictionaries]: <www.dsl.dk>.

Det norske språk- og litteraturselskap [repository of critical editions of Norwegian classics]: <www.bokselskap.no>.

Litteraturbanken [repository of critical and facsimile editions of Swedish classics]: <www.litteraturbanken.se>.

National Library of Norway: <www.nb.no> [searchable facsimile editions of Norwegian books, periodicals, newspapers, ephemera and other media publications].

National Library of Norway's bibliographies (links from entries to facsimile editions): <www.nb.no/ressurser/bibliografier>, including:

   Norske tidsskrifter 1700–1820: <www.nb.no/bibliografi/notids1700> [periodicals].

   Norske bøker 1519–1850: <www.nb.no/bibliografi/nor1519> [books].

Royal Library, Copenhagen – bibliographies and repositories:

   Arkiv for dansk litteratur [repository of Danish literary classics]: <https://tekster.kb.dk/adl>.

   Facsimile editions of selected books and periodicals available from the main catalogue: <www.soeg.kb.dk>.

Mediestream [searchable facsimile editions of Danish historical newspapers]: <www2.statsbiblioteket.dk/mediestream/avis>.

Trykkefrihedens Skrifter [bibliography of press freedom publications 1770–73, linked to facsimile and text encoded edition]: <https://tekster.kb.dk/tfs>.

Royal Library, Stockholm – bibliographies and repositories:

Links to digital collections: <www.kb.se/hitta-och-bestall/fritt-digitaliser-at-material.html>.

Svenska dagstidningar [searchable facsimile editions of Swedish historical newspapers]: <https://tidningar.kb.se>.

Index

Printed and bound by CPI Group (UK) Ltd, Croydon, CR0 4YY

09/06/2025

14685705-0004